New Perspecti

Japanese Occupation

Malaya and Singapore, 1941-1945

New Perspectives on the Japanese Occupation in Malaya and Singapore, 1941–1945

Edited by

Akashi Yoji
&
Yoshimura Mako

NUS PRESS
SINGAPORE

© 2008 NUS Press
National University of Singapore
AS3-01-02, 3 Arts Link
Singapore 117569

Fax: (65) 6774-0652
E-mail: nusbooks@nus.edu.sg
Website: http://www.nus.edu.sg/npu

ISBN   978-9971-69-299-5 (Paper)

National Library Board Singapore Cataloguing in Publication Data

New perspectives on the Japanese occupation in Malaya and Singapore, 1941–1945 /
    edited by Akashi Yoji & Yoshimura Mako. – Singapore : NUS Press, c2008.
    p. cm.
Includes index.
ISBN-13 : 978-9971-69-299-5 (pbk.)

    1. Malaya – History – Japanese occupation, 1942–1945.   2. Singapore –
    History – Japanese occupation, 1942–1945. I. Akashi, Yoji, 1928–
    II. Yoshimura, Mako, 1961–

D802
940.5337 – dc22   SLS2007015914

Photos published in this book are provided by the authors.
Cover photos: (Left)   War memorial at Bukit Timah
                (Top)   A Japanese officer instructing a Malay on making rope
                          with rice straw
                (Bottom) Maj. Gen. Tatsumi Hiroshi (third from left) with the
                          Sultan of Kelantan

Typeset by: International Typesetters Pte Ltd
Printed by: Vetak Services

Contents

List of Illustrations

List of Contributors

Akashi Yoji is Professor Emeritus at Nanzan University, Nagoya. His publications include *The Japanese Occupation in Southeast Asian History* (1997), Kurasawa Aiko, ed., *Interview Record. The Japanese Occupation of British Malaya and Singapore, 1941–1945* (Tokyo: Ryukei Shosha, 1998); *Major General Watanabe Wataru: Papers Relating to Malay Military Administration* (Tokyo: Ryukei Shosha, 1998); *Documents Relating to Education in Occupied Malaya and Singapore, 1941–1945* (Tokyo: Ryukei Shosha, 1999); *Nanpogun Gunsei Sokanbu Kankei Monjo (Sakakibara Collection)* 9 volumes (Tokyo: Ryukei Shosha, 2004). *Nanpogun Gunsei Sokanbu Chosabu, Malai Gansei Kambu Chosabu Field Study Reports*, 22 volumes (Tokyo: Ryukei Shosha, 2006)

Hara Fujio is Professor at Nanzan University, Nagoya. His publications include *Japanese in British Malaya* (Tokyo: Institute of Developing Economies [IDE], 1986); *Chinese in Southeast Asia and China* (Tokyo: IDE, 1993); *Malayan Chinese and China* (Tokyo: IDE, 1997); *The Formation and Reorganization of Entrepreneur Groups in Malaysia* (Tokyo: IDE, 1994); *Malayan Chinese and China* (Tokyo: Ryukei Shosha, 2001).

Yoshimura Mako is Professor at Hosei University, Tokyo. Her publications include *Malaysian Economic Development and the Labour Structure* (Tokyo: Hosei University Press, 1998); *Asian Big Cities (3): Kuala Lumpur and Singapore* (Tokyo: Nihon Hyoronsha, 2000); "Social Safety Net in Malaysia", Teranishi, ed., *Social Safety Net in Asia* (Tokyo: Keiso Shobo, 2003); "Asian Female Migrant Workers", Aoki *et al.*, eds., *Asia's New Century (5) The Market* (Tokyo: Iwanami Shoten, 2003).

Ota Koki is Professor Emeritus at Tohoku Women's University, Aomori. His publications include "Religion under Naval Administration", *Nippon Rekishi* (Japanese History), no. 527 (1992); "Official Commitment to

Indonesian Independence and the Naval Administrative Area — Focused on the Eve of Japanese Surrender", *Gunji Shigaku* (Military History), nos. 121–22 (1995).

Nakahara Michiko is Professor Emeritus at Waseda University, Tokyo. Her publications include "The Thai-Burma Railway and Dato Yusoff Bangus — A British Planter in the Japanese Military Administration", *Shakai Kagaku Tokyu*, no. 117 (Waseda University 1994); *The Japanese Occupation in Southeast Asian History* (Tokyo: Waseda University Press, 1997); "Labour Recruitment in Malaya under Japanese Occupation", in *Rethinking Malaysia*, ed. Jomo K.S. (Kuala Lumpur: Malaysian Social Science Association, 1998).

Frei, Henry was Professor at Tsukuba Women's Junior College. He passed away in 2002. His publications include *Japan's Southward Advance and Australia* (Melbourne: Melbourne University Press, 1991); "Japan's Reluctant Decision to Occupy East Timor, 1 January–20 February 1942", in *Australian Historical Studies* (Melbourne: University of Melbourne, 1996); *Guns of February: Ordinary Japanese Soldiers' View of the Malayan Campaign and the Fall of Singapore, 1941–42* (Singapore: Singapore University Press, 2004).

Hayashi Hirofumi is Professor at Kanto Gakuin University, Tokyo. His publications include *Chinese Massares: The Malay Peninsula under Japanese Occupation* (Tokyo: Suzusawa Shoten, 1992); *Tried War Crimes: British War Crimes Trials of Japanese* (Tokyo: Iwanami Shoten, 1998); *BC Class War Crimes Trials* (Tokyo: Iwanami Shoten, 2005).

Preface

This book is the product of a project known as the Forum on the Japanese Occupation of Malaya and Singapore, 1941–45. Supported by a grant from the Toyota Foundation, the Forum was organised in 1994 and operated for four years. The Forum had three objectives: to identify hitherto undiscovered primary sources in archives in Japan and the former Allied Powers; to interview surviving Japanese military and civilian officials who took part in the military administration as well as people in Malaysia and Singapore who lived through the period; and to publish the interview records and other research results in order to elucidate the history of the Japanese occupation from a new perspective. Members of the Forum interviewed more than 50 people — Japanese, Malaysians and Singaporeans — and visited national archives and libraries in the United Kingdom, Malaysia, Singapore, India, Australia and the United States to locate primary documents.

Of the seven contributors to the present volume, Akashi, Hara, Nakahara and Yoshimura are scholars concerned with Malaysian studies. Ota is a military historian, and Hayashi is a historian of Japan who wrote on war crimes and the Second World War. The late Henry Frei studied relations between Japan, Australia, and Southeast Asia. Other participants in the Forum discussions were Hata Ikuhiko, a military historian, and Iwatake Teruhiko, a former official of the Gunsei Kambu. Masutani Satoshi, a historian of Chinese literature on the Japanese occupation in Southeast Asia, worked on bibliography with his students, together with Yoshihisa Akihiro who kindly advised on the bibliography.

The Forum has published five volumes in Japanese: *A Collection of Primary Sources on the Military Administration of North Borneo* (1997); *An Interview Record. Japanese Occupied Malaya and Singapore 1941–1945* (1998); *A Collection of Primary Sources on Education in Occupied Malaya and Singapore 1941–1945* (1999); *The Watanabe Wataru Papers on the Malay Military Administration 1941–1945* (1999); *Essays on Japanese Occupied Malaya and Singapore* (2001). The final project of the Forum is the publication of a comprehensive bibliography of references, published and unpublished in Japanese, English, Chinese, Malay languages during pre-war, inter-war, post-war periods, on Japan's relations with Malaysia (Malaya) and Singapore. Its publication is due in late 2007. Future plans call for the publication of diaries written by Maj. Gen. Inada Masazumi, Col. Ishii Akiho, Maj. Gen. Sukegawa Seiji, Col. Kushida Masao, as well as memoirs written by Col. Imaoka Yutaka. Inada was a deputy chief of staff, Southern Army; Ishii was a staff officer in charge of military administration, Southern Army; Sukegawa was the governor of Kedah/Perlis; Kushida was a staff officer in charge of operations, Southern Army; and Imaoka was a staff officer in charge of military administration and logistics, Southern Army, and 7th Area Army.

Independent of the Forum but related to its project, Akashi compiled and edited a 22-volume collection of the *Nanpogun Gunsei Sokambu Chosabu* and the *Malai Gunsei Kambu Chosabu* Field Study Reports, published in 2006 (Tokyo: Ryukei Shosha). These reports, covering agriculture, commerce, economy, ethnology, education, hygiene, industry, society, religion, and trade, were prepared by academics recruited for the Research Department (Chosabu) of the Gunsei Sokambu and the Malai Gunsei Kambu.

The present book is largely drawn from a Japanese-language volume titled *Nihon Senryoka no Eiryo Maraya, Shingaporu* [British Malaya and Singapore under the Japanese Occupation], published in Tokyo by Iwanami Shoten Publishers in 2001. Two articles that appeared in the original volume (by Masutani Satoshi on Chinese literature on World War II in Southeast Asia and by Yamazaki Isao on natural resource in South Borneo) are not included in this English edition because of the topics and region. The article by Hayashi (Chapter 9) is added.

Members of the Forum have delivered research papers prepared in connection with their research at a number of international conferences. Akashi and Hara participated in a panel on the Japanese Occupation in South East Asia at the Annual Meeting of the Association of Asian Studies, USA in Honolulu in 1998; Yoshimura organised a panel on the Japanese Occupation in Malaya, with a grant from the Japan Foundation at the Second International Malaysian Studies Conference organised by the Malaysian Social Science Association in 1999, at which Akashi, Hara, Nakahara, Yoshimura and Masutani presented papers with comment by Prof. Cheah Boon Kheng of Universiti Sains Malaysia. Akashi, Nakahara, Yoshimura and Masutani presented papers at the Annual Meeting of the Association of Asian Studies in San Diego in 2000; in 1995 Akashi read a paper at an international conference marking the 50th anniversary of the Fall of

Singapore held in Singapore and sponsored by the Department of History at the National University of Singapore, and by the Toyota Foundation. Akashi and Masutani delivered papers at the 4th International Malaysian Studies Conference organised by the Malaysian Social Science Association in 2003, and at a conference marking the 60th anniversary of the end of World War II held in Singapore in 2005, where Hayashi also presented a paper.

It is hoped the present volume and these papers will contribute to enhancing the studies of the Japanese occupation of Malaya and Singapore.

The Forum members wish to express their appreciation to the Malaysian Social Science Association (Persatuan Sains Sosial Malaysia) and its President, Professor Abdul Rahman Hj. Embong, for permission to reprint Akashi Yoji's article, "Colonel Watanabe Wataru: The Architect of the Malayan Military Administration, December 1941–1943", which first appeared in *Reinventing Malaysia: Reflections on its Past and Future*, ed. Jomo K.S. (Bangi: Penerbit Universiti Kebangsaan Malaysia) and to the Department of History, University of Malaya (Universiti Malaya) and the head of the department, Assoc. Prof. Mohammad Redzuan Othman, for permission to reprint Yoshimura Mako's article, "Japanese Occupation and Economic Policy in Malaya: Exploitation of Materials and Japanese Rubber Estates", first published in *Sejarah*, the Journal of the Department of History, University of Malaya (no. 10, 2002, pp. 21–51).

The four-year-Forum and its subsequent publication projects have been generously subsidised by the Toyota Foundation, and Forum members wish to express their deep appreciation to the Foundation and particularly to Ms. Himemoto Yumiko, the programme officer concerned, who supported the Forum from the beginning to the end. We would also like to acknowledge the assistance rendered by the late Professor Itogaki Yoichi and the late Professor Yamada Hideo of Hitotsubashi University for allowing Forum members access to its Library and the editorial advice of Dr. Paul Kratoska, Managing Director of NUS Press, National University of Singapore. The illustrations in this publication are scanned by Mr Sagara Go for which we would like to extend our thanks. It is unfortunately impossible to mention all of the many individuals and organisations that cooperated with our Forum project, but without their support it could not have been carried out successfully, and our debts in this regard are great. We would like to conclude with a note of appreciation for the understanding and encouragement of our colleagues at home and abroad, and a wish that we will be able to work together on other projects in the future.

Akashi Yoji and Yoshimura Mako
*Chairman and Secretary General of the Forum on the
Japanese Occupation of Malaya and Singapore, 1941–45*

January 2008

Introduction

The Pacific War commenced in Malaya at 12.35 a.m. on 8 December 1941. One and one half hours before Japanese aircraft attacked Pearl Harbour, the Takumi detached troops of the 25th Army under Lt. Gen. Yamashita Tomoyuki's command carried out landing operations at Kota Bahru, Kelantan, in the northeastern corner of the Malay Peninsula and several places at Songkla, Dhebhe, Pattani, Nakhom Si Thammarat, Chumphon, Jumbhorn, and Prachuap Khiri Khan in Southern Thailand.

Yamashita's army (code named "Tomi") consisted of three divisions — the 5th, 18th and Imperial Guards — with a total strength of 49,000 (the main force of the 18th Division about 15,000 men joined the 25th Army on 30 January 1942). After landing, Yamashita's army launched *Kirimomi* (penetration) operations and drove south down the peninsula towards Singapore, Britain's military bastion in the Far East. Lt. Gen. A. E. Percival, commander in chief of the British force that numbered 100,000 men, surrendered to the Japanese Army on 15 February 1942. Following the British surrender, the 25th Army established a military administration throughout Malaya, Singapore and Sumatra, and these territories remained under Japanese military administration for three years and eight months, until the war ended in August 1945.[1]

Prior to the war, the British colonial administration had built an economic system in which income from the export of rubber and tin supported the import of food and daily necessities. Malaya's economy was not self-sufficient, and when the Japanese came into power, the country lost its export markets for rubber and tin, and faced the disruption of the inflow of food, especially rice, and of daily necessities. Japan was unable to arrange alternative sources of supply, and the economic situation deteriorated rapidly. After 1943, the people of Malaya suffered from acute shortages and from spiralling inflation. They also endured other kinds of suffering: unemployment, forced labour, torture, rape, plunder, violence and censorship. Why did these injustices occur during the Japanese Occupation? What sort of military rule did the Japanese create?

Through the 1960s, Akashi Yoji was one of just a small number of academics to seriously study the issues such as these, and in a series of articles, based on archival documents and interviews, he began to shed light on the period that had been known only through anecdotal accounts. In 1969, he expanded his research by systematically interviewing people with first-hand experience of the Malayan military administration, including Japanese military and civilian officials as well as people who had lived in Malaya during the war years. Akashi's studies of the Japanese Occupation of Malaya and the military administration attracted considerable interest and attention in academic circles in Japan and abroad, and generated further studies. For example, Dr. Iwatake Teruhiko, a former official with the Malay Military Administration (hereafter Malay Gunsei Kambu) who was in charge of mobilisation of resources from February 1942 to May 1944, published a two-volume work, *The Economic Policy under the Japanese Military Administration: Its Record in Malaya and Java* (南方軍政下の経済施策―マライ・ジャワの記録),[2] based on his experience and information from documents in the Tokugawa Collection (徳川コレクション), Waseda University's Nishijima Collection (西島コレクション), and the Kishi Collection (岸資料). Iwatake undertook a critical analysis of the economic policy in Malaya and Indonesia during the Occupation, focusing on mobilisation of materials, plantation administration, food production, industrialisation, money, currency and finance. While the scope of the work is broad, it deals specifically with the economic sector but is not a comprehensive study of the Malay Gunsei Kambu.

In the 1980s, Malaysia and Singapore launched a project to study the Malay Gunsei for collecting primary sources. The National Archives of Singapore as well as Universiti Sains Malaysia (USM) in Penang, undertook an oral history project in which citizens who had experienced the Occupation were interviewed on tape. Hundreds of people were interviewed in Singapore, where tapes and transcripts are available in the National Archives, while USM amassed a collection of tape recordings that is partially available to the public.[3] University students in Singapore and Malaysia have used these sources and supplemented them with primary field research to produce numerous honours and master's theses. In 1998, Paul H. Kratoska of the National University of Singapore produced a comprehensive study of the socio-economic history of occupied Malaya, based in part on oral histories but drawing primarily on British and American documents held by archives in Malaysia and Singapore. Abu Talib also published a book on the Japanese policy toward Islam and Malay Muslims.[4] Academic works such as these are indicative of continuing interest in the subject in both Singapore and Malaysia.

There is a bibliographical problem in the monographs by Iwatake, Kratoska, and Talib. Iwatake did not have full access to British, Singaporean and Malaysian sources, while Kratoska and Talib used Japanese sources in translation. Because of this, Iwatake's work does not adequately elucidate policy development as it was implemented to the Malayan people, and Kratoska's study does not sufficiently analyse the policy making process and the philosophical principles that underlay the military administration. The articles in this book hope to remedy these deficiencies.

Policies for the Occupied Regions

In early February 1941, the General Staff formed a study group to draft a general outline of the administration for occupied areas. Col. Obata Nobuyuki, Lt. Col. Nishimuta Otoji and Lt. Col. Tofuku Seijiro were asked to draw up a study of military government, which they were to present directly to the chief of the Operations Bureau.[5] The study was titled "Draft of the Administrative Principles for the Occupied Regions in the Operations of the Southern Area" (南方作戦ニ於ケル占領地統治要綱案).[6] It asked for:

1. acquisition of vital materials as rapidly as possible for national defence;
2. restoration of law and order;
3. self-sufficiency for troops in occupied territories;
4. respect for established local organisations and customs; and
5. no hasty statement about the future status of sovereignty.

The first three of these points were subsequently incorporated into "Principles for the Administration of the Occupied Southern Regions" (南方占領地統治要綱), a document adopted by the Imperial Headquarters-Government Liaison Conference on 20 November 1941 as the "Three Objectives of the Military Administration".

Another policy paper, the "Draft of Implementing Principles for Each Region", contained the following tenets in its section on Malaya:

1. because the Straits Settlements of Singapore, Malacca and Penang were important military administrative centres, they were to be controlled by the Japanese Army;

2. the four Federated states (Perak, Selangor, Negri Sembilan and Pahang) were to be supervised and recognised under the rule of their respective sultans;

3. the four "Unfederated states" that were former Thai territories — Trengganu, Kelantan, Kedah and Perlis — were "expected" to revert to Thailand in the future.

On 6 November 1941, the supreme command issued the order of battle for the Southern Army, which placed the 25th Army and its military administration department (Gunseibu) under its command. In July 1942, the Gunseibu was restructured into a Military Administrative Superintendency, the Gunsei Kambu (軍政監部). The chief of staff of the 25th Army became the Gunsei Kambu's superintendent and the chief of the General Affairs Department its executive officer, the person charged with drafting and implementing policies.

The early military administration period (February 1942 to March 1943) was characterised by "hardline" policy (武断軍政). Akashi's article on Watanabe Wataru, in Chapter 2 of the present book, attributes this stance to Watanabe, the second chief of the Gunseibu and the chief of the General Affairs Department in July 1942, whose thinking lay behind the nationality policy implemented in the early stages of his administration.

The presence of some two million Chinese living in Singapore and Malaya and their anti-Japanese movement there underlay Watanabe's nationality policy. Since the late 1920s, Chinese communities in Southeast Asia had been active in anti-Japanese "national salvation" movements, responding to growing anti-Japanese sentiment in mainland China. Following the Manchurian Incident of 1931 and the outbreak of the Sino-Japanese war in 1937, an anti-Japanese boycott and "Aid Chiang Kai-Shek" campaign became very animated, with various Chinese associations in British Malaya as the core of these movements.[7] Early in the period of military rule, Watanabe's Gunsei introduced a series of repressive and discriminatory policies directed towards the Chinese, including a forced payment of ¥50 million, closure of Chinese schools, a ban on the use of the Chinese language in schools, and suspension of remittances to China. Throughout Watanabe's tenure, which lasted until March 1943, he looked upon the Chinese community with suspicion.

By the time Watanabe left Malaya, Japan's war situation had deteriorated significantly. In an effort to improve conditions in Malaya, Watanabe's successors modified his repressive policies towards the Malayan Chinese because it had become obvious that Gunsei authorities could not acquire rice and daily necessities without Chinese cooperation. The Japanese took a further step in March 1944 when Col. Hamada Hiroshi, Director of the General Affairs Department, established a Public Reading Room (閲報処) as a way of improving relations with the Chinese and of exchanging and listening to the views of community leaders and young people. In July 1945, Maj. Gen. Umezu Hirokichi, newly appointed director of the General Affairs Department, admitted frankly to Malay leaders that Japan's nationality policy in Malaya had made "serious mistakes", and assured them that the situation would be rectified.[8]

As for the Malays, the Gunsei Kambu had no concrete policy for the sultans until after July 1942. This lack of interest in the Malays stemmed in part from a generally shared preconception amongst the Japanese that the Malays were lazy and pusillanimous. The Japanese at first tried to win Malay support by utilising the Kesatuan Melayu Muda (Malay Youth League) of Ibrahim Yaacob to practical use, but the Gunsei Kambu later banned all political associations and dissolved the Malay Youth League. The "Principles for the Disposition of Sultans" adopted in July 1942 stated that though the military would "not authorise the institution of the sultanates in the future", it was "not appropriate to disestablish the sultanate from the point of administrating the Malays, and sultans might be advised to give up voluntarily their political prerogatives to the military". It was further specified that the throne, the land and the people should be made subject to the Emperor through the commander of the Japanese Army, and that by swearing loyalty to the Emperor, the sultans as Japanese subjects must set the example to the people.

To induce the sultans to voluntarily surrender their authority, the Japanese guaranteed them certain prerogatives, for example, in religious matters, and assured them that they would receive a minimum stipend and a pension and allow them to maintain their inherited assets. This policy was the brainchild of three men: Watanabe, Takase Toru (Watanabe's key advisor) and Marquis Tokugawa Yoshichika, supreme advisor to the Gunsei and a self-appointed protector of the sultans. Prior to the war, Tokugawa had advised Watanabe to deal with the sultans firmly, and he took on the task of persuading them to hand over their authority to the Emperor.[9]

The vice-war minister, however, believed that such repressive measures towards the sultans and the punitive reduction of their pensions would not help the Japanese win popular support, and he requested that the 25th Army ameliorate this harsh treatment.[10] Though Watanabe was unhappy with the request, he reluctantly complied with it and increased the sultans' stipend, while insisting that the discriminatory policy should be applied to all of the sultans, regardless whether they were friendly towards the military administration, sympathetic to Britain or sitting on the fence. Tokugawa also disagreed with the vice-war minister's request, but nevertheless he gave way.[11]

The vice-minister's comments on the policy towards the Malay sultans had a mollifying effect, and the Gunsei Kambu subsequently worked out policy to improve relations with the sultans and with the Islamic leaders, holding a series of conferences with leaders of these groups drawn from Malaya and Sumatra, granting sultans the right to appoint Islamic scholars for the study of the Koran, appointing sultans as vice presidents of state councils, and giving priority to Malays over other ethnic groups in making appointments to local administrative posts. The Gunsei Kambu recruited Ibrahim Yaacob to organise a Giyugun (volunteer army) and drafted Malays as Giyutai and Heiho (auxiliary soldiers). It also helped organise the KRIS (Kekuatan Rakyat Istimewa Semenanjung, literally, The Strength of Special People on the Peninsula) movement, which was to prepare for Malayan independence.

The Gunsei Kambu had little to do with the Indian community, which fell under the Japanese government and military authorities in Tokyo. The Japanese military's Indian policy aimed at inducing Indian soldiers in the British army to surrender to the Japanese. Responsibility for this effort lay with the Fujiwara Unit (Fujiwara Kikan), commanded by Maj. Fujiwara Iwaichi, and it succeeded in persuading more than 1,000 Indian soldiers to lay down their arms, while several thousand surrendered Indians later joined the Indian National Army (INA).

The Iwakuro Kikan (commanded by Fujiwara's successor, Col. Iwakuro Hideo), Imperial Headquarters, the INA, and the Indian Independence League (IIL) were deeply divided over the issue of autonomy for the Indians, a point upon which the INA and the IIL insisted, and as a result of this dispute, the INA was disbanded. After the arrival of Subhas C. Bose in Singapore in July 1943, Bose helped resuscitate the moribund INA and turned it into a revolutionary army striking for Indian independence, while he himself became head of the Provisional Government of India backed by the Japanese government. Bose's INA joined the Japanese Army in the Imphal operation on Burma's western front, but suffered heavy casualties and was defeated. Bose died in an airplane crash on 16 August 1945 at Taipei Airport. The Indian question remained a peripheral issue to the Gunsei Kambu in Malaya.

Collaboration and Resistance

There was relatively little controversy in post-war Malaya over the question of collaboration, as happened in the Philippines. Many Malays, Chinese and Indians in occupied Malaya cooperated with the Japanese Army in one way or another, although they might not have accepted or even fully understood grand slogans such as "Greater East Asian Co-Prosperity Sphere" or "Asia for the Asians". Many Malay leaders, including the sultans, cooperated actively or passively, while others sat on the fence, but there was hardly any public demand after the war for collaborators to be tried or punished. In fact, the Malays protested strongly when the British attempted to punish the sultans who had cooperated with the Japanese, for example by dethroning three sultans appointed by the Japanese, and forced the British to retract their reprisals.

The majority of the Chinese sided with the anti-Japanese movement, but some cooperated with the Gunsei Kambu even though the Gunsei's policies discriminated against the Chinese community. Some did it as a way of protecting the Chinese community, some to protect their own lives, and still others to make money. For the most part, the Chinese who cooperated with the Japanese did so reluctantly. Some collaborators were assassinated by soldiers of the Malayan People's Anti-Japanese Army (MPAJA) during the Occupation and after, while a post-war People's Court put collaborators on trial, and people unable to prove their innocence were ostracised by the community.

Should INA soldiers and Bose be seen as collaborators? Bose was a nationalist who dedicated himself to the liberation and independence of India. To achieve this goal, Bose did not "hesitate to join hands with devil" and parted company with Nehru and Gandhi, who insisted on non-violence. Teaming up with Japan was for Bose, part of the effort to achieve his objective, although Bose could not have been altogether sanguine about future prospects of allying with Japan, having once sadly revealed his inner thought: "There is no real statesman in Japan", and "Tojo is not a man of calibre capable of dealing with world problems".[12] Judging from Bose's sense of independence, his keen perception of international affairs, and his strong leadership style, he could hardly be labelled a collaborator.

The largest anti-Japanese resistance organisation was the MPAJA, largely led by the Malayan Communist Party (MCP), which harassed the Japanese with guerrilla warfare. Throughout the Occupation, the Kempeitai, police and garrison army were constantly ferreting out guerrillas, but supported by the Chinese community and particularly by the Malayan People's Anti-Japanese

Union, supplying food and money, sustained the MPAJA's anti-Japanese campaign. The British military began sending support early in 1944, and by the time the Japanese surrendered, the MPAJA had organised eight battalions deploying in every state and had boasted an army of 7,800 soldiers. The British Government rewarded MPAJA leaders after the war, but the partnership was nothing more than a marriage of political convenience to fight the common enemy, Japanese Army.

Objectives of the Book and Chapter Summaries

In October–November 1995, a group of scholars gathered in Japan and Singapore for conferences on "The Japanese Occupation in Southeast Asian History". The participants presented papers that drew on Japanese, English, Malay and Chinese sources to re-evaluate from an international perspective on the actual state of Southeast Asian countries during the war years and the historical significance of the Japanese Occupation for the region. The participants adopted a much broader approach to the Japanese Occupation than ever before, dealing not only with history, politics and race but also with economics, food, religion, labour, education, transportation and bibliography. The conference led to a number of publications, and stimulated new directions for further research.[13]

The Toyota Foundation supported a project in 1986 for the study of the Japanese Occupation and administration of Southeast Asian countries from 1941 to 1945. The project's objective is threefold; first, to collect primary sources and references (published and unpublished books and articles) that are indispensable for the study of the Japanese military administration; second, to compile a bibliography and publish research results; and third, to conduct interviews with military and civilian officials, as well as soldiers who took part in the Occupation.

Under the project, the Indonesian Forum started in 1986 followed by the Philippines, Malaysia/Singapore, Burma and Timor Forums. With a team of eight academics, we organised the Malaysia-Singapore Forum in 1994, which ended in 1997. During the period, we regularly held meetings and invited persons involved in the administration for interviews. We also scoured archives and libraries, not only in Japan but also in Britain, Malaysia, Singapore, Australia, India, America for published and unpublished materials, particularly personal diaries and memoirs hitherto undiscovered.

Later these primary documents, interview records and a monograph collected as a result of our studies have been published. A bibliography of

Japan-Malaysia-Singapore relations in Japanese, Chinese, Malay and English languages is now being prepared.

The present volume is part of a new, broader approach to the study of the Japanese Occupation. The authors have analysed taking into account broad perspectives. The volume has not only discussed topics of politics and race but also a much wider range of topics including Watanabe's administrative philosophy and its implementation, the wartime economy, the internment of women of the Allied countries, the wartime operations of the Malayan railway system, leaders of the wartime Malayan Communist Party, the massacre of Syonan Chinese and its coverage in postwar Japan, Japanese surrender, Gunsei Kambu research activities, and bibliographical study on the occupation and Japan's relations with Malaysia and Singapore. It includes published and unpublished primary sources, diaries, memoirs, monographs, as well as books published as of around 2000 written in Japanese, English, Chinese and Malay languages.

The first chapter, written by Akashi, concerns the Nanyo Kyokai (South Seas Society), established in 1915 by Inouye Masaji, president of Nan'a Kung-ssu, and Uchida Kakichi, director of the General Affairs of the Government General of Taiwan, was the principal organisation dedicated to the studies of Nanyo affairs during the Taisho (1912–26) and early Showa (1926–45) periods. It was founded following the outbreak of World War I to meet the rising interest in Nanyo in the business circles. The Kyokai's objectives were to disseminate through its monthly journal, *Nanyo*, information for promoting trade, business, economic relations and cultural exchanges, and for training human resources necessary to expand Japanese business in the region. For this purpose, the Kyokai established its office and a commercial museum in Singapore in 1915 and 1916, respectively, to assist business activities and introduce Japanese products to the local market.

As part of expanding its activities in the 1920s, the Kyokai encouraged capital investment and promoted an emigration project. Supported by the government in Tokyo, Inouye persuaded the Kuhara Mining Co. to invest capital for purchasing a rubber plantation estate at Tawau, North Borneo and for emigrating Japanese there.

In cooperation with the government, it also coordinated an ambitious emigration project in Peninsular Malaya for settling several hundred Japanese farmers in Cameron Highlands. The first group of families arrived in 1932 but it turned out to be a failure. By late 1941, only three families had remained there.

After the mid-1930s, with a government subsidy and the appointment of ranking government officials to the Kyokai's executive offices, Kyokai transformed itself from a private association to a semi-government organisation.

Following the outbreak of the Sino-Japanese war in 1937, the journal *Nanyo* reported detailed information on Chinese boycotts and the Kyokai published an English language newspaper in Singapore to inform English-speaking readers of Japan's China policy in order to counter the Chinese anti-Japanese propaganda.

The Kyokai ceased its 30 years of activities in 1945. During the period, it maintained the publication of its monthly journal consisting of 30 volumes; published numerous monographs; presented a series of lectures through which it promoted trade relations with Nanyo and contributed to enlightening people in Nanyo affairs. The Kyokai's collected information provided the Army General Staff with a vital intelligence for the Malayan campaign.

Chapter 2, also by Akashi, describes Watanabe Wataru's administrative philosophy and how he dealt with nationality issues, the economy, industry, finance, bureaucratic problems, the training of young people and Japanese language education. Watanabe developed his administrative policy in occupied China while serving with the *Tokumu Kikan* (Special Service Agency), and he got his appointment in Malaya in recognition of his long career in the political arena. His philosophy is summed up by three principles: "spiritual purification" (禊), "simple rules" (法三章) and "leave things as natural as possible" (無為に化す).

In putting these ideas into practice, Watanabe implemented a hardline policy to deal with the occupied people, especially the Chinese. He wanted indigenous people to repent their subserviency and to be born again through a spiritual purification. Until this was accomplished, Watanabe intended to treat them harshly. The civilians who made up the bureaucratic administration considered Watanabe autocratic. He drafted policies without consulting them, relying on top-down decision-making with a small group of his cronies, and the bureaucrats resented being ignored. A case in point was Watanabe's attempt to make Japanese the official language of government within just a few months. The measure was so radical, unrealistic and impractical that it aroused strong resistance among the bureaucrats and was finally rescinded. On the other hand, Watanabe demonstrated a considerable acumen in dealing with rubber plantations owned by enemy nationals, and with requisitioning rice and providing training for young people.

Watanabe was effective largely because influential Yamashita Tomoyuki, Commanding General of the 25th Army, shared his administrative philosophy and appreciated his ability. After Yamashita left Syonan in July

1942, Watanabe became increasingly isolated in the administration and was unable to exercise power as he wanted. He lost his initial enthusiasm for the administration of occupied Malaya, and returned to Tokyo in March 1943 with mixed feelings of disappointment and relief.

The third chapter, by Hara Fujio, provides a precise analysis of leaders of the wartime Malayan Communist Party (MCP) and of the MPAJA. It is based on hitherto unavailable Chinese language primary sources made public and accessible by the MCP after it concluded an armistice agreement with the governments of Malaysia and Thailand in late December 1989.

The study of wartime MCP leaders has focused mainly on Secretary General Lai Teck, a spy for the Kempeitai whose betrayal led to the arrest and execution of many MCP members. Hara has studied the careers of other top MCP leaders in detail, revealing that the two top leaders of the MCP Central Committee were members of the Chinese Communist Party (CCP) sent to Malaya by the party in the 1930s. The majority of MCP leaders, he said, came from China to Malaya in their childhood, but key pre-war leaders were also members of the CCP sent to supervise the MCP.

Hara has also re-interpreted why the MCP laid down their arms and failed to launch an anti-British struggle after the war ended. The prevailing explanation for this has been that Lai Teck was a double agent of the British. Hara, however, has challenged this interpretation and offered an explanation that it stems from the situation existing in the Chinese community at the time and the awareness MCP leaders had of post-war conditions.

In Chapter 4, Yoshimura Mako surveys the economic policy of the military administration on the Southern region, specifically Japan's policy of acquiring raw materials in Malaya. She has studied the rubber policy examining Showa Rubber Co. as a case study. The Showa Rubber case describes the closure of estate and local workers' lives during the war. In addition to archival materials, the research draws on interviews with villagers living in the neighbourhood of Showa Rubber plantation.

Yoshimura considers the policies and local people's lives in occupied Malaya. When an acute shortage of rice and other daily necessities in Malaya caused prices to skyrocket, the Gunsei Kambu established *kumiai* (associations) for each industry to control production and marketing. When this measure failed to overcome the difficulty, the Gunsei Kambu authorised the felling of unproductive rubber trees in government administrated plantations to make way for food production, and encouraged citizens to grow food on unused land. Owing to a critical shortage of ships and a decline in shipbuilding, stockpiles of rubber and tin waiting to be sent to

Japan accumulated in overflowing storage facilities in harbours throughout Malaya. The failure of the Gunsei Kambu's economic measures had disastrous consequences for the Malayan economy.

She looks at the implications of policies for reparations and for post-war economic recovery and development.

After Japan's surrender, the Allied Powers confiscated Japanese-owned rubber plantations and auctioned off the assets of Japanese subjects and used the proceeds to help meet claims for war damage compensation. These funds were paid off principally to large businesses and ordinary citizens were not compensated for their losses. At the request of the United States, the British Government renounced the right to demand reparation compensation from Japan at the San Francisco Peace Treaty. Residents of Singapore and Malaya, that were then British colonies, thus lost their right to seek redress for the heavy losses they had suffered.

Chapter 5 by Ota Koki, "Railroad Operations in Japanese-occupied Malaya" explores a subject that has not been studied previously. Immediately after the British surrendered, the Japanese Army restored some railway services on the west coast of Malaya to pre-war levels. The east coast railway between Gemas and Kota Bharu was of little value to Japan, and when the Japanese Army needed supplies for Thailand-Burma railway construction, tracks from the Eastern Line and from a branch line that ran between Malacca and Tampin were removed for the purpose.

Ota points out the dual importance the Malayan railway had during the Japanese Occupation. It was not only a means of transporting passengers, materials and munitions locally but also it was an important link with railway networks in French Indochina and, after completion of the Thailand-Burma railway in October 1943, with the Burmese railway system as well.

As the war situation worsened, Allied planes frequently bombed Malayan railway lines and inflicted heavy damages. Ota elaborates the damages as well as train schedules and the frequency of train services using diagrams, tables, graphs and statistics drawn from the Kawahara File. Ota's contribution is a valuable source of information that elucidates this little known area in the history of the Malay Gunsei.

In Chapter 6, Akashi explores the work done by the Chosabus (research departments). In July 1942, the War Ministry organised the Chosabus and dispatched their staff to occupied Burma, Java, North Borneo, Syonan and the Philippines, and it requested Tokyo Shoka Daigaki (alleviated hereafter as Toshodai, now Hitotsubashi University) to form a research group to be attached to the Southern Army General Headquarters at Saigon and later

Syonan after April 1943. Its staff members were recruited largely from the Toshodai faculty and were headed by Professor Akamatsu Kaname. They launched research activities on various aspects of the Malayan society.

Based on field studies on agriculture, economy, education, employment and wages, ethnicity, hygiene, industry, population, religion, and the sultanate, the Chosabu prepared reports known as *Sochoshi* (Nos. 1–36), Malai *Choshi* (Nos. 1–32), and fortnightly Chosabuho (Nos. 1–34), which were to help the military government (Gunsei Kambu) formulate administrative policy.

Col. Hamada Hiroshi, appointed in January 1944 as chief of the General Affairs Department of the 29th Army to which the Chosabu was attached, was receptive to the Chosabu' s advice. Persuaded by Chosabu staff members, he authorised them to engage in political activities and policy making in order to win the cooperation of Chinese and Malays. This was the beginning of the end of the Chosabu as a research body, as it transformed itself to a policy making body.

Hamada appropriated funds to Chosabu staff members for organising the All Malay Muslim Supreme Council held in December 1944 for winning religious leaders and the Epposho (public reading room) for allowing Chinese to air their complaints and to import rice by junks from Thailand. Itagaki Yoichi of the Chosabu helped Ibrahim Yaacob of the Young Malay Union organise the *Kekuatuan Rakyat Istimewa Semenanjung* (KRIS) aimed at achieving national independence.

The Gunsei Kambu at first regarded the Chosabu as a white elephant, and the latter's reports were hardly utilised to reflect them on *gunsei* policy making. Only in 1944, the Gunsei Kambu listened to the Chosabu's suggestions to win popular support.

For nearly two decades in the postwar years, Chosabu activities were hardly known and its reports were not used by scholars partly because the study of World War II had not been popular in those years and access to the archives of the Defence Agency had been restricted until the 1970s with the consequence that a serious academic study of the Chosabu had not been undertaken in Japan.

Chosabu field study reports are of scholarly quality and they are invaluable sources of information on the Occupation period that remains a vacuum in the historical study of contemporary society of Malaysia and Singapore.

In Chapter 7, "The Civilian Women's Internment Camp in Singapore: The World of *POW WOW*", Nakahara Michiko analyses the experiences of women interned in Changi Prison as revealed through a newspaper published in the camp, and the effect of internment on these women's lives after the war. Following the fall of Singapore, 2,800 male and female civilians were interned under harsh conditions. In order to survive, women internees — who comprised different nationalities, religions and social status — established and managed their own prison community. Copies of their camp newspaper, *POW WOW* are held by the Imperial War Museum in London, and they provide a great deal of information about the experiences of the internees. Other sources of Nakahara's article included unpublished diaries, reports and interviews.

In Chapter 8, "Surrendering Syonan", Henry Frei describes events during the final months of the Japanese Occupation of Singapore. He discusses steps taken by Japan to strengthen the city's defences, British plans to recapture Syonan, the movements of the Southern Area Army after the war, the relief activities of Hans Schweizer — a resident of Singapore and the local Red Cross delegate, how the local population reacted to the returning British army, the arrogance of British officers and the life of Japanese soldiers held on Rembang Island.

Using Schweizer's testimony, Frei shows that the British Army's treatment of Japanese soldiers often violated International Law and the principles set down by the Red Cross.[14] Around 600 out of 1,200 Japanese soldiers in Tengah Air Field died from overwork, and another 600 internees on Rembang Island, died from starvation or malnutrition within a few months of being sent there.

According to Frei, Japan's defeat brought about significant changes in Southeast Asian countries during the post-war years, including the retreat of European colonial powers and the independence of Southeast Asian nations. With regards to Australia, Frei argues that 15 August 1945 was a turning point, after which Australia aligned itself more with Southeast Asian nations and Japan rather than with the United Kingdom.

Chapter 9 by Hayashi Hirofumi is in two parts. In the first part, Hayashi traces the origins of massacres committed by Japanese troops to the Sino-Japanese war in the 1930s, when the execution of anti-Japanese prisoners without trial (*genju shobun or genchi shobun*) was condoned, and he examines when and how the policy of killing Chinese in Singapore and Malaya was made and carried out.

The decision for the massacre was made in late January or early February 1942 at the 25th Army headquarters and its commanding general, Yamashita Tomoyuki, gave the order for the severe punishment of the

Chinese. Hayashi argues in rebuttal, that the massacre was carried out because the Dalforce had fought fiercely in the battle of Singapore thereby inflicting heavy casualties on Japanese troops. Chinese guerrillas and supporters had also engaged in subversive activities with the Chinese preparing for an armed insurrection. He also attributes the atrocity to the Japanese culture of discriminating against the Chinese. He concludes that the war crimes committed were not the "conduct of a few evil people but rather a result of a long period of Japanese aggression against China". Therefore, Tsuji Masanobu was not a major figure of the massacre, though he was the principal culprit of the crimes.

In the second part Hayashi examines how postwar Japan has narrated the Singapore massacre. Since regaining sovereignty in 1952, after the ratification of the San Francisco Peace Treaty, there were negative campaigns in the 1950s against war crimes trials, denouncing them as mock trials, or victor's justice or acts of reprisal. In the 1960s, the Japanese government and the mass media had tried to play down the number of the people killed when a large quantity of human remains alleged to be those of the war victims were discovered in Singapore. The Japanese newspapers covered the incident as minor news. In the 1970s, a few Japanese scholars at last came to grip with the study of war crimes, disclosing the atrocities perpetuated by Japanese soldiers in Singapore and Malaya and also some former Kempeitai officers admitted their inhumane treatment of the Chinese.

In the 1980s through the 2000s, several Japanese scholars engaged in documented studies of the war crimes in Singapore and Malaysia and published their works. Government authorised high school history textbooks, however, mention the war crimes only in several lines and revisionists even deny the war crimes had taken place.

Hayashi concludes that there is an abysmal chasm of knowledge about this issue between the Japanese and the Asian neighbours, and that it is necessary for further studies based on Japanese, Chinese, English, and Malay sources.

In the final chapter, Akashi has contributed an article on the study of a selected bibliography, written in Japanese, of published and unpublished primary sources including official papers, personal diaries memoirs, and monographs as well as books published in the period from the late 1940s to around 2000.

The study shows that there were few publications through the late 1960s. It was considered a taboo to write or study about World War II and the Japanese military occupation of Southeast Asian countries, reflecting the post-war pacifism and anti-war and anti-military sentiments prevailing in Japan. The Nishijima Kishi study of Japanese military administration (published in 1959) was virtually ignored in the academic circle. By the time the Japanese had got over the trauma of defeat in war and regained national confidence in the mid-1960s, former soldiers began to write about their experiences in war and journalists and writers published books and articles relating to war. Senki-mono (books about war) created a part of boom in the 1970s through the 1980s.

The record of published books about the war and occupation in Malaya/Singapore statistically and generally followed a similar pattern. They are predominantly about battles and very few are about the military administration.

The one hundred and one volume work of the official history of World War II edited by the War History Department, Institute of National Defence is a useful source of information. The first volume (1966) deals with the Malayan campaign and the last one with Gunsei (1985). They are gold mines for the study of the battle, occupation and gunsei. Also the publication of the Watanabe papers and diary, the Sakakibara papers and diary, the Tokugawa collection and interview record has enhanced the study of gunsei.

Based on these sources, academics have published their works on history, economics, politics, Chinese, *Ianfu* (Comfort women/sexual slavery), *Romusha*, and war crimes.

The Historical Significance of the Japanese Occupation

Malaya and Singapore ended the Occupation in an impoverished state. The people were suffering from acute shortages of foods, clothing, medicines, and daily necessities. The rubber and tin industries — the mainstays of the prewar economy — had been devastated. A sense of uncertainty about the future was pervasive, and the people were restive, mixed with joy from being liberated from the oppressive Japanese rule. The Occupation and the wartime administration brought about radical changes to Malaya and Singapore and they had both positive and negative elements, depending on the experiences of individuals and of various racial communities, and subsequent evaluations of the Occupation similarly vary among Malays, Chinese, Indians, and Eurasians.

Anti-Japanese feelings are most intense and lingering in the Chinese community, as shown in the case of a violent demonstration in August 1958 against Ogata Shinichi, former police superintendent of Singapore. When he made a stop-over there, both Chuan Hui Tsuang, director general of the Singapore Chinese Committee for Calling Attention to Wrongs, and the *Straits Times* accused him of being responsible for the massacre of Chinese carried out by the Japanese army.[15]

In 1962, when human remains, believed to be those killed by the Japanese army, were excavated in the Changi area, Chinese in Singapore and Malaysia demanded a repayment of "Blood Debt", and staged an anti-Japanese boycott. These incidents show that deep-seated anti-Japanese feelings were persistent in the Chinese community of the two countries. On the other hand, there were Chinese who made enormous profits by cooperating with the Gunsei Kambu in the procurement of provisions.

In the early stages of the wartime administration, the government and the military had no concrete policy towards the Malays, apart from the sultans and the Islamic religion. Most Malays living in villages remained passive. Only after 1942, when the tide of the war situation turned against Japan, did the Gunsei Kambu see the need for a policy directed towards the Malays, and it took a series of steps to win popular support within the Malay community. The treatment of the sultans and Islamic religious leaders improved, and the Japanese appointed Malays to local administrative posts over the other racial groups, along with organising the Giyugun. Furthermore, they authorised the organisation of the KRIS movement with a view to granting independence in the future. These policies helped kindle Malay patriotism and a sense of national unity, and contributed to activating a desire to achieve independence. Malay women mobilised for labour service and Tonarigumi (neighbourhood association) activities were freed from household chores, and some Malay women became active participants in politics in post war years, contributing to raising women's social status.

Malays who witnessed the ignominious surrender of the British Army and were inspired by propaganda slogans such as "Asia for Asians" were no longer the "docile" Malays of pre-war years.[16] They fiercely opposed the constitution of the Malayan Union proposed by the British, supported the demand that the scheme be withdrawn, and organised the United Malays National Organisation to assert their rights and identity.

The Occupation had a profound impact on the Indians. Under the charismatic Suhbas Chandra Bose, the INA joined in the Imphal operations for the liberation of India under the slogan "Chalo Delhi" (On to Delhi). Though the INA failed to enter India, it helped raise the political awareness of the Indian people. Not all Indians joined the INA, and the Tamils in particular were skeptical about joining what they saw as a north-Indian dominated organisation. Some Indians acquired skills in mobilising and organising people that allowed them to become leaders after the war.

Communal conflicts between the Malays and the Chinese, both awakened to national aspirations, and an increase in MCP power were indelible legacies of the Occupation, although there is no indication that the Japanese deliberately incited racial or communal strife between Malays and Chinese. The conflict intensified when the Japanese army and police mobilised Malay policemen for an anti-MPAJA campaign. The MPAJA responded by attacking Malay villages and kidnapping collaborators, and the Malays in turn attacked and raided Chinese settlements. The repetition of the reprisals planted the seeds of postwar communal conflict between the two communities.

One of the controversial questions in evaluating the impact of the Occupation is the extent to which it contributed to the independence of Singapore and Malaya. Japan drove out the British colonial power from Malaya and Singapore, but the Japanese government did not intend to grant independence to Malaya, as evidenced by the adoption of "General Guiding Principles for Political Strategy in Greater Asia" (大東亜政略指導大綱) at the Imperial Conference of 31 May 1943, a document stated that "Malaya was to remain Japanese territory", and this decision was "not to be announced for the time being."[17] A Japanese foreign office position paper prepared in June 1945 also concluded that it was difficult to grant independence to the Malays on the account of the country's low economic and cultural standards.[18] In short, Japan planned to retain Malaya as a colony, replacing Britain as the controlling colonial power.

Judging from these statements, Japan did not fight the war for the independence of Malaya and Singapore. The Japanese Occupation reactivated Malay nationalism, and the Malays won independence by themselves, and helped strengthen Singapore residents as "Singaporeans".

As a result of Japan's invasion of China and of the harsh policy towards the Chinese, many of them joined or supported the MPAJA by taking up arms or by aiding it with provisions and funds. After the war, the MPAJA had the strongest and best trained army under the MCP command. Rise of the postwar Malayan People's Liberation Army that threatened law and order in Malaya was attributed to the failure of the Japanese policy in the Occupation period.

Notes

1. The 25th Army Gunseibu administrated Malaya and Sumatra and appointed governors of ten states in Malaya and ten states in Sumatra, and the Mayor of Syonan. On 20 April 1943, following the deployment of the 25th Army to Sumatra, the Southern Army established the Gunsei Kambu directly under its command. On 30 January 1944, when the 29th Army was organised, the Gunsei Kambu was attached to the 29th Army at Kuala Kangsar and later at Taiping (October 1944). With the conclusion of the Japan-Thailand Treaty, Japan transferred Kelantan, Trengganu, Kedah, and Perlis to Thailand in October 1943. In March 1945, the Gunsei Kambu of the 7th Area Army administered Syonan and Johor. In December 1942, "Malay" was designated "Malai". For the structure of the Gunsei Kambu, see Hata Ikuhiko, ed., *The Structure of the Military Administration in the Southern Region and Its Principal Administrators* (南方軍政の機構・幹部軍政官一覧) (Dec. 1998; privately published).

2. Privately published in 1981 and reissued in 1998 by the Ryukei Shosha Publication. Iwatake also published several articles relating to military administration. They are reprinted in the volume, *A Collection of Articles Relating to Military Administration in the Southern Region* (南方軍政論集).

3. *Syonan: Singapore under the Japanese*, a catalogue of oral history interviews, Oral History Department, Singapore, 1986. Force 136 (1), (12), (Pulau Pinang: Universiti Sains Malaysia, 1991). *Reminiscences of Tungku Abdul Rahman on the Japanese Occupation 1941–1945* (Pulau Pinang: Universiti Sains Malaysia, 1989).

4. Paul H. Kratoska, *The Japanese Occupation of Malaya 1941–1945* (London: C. Hurst, 1998); Abu Talib Ahmad, *The Malay Muslims, Islam and the Rising Sun 1941–45* (Kuala Lumpur: Malaysian Branch of the Royal Asiatic Society, 2003).

5. Obata was the section chief of Intelligence, Southern Army, at the beginning of the war. Nishimura was director of the General Affairs Department, 16th Army Gunsei Kambu (Indonesia) Dec. 1944. Tofuku was on the staff of the Accountant's Department, Southern Army.

6. This document was deposited in a safe by the General Staff because Japan-U.S. negotiations had started and the tension of world affairs had somewhat subsided. By the fall of 1941, however, war between Japan and the United States appeared unavoidable, and the General Staff drafted its "Principles for the Administration of the Occupied Southern Region" based on the March document.

7. The Japanese Army accused the Chinese of supporting the British and obstructing Japanese operations. The fierce resistance of the Chinese Voluntary Army (Force D) in the battle of Bukit Timah was viewed as an example of anti-Japanese activities. The soldiers of the 5th and 18th Divisions had been harassed by Chinese guerrillas while fighting in China, and because of that, harboured a strong hostility towards the Chinese. The 25th Army was apprehensive of maintaining the security of Syonan in view of its troops being deployed to Burma and Sumatra, and of anti-Japanese operatives hiding in the city. This insecurity and hostility drove the Japanese soldiers to an extraordinary psychological

state of battle and led them to commit atrocities in Malaya and Singapore. Colonel Sugita [Ichiji], Colonel Oishi [Masayuki] and Lieutenant Colonel Hashizume [Isamu], "A Report on the Investigation of Inhumane Conducts (mainly Chinese) Committed During the Malay (Singapore) Operations", (22 Nov. 1945, top secret). This report was submitted to the Central Committee for the Investigation of Prisoners of War. Sugita and Hashizume were intelligence officers of the 25th Army and Oishi was the commander of the Second Field Kempeitai. (For a different view of the Chinese resistance at Bukit Timah and the Postwar "Report", see Hayashi's article in Chapter 10)

8. Itagaki Yoichi, *Dialogue with Asia* (privately published, Shin Kigensha, 1968).
9. Diary of Tokugawa Yoshichika, entries for 7, 17 and 20 July 1942. Tokugawa induced the sultans to contribute funds for the construction of a memorial for fallen soldiers (13 Sept. 1942), and was involved in the succession of the Sultan of Trengganu (27 Sept. 1942).
10. Directive for the Treatment of the Sultans, Dec. 1942. Telegram from the vice minister of war to the chief of staff, 25th Army.
11. See Itagaki's report on the payment of stipends to sultans: "On Sultan's Political and Religious Prerogatives Prior to War: Pahang and Selangor", *Chosabuho* (調査部), No. 1 (1 May 1944); "The Sultan of Perak", *Chosabuho*, 4 (20 June 1944).
12. Statement of Seki Michisuke. Seki was a Kempeitai sergeant and served as Bose's body guard in 1943.
13. Paul H. Kratoska, ed., *South East Asian Minorities in the Wartime Japanese Empire* (London: Routledge Curzon, 2002); *idem.*, *Food Supplies and the Japanese Occupation in Southeast Asia* (London and Basingstoke: Macmillan Publishing Co., and New York: St. Martin's Press, 1998); *idem.*, *Malaya and Singapore during the Japanese Occupation* (Singapore: Journal of Southeast Asian Studies, 1995); *Journal of Southeast Asian Studies* 27, no. 1 (Mar. 1996): Special Issue on The Japanese Occupation in Southeast Asia.
14. The Japanese side wanted its soldiers not to be treated as POWs. As a result, the British regarded them as "surrendered personnel" and treated them worse than POWs.
15. *Sekai* (世界) (Oct. 1958), pp. 240–4.
16. Zainal Abidn bin Abdul Wahid, ed., *Malaysia no Rekishi* (translation of *Glimpses of Malaysian History* by Nomura Toru) (Tokyo: Yamakawa Shuppansha, 1983), p. 193.
17. Army General Staff, ed., *Sugiyama Memo. A Shorthand Record of Imperial Headquarters — Government Liaison Conferences* (杉山メモ. 大本営・政府連絡会議速記録), vol. 2 (Tokyo: Hara Shobo. 1957), pp. 401, 404. Besides Malaya, Sumatra, Java, Borneo, and Celebes were to be incorporated into Japanese territory.
18. "Papers Relating to the Ministry of Greater East Asian Affairs", in Foreign Office Archives File.

1

The Nanyo Kyokai and British Malaya and Singapore, 1915–45

AKASHI YOJI

The Nanyo Kyokai (South Seas Society) was one of a number of institutions founded in January 1915 in response to Japan's rising interest in the South Seas region following the outbreak of World War I. It was the sole organisation in the Taisho (1912–26) and early Showa (1926–45) periods devoted to the studies of the South Seas region, and played an important role in disseminating information about the region and in training the manpower necessary for Japanese business operations in Nanyo. This chapter examines the activities of the Nanyo Kyokai during its 30-year existence, focusing on British Malaya, Borneo, and Singapore.

Japan's entry into World War I, its occupation of German-held protectorates in the central Pacific and a sharp increase in its exports to the region prompted the establishment of the Nanyo Kyokai. Japan had close geographical, historical and economic ties with Nanyo, Nanyo Kyokai said, and the purpose of founding this association was to promote Japan-Nanyo relations with the aim of expanding mutually beneficial economic and cultural dealings. The efforts of Inouye Masaji, President of Nan'a Company, which operated a rubber plantation in British Malaya, and Uchida Kakichi, Director of the Civil Affairs Department of the Taiwan Government General, got the association off to a promising start in 1913, but it ended up being dissolved two years later, owing to a lack of interest from Japan's business circles. Inouye and Uchida reorganised it in 1915.

To achieve the objective for promoting Japan-Nanyo economic and cultural relations, the Nanyo Kyokai proposed to undertake the following projects:[1]

1. study the industrial, social and cultural affairs of Nanyo;
2. disseminate information about Nanyo and Japan to both parties;

3. promote a good-neighbour policy with the countries of Nanyo through the development of trade and cultural exchanges;
4. train human resources necessary for businesses in Nanyo;
5. publish journals, reports and bulletins;
6. establish museums and libraries.

To carry out research activities and promote economic and business relations, the Nanyo Kyokai established an office in Singapore at 77 Bras Basah Road in 1916 and, in 1918, the Singapore Commercial Museum in the same location.[2] The Museum office published *Nanyo keizai iho* (the Nanyo Economic Bulletin) from 1919 to 1924, after which it was absorbed into a monthly journal called *Nanyo kyokai kaiho* (later renamed *Nanyo kyokai zasshi* and *Nanyo*), first published in 1915. The Museum office also published a monograph series, *Nanyo keizai sosho*, which numbered nineteen volumes by 1935, and it regularly issued reports on economic affairs, including the commodities market, the local economic situation, trade regulations relating to customs, exports and imports, ethnic problems, overseas Chinese and their boycott of Japanese goods, immigration, Japanese economic activities and trade with Japan. These reports were made available to the Nanyo Kyokai members in the *Nanyo*. So valuable was the raw data gathered by the Museum that some of it was distributed to government agencies and business circles as classified information.[3]

The *Nanyo* was the principal publication of the Nanyo Kyokai. The first issue appeared in January 1915 and the last in October 1944, for a total of 30 volumes. A typical number of this monthly periodical contained 100–130 pages, and included an editorial, reportage contributed by government company, the Nanyo Kyokai and officials trading with the Nanyo, miscellaneous articles about local customs, travelogues and news of recent events.

Besides publishing the *Nanyo* journal, the Kyokai managed a language school and on-the-job training institutes to deal with anti-Japanese movements organised by overseas Chinese whose boycotts threatened Japanese trade and business in the region and expand business and commercial opportunities.

Emigration Project[4]

One of the Nanyo Kyokai's major projects was to promote the emigration of Japanese farmers to North Borneo and peninsular Malaya. Several field studies were conducted to ascertain the feasibility of the project. This initiative dates back to 1913 when the Governor of North Borneo, A.C. Pearson, invited Japanese emigrants to North Borneo and thereby generated Japanese interest in a project of this nature. Subsequently, the Nanyo Kyokai and the Japanese government sent researchers to North Borneo to conduct a feasibility study. Sakai Rikita, a rubber plantation engineer and an associate of the Nanyo Kyokai, made survey trips in 1914 and 1915, visiting Tawau and the Mt. Kinabalu area, respectively. Other trips were made in early 1915 by a man named Kato of Toyo Immigration, in mid-1915 by Miho Goro, Secretary of the Japanese Legation in Bangkok (and Director of the Singapore Commercial Museum from 1921 to 1924), and by Goto Fusaji, a forestry specialist attached to the North Borneo Government and later to the Agriculture and Commerce Ministry. Matsuoka Wasaji, a research specialist of the Government General of Taiwan and Fujii Minoru, Consul of Singapore, also made visits to North Borneo.

All of them, but especially Miho, strongly recommended that Japanese settlers be sent to North Borneo, and prospects for the emigration project looked rosy. In a lecture at a Nanyo Kyokai meeting, Miho extolled the scheme, encouraging Japanese farmers to go to North Borneo to plant rice because the country depended upon rice imports. The Government of North Borneo, he said, would welcome Japanese settlers with open arms by "providing transportation fares and free land with an advance loan for living expenses and by building houses", if they brought with them the cash necessary for cultivating the land. He also promised that the settlers would be entitled to hold the land they cultivated for 999 years. Miho cautioned individuals with meager capital not to take on this risk, but strongly urged corporations to invest capital in the scheme. Miho was optimistic that if corporations provided large initial capital investments, the emigration scheme would succeed. Consul Fujii, in a series of five lectures, supported Miho's recommendation and urged the business community to inject ¥500,000 to help promote the project.[5]

Inouye Masaji, Nanyo Kyokai's executive director, was known as the "father of emigration". He commissioned the study of the North Borneo emigration project, and after reading the Miho-Fujii reports, concluded that the project held potential for the expansion of Japanese activities in North Borneo, and purchased a rubber estate owned by the North Borneo government. Inouye used the good offices of Prime Minister Okuma Shigenobu and Prince Yamagata Aritomo, an influential senior statesman, to convince Kuhara Fusanosuke,[6] President of Kuhara Mining Company, to invest the capital needed to buy the property. The acquisition of the estate, Inouye said, was not only for settling Japanese emigrants but also for blocking "the southward movement of the United States from the Philippines and expanding [Japan's influence] in the Dutch East Indies".[7] Thus Inouye and the Nanyo Kyokai helped launch the Kuhara mining company into the rubber plantation business.

In the 1920s, the Nanyo Kyokai and its officials consistently appealed to businessmen and ordinary people to visit the southern areas, and stressed the need to create a strong financial institution to support Japanese trade and business there. They felt that the investment of a few hundred million yen over the next twenty to thirty years would lay a solid foundation for Japan's economic expansion into Nanyo. At the time, Japan faced serious political, economic and social problems that were giving rise to instability domestically, and it was in this context that the Nanyo Kyokai called upon people to embark on overseas ventures. The editorials in its periodicals expounded the view that North Borneo and peninsular Malaya were ready to accept young, skilled Japanese craftsmen and entrepreneurs as immigrants.

To implement its emigration programme, the Nanyo Kyokai carried out feasibility studies betweeen 1926 and 1932 with the help of government agencies, resulting in the following reports: "Siam as an Investment Opportunity for Japanese Entrepreneurs" (1926), "A Study of Rice Cultivation Experiments in Sarawak" (1929), "A Study of Emigration to Peninsular Malaya" (1930) and "A Study of Emigration to North Borneo" (1932). The Malay study of 1930 was a classified project that secured support from the Ministry for Colonial Affairs, which was searching for suitable places for Japanese migrants to settle as independent agriculturists.[8]

The study was carried out by a Nanyo Kyokai officer named Iiizumi Ryozo, who was instructed by Minister Matsuda Genji to keep this assignment secret lest it arouse suspicion on the part of the British colonial authorities. Prior to Iiizumi's departure, Foreign Minister Shidehara Kijuro also instructed the acting Japanese Consul General in Singapore to provide any assistance needed to carry out the field study, and to supervise his activities. The consulate took elaborate measures to keep this sensitive mission secret.

Iiizurni travelled for four months in the Netherlands Indies and Singapore before arriving in Malaya, where he joined Sakai Rikita of the Colonial Affairs Ministry and Masubuchi Sahei, Director of the Singapore Commercial Museum. Together they went to Cameron Highlands in the western part of the state of Pahang and spent several days there on a field study so well hidden that the British Special Branch was unware of it. It was only by 1936 or thereafter when fourteen families had settled in Cameron Highlands that the police found out about the Nanyo Kyokai's involvement in a Cameron Highlands project.[9] Eric Robertson of the British Forest Service[10] said in his book *The Japanese File* that the Cameron Highlands scheme was an example of Japanese illegal activities, and that the Japanese frequently approached Europeans living in Cameron Highlands to ask if they were interested in hiring Japanese farmers. One of the leaders of the scheme, he said, was the director of the Singapore Commercial Museum.[11]

In subsequent issues of *Nanyo*,[12] Iiizumi described the Cameron Highlands as a place with fertile soil and a mild climate, a land of opportunity for enterprising small Japanese farmers willing to settle there. Farmers could make as much as $1,000 a year growing vegetables and raising hogs and save $500. According to Consul General Tamura of Singapore, the British Governor General was enthusiastic about the settlement project. Advertising Cameron Highlands as well-suited for growing highland vegetables and fruits, Iiizurmi suggested that only Japanese farmers with their superior skills were capable of developing Cameron Highlands, and that British residents in the area felt the same.

After visiting the Cameron Highlands again in late September 1936, Inouye was firmly persuaded that conditions there would allow Japanese vegetable growers to raise their businesses to a higher level, and that the scheme would become a symbol of Anglo-Japanese collaboration. His real intention for the project, however, was for "the vegetable growers of Cameron Highlands [to] form the base of our advance north", a movement that would not only include Pahang but also Siam.[13] This statement understandably further aroused British suspicions.

The Cameron Highlands scheme envisaged the settling of several hundred farmers, and the first group of families arrived in 1932, but in the event only twenty families came. A few made a profit, but most families returned home broke before the outbreak of war in December 1941, while others were arrested and sent to India where they remained in an internment camp until after the war was over.

The agricultural colonisation scheme supported by the Nanyo Kyokai was not a success. Hara Fujio attributes its failure to several factors, including the difficulty of acquiring large non-hillside tracts of lands that were profitable, competition from Chinese farmers, and the Chinese boycott of Japan that erupted in the wake of the Sino-Japanese war of 1937. Just three families remained in the Cameron Highlands at the end of 1941, sustained by the successful cultivation of tomatoes.[14]

Nanyo Kyokai's Singapore Office and the Commercial Museum

The Nanyo Kyokai opened a Singapore office in 1916 to help protect the interests of the Japanese business and trading community in the British colony. In 1917 the colonial administration passed a "The Rubber Lands Restriction Enactment" that prohibited foreigners from acquiring title to more than fifty acres of land. The Singapore office presented a petition to the Ministry of Foreign Affairs requesting that it raise the issue with the British government on grounds that the ordinance was contrary to the spirit of Japanese cooperation with Britain in World War I under the Anglo-Japanese Alliance, and would bring to naught the current endeavours of Japanese estate owners and undermine their future projects. Subsequently the Singapore office, acting on behalf of Japanese rubber estate owners, submitted to the Ministries of Agriculture and Finance a request for compensation for financial losses sustained as a result of a sharp drop in rubber prices in 1920.[15] The office also helped arrange the itinerary of the Sultan of Johor's 1934 visit to Japan; he was invited by Marquis Tokugawa Yoshichika, and Fujiyama Raita, vice-chairman of the Nanyo Kyokai, who also hosted a luncheon party and a tea party for the royal couple at his residence.

The Singapore Commercial Museum was founded in 1918 with four objectives:

1. studying economic policy for Nanyo;
2. planning policies and promoting the export of Japan's high quality commodities to Nanyo;
3. improving the quality of Japan's export products for sale in the Nanyo and improving business knowhow;
4. developing and utilising Nanyo's natural resources.

In support of these goals, the Commercial Museum exhibited Japanese and local products, advised manufacturers to improve quality and design, facilitiated business transactions and sales of consigned commodities, investigated credit inquiries, conducted economic research, published monographs and organised bazaars in Japan and Nanyo displaying sample goods.[16]

In addition to these activities, the Commercial Museum instituted a one-year *shogyo jisshusei* programme (on-the-job practical business training) in 1919 to train young men needed to carry out business operations in Nanyo. Students in this programme lived together in dormitories, studied Malay (or Dutch or Chinese) and English and economic and regional affairs; they also gleaned practical business skills from internship at local Japanese shops. The Museum office, however, closed the programme in 1921 due to financial problems and difficulties in placing its graduates with local firms.[17]

Responding to demands from Nanyo that arose from the Chinese boycott, Nanyo Kyokai headquarters in Tokyo instituted a similar *shogyo jisshusei* programme in 1929. The new version trained male middle school graduates, who were about 18 years of age, in practical business skills so that they would be able to establish their own shops and develop new business connections to sell Japanese goods without having to rely on Chinese intermediaries.

The institute trained 798 young men as of 1943, of whom 669 remained in the Nanyo, and 116 became independent shop owners. Beginning in 1931, the Museum office helped trainees find positions in Singapore and peninsular Malaya. As of 1938 a total of 39 trainees had settled in British Malaya, 28 of them in Singapore, but very little information is available about their activities.[18] Like the Japanese farmers in Cameron Highlands, most of these trainees were presumably arrested when the Pacific War broke out and sent to India, while others may have worked for the wartime Japanese military administration.

Nanyo Kyokai in the 1930s

Until 1927, the Nanyo Kyokai remained a private organisation primarily interested in the economic activities of Nanyo, as reflected in the profile of the members of its executive board — predominently professionals who represented business interests. With the Nanyo *shogyo jisshusei* programme, the Nanyo Kyokai received in 1938 a subsidy of ¥135,000 plus a further subsidy of ¥50,000 for cultural and economic operations from the Foreign Affairs Ministry for the association's annual budget, and was transformed into a *hankan hanmin* (semi-government) organisation.[19] In 1938 businessman Fujiyama Raita resigned from his post as vice chairman of the executive board, and Inouye from his post as executive director. Fujiyama's replacement was Kodama Hideo, a former Minister of Colonial Affairs, and the new executive director was Hayashi Kyujiro from the Foreign Office. Following this change, the Nanyo Kyokai came increasingly under bureaucratic government control.

Hayashi made it clear that under his leadership, Nanyo Kyokai would pursue a peaceful policy aimed at "developing cultural exchanges and economic cooperation, for the happiness of all peoples concerned and for the benefit of mutual co-existence and co-prosperity". Possessing human resources and capital, Hayashi said, Japan was on a mission to develop Nanyo's abundant resources for world peace and the prosperity of humanity.[20]

Inouye in his parting statement warned against the "southward movement" fever, a sentiment popularised by various publicists and by Murobuse Tananobu's *Nanshinron* (A Discourse on Southward Movement) in 1936, the publication coincided with the government's adoption on 7 August 1936 of *Kokusaku no Kijun* (The Fundamental Principles of National Policy), that pronounced *Nanshin* as the national policy, espoused particularly by the Navy. Inouye cautioned against idle talk about *Nanshinron* lest it aroused suspicion. He advised his colleagues to adhere to the Nanyo Kyokai's founding principles of researching and studying the industry, society and culture of the Nanyo, and promoting good relations and trade between Nanyo and Japan.[21]

A few weeks after the reorganisation of the Nanyo Kyokai, the association's new executives held a meeting with government and navy officials to discuss its future policy. They invited navy officers because the Navy had a keen interest in Nanyo affairs, as reflected in the establishment of the Committee for Policy Study of the Southern Region (*Tai Nampo hosaku kenkyu iinkai*) in July 1935. Asked by Ishizawa Yutaka of the Foreign Affairs Ministry about the Navy's position towards the Nanyo Kyokai, Captain Oka Takasumi, a member of the Committee and Chief of the First Section of the Military Affairs Bureau, which was responsible for political affairs, assured Ishizawa that the Navy would positively support the Nanyo Kyokai's economic and cultural policies and would not interfere with the association's civilian control.[22]

Following the establishment of the Committee and the adoption of the "Fundamental Principles of National Policy" by the cabinet in August 1936, officers of the Army Ministry, Army General Staff, Naval General Staff and Planning Board were regularly present at the Nanyo Kyokai's intelligence gathering lectures.[23]

The outbreak of the Sino-Japanese war in July 1937 and the ensuing Nanyang Chinese boycott confronted the Japanese government with serious problems such as a decline in the volume of business and trade as well as the safety of Japanese residents. The opening article in the October 1937 issue of *Nanyo* was a detailed report about the Chinese boycott and the anti-Japanese national salvation movement. The Nanyo Kyokai's Singapore Commercial Museum office kept the journal's subscribers informed about the boycott movement in Singapore and peninsular Malaya, where the anti-Japanese movement was most intense, and inflicted serious damage upon Japanese businesses and trade for many months. To cope with the worsening situation, the Nanyo Kyokai in September 1938 published *Bulletin of the South Seas Society*, a monthly journal in English catered to an English speaking audience. It called for a better understanding of Japanese history and culture.

The Chinese boycott was a major topic in reports presented by delegates who attended a Conference of Nanyo Economic Problems held in September 1939 in Tokyo, Osaka-Kobe and Nagoya under the auspices of Nanyo Kyokai. Matsumoto Saburo of Showa Rubber, Sakano Kazuichi of Sakano Co., Uo Eijiro of Senda Trade Co. and Ichihara Akinori of Nippon Yusen from Singapore presented their views on the Chinese boycott and its effects on Japanese trade and businesses in British Malaya.[24] Quoting statistics compiled by the Museum office in Singapore, Ichihara reported that imports from Japan dropped from $32,546,000 in 1936 to $12,426,000 in 1938, a decline of 60 per cent. Speaking of the boycott's effect on merchant shipping, Ichihara said Nippon Yusen lost business with Chinese who were formerly their best clients for the export of canned pineapple, a major export commodity of Malaya, from Singapore to England. In addition, Chinese coolies at Muar, Malacca, Port Swettenham and Penang refused to handle Japanese freight. The British administration, Ichihara suspected, acquiesced the Chinese boycott going as long as it did not get out of hand.[25]

Sakano, who owned his own company and had been a resident of Singapore for 20 years, reported on the plight of 1,000 displaced Japanese fishermen (one-quarter of the Japanese population in the city) and of mining companies that were forced to suspend their operations as a result of Chinese labourers going on strike. Small Japanese and indigenous shops were also reported to have suffered sharp losses, with a number of business owners losing their bank credit and thus being forced out of business. Sakano was pessimistic about the prospect of an early end of the Chinese boycott, partly because the colonial administration had turned a blind eye to the boycott, insinuating that Chinese could carry it on as long as they did not harm Japanese residents, and partly because Tan Kah Kee, a leader of the Chinese community, and his cohorts had been actively inflaming anti-Japanese feelings.

In 1939, Sakano said, the Japanese community had tried to counteract the Chinese boycott with a public relations campaign conducted through the *Singapore Herald*, a Japanese-owned English language newspaper subsidised by the Japanese Consulate General, but the press campaign did little to remedy the situation. Sakano said Wang Ching-wei's government would be no help to diffuse the boycott.[26] Uo Eijiro, an executive of Senda Trade Co., like Sakano, had lived in Singapore for 20 years, reported that this difficult situation would not end soon. He saw no immediate abatement of the boycott and asked the government to do its utmost to subdue the Chiang Kai-shek government in order to end the boycott.[27] The Conference resolved to request the government to promote trade and friendship, protect retail merchants and train human resource.

In December 1940, Imperial General Headquarters organised Taiwan Army Unit 82, the Research Department of the Japanese Army in Taiwan. It took over the task of reconnoitring all territories in the Southern region which Japan aimed to invade, and became an intelligence and planning nerve-centre for the Malaya-Singapore campaign. The brain behind the intelligence operation in Malaya was Lt. Col. Tsuji Masanobu, the "god of operations", who was later joined by Maj. Asaeda Shigeharu and Maj. Hayashi Tadahiko. The Unit was told to accumulate the latest intelligence on military formations, equipment, weapons, medicine, hygiene, and geographical information, and to devise administrative machinery suitable for Malaya and Singapore. Because the Army was very poorly off in terms of information and maps of Malaya, the Unit tapped the library resources of the Nanyo Kyokai's Taiwan office, Government General of Taiwan's Nanpo Kyokai, and the Taiwan Bank.[28]

By the time war broke out in December 1941, the Unit had prepared a booklet titled, "Read This Booklet. You Win Victory" (*Kore wo yomeba katsu*). This booklet was distributed to soldiers of Yamashita's 25th Army. Tsuji, Asaeda and Hayashi all became staff officers of this Army, and they were responsible for the *Sook Ching* (massacres) in Singapore in February and March 1942. With the occupation of Malaya and Singapore in February 1942, the Nanyo Kyokai ceased its business in those territories. The Malay military administration did not authorise the reopening of the Nanyo Kyokai's Singapore office, nor did it utilize Nanyo Kyokai's human resources for research or seek advice from Inouye. In fact, Inouye was practically ignored by the government and military officials throughout the war years.[29]

The Nanyo Kyokai administered the government sponsored *Nanyo Gakuin* established in Saigon in 1942. It was a three-year programme to train young men aspiring to dedicate themselves to Japan's economic development in Nanyo. 112 trainees went through the programme before it closed in August 1945. The army drafted the first and second batches of

60 students in October 1944, and they took part in the "Meigo" Operation for the occupation of French Indochina.[30]

Conclusion

From its inception, the Nanyo Kyokai played a major role in facilitating Japanese economic penetration into British Malaya. The Singapore office accumulated a vast store of useful information about British Malaya evaluation related to business and trade opportunities. It also helped train young men who went on to build a retail network for Japanese commodities that did not depend on Chinese retailers, but the number of trainees was too small to permit an evaluation of the programme's success.

As a lobbying organisation, the Nanyo Kyokai successfully represented the interests of the Japanese business community in British Malaya and Singapore. Its emigration scheme, however, was not only a failure but also engendered British distrust and gave the Nanyo Kyokai a negative image in the British eyes.

During the Allied occupation of Japan (1945–52), the Nanyo Kyokai was dissolved and its treasure trove of materials dispersed. The Allied Powers seized its accumulated assets at home and abroad, and much of its library holdings was lost or dispersed. In 1956, a group of people interested in Malaysia resuscitated what was left of the Nanyo Kyokai's activities and created the Japan-Malaysian Society, with Aoki Kazuo, former Minister of Greater East Asian Affairs as the first chairman and Raja Non Chik as an advisor. Other leading figures in Malaysia who have held this position, including Tun Dato Seri Hamdan Tahir, a former head of state in Penang. The Society, following in the footsteps of the Nanyo Kyokai, devotes its activities entirely to promoting mutual friendship and understanding and cultural exchanges between Japan and Malaysia.

Notes

1. Nanyo Kyokai, *Nanyo Kyokai 10 nenshi* (Tokyo: Nanyo Kyokai, 1915), p. 7.
2. Ibid., p. 145.
3. See a list of titles classified as restricted, *Nanyo Kyokai Zasshi* 10, no. 9 (1923): 117.
4. I am grateful to Hara Fujio for information provided in this section. See his *Eiryo Maraya no Nipponjin* (Tokyo: Ajia Keizai Kenkyujo, 1986), pp. 75–115.
5. Inouye Masaji, *Kensoroku* (Tokyo: Daisansha, 1944), pp. 533, 585; *Nanyo Kyokai Kaiho* 2, 3 (1916): 21, 22, 41–4; 2, 6 (1916): 35–7; 2, 7 (1916): 11–3; 2, 10 (1916): 33.
6. Kuhara was a conservative politician, whose mining company became Nissan Sangyo, or Nissankozan.

7. Inouye, *Kensoroku*, p. 533.

8. Gaimusho Gaiko Shiryokan Monjo, *Honpo Imin Hogo Shorei oyobi Kyusai Kankei Zakken: Eikoku Kankei* (*Zokkoku Chiho wo fukumu*), "Eiryo Marei ni okeru Chusho Gomuen Shirabe", 1932, quoted from Hara, *Eiryo Maraya*, p. 75.

9. Nanyo Kyokai, *Nanyo Kyokai 10 nenshi*, p. 145; Eric Robertson, *The Japanese File: Prewar Japanese Penetration in Southeast Asia* (Hong Kong: Heinemann Asia, 1979), p. 11.

10. Robertson served in Malaya from 1938 to 1942. In 1940 he was transferred to a unit called Frontier Patrol, which gathered intelligence along the Thailand-Malaya border.

11. Robertson, *The Japanese File*, p. 12.

12. *Nanyo*, 21, 8 (1935); 22, 4, 7, 8 (1936).

13. Robertson, *The Japanese File*, p. 12.

14. Hara, *Eiryo Maraya*, pp. 82–113.

15. Nanyo Kyokai, *Nanyo Kyokai 10 nenshi*, pp. 115–6, 120–1.

16. Ibid., pp. 202–6.

17. Ibid., pp. 211–4; Nanyo Kyokai, *Nanyo Kyokai 20 nenshi*, p. 317.

18. Teisei [Nomura Sadao], "Jinbutsu no Yosei wa ikan", *Nanyo Kyokai Zasshi*, 8, 2 (1922); "Jinko Mondai kara mita Nanyo Hattensaku", *Nanyo oyobi Nipponjin* (1924): 2–3; Nanyo Kyokai, *Nanyo Kyokai 20 nenshi*, pp. 289–93, 321–7; Ikeda Yo, "Nanyo Kyokai no Jigyo", *Nippongo* (1944): 34; Kawanishi Akihiro, "Nanyo Kyokai to Nampo Shinshitsu no Shoso", MA thesis, Faculty of Literature, Sophia University, 1998.

19. Kawanishi, *Nanyo Kyokai*, pp. 78–83. Originally it was proposed ¥120,000.

20. "Rijicho Shunin ni saishite", *Nanyo* 24, 5 (1938): 2–5.

21. "Senmuriji yori Sodanyaku e", *Nanyo* 24, 5 (1938): 11.

22. O-A Kyoku Dai Sanka, "Nanyo Kyokai Kongo no Hoshin ni kansuru ken", 9 May 1938.

23. Daitobunka Daigaku Toyo Kenkyujo, ed., *Showa Shakai Keizai Shiryo Shusei 2: Kaigun no Shiryo* (*1*) (Tokyo: Ochanomizu Shobo, 1978), p. 68. Among those who attended were: Maj. Manaki Takanobu who was to become deputy chief of staff of the 25th Army, the force that invaded Malaya, and Maj. Sugita Ichiji, who would become an intelligence staff officer in the 25th Army.

24. Nanyo Kyokai, *Nanyo Keizai Kondankai* (Tokyo: Nanyo Kyokai, 1940), marked with "top secret", pp. 46–50.

25. Ibid., pp. 51–4.

26. Ibid., pp. 91–6.

27. Ibid., pp. 303–8.

28. Masanobu Tsuji, *Singapore 1941–1942: The Japanese Version of the Malayan Campaign of World War II* (Singapore: Oxford University Press, 1988), pp. 6–13.

29. For the area administered by the 25th Army, a research department was established with members appointed from the faculty of the Tokyo College of Commerce (now Hitotsubashi University). See Chapter 6 for information.

30. Kameyama Tetsuzo, Nanyo Gakuin (Tokyo: Fuyo Shuppan Shobo, 1996).

2

Colonel Watanabe Wataru: The Architect of the Malayan Military Administration, December 1941–March 1943

AKASHI YOJI

The 25th Army of General Yamashita Tomoyuki made landings in the early morning hours of 8 December 1941 at Singora in Southern Thailand and Kota Bahru in the northeast corner of the Malay peninsula. As its troops occupied city after city, the 25th Army's Gunseibu (Military Administration Department) established provisional military administrative offices, each staffed by a small number of officers.

On 15 February, Yamashita's Army captured Singapore, and the British forces surrendered. The Gunseibu, headed by Maj. Gen. Manaki Takanobu, deputy chief of staff of the 25th Army, then became responsible for the administration of Malaya. His deputy, Col. Watanabe Wataru, effectively ran the administration because, in Watanabe's opinion, it was impossible for Manaki to carry out the task of deputy chief of staff and supervise the Gunseibu at the same time. Besides, Manaki had no expertise in military administration, while Watanabe had spent ten years in occupied north China as an administrator of the Special Service Agency (Tokumu Kikan) and a political liaison officer with responsibility for political and economic affairs. For his military career record, he was known as a political officer and as a *Shinaya* (China expert).[1] In addition, he had spent a year (October 1940 to November 1941) at the Institute of Total War, where he studied military administration and the use of military resources.[2]

Proud to the point of conceit about his expertise in military administration, Watanabe was disgusted with Manaki's haphazard approach, and his ideas that did not rest on principles, which he felt compromised the military administration. Watanabe eventually pushed Manaki into the position of mayor of Syonanto (the wartime name for Singapore) in order to remove him from the Gunseibu.[3] Odachi Shigeo replaced Manaki as mayor on

11 March 1942, and Manaki became chief of staff of the North Borneo Garrison Army in April.

Watanabe now became head of the Gunseibu, and in July, head of the General Affairs Department. He held this position until March 1943, and developed what is known as the "Watanabe *Gunsei*".

The Watanabe Gunsei Philosophy

During his military career in northern China and Manchuria, Watanabe had developed a unique gunsei philosophy for use in administering occupied people. At the start of the Occupation, he considered it both necessary and feasible to "coerce the occupied people with resolution responding to the needs of military operations." To begin with a "claptrap policy of sympathy and promises that could not be implemented," he insisted, was "absolutely to be avoided". In Malaya, according to Watanabe,

> The indigenous people who had submitted themselves to British rule for such a long time must be made aware of their need to reflect on their conduct and must be taught to endure hardship as citizens of greater Asia for its prosperity. They can no longer be allowed to indulge themselves in a hedonistic and wasteful way of life that is eating up their mind and spirit.
>
> The fundamental principle of my nationality policy is to require them to account for their past mistakes and to make them ready to give up their lives and property. Only when they repent their wrongdoing, will I allow them to live, and I will return their property once they repent.[4]

This nationality policy can be summarised by the concept of *misogi*, or spiritual cleansing, and it was the cardinal *gunsei* principle that he had derived from his long experience in the administration of the occupied people in Manchuria and China.[5] He also demanded *misogi* from his fellow Japanese, seeing in Greater East Asia an opportunity for them to correct their depraved way of life tainted by liberalism, materialism, and epicurianism, and to restore an indomitable spirit embedded in Japan's traditional culture.

Watanabe's second *gunsei* principle, derived from his ten years of experience in the reconstruction of an occupied territory, is *mui ni kasu*, or leave things as natural as possible. What he meant by *mui ni kasu* was that the most important thing in politics was to refrain from giving unwanted policy guidance in an attempt to provide people with a more civilised way of life. Actually, he said, such a policy was uncalled-for meddling that resulted in "misgovernment with a good intention" and was contrary to the spirit of *mui ni kasu*.

The third *gunsei* administrative principle Watanabe espoused was *ho sansho*, or the fewer regulations and laws there are, the better it is for the administration of occupied territory, because a government hedged with regulations would become inflexible and discourage people from taking any initiative. To run a government, Watanabe maintained, is to leave the administrative responsibility to trusted staff, allowing them to exercise their ability to the fullest.

Prior to his appointment to the Institute of Total War, Watanabe had maintained that war against the Anti-Axis Power was inevitable, and that Japan should declare war without delay against the Anti-Axis Power, because the longer the delay, the more Japan would face an unprecedented crisis. But as he studied Japan's resources and power at the Institute, he became convinced that hostilities should be postponed to as late as possible, on the grounds that the nation's military strength was yet inadequate for war and prospects for winning would not be in Japan's favour. Watanabe's misgivings about hostilities against Britain and the United States were due to Japan's vulnerability against economic blockade, inadequate anti-air defence, and difficulties in defending and administering the vast occupied territory of the southern area, which spanned tens of thousands of miles, while Japan was still fighting an unfinished war in China that had sapped the nation's strength and resources.[6]

With such apprehensions, Watanabe, on orders from the chief of staff of the 25th Army, left Tokyo for Saigon on 26 November 1941 still unprepared for his task.

Upon his appointment to Gunseibu deputy chief, Watanabe examined the "Principles for the Implementation of Military Administration in the Occupied Southern Area" that had been adopted on 20 November by the Imperial Headquarters-Government Liaison Conference. He severely criticised the three *gunsei* principles of the document: acquisition of strategic materials, establishment of the self-sufficiency of the occupying army, and restoration of law and order.[7]

Watanabe was dissatisfied with the document because it had no fundamental principles for constructing a Greater East Asia Co-Prosperity Sphere nor did it have the spirit of *misogi* that was required of the Japanese and indigenous peoples of Asia for the administration of the southern area. He was also dissatisfied with the organisation of the Gunseibu, which, according to the "Principles", was just a department with no executive power, attached to the 25th Army command. He insisted that the Gunseibu, instead of being just a *gunsei* guidance department, should have the power to execute policy for the restoration of law and order and for the postwar administration of occupied territory.[8]

Watanabe was also dismayed at the incompetence of elite staff officers at the Army's central headquarters who, out of ignorance about the extremely difficult task of restoring law and order in a war-devastated occupied country, assigned only 70 officers for the mission. He was disgusted with the unrealistic number of personnel which the "elite" armchair staff officers at Army Central Headquarters were planning to assign.[9]

Faced with the almost impossible task of administering an occupied territory whose administrative machinery was practically non-existent as a result of wartime destruction, Watanabe requested an emergency measure of an additional 500 personnel. The Army General Staff rejected the request as an astronomical figure but authorised the allocation of an additional 25 officers,[10] supplemented by 50 volunteers Watanabe himself recruited in Japan and Malaya. The personnel Watanabe recruited were cronies of his who had worked with him in Manchuria and North China when he was director of the *Tokumu Kikan* (Special Service Agency) and who came from his home province of Okayama.[11] They soon formed the core of the Watanabe Gunsei, characterised as a "brain-trust-staff *gunsei*".

With the reorganisation of the Gunseibu into a Gunsei Kambu in July 1942, the Army Ministry dispatched numbers of bureaucrats recruited from various government agencies. The arrival of the bureaucrats, who were accustomed to government by regulations, soon caused serious friction with Watanabe and his brain trust *gunsei*, who exercised *dokudan senko* (the power of arbitrary decision-making and execution exercised by staff officer) based upon Watanabe's principle of *ho sansho*. The Watanabe brain-trust *gunsei* was impatient with inflexible bureaucrats who, Watanabe lamented, had little sense of the crisis the nation was facing.[12]

Furthermore, Watanabe was displeased with interference from staff officers of the 25th Army Headquarters in military administrative matters. From the very beginning they maintained that the army commander had the power for decision-making in matters to do with *gunsei*; therefore, his staff officers should be involved in *gunsei*. Because the staff personnel of the Gunseibu were of poor stuff, staff officers should advise them with their superior intelligence. The result was the establishment of a Gunsei Council which was to deliberate all important *gunsei* policy.[13]

Once established, the Council did not function at all except interfering in the operation of the *Gunseibu* and created conflict. According to Watanabe, the Council hardly deliberated what might be considered important policy and died a natural death in late April, when the senior staff officer who originally pushed for the Council was transferred to a new post in Tokyo. Watanabe blamed the friction created against his staff on that officer's "casual idea hatched out of a desk plan" and also upon a chief of staff who, having "no firm administrative principle of his own", was easily swayed by his subordinate.

Watanabe attributed the incompetence of desk-bound elite staff officers to the seniority system of promotion based on academic record at the Military Academy and the War College. Under that system, top graduates were promoted faster and appointed to important posts at the central command.[14] With his practical experiences in the field, Watanabe was apprehensive about *gunsei*'s future, because he wondered whether he would be able to exercise his power while having to cope with these armchair staff officers toying with their impractical ideas.

He also clashed with his senior officers over the appointment of retired older generals to be governors of occupied territories.[15] Watanabe proposed that retired generals be drafted to the posts because of their familiarity with the army system and military discipline and their eagerness to serve their country again. His superiors, however, were reluctant to accept this idea, saying that the appointment of such older generals would create complications in the command system. He insisted that there would be "no problems in handling them" if the chief of staff and his deputy had the ability to deal with them. The only reason for their reluctance was their own inability to control them. Gaining Yamashita's endorsement, Watanabe had his way on this point.[16] From among 14 retired generals, Watanabe nominated seven to be appointed as governors in Malaya and Sumatra (which had been merged in March 1942 with the Malay Gunseibu). Through the mediation of the editor-in-chief of the *Asahi* newspaper, Watanabe also recruited Odachi Shigeo, former vice minister of the all-powerful Ministry of Internal Affairs, who was to become the first mayor of Syonan Special Municipality. Ironically, Watanabe would clash with Odachi later.[17]

Watanabe also took exception to the *gunsei* advisory system when four advisors, including Marquis Tokugawa Yoshichika, were appointed. He thought that the number was just too many, and that only two were needed to be in charge of industry, transportation and culture but he remained skeptical about whether his superiors were capable of tapping the talents of the advisors. He was not, however, completely negative about the advisory system, because it could function effectively if a person of Yamashita's calibre handled the system.

As Watanabe feared, the advisory system did not function properly in his view after Yamashita left Malaya in July 1942. Watanabe had a very low opinion of Yamashita's successor, General Saito Yaheita, who had no understanding of how to use the advisors and contributed to failure in utilising the advisory system. They failed in coordinating working relations between the Gunsei Kambu and a bureaucratic group headed by advisor Otsuka Isei. Saito's failure to utilise the advisors added fuel to the conflict between the two parties. Watanabe recorded that the advisors did "nothing but while away their leisure time. They are not needed."[18]

Watanabe's Relations with Yamashita

Under Yamashita, Watanabe was able to exercise strong power because the commanding general had complete trust in him in regard to drafting and executing *gunsei* policy. They had known each other since late 1937, when they served together in north China. When Yamashita learned that Watanabe was assigned as a staff officer in charge of *gunsei* to his command, the General was so pleased that he said he "felt relieved" of his worry about *gunsei* matters.[19] They were bound together by a mutual understanding and respect and were in complete agreement on the *gunsei* policies that Watanabe and Takase Toru, Watanabe's confidant, formulated. Watanabe arrived at Taiping on 28 December 1941 and, together with Takase, spent a few days drafting policies for general *gunsei* principles: Gunseibu organisation, personnel training, Chinese affairs, finance and money, and industry. Yamashita gave them his seal of approval.

Watanabe took a trip to Tokyo in late January to finalise the *gunsei* policies he and Takase had drafted. On 8 February, he reported back to Yamashita what he had discussed in Tokyo while the General in Johor Bahru was preparing his troops for the assault of Singapore.[20] Yamashita's presence in Syonan and his support characterised what is called the Yamashita-Watanabe *gunsei* in the first six months of hardline *gunsei*.

Takase, the Brain Trust

Takase was another person who, as Watanabe's brain trust, played an important role in policy implementation. It was Colonel Tsuji Masanobu, operations officer of the 25th Army, who had introduced Takase to Watanabe. Takase used to serve as a Special Service agent in China and had studied overseas Chinese affairs in Southeast Asia, which he visited once or twice, and he reported his findings on overseas Chinese attires to the Army General Staff.[21]

Watanabe took Takase in as his confidant, though the latter had a personality problem. Watanabe described Takase as of "complicated character, simple-minded, self-conceited, quarrelsome, and aggressive, but of considerable intelligence".[22] Despite these personality problems, Watanabe appreciated Takase's decisiveness and energetic vitality, which were useful for policy implementation, and he was confident that he could utilise positively what might otherwise be Takase's negative aggressive character in order to carry out *gunsei* policy.[23] Watanabe's confidence in Takase's ability was quite evident in his diary description of Takase as being indispensable for the Gunseibu.

The Chinese under the Watanabe *Gunsei*

Watanabe and his Gunseibu entered Singapore on 16 February 1942, the day after the Japanese conquest of the British fortress. As chairman of the Political Affairs Committee representing the 25th Army, he had planned, on his own responsibility, to negotiate with a British representative for the takeover of British facilities. According to his original plan, he wanted to prevent Japanese troops from entering the city for several days, completely shutting out the city from outside contact and ordering British prisoners of war to remain where they were. He planned, during this interval, to complete the task of takeover without interference. Much to his chagrin, his take over scheme was not carried out to his satisfaction, because the 25th Army staff officers changed it while Watanabe was away in Tokyo.[24]

While Japanese troops were kept out of the city for a few days, citizens were free to plunder and hide their loot and British and Australian prisoners of war were in a state of chaos and despair disturbing law and order.[25] There was no central body until the Gunseibu took over the city to coordinate the task of maintaining security. Immediately, Watanabe protested, appealing directly to Yamashita over the head of the chief of staff, and he obtained Yamashita's approval of his plan for the takeover of the city's administration.[26]

With the arrival of 20 additional staff members, Watanabe's Malay Gunseibu officially started on 24 February.

In the meantime, the 2nd Field Military Police had been carrying out a *sook ching* (liquidation) in the city. Watanabe said that he had not been aware of the *sook ching* until after dozens of Chinese residents came to the

Gunseibu to appeal for help in finding the whereabouts of their kinfolk.[27]
Though the Gunseibu had no part in the *sook ching*, Watanabe was inwardly
in favour of meting out severe treatment to the Chinese. His hard line
policy toward the Chinese was evident in the "Policy Principles toward the
Chinese" that he and Takase drafted in December 1941 and in his speech
on nationality policy given to officers of the War College in May 1941.[28]
Describing the Chinese character, Watanabe was recorded as saying, "The
Chinese, accustomed to foreign rule, are prone to maintain a false obedience,
and they are as crafty as anything and hard to control. They ought to be
dealt with unsparingly."

The "Policy Principles toward the Chinese" adopted on 24 February
1942 by the Imperial Headquarters-Government Liaison Conference had
undergone modifications but incorporated the general principles set down
by Watanabe and Takase two months earlier.[29] The earlier document made
it clear that hostile Chinese would be subjected to deportation and severe
punishment, but cooperative Chinese would be assured of a "peaceful
and comfortable life," and that the Gunseibu would demand ¥50 million
from the Chinese community. The ¥50 million contribution, Watanabe
noted, offered the Chinese an opportunity to "atone" for their past crimes
against Imperial Japan,[30] and Ishii Akiho considered the idea a master
stroke in that it also raised funds to defray the expenses of military
administration.[31]

It was Takase who coerced the Chinese to make the contribution in
time for the emperor's birthday celebrations on 29 April. Using cajolery and
threats, Takase extorted the money despite repeated pleas from Chinese
leaders for a later deadline. Chinese community leaders finally presented
the ¥50 million to Yamashita on 25 June, thanks to a loan of ¥22 million
from the Yokohama Specie Bank.[32]

The "gift" by coercion aroused concern among officials in the Army
Ministry about the adverse effect it would have on the policy of winning
the support of the occupied people — not only the Chinese but also the
other nationalities. The vice war minister sent a message on 21 March
to the chief of staff of the Southern Army and the chief of staff of the
25th Army expressing concern that the contribution was contrary to the
principles of the nationality policy and would have a "negative effect upon
our future policy".[33] Watanabe insisted, however, that the amount was not
exorbitant, because the Overseas Chinese Association voluntarily donated
half of the assets of the Chinese community. He also contended that the
contribution would not interfere with the central government's plan to tax

the indigenous people as a way of sharing the cost of defending the Co-Prosperity Sphere.[34]

The explanation placated the vice minister,[35] but he demanded an explanation of how ¥50 million would be spent, and Watanabe provided a list of seven items for which the money would be used:[36]

(1) depositing in the National Treasury: ¥1.5 million;
(2) creating a fund to help refugees and to subsidise the first three-month expenditure for maintaining civil administration: ¥5 million;
(3) making policy research on nationality, culture, industry and economic affairs: ¥3 million;
(4) reconstructing roads, harbour facilities and bridges: ¥10 million;
(5) young people's manpower training and opening and maintaining educational facilities: ¥5 million;
(6) floating a "reconstruction bond": ¥10 million;
(7) reopening the Overseas Chinese Bank: ¥4 million.

The vice war minister notified the chiefs of staff of the Southern Army and the 25th Army that he had approved the appropriation of ¥50 million for these purposes.

The ¥50 million contribution was characteristic of Watanabe's hard line *gunsei* principles, whereby he first intimidated the Chinese with a threat of life or death and then forgave them, sparing the lives of those who showed sincere remorse for their past wrongdoings.

"This principle is the essence," Watanabe insisted, "of what I have learned from ten years of experience in administering alien nationals."[37] Takase denied that the contribution was extortion, explaining it as a justifiable preventive measure whereby the Chinese would not be double taxed by incoming Japanese troops.[38] Recalling the ¥50 million episode several months later, Watanabe wrote in his memoir:[39]

> I am aware of many people have expressed opposing and critical opinions about this affair, but in a few years they will think it over with a fair and coolheaded judgment. I am afraid of the resurgence, as a result of abstract Japanese idealism, of a "make use of Chinese" policy, with the result that Japanese could be made use of by the Chinese. I regret that even today [1 January 1943] officials in higher circles are beginning to entertain the idea of dealing with the Chinese with generosity.

The ¥50 million incident left an indelible stain on Malay *gunsei* history. Colonel Otani Keijiro, a former Gunsei Kambu police chief, criticised it strongly, saying that the coercive donation was the worst single measure the administration had adopted, and that it had an irreversible adverse effect on the efforts to win cooperation from the Chinese community and implanted the seeds of uncertainty among other racial groups. According to Otani, it also provided the Anti-Japanese Malayan People's Army with a "propaganda windfall, contributing to their anti-Japanese solidarity and legitimising their resistance".[40]

Watanabe's hard line Chinese policy extended also to education, employment opportunities, and communication with the Chinese mainland. The Gunseibu delayed the opening of Chinese schools for a few months longer than other schools and banned the teaching of Chinese in the school curriculum. It also excluded Chinese from government employment, and prohibited communication with and remittance to the mainland of China.[41]

The Policy Towards Sultans

The draft "Principles for the Administration of Occupied Areas Following Southern Operations", prepared in March 1941 by the First Bureau (Operations) of Army General Staff, said that all Malay states were to be "incorporated into Japanese territory and administered by a military government". Sultans were to be "placed under Japanese supervision allowing them to remain nominal rulers", with the supervisory system transformed into an advisory system following restoration of law and order.[42] The "Principles for the Administration of the Occupied Southern Area" adopted by Imperial Headquarters and the Government on 20 November 1941 generally followed the policy lines set down in the March document, but stressed the utility of using the sultans to restore law and order and win popular support.

Following the completion of operations in Malaya, the Army General Staff and the War Ministry re-emphasised the policy stated in the November document. War Minister Tojo Hideki also reminded staff members drafted from government agencies for assignment to Malaya that they should "refrain from acting as if the Japanese were superior and from such conduct that would be insulting to the dignity of the sultans and would cause people to lose their trust in them". He added that it was "of vital importance to pay respect to sultans outwardly in order to bring them under our control".[43] In short, the Army's policy toward the sultans was to appease them so they would cooperate with *gunsei* and use them to win popular support, but also to reduce their political authority.[44]

Watanabe thought that appeasement was absurd and would "end up a waste of time and form a source of future trouble". He had met some of the sultans during his tour of the Malay states, and they had struck him as being incompetent.[45] His pre-war consultations with His Most Highness Otani Kozui of the *Nishi Honganji* Buddhist sect and with Marquis Tokugawa Yoshichika, the "tiger hunter of Malaya", had led him to formulate a hard line policy toward the sultans, and strengthened his impression that appeasement was undesirable. Otani had suggested that the sultan system be abolished and Japan should rule a Malay kingdom under a constitutional monarchical government.[46] Tokugawa had proposed a unique but complicated reform plan under which the five kingdoms of precolonial days should be restored and federated, each kingdom ruled by a monarch.[47] The five kingdoms he proposed were Johor (with its capital at Kuala Lumpur), which would control Perak, Selangor, Negri Sembilan, and Melaka, and the other four kingdoms were Trengganu, Kelantan, Kedah-Penang, and Perlis. Under the scheme, an area of 800 square miles in the southern part of Johor would be incorporated into Singapore as Japan's strait settlement for strategic defence purposes. The sultans of the five kingdoms would be obliged to "pledge loyalty to the sacred land of Japan, pay a visit to the Japanese royal family once every two years, report all laws to the imperial government of Japan, assure freedom of religion, worship, employment, and private ownership of property to all people, and accord Japanese residing in the kingdoms with treatment equal to indigenous people". As the suzerain power, Japan was duty-bound to "oblige each monarch to give Shinto a concrete expression, guide the foreign policy of each kingdom, and appoint a Japanese superintendent assisting the monarchs of the federated kingdom and the other four kingdoms".

Tokugawa arrived at Syonan in March as an advisor on sultan affairs for the 25th Army.[48] In mid-May he and Takase travelled to Tokyo, where they remained for several weeks to consult with officials of the War Ministry and General Staff on how to deal with the sultans. In meetings with Premier Tojo, the chief of Army General Staff, the vice war minister, and the chief of the Political Affairs Bureau of the Army Ministry, Marquis Tokugawa suggested that "sultans be persuaded to voluntarily surrender their political power, allowing them to retain only a religious position", and that "Malays be indoctrinated in the Japanese spirit to be the emperor's subjects and pay a visit to Syonan Jinja enshrined with the ancestral god of the imperial family". Takase, with whom Tokugawa met six times while in Tokyo, was reported to have suggested to a ranking official of Imperial Headquarters that the "sultan's sovereign political power, except in religious matters, be turned over to Japan".[49] The proposals advanced by Tokugawa and Takase thus totally ignored the principles of respect for religion and the traditional customs of the indigenous people.[50]

Following their return to Syonan in early July, Tokugawa and Takase met frequently with Watanabe to discuss the matter, and on 17 July they produced a document called "A Policy for the Treatment of the Sultan." The policy was in fact a demand that his "sovereign power over people and land be surrendered to the emperor through the commander of the Japanese Army". In other words, the Gunsei Kambu demanded that the sultans give up their power in a manner reminiscent of the way the Tokugawa shogun surrendered his power to the emperor in 1868.[51]

While the Gunsei Kambu formulated this hard line position, higher circles in the Army Department were contemplating a softer line. At a conference of senior *gunsei* administrators of the occupied southern region held on 14 July, War Minister Tojo re-emphasised the importance of adopting a conciliatory policy to gain the support of the sultans for *gunsei* activities. Tojo also instructed a newly-appointed chief of staff of the Southern Army, who served concurrently as *gunsei* superintendent general *(Gunsei Sokan)*, to ensure that his position was fully understood by all the Gunsei Kambu under Southern Army command.[52] The new chief of staff ordered *gunsei* superintendents to observe the moderate policy demanded by central Army authorities, adding that the sultans were to be provided with sufficient remuneration to enable them to maintain their pre-war living standards, and that Japanese officials were to refrain from an excessive imposition of Japanese culture on them.[53] Watanabe was unhappy with the conciliatory policy but reluctantly implemented, with conditions, the wishes of the higher authorities that sultan's stipends be restored to pre-war levels. He felt that the stipends should be based on "how much sultans would prove themselves useful to us".[54]

Allowances in the first few months of the *gunsei* period were only 10 per cent of what the sultans had received from the British colonial government. Later the Gunsei Kambu gradually increased the stipends, yet at the end of 1942, they still were no more than 28 to 46 per cent of the pre-war level. The cold treatment accorded to any recalcitrant sultan was a "warning to others", as stipulated in a document prepared in October by Watanabe's office entitled *"Reference Material for Nationality Policy and Its Explanation"*.[55] Thus, for instance, the Sultan of Selangor, who was installed by the Japanese because of his pro-Japanese sentiments, and the acquiescent though slightly hostile Sultan of Perak, were better paid than the Sultan of Pahang, who was less cooperative. Watanabe thus dealt the sultans with carrot-and-stick.[56]

Tokugawa complained about Watanabe's qualified compliance with the wishes of the central Army authorities. His diary records his disappointment at Watanabe's retreat from the hard line position, "I talked with Watanabe and he asked me to treat the sultan with leniency. His position was contrary to that of Commanding General Yamashita."[57]

The central Army authorities, meanwhile, were increasingly concerned with Watanabe's half-hearted adherence to their instructions regarding the sultans. So concerned was the vice war minister that he sent an urgent telegram to the *gunsei* superintendent of the 25th Army ordering him to implement without delay a moderate policy toward the sultans. Reminding him of the importance of such a policy for winning over the maharajas of princely states in India, against which imperial armies had been preparing invasion plans, the vice war minister said,[58]

> For the administration of the occupied southern region, it is extremely important for the execution of the war to win the confidence of the indigenous peoples. High government officials have reiterated the need to exercise prudence in dealing with their customs, religion, and sultans. It is reported lately that the sultans' allowances have been sharply reduced and their dignity has been undermined. They must be treated with circumspection and accorded with honour. You are requested to report the present state of affairs of each sultan in regard to his political, religious, and social status and his stipends compared with those in pre-war years.

Watanabe complied with the vice war minister's instruction, and the *gunsei* superintendent held a conference of representatives of the sultans of Malaya and Sumatra on 20–21 January 1943. At this gathering, both commanding general Saito and superintendent Nishioeda Yutaka officially reaffirmed the sultan's position and honour as the supreme head of the Islamic religion, his rights to the ownership of private property, and the pledge of cash allowances and pensions, though the latter still fell somewhat short of pre-war levels. They asked the sultans to accept a reduced annuity because the people were still suffering from the terrible effects of war. Terauchi Hisaichi, supreme commanding general of the Southern Army, received the representatives and presented a Japanese sword to each one of the eleven sultans.[59]

Watanabe, however, remained unconvinced of the advisability of the conciliatory policy and held a contemptuous view of the sultans and *penghulus* (local chiefs). He said, "Sultans, especially the Sultan of Johor, are too Anglo-Saxonised and the *penghulus* have no creative mind and are subservient to the British. It is better to ignore them."[60]

Watanabe and the Bureaucrats

The 25th Army and the Gunseibu underwent in July 1942 major personnel and organisational changes. Yamashita, Watanabe's most sympathetic superior, left Syonan and Saito replaced him, and a new chief of staff (concurrently *gunseikan* or superintendent) arrived later. The Gunseibu was reorganised as the Gunsei Kambu thereafter in order to launch a full-scale *gunsei* business with the arrival of a large troop of bureaucrats, and Watanabe was "demoted", as he said, to become *Somubucho* (director of the General Affairs Department). He was skeptical of the internal reorganisation in which the *Somubucho*, as one among equal department heads, was expected to control his peers. Watanabe considered the task extremely difficult, but felt that only he, with his experience and expertise, could fill the new post. He was also pessimistic about the management of the Gunsei Kambu in the future when a lesser capable man would succeed him.[61]

Watanabe was also apprehensive about the calibre of the new *gunseikan*, who would simultaneously be chief of staff. He wondered whether he would be able to assist the new chief of staff, because the new *gunseikan* was a very narrow-minded man who, having no *gunsei* experience, wanted to poke his nose into everything. The new commanding general likewise had little experience in *gunsei* administration, though he had a strong reputation as a fighting field army general. Watanabe thought Yamashita's departure removed a guiding light from the *gunsei* government and would have an adverse effect on it.[62]

Following the arrival of bureaucrats from Tokyo, Watanabe faced numerous problems. No sooner they arrived in Syonan than they encountered a blast of rough treatment from Takase, something to which the ranking bureaucrats were not accustomed. Their relations with Takase became uglier day by day, and they directed their criticism against Watanabe who, exercising power in Syonan "as if he were a prime minister",[63] supported Takase. The bureaucrats expressed their disapproval of Watanabe's hard line policy towards the Chinese, surtax, and the "crony staff ".[64] Ignoring the criticism, Watanabe said that a military government under civilian control would inevitably generate conflict, and the political subtlety was to coordinate the two opposing elements. He justified his militantly oppressive policy and "crony-staff" government of top-down decision making with the argument that an administration with too many bureaucrats would degenerate in political chaos.[65] A ship of government with "too many captains", he argued, would go nowhere. He could not help but foresee a gloomy future for the Malay *gunsei* with Yamashita gone.[66]

Watanabe held a low opinion of bureaucrats with whom he had associated for many years. Accustomed to *dokudan senko* (arbitrary decision-making and execution) and to *ho sansho* (the fewer regulations there are, the better it is), Watanabe was irritated by bureaucrats, finding them precedent-bound men with sterile mind, who believed in the omnipotence of law. He denounced them as a bunch of "good-for-nothings", and disparaged their inflexibility.[67]

The strife between the Watanabe group and the bureaucrats, however, centered on Takase, a man whom the bureaucrats resented deeply for his aggressive and abrasive behaviour. The rivalry intensified when Odachi and Otsuka joined attacking Takase, and it continued until Takase's departure in late September.[68]

Watanabe's cronies were also transferred, one after another, in the following months until he found himself isolated, with no one to support his *gunsei* policies. At the same time, he grew increasingly disgusted with his two superior officers, Saito and Nishioeda who, according to him, had no political principles or administrative acumen. He was increasingly tired of his job and wished for a transfer, but was persuaded to stay until March 1943, when he finally left Syonan.[69]

Reflecting upon the Malay Military Administration of the past one year, Watanabe wrote a memorandum in January and presented it to commanding general Saito, hoping that it would serve as a guide for him to carry on the *gunsei*. In this memorandum, Watanabe suggested *gunsei* guiding principles, argued for the use of the *gunseikan* and advisors, and offered suggestions for invigorating the *gunsei*.[70] To Watanabe's great disappointment, the "quixotic" general was displeased, and made no comments. Disgusted at what he considered Saito's lack of intelligence, Watanabe bitterly criticised his superior officer. "He is worse than a boor, he has no philosophy, leadership quality, and inspirational intelligence. I wonder how the Army made him a general." Saito confided his views about Watanabe's memorandum in his diary, writing curtly, "The memorandum is too abstract and impractical to be of any use."[71]

Japanisation and Education

In March 1942 the Japanese government adopted an educational policy as part of the "Principles for the *Gunsei* Disposition of the Occupied Area".[72] The objectives of the policy were to unite the cultures of the indigenous peoples of the southern region with Japanese culture under the spirit of *Hakko Ichiu* (universal brotherhood), to teach industrial technologies and the Japanese language as the lingua franca of the Co-Prosperity Sphere, and to promote the spirit of labour.

Watanabe had been pushing the idea, based upon the emperor system, of creating an Oriental moral culture and of Japanising local people in order to construct a new order under Japan's leadership. To achieve these objectives, he wanted to abolish the Western educational curriculum and cultivate the Japanese spirit based on an ideology of universal brotherhood as a guiding principle for the education of young men. He regarded the retraining of local teachers as extremely important, a "spiritual *misogi*" that would eliminate the materialistic and individualistic Western way of life that had stained the indigenous culture, and that would generate an Oriental morality based upon *seishin* (the spirit of the Imperial Way).[73]

Watanabe spelled out his ideas in "Principles for Reforming School Education", a notice given to governors on 6 October 1942, which said that the core curriculum ought to be centred on the Emperor system with the understanding that the indigenous people of Malaya were to be citizens of Imperial Japan in the future. Watanabe instructed them as follows:

> Spiritual training in all levels of Japanese language education must be emphasised to educate the people in their everyday life in discipline, obedience, and cooperation. Such education must be aimed at strengthening their bond of trust in Imperial Japan and at teaching basic knowledge, skills, the spirit of labour, and self-sacrifice, while deemphasising intellectual education.

In instructing governors on the implementation of the "Principles", Watanabe directed primary schools to offer the instruction using only Japanese or Malay, to abolish the use of English and Dutch, and to ban Chinese for the time being. Moreover, he stated that the Gunsei Kambu was not "planning for the time being to enforce and popularise education".[74]

As part of this *kodo seishin* (spirit of Imperial Way) education policy, the Gunsei Kambu observed Japan's national holidays and enforced on people to participate in a ceremony in which they bowed in the direction of the Imperial Palace, shouted three cheers for the emperor, and sang the *Kimigayo* (Japan's national anthem), and on 8 December listened to a reading of the Imperial Rescript for Declaration of War on the Allied powers.[75]

The Japanisation policy included changing names of cities, streets, hotels, and theatres to Japanese, and adopting Tokyo time and the name of the Japanese imperial era.[76] Watanabe's most controversial Japanisation measure, to be enforced in just a few months, was to make Japanese the official language in government communications and to ban the use of English in public. The policy stirred up a hornet's nest in Syonan Municipality, the stronghold of the anti-Watanabe group led by Mayor Odachi.[77] Denouncing the policy as absurd that would only help alienate the people, Odachi refused to comply with it. It was widely thought to be impracticable and unenforceable. Though he attempted to challenge Odachi in this controversy, Watanabe was completely isolated in the Gunsei Kambu, so much so that he was compelled to postpone the enforcement deadline, and the administration eventually withdrew the policy.[78]

Youth Training

Watanabe had a keen interest in training manpower, something that was badly needed to reconstruct a war-torn society, and to unite young men around a common objective. Because Watanabe was sceptical about the leadership quality of the Malay establishment, he established the Syonan Koa Kunrenjo (Asia Development Training Institute) in May 1942 to train young men.[79] Selected young men from 17 to 25 years old, upon whom Watanabe pinned his hopes for the construction of a new born Malaya, were trained for three months (later six months), undergoing a rigorous physical and spiritual training along with language study. Selected trainee graduates were later given the opportunity to study in Japan. When Watanabe attended the Kunrenjo's first commencement exercise, the cadets impressed him with their spiritual discipline and vigorous physical appearance. He recorded his excitement in his diary, saying, "Nothing gives me more pleasure than educating young men, and they have a great future ahead of them."[80] Many of the approximately 1,000 graduates of the Kunrenjo (both in Syonan and Melaka) became leaders in Malaysian society, and created a bridge of friendship between Japan and Malaysia.[81]

Economic Policies

Finance

One of the urgent problems the Gunseibu faced in its early months was how
to raise revenue and allocate the limited budget for administering the *gunsei*
government.[82] As an emergency measure, Watanabe and Takase drafted,
on 28 December 1941, a set of "Principles for the Disposition of Malay
Finance". The policy divided the first several months into three periods
aimed at restoring the chaotic financial situation created by the war.

In the first stage, the Gunseibu hoped to raise revenue through emergency measures by charging various fees and by selling rice, cigarettes,
and opium. The Gunseibu allocated an advance payment of ¥50,000 to
local *gunsei* offices to tide over the emergency period, allowing them to
pay wages owed to policemen and government employees, and to repair
highways and bridges.

In the second stage, the Gunseibu planned to reorganise the country's
financial structure on the basis of a three-year budgetary system. Because of
the difficulties experienced in raising revenue from various sources to meet
the expenditure in the three-month period, Watanabe decided to introduce
a special wartime surtax and to demand a contribution from the Chinese.
With these sources of income, and the development of industry and trade
with Japan, Watanabe hoped that the financial situation would be stabilised
in the third stage, thus enabling him to draw up a six-month budget.

Notable in the budget are revenues from opium, the contribution from
the Chinese, and wartime surtax. Watanabe's extortionate demand of a
¥50 million "gift" from the Chinese is discussed above. The revenue from
opium was estimated at ¥19 million, or 78 per cent of the budget of the
first quarter.

The "provisional wartime special surtax" was devised by Watanabe and
Takase. According to their proposal, they would collect ¥60 million from
all residents every year for five years, for a total of ¥300 million, of which
residents of Malaya, including Japanese, were to pay ¥150 million and those
in Sumatra the other half. The taxation was a surcharge, disguised as an
income tax of the next five years charged in advance that people should
bear the burden of war expenditure. The *Malay Gunseibu* was the only
gunseibu that actually drafted such a proposal.[83] The surtax plan, however,
was never carried out, because of objection by central Army authorities on
grounds that the surtax would have an adverse effect upon the policy of
winning popular support.

Monetary Policy

On 1 May 1942, the Gunseibu promulgated "Principles for Establishing Monetary Policy" that highlighted the problems of monetary policy at the outset of the *gunsei* period. To help restore normal economic activity, the Gunseibu authorised Indian and Chinese money lenders to resume business, established a people's bank for the population, guaranteed loans for labourers working on rubber estates and in mines, and authorised overseas Chinese banks to remit money within Malaya for the time being. To establish a monetary policy, Gunseibu planners sought to appoint more monetary specialists, found a central bank, and suspend payment of monies owed to defunct colonial government agencies. To maintain the value of military notes declared the legal tender on 23 February 1942 valued at par with the Straits Settlements dollar, the Gunseibu planned to withdraw the notes by selling rice, cigarettes, opium, sugar, and salt in the market, and by removing money paid for these items from circulation. In August, the Gunsei Kambu annulled the May "Principles" and issued a new law regulating monetary organisations.[84] The Gunsei Kambu now put an end to the Indian business of money lending but allowed Chinese money lenders to operate for the time being. A new government fund of ¥2.5 million offered an alternative source of loans to small and medium entrepreneurs and lower middle income people.

For banking reorganisation, the Gunsei Kambu took control of Japanese banks (the Bank of Taiwan and the Yokohama Specie Bank) and helped overseas Chinese banks resume lending services, that were to be succeeded by a Nanpo Kaihatsu Ginko (Southern Development Bank) in the future when it would start its business. The administration itself assumed the responsibility for financing economic activities, regulating the circulation of money, controlling yen exchange, and managing industrial finance and development activities. It also established a fund of ¥10 million for floating reconstruction bonds, out of the ¥50 million contribution from Chinese.

In addition to these measures designed to control inflation, the Gunsei Kambu launched the sale of *Konan Saiken* lottery in July 1942 each ticket costing ¥1. The top prize was ¥50,000, and initially there were 2,507 prizes worth a total of ¥139,500.

The Gunsei Kambu followed the colonial government's practice of operating an opium monopoly and kept exclusive rights over the opium trade as a revenue source in order to withdraw the military notes from circulation. In the first seven months, from March to September, the proceeds of opium sales totalled ¥5,705,500. This sum was equivalent to the general revenue (¥5,790,000) for the second quarter of 1942 (July to September). The sales of opium thus represented a significant part of the *gunsei* budget.[85]

Rubber

With the conquest of Malaya and Sumatra, the 25th Army occupied an area that produced 882,000 tons of rubber per year, or about 64 per cent of the world's total production (based on 1940 figures). At the beginning of the Occupation, the Japanese government had no definite policy as to how to administer the rubber estates, except that it wanted to protect rubber plants in order to maintain pre-war productivity.[86]

The Japanese government planned to requisition 170,000 tons of rubber in 1942 (100,000 tons from Malaya and 70,000 tons from Sumatra), and 200,000 to 250,000 tons for 1943. Watanabe thought the demand would not be difficult to meet if he placed the rubber estates under direct Gunseibu administration and adjusted production capacity, and he carried out this plan in accordance with the policy he had drafted as part of the "Implementation Plans for Important Industries".[87] As a stopgap measure until the arrival of rubber specialists from Tokyo, the Gunseibu took over the administration of enemy rubber estates, and also purchased stocks of rubber sheets for 1.2 cents a pound. It closed unproductive estates, but assured estate workers of their livelihood. With the arrival of specialists, the Gunseibu created (on 1 May 1942) the *Syonan Gomu Kumiai* (Syonan Rubber Association) to oversee the rubber industry. The association took the custody and management of all rubber estates in Malaya and Sumatra, although their ownership remained with the Custodian of Enemy Property.

To Watanabe's great surprise, the War Ministry, influenced by rubber firms seeking concessions, did not authorise the establishment of the association, opposed his rubber production readjustment initiative, and urged him to reverse the policy.[88] In response to this demand, the Gunseibu on 17 May drafted a provisional plan granting the association administrative authority over Japanese and enemy rubber estates and over collection, distribution, and export, regardless of profitability. Under this policy the Gunseibu would not curtail the production, allowing all estates to resume business in order to maintain a maximum production capacity.[89] Sunada Shigemasa, advisor to the 25th Army, Tanabe Toshio (Watanabe's deputy), and Takase drafted, in July, a plan for the disposition of rubber estates under which the government would transfer to several public corporations all of the enemy property and facilities including rubber estates as an investment in kind. They would issue equities and invite shareholders of war bonds to subscribe them, with a fixed dividend rate guaranteed.[90] Watanabe sharply criticised the proposal, denouncing it as "nothing but dividing up war booty" while the future of war still remained uncertain. "How could we", he wrote in his diary, "lead our people to victory and realise the ideal of universal brotherhood with such a materialistic idea? I cannot help but conclude that, having no principle of war, they would lead this country to certain defeat."[91]

The Gunsei Sokambu of the Southern Army turned down the proposal on the grounds that the idea was premature and requested the 25th Army Gunsei Kambu to develop a fresh plan. Later in October, the Agriculture and Forestry Section reaffirmed the Syonan Rubber Association's administrative control over rubber estates in Malaya and Sumatra.[92] Furthermore, with little discussion with Watanabe, who was steadily losing his influence in the Gunsei Kambu, Tanabe of the Planning Section devised a "Policy Dealing with Rubber" (19 December 1942) and a "Principle of Principles Enemy Rubber Estates Allotment" (15 February 1943).[93] The December policy was a long term plan for rubber estates extending a three-year period, aimed at reorganising rubber estates and designed for rationalising rubber production with the idea of idle estate land and part of a surplus of the labour force diverted to food production. The February document entrusted productive estates (40 per cent of the total acreage) to the management of seven concession-hunting Japanese rubber companies. The rest were consigned to the Gunsei Kambu or to state governments as reserve estates. With the implementation of these policies, the Gunsei Kambu dissolved the Syonan Rubber Association, and created the Rubber Central Association.[94]

Thus, within one year, the rubber policy underwent a kaleidoscopic series of changes. The Gunsei Kambu and the War Ministry disagreed over the treatment of concession-hunting rubber companies, and the process left Watanabe disgusted with the stupidity of the myopic short-term rubber policy espoused by his colleagues in Syonan and Tokyo. It was politically very unwise, he said, to change policy so frequently without guiding principles. He insisted that the Syonan Rubber Association should have been placed under government control, as he had proposed, and he held the commanding general, his chief of staff, and Tanabe responsible for the policy confusion.[95]

Food Supplies

Rice supplies in pre-war Malaya largely depended upon imports from Thailand
and Burma, purchased with the proceeds of rubber and tin exports. In 1938,
Malaya's rice self sufficiency was only 35–40 per cent, largely depending on
the supply from Thailand, Burma and French Indochina. In 1939, Malaya
imported 983,000 tons of rice from the three countries, and by the end
of 1941, the Malayan authorities had stocked rice to meet the country's
needs for six months, mostly imported from Burma.[96] Control over foreign
exchange payable outside the sterling bloc impeded imports of Thai rice. In
July 1939, the Straits Settlements Colonial Government introduced controls
over staple foods.

In Saigon on the eve of hostilities, Watanabe grew concerned over an
anticipated critical food shortage in Malaya once war started. An entry in
his diary records his concern that people in occupied territories "must not
be allowed to starve to death".[97] Immediately after the fall of Singapore,
Watanabe negotiated with the 15th Army deployed in Bangkok for the
purchase and shipment of Thai rice.[98] Seventeen thousand tons of Thai rice
arrived in Syonan between late March and May.[99] In the subsequent months,
it became a matter of the most important problem for the Gunseibu, under
the "Policy for Mutual Exchange of Materials in the Southern Region", to
import rice from Thailand by means of land and marine transportation.[100]
The Gunseibu managed to import 62,000 tons of foodstuffs per month
from Thailand, Burma, and Java. Its monthly report for June noted that
it had helped relieve the food shortage and alleviate people's uneasiness.[101]
It consigned responsibility for distribution of rice and other food grains to
Mitsubishi Trading Co., and of sugar and salt to Mitsui Trading Co.[102]

In June 1942, the Malay states adopted a rationing system that followed
the pre-war British practice, under a food controller. In Syonan, the Gunseibu
appointed special retailers to handle all wholesale rice sales from April
until the end of July. On 1 August, a new rice rationing system allowed
registered residents holding identification certificates (*ankyosyo*) to buy rice
upon presenting a purchasing card.[103]

After the autumn of 1942, rice supplies fell well below the level of
pre-war imports because of the deteriorating war situation, irregular railway
and marine transport services, and damage to the Thai rice crop as a result
of flooding. In December, the Gunsei Kambu opened rice import trade by
junks between Moulmein in southern Burma and Penang to relieve the
acute food situation.[104]

Despite these measures, the Gunsei Kambu's efforts fell short of 62,000 tons of food stuffs per month. In 1942, the total quantity of rice imports came to 466,786 tons, or 46,679 tons per month (March to December).[105] Malay state governments thus had to reduce rations. For instance, the Selangor government reduced the rice ration for males over 12 years old from a generous 36 *katis* per month (about 48 pounds) to 17 *katis* by late January 1943. Quantities of rice issued by the Penang and Malacca governments were also less than the announced ration — amounting to 60 per cent of the stated quantity in Penang, and one-third or one-fourth of the published figure in Malacca.[106]

Table 1: Changing Average of Rice Ration (October 1942–March 1943)

		Unit: ton
Oct.–Nov. 1942	Syonan	10,500
	Johor	6,000
	Malacca	3,000
	Negri Sembilan	2,200
	Selangor	7,500
	Perak	6,000
	Penang	3,000
	Pahang	1,000
	Trengganu	1,000
Dec. 1942–Mar. 1943	Syonan	10,500
	Johor	4,500
	Malacca	1,800
	Negri Sembilan	1,800
	Selangor	6,000
	Perak	4,800
	Penang	2,800
	Pahang	800
	Trengganu	1,000

The food situation went from bad to worse in the coming months. Tapioca became a rice supplement. The Gunsei Kambu urged people to grow their own food crops by utilising empty space, and later it experimented with double cropping rice, plants, introducing a variety of short growing strain for producing more rice. The food shortage caused malnutrition and contributed to a substantial rise in the number of deaths, and it forced the Gunsei Kambu to relocate people from towns and cities to rural areas such as Endau in Johor for Chinese and Bahau in Negri Sembilan for Eurasians, where they grew their own food. No food relief was in sight until the end of war.[107]

Conclusions

Watanabe Wataru was a political officer with extensive experience in administering occupied territories. He had developed a unique politico-administrative philosophy that was summarised in three phrases: *misogi*, *mui ni kasu*, and *ho sansho*. He executed gunsei policies on the basis of this philosophy when he dealt with peoples of occupied territories, and it remained the cardinal principle of his policies on nationality, education, and youth training. It also caused friction with bureaucrats, a problem aggravated by Takase's haughtiness in dealing with bureaucrats. Yamashita's understanding and support allowed Watanabe to pursue his hard line policy and exercise it with power, but Yamashita's departure undermined his authority and he became increasingly isolated in the administration and lost his initial enthusiasm for *gunsei* government. The arrival of a new commanding general and a chief of staff, men who in Watanabe's opinion had no understanding of how to administer conquered territories, isolated him with no friends who really appreciated his administrative philosophy. Watanabe recorded his bitterness and frustration without mincing words in his diary, criticising his superiors and subordinates. To divert his irritation at having everything turned against his will, he spent more and more time on his hobby of fishing. He was anxious to leave Syonan on a transfer expected in March 1943.

Watanabe developed his unique *gunsei* philosophy on the basis of practical experience rather than on desk planning, as was the case of armchair staff officers in the central Army command. The policies he formulated at the initial *gunsei* stages of the administration, and his ability to draft and execute them, were outstanding. On the other hand, he was arrogant about his ability to exercise his power, and consequently earned the dislike of bureaucrats for his stinging criticism against them.

His arbitrariness is evident in policy making and *dokudan senko* approach. The proposed ¥50 million contribution from the Chinese was unpopular not only among bureaucrats but also in Army circles in Tokyo, where it was regarded as going too far in dealing with the Chinese. Overconfidence in his ability led him to underestimating Chinese resilience to survive in the most adverse situations. With his hard line policy, he drove many Chinese to the jungle, where they joined the Malayan People's Anti-Japanese Army. It is all the more regrettable that he, as a China expert, alienated the Chinese at the very beginning of the *gunsei* administration in ways that left ill feeling among the Chinese that has lingered to the present.

The policy towards the sultans and Malays was consistent with his hardnosed administrative philosophy. He would not court them with easygoing promises in order to win their cooperation, but first demanded their *misogi* to rid themselves of the degenerate Western way of life in which had indulged. The lesson Watanabe drew from his experience in governing occupied people in China was that he should not to be soft with them at the beginning, and that he should remain unapproachable and aloof; it was preferable that people feared him. His nationality policy failed to produce the expected results from the native people.

Nonetheless, Watanabe ably managed in the early gunsei stages the extremely difficult tasks of restoring law and order, banking, and the monetary system, of repairing and reconstructing public facilities and industrial plants left in ruins, and of securing food.

Notes

This article originally appeared in *New Perspectives in Malaysian Studies*, ed. Mohd. Hazim Shah, Jomo K.S. and Phua Kai Lit (Malaysian Social Science Association, 2002), pp. 115–38. Reprinted with permission.

1. Watanabe was appointed to the China Affairs Section, General Staff in 1929 and had spent 12 years in China serving mostly as a special service agent.
2. The Total War Institute was established by War Minister Tojo Hideki. Watanabe was pleased with the appointment at the Institute, because he would have time to study world history and future trends of the world. Watanabe Wataru, *Daitoa Senso Kaisoroku*, Part I, *Syonanhen*, p. 461 (hereafter *Watanabe Kaisoroku*).
3. *Watanabe Kaisoroku* I, p. 466. Watanabe *Wataru Daitoa Senso Sanka Nisshi* 1, 3, 19, 28 Dec. 1941 (hereafter *Watanabe Nisshi*).
4. *Watanabe Kaisoroku*, pp. 437–8. *Senryochi Tochi (Chian Shukusei) ni kansuru Watanabe Wataru Taisa Koen* Sokkiroku, 7 May 1941.
5. *Watanabe Kaisoroku* I. *Gunsei Ichinen wo Kaerimite*, 19 Jan. 1943.
6. Ibid., p. 462.

7. This document was based on a draft prepared by a study group in the Operations Bureau of General Staff in March 1941.
8. *Watanabe Kaisoroku* I, p. 462.
9. Ibid., p. 463.
10. Ibid., p. 466.
11. Interview with Tanabe Toshio, 20 July 1966. Major Tanabe was chief of the *Gunseibu* General Affairs Section. Mori Shozo, *Senpuu 20nen*. I (Tokyo: Kojinsha 1968), p. 157.
12. *Watanabe Kaisoroku* I, p. 466.
13. Ibid., p. 476.
14. Ibid., *Watanabe Nisshi*, 18 Dec. 1941. Watanabe graduated from the War College the 41st out of 56 classmates. The officer who proposed the Council was the first in his class of 72 officers.
15. *Kushida* Nisshi, 22 Jan. 1942. Lt. Col. Kushida was a staff officer in charge of material mobilisation on the General Staff.
16. Author's interview with Watanabe, 9 July 1966. *Watanabe Kaisoroku* I, p. 473.
17. Odachi Shigeo Denki Kankokai, ed., *Odachi Shigeo* (Tokyo: Odachi Shigeo Denki Kankokai, 1956), pp. 169–70.
18. *Watanabe Kaisoroku* I, p. 480.
19. Ibid., p. 471. Watanabe was acquainted with Yamashita when in 1937 he was, as a special agent, attached to the North China Area Army, while Yamashita was a brigade commander of the same Army. Thereafter, they met frequently.
20. Ibid., p. 472. Watanabe recorded that it was a historic event when Yamashita's assault operations and Watanabe's *gunsei* plans were to be executed simultaneously.
21. Interview with Takase Toru, 30 Aug. 1966. He probably visited Southeast Asia in late 1940. Tsuji and Takase might have worked together in late 1940 at an intelligence gathering team in Taiwan in preparing operational plans for Malaya and Singapore. Takase claimed to be an expert of overseas Chinese.
22. Watanabe asked Lt. Gen. Morioka Susumu, former chief of the Hankow Special Agency, about Takase's personality, and was told: "He is clean of money and women but is stubborn and quarrelsome." *Watanabe Kaisoroku* I, p. 465.
23. Interview with Watanabe Wataru, 9 July 1966.
24. *Watanabe Kaisoroku* I, p. 472.
25. Ibid.
26. Ibid.
27. Interview with Watanabe Wataru, 9 July 1966. Interview with Takase Toru, 30 Aug. 1966. There is no reference to the *sook ching* in Watanabe's diary. Onishi Satoru, who was a platoon leader of the Second Field Military Police Unit, pointed at Tsuji Masanobu and Asaeda Shigeharu, both staff officers of the 25th Army, as the instigators of the *sook ching*. *Hiroku Syonan Kakyo Shukusei Jiken* (Tokyo: Kongosha, 1976), pp. 75–9. Kawamura Saburo, commander of

Syonan garrison army in charge of the *sook ching*, received the order from the chief of staff of the 25th Army to deal "hostile Chinese" with severe punishment. In military terms it means execution. *13 Kaidan wo Noboru* (Tokyo: Ato Shobo, 1952), pp. 162–8. According to Asaeda, Tsuji made up the *sook ching* order without getting Yamashita's authorisation and passed it to the chief of staff as if Yamashita had authorised it. Interview with Asaeda by Masutani Satoru, 10 Mar. 1997. See my article, "Japanese Policy Towards the Malayan Chinese, 1941–1945", *Journal of Southeast Asian Studies* 1, 2 (Sept. 1970): 61–89.

28. *Watanabe Koen Sokkiroku*, p. 17; *Watanabe Kaisoroku* I, pp. 437–8.

29. Interview with Takase Toru, 30 Aug. 1966. *Kushida Nikki*, 3 Feb. 1942. Takase originally proposed a figure of ¥100 million. The ¥50 million was based on a calculation that there was ¥210 million circulated in pre-war years and it increased to ¥260 million at the time of the fall of Singapore. It was decided to demand the balance of ¥50 million. Top Secret. *Marai (Shingaporu) Sakusen kan ni okeru Hijindoteki koi (Kakyo Mondai wo Shu tosu)*, 22 Nov. 1945.

30. 25gun Gunseibu. *Kakyo Kosaku Jisshi Yoryo.*

31. Ishii Akiho, *Ishii Gunsei Nikki*, pp. 146–7. Ishii was a staff officer for the Southern Army Headquarters in charge of *gunsei* affairs. According to Ishii, Tojo personally approved the ¥50 million contribution.

32. Shinozaki Mamoru. *Shingaporu Senryo Hishi* (Tokyo: Hara Shobo, 1976), p. 62. Chin Kee Onn, *Malaya Upside Down* (Singapore: Jitts & Co., 1946), pp. 72–83. Fujioka Taro of Yokohama Specie Bank's Syonan office cancelled the loan of ¥22 million.

33. "Kakyo Kenkin Shori. Rikugun Jikan yori Nanpo Hakengun Sosanbocho, 25 gun Sanbocho". 1942 *Riku A Mitsu Dainikki* XI. 4/1. Interview with Tarora Sadao, 26 Nov. 1968. Tarora was a staff officer of the Southern Army in charge of overseas Chinese affairs, and felt that the Army should not accept the ¥50 million.

34. "Kakyo Kenkin Shori". The vice war minister asked the Gunseibu to dispose the ¥50 million with discretion. "Marai Kakyo Nokin Shito, Jikan yori Oka Butai Sanbocho", 22 Mar. 1942. 1942 *Riku A Mitsu Dainikki* XI. 4/1 "*Oka*" was the code name of the Southern Army.

35. "Kakyo Nokin. Tomi Butai Sanbocho yori Sanbo Jicho, Heitan Sokanbu Sanbocho", 27 Mar. 1942. 1942 *Riku A Mitsu Dainikki* XI. 4/1. "*Tomi*" was the code name of the 25th Army.

36. "Kakyo Nokin oyobi Kokubohi Futan. Jikan yori Oka, Tomi Sanbocho", 18 Mar. 1942. 1942 *Riku A Mitsu Dainikki* XI. 4/1.

37. *Watanabe Kaisoroku* I, p. 469.

38. Interview with Takase Toru, 31 Aug. 1966.

39. *Watanabe Kaisoroku* I, p.467. In an interview with me on 9 July 1966, Watanabe admitted that he "went a little too far" in demanding the ¥50 million contribution.

40. Otani Keijiro, *Dai 25gun Marei, Sumatora Gunsei ni okeru Jakkan no Shiryo*, 1969, p. 74.

41. See my article, "Educational and Indoctrination Policy in Malaya and Singapore under Japanese Occupation, 1942–1945", *Malayan Journal of Education* 13, 1–2 (Dec. 1976): 1–46. In a "Directive from Gunsei Superintendant General" issued on 7 August 1942, he warned "Chinese who are disloyal to Imperial Japan will be expelled from the Southern area or regarded as temporary residents" and "they are neither given the rights to employment at public facilities nor are they entitled to own property". "Even if they pledge loyalty, they are to be restricted from participating in all kinds of activity."

42. Sanbo Honbu, *Senryochi Gunsei Jisshi ni kansuru Kiso Yoryo*, Mar. 1942. See my article, "Japanese Military Administration in Malaya — Its formation and evolution in reference to sultans, the Islamic religion, and the Moslem Malays, 1941–1945", *Asian Studies* 7, 1 (Apr. 1969): 81–110.

43. *Gunseibu Yoin in taisuru Daijin Kondan Yoshi.* This document is not dated. According to *Tojo Naikaku Soridaijin Kimitsu Kiroku*, ed. Ito Takashi, Hirohashi Tadamitsu and Katashima Norio (Tokyo: Tokyo Daigaku Shuppankai, 1990), Tojo had a meeting on 9 Feb. 1942 with staff members to be assigned to various gunseibu in the Southern area. Tojo also gave the same talk at a meeting of senior *gunsei* administrators on 14 July 1942. *Kushida Nikki*, 14 July 1942.

44. Sanbo Honbu, *Senryochi Gunsei Jisshi ni kansuru Kiso Yoryo*, Mar. 1942. See my article, "Japanese Military Administration in Malaya — Its formation and evolution in reference to sultans, the Islamic religion, and the Moslem Malays, 1941–1945", *Asian Studies* 7, 1 (Apr. 1969): 81–110.

45. *Watanabe Kaisoroku* I, p. 462.

46. Otani Kozui, *Marei Hanto Zengosaku*, no date.

47. Tokugawa Yoshichika, *Nanpo Shokoku no Juritsu Mokuhyo*, no date.

48. Ibid., Tokugawa volunteered to serve as an advisor for the 25th Army ostensibly to protect the lives and property of the sultans, as he said in his diary (18 Dec. 1941) and in his autobiography (*Tokugawa Yoshichika Jiden* [Tokyo: Kodansha 1993], p. 182). He was well acquainted with the Sultan of Johor and he invited the Sultan of Johor to Japan in 1934. The 16th Army Gunseibu in Java set up a department of religious affairs staffed by Japanese Muslims, but the 25th Army had no such organisation.

49. *Tokugawa Nikki*, 3, 4 and 14 June 1942. He met with Takase six times over five days: 29 May and 1, 4, 6, 7 June 1942. *Kushida Nikki*, 2 June 1942.

50. Ibid., 9 May 1942. Maj. Gen.Tanaka Shin'ichi, chief of the Operations Bureau, General Staff, said at a meeting held on 27 June to chiefs of staff of armies under the command of the Southern Army that the General Staff would allow sultans to retain religious position, honours, and stipends, but would strip them of political power. His speech was very much in line with Tokugawa's position. Boeicho Boei Kenshujo Senshi Shitsu, ed., *Daihon'ei Rikugunbu* IV (Tokyo: Asagumo Shinbunsha, 1972), p. 306.

51. *Tokugawa Nikki* 4, 11, 12, 16, 17 July 1942. Tokugawa tried through, Abdul Aziz, to persuade the Sultan of Johor to turn over his sovereignty to the Japanese emperor. (*Tokugawa Nikki*, 17, 20 July). He also served as an intermediary for collecting donations from sultans for the construction of a memorial tower of

fallen soldiers (13 Sept., 9 Oct. 1942). He was involved in the succession of the deceased Sultan of Trengganu.

52. *Kushida Nikki*, 14 July 1942.
53. Gunsei Sokanbu, *Gunsei Sokan Shiji*, 12 Oct. 1942. War minister Tojo and vice minister Kimura said at a *gunsei* meeting held on 12 Oct. 1943 that sultans should be treated with prudence. *Kushida Nikki*, 13 Oct. 1942. 25th Army commander, Saito Yaheita, and *gunsei* superintendent, Nishioeda Yutaka instructed state governors to enforce the policy.
54. Syonan Gunsei Kambu, *Marei, Sumatora Kakushu (shi) Chokan Kaigi*, 26–28 Nov. 1942.
55. Gunsei Kambu Somuka, *Minzoku Taisaku Sanko Shiryo oyobi Setsumei*, 28 Nov. 1942.
56. Yamashita Kakutaro, Itagaki Yoichi, "Pahan, Serangoru Ryoshu Shucho Hokoku Gaiyo — Doko Shikyu Jokyo", *Chosabuho* no. 1 (1 May 1944). Itagaki Yoichi, "Pera Doko Jijo ni tsuite". Ibid., no. 4 (20 June 1944).
57. *Tokugawa Nikki*, 18 Nov. 1942.
58. "Doko (sultan) no Toriatsukai ni kansuru ken". 1942 *Riku A Mitsu Dainikki* vol. 64, no. 12. According to *Kotani Gyomu Nikki* (18 Oct. 1942), the emperor told Tojo to "respect the national characteristics" of the Malays, cautioning not to go too far in changing their customs. Kotani Etsuo was a staff officer of General Staff.
59. Syonan Gunsei Kambu, *Marei, Sumatora Sultan Kaigi. Tokugawa Nikki*, 20, 21 Jan. 1943. The Gunsei Kambu, however, insisted on sultans and Malays visit Syonan shinto shrine.
60. *Watanabe Nissh*, 10 Jan. 1943.
61. Ibid., *Watanabe Kaisoroku* I, pp. 477–8. *Watanabe Nikki*, 20 Feb., 30 Mar., 22, 28 July, 27 Nov. 1942, Watanabe said chief of staff Suzuki lacked leadership and statesmanship.
62. *Watanabe Kaisoroku*, pp. 477–8.
63. Kuroda Hidetoshi, *Gunsei* (Tokyo: Gakufu Shoin, 1952), p. 187.
64. *Watanabe Kaisoroku* I, p. 477.
65. *Watanabe Nikki*, 16 Nov. 1942.
66. *Watanabe Wataru, Soryokusen Kenkyusho Jidai* 1940; *Tokyo ni kinmu shite*, Jan. 1941.
67. *Watanabe Kaisoroku* I, p. 479.
68. Ibid., p. 478. See my article, "Bureaucracy and the Japanese Military Administration with Special Reference to Malaya", in *Japan in Asia*, ed. William H. Newell (Singapore: Singapore University Press, 1981), pp. 46–82. The friction between the Watanabe-Takase group and the bureaucrats intensified with the arrival of the Restaurant *Yamato* that Takase patronised in Japan. Abusing his power, he brought it to Syonan. *Watanabe nikki*, 14 July 1942. Commenting on Watanabe's highhanded administration, Odachi expressed his displeasure saying, "There is no statecraft here. I, as the mayor of Syonan, am only nominal. We have nothing to do under the military administration." Kuroda, *Gunsei*, pp. 184–5.
69. *Watanabe Kaisoroku* I, p. 478.

70. *Watanabe Nisshi*, 27 Jan., 5 Feb. 1943.

71. Saito Yaheita. *Jinchu Nisshi*, 24 Jan. 1943.

72. For a detailed study of this topic, see Matsunaga Noriko, *Nippon Gunseika no Maraya ni okeru Nippongo Kyoiku* (Tokyo: Kazama Shobo, 2002).

73. *Watanabe Kaisoroku* I, pp. 468–9.

74. Dai 25gun Gunsei Kambu, *Kyoiku ni kansuru Shiji*, 6 Oct. 1942. *Tomi Shu Sei So* No. 269. "Gunseikan yori Kakushu Chokan, Tokubetsu Shicho ate". *Gunsei* advisor Sato Toshihisa also proposed that the education policy should "emphasise on teaching industrial, technical and artistic skills, avoiding education on political ideas". *Marei oyobi Sumatora no Kokudo Keikaku Taiko*, Sept. 1942.

75. Shinozaki, *Shingaporu*, pp. 76–8. "Tenchosetsu Hoshuku Gyoji Jisshi ni kansuru ken", *Tomi Shu Sei So* No. 8 (Apr. 1942). Despite an instruction from Army central authorities not to celebrate the emperor's birthday with elaborate events, Yamashita celebrated the occasion with a city-wide event.

76. *Tomi Shu Sei So* No. 28 in Tomi Shudan Gunseibu, *Senji Geppo* (11 May 1942): 78. *Marei Gunsei Kambu.Senji Geppo* (Oct. 1942). On 21 July 1942, the Education Section of the Council for the Construction of Greater East Asia chaired by Premier Tojo presented a report resolving that "the Japanese language should be propagated as the *lingua franca* of Greater East Asia" and the indigenous people should be "indoctrinated in the superiority of Japanese culture". Daitoa Kensetsu Shingikai, *Daitoa Kensetsu Shingikai Kankei Shiryo — Sokai, Bukai, Sokkiroku*, edited by Akashi Yoji and Ishii Hitoshi (Tokyo: Ryukei shosha, 1995), pp. 10–1.

77. Dazai Hirokuni, "Eigo Kinshi Mondai to Odachi Shicho", *Odachi Shigeo*, pp. 126–7. Dazai was education section chief of Syonan Municipality. Shinozaki, *Shingaporu*, p. 89. Shingaporu Shiseikia, ed., *Syonan Tokubetsushi. Senjichu no Shingaporu* (Tokyo: Shingaporu kyokai, 1986), pp. 208–9. Marai Gunsei Kambu, "Yubinbutsu no Tsushinbun ni Eigo Shiyo Kinshi Enki Kokuji", *Marai Koho Gogai*, 15 May 1943.

78. Watanabe's successor, Fujimura Masuzo, announced on 12 May that the ban on using English was permanently rescinded.

79. *Watanabe Kaisoroku* I, p. 469. Watanabe wanted to use ¥3 million out of the ¥50 million contributed by the Chinese to establish schools in Syonan and Japan to train young men for future leadership. See my article, "*Koa Kunrenjo* and Nanpo Tokubetsu Ryugakusei: A study of cultural propaganda and conflict in Japanese-occupied Malaya 1942–45", *Shakai Kagaku Tokyu* 67, 23, 3 (Mar. 1978): 39–66. Gunsei kambu, *Bunkyoka. Marai Kyoiku Tsuran 1944*, p. 30.

80. *Syonan Times*, 22 May 2602 (1942).

81. Akashi, "*Koa Kunrenjo*". The Syonan *Koa kunrenjo* closed in July 1943 after having graduated 280 cadets. The Melaka *Koa kunrenjo* opened in Feb. 1943, and continued to operate until the end of war. About 1,000 young men were trained in the two programmes. Another 12 young Malay men went to Japan in 1943 and 1944 as *Nanpo tokubetsu ryugakusei* (special foreign students), and Tokugawa Yoshichika established scholarships for five young men and

women related to the Sultan of Johor. Of the 12 men who went to Japan, two Malays died by the atomic bomb — one instantly and the other on 4 Sept. in Kyoto, and a third died of tuberculosis on 21 Dec. 1946 in Fukuoka. See my article, "Koa Kunrenjo" for a list of prominent men who went through the *Koa kunrenjo*.

82. Iwatake, Teruhiko, *Gunseika no Keizai Shisaku — Marai, Sumatora, Jaba no Kiroku*, 2 vols., 1976. Privately published. The work was reprinted by Ryukei Shosha in 2003. I am indebted to Iwatake's work for the discussion of this section.

83. Ibid., pp. 345–9. Remittance only to Shanghai was authorised on 17 Nov. effective 15 Jan. 1943.

84. *Gunsei kambu. Shojosei ni Sokuo suru Aratanaru Kinyu Taisaku Yoryo*, no date. The document bears Takase's seal, indicating that he probably took part in drafting the policy.

85. *Marai Gunsei Kambu.Senji Geppo* (Oct. 1942). Otabe Yuji, *Tokugawa Yoshichika no 15nen Senso* (Tokyo: Awoki shoten, 1988), pp. 141–2.

86. *Daitoa Kensetsu Shingikai. Dai Rokubu*, 1 July 1942

87. This document is not dated, but was presumably drafted before the fall of Singapore.

88. *Watanabe Kaisoroku* I, p. 468.

89. Gunseibu, *Syonan Gomu Kumiai Zantei Yoryo.*

90. *Gunsei Kambu. Senryochi Juyo Shigen no Shori Yoryo Kosshian.* Iwatake Teruhiko commented highly on the draft as being an "original and outstanding idea". "Shoki Nanpo gunsei no futatsu no taipu — Yamashita-Watanabe gunsei (Marai) to Imamura-Nakayama gunsei (Jaba)". Iwatake Teruhiko, *Nanpo Gunseironshu* (Tokyo: Gannando, 1989). Iwatake assumed that Watanabe and Sunada were involved in drafting the policy.

91. *Watanabe Nisshi*, 23 July 1942. Judging from Watanabe's critical remark, he seems to have been left out of the deliberation and it is interesting to note that the provisional plan was prepared in the Planning Section that Watanabe supervised, and that Takase, Watanabe's brain trust, was one of the men who drafted it without Watanabe's knowledge.

92. Gunsei Kambu Sangyobu Norinka. *Dai 25gun Norin kankei Un'ei Yoko.* Tomi Shudan Gunsei Kambu. *Tomi Shuan Kanka gomuen kankei Un'ei Yoko.* 21 Oct. 1942. Iwatake, *Nanpo Gunsei no Keizai Shisaku* l, p. 225.

93. Iwatake, *Nanpo Gunsei no Keizai Shisaku* I, pp. 226–30.

94. *Watanabe Kaisoroku* l, p. 267. Watanabe said that seven rubber companies were hand in glove with the Military Preparations Section of the War Ministry to get the concessions. For more information in the rubber policy, see Yoshimura's article (Chapter 4).

95. *Watanabe Kaisoruku* l, p. 484.

96. Iwatake, *Nanpo Gunsei no Keizai Shisaku* I, p. 142, quoted from the Government General of Taiwan, ed., *Nanyo Nenkan* (Nanyo Yearbook), 4th ed., Vol. 1 (Taipei, 1939), p. 1094. According to *Malayan Statistics*, the Malayan authorities paid $62.4 million for rice import, quoted from *Nanyo Nenkan*

(1943), p. 780, *Nanyo Nenkan Kanko kai*, ed. (Tokyo: Tokosha, 1943), Paul H. Kratoska, *The Japanese Occupation of Malaya 1941–1945* (London: Allen & Unwin, 1998), p. 32.

97. *Watanabe Nisshi*, 1 Dec. 1942.
98. Dai 25gun Shireibu, *Senji Junpo* (late Mar. 1942).
99. Dai 25gun Shireibu, *Senji Geppo* (June 1942).
100. Dai 25gun Shireibu, *Senji Junpo* (mid-June 1942).
101. Dai 25gun Shireibu, *Senji Geppo* (June 1942). The *Gunseibu* was able to import rice, sugar and salt and other items from Burma, Thailand and Java.
102. Ibid.
103. Paul H. Kratoska, *The Japanese Occupation of Malaya*, p. 251.
104. Dai 25gun *Shireibu. Senji Junpo* (early Dec. 1942).
105. Marai wo Katarukai, ed., *Marai no Kaiso*. Tokyo, July 1976, p. 114. Private publication.
106. Kratoska, *The Japanese Occupation*, p. 255.
107. Ibid., p. 277.

3

Leaders of the Malayan Communist Party During the Anti-Japanese War

HARA FUJIO

Anti-Japanese movements gained a considerable momentum in Malaya during the 1930s and the period of the Japanese occupation (1941–45),[1] driven by the Malayan Communist Party (MCP) and the Malayan People's Anti-Japanese Army (MPAJA), the latter organised by the MCP leadership. These movements have received a considerable scholarly attention, but there have been few studies of the MCP cadres with the exception of Lai Teck, the MCP Secretary General. Following the outbreak of the MCP armed rebellion in 1948 and the subsequent British ban on the MCP, large numbers of Party members active in pre-war anti-Japanese resistance went underground, or were banished to China and forced to remain silent. As a result, little information about the MCP's wartime activities is available to scholars apart from details that the British authorities have made public for specific purposes. Scholars studying the MCP have largely relied on primary sources made available by the British colonial government and have not been able to check the information from those sources against MCP sources, thus creating an imbalance in their research.

After the MCP ceased its political activities following an armistice between the Party and the governments of Malaysia and Thailand, MCP official documents and information have gradually been published and made accessible to scholars. Former MCP members banished to China began to talk about their own history. Typical examples are two books edited by the Friendship Society of Returned Chinese from Singapore and Malaya (Xin Ma Qiaoyou Hui, 新馬僑友会): *Malayan People's Anti-Japanese Army* (Malaiya Renmin Kangri Jun, 馬來亞人民抗日軍), hereafter *Anti-Japanese Army*,[2] and *Malayan People's Anti-Japanese Struggle: Selected Historical Sources* (Malaiya Renmin Kangri Douzheng Shiliao Xuanji, 馬來亞人民抗日鬪爭史料選輯), hereafter *Selected Sources*.[3] These sources are roughly edited nor do they offer a systematic analysis. However, these and other materials made available in recent years provide important new information concerning the MCP's anti-Japanese activities and the MPAJA, and a reassessment of this period has become necessary.[4] The present article takes a step in this direction by examining the birthplaces and careers of MCP wartime leaders as much detail as possible, and on this basis offers a revised picture of the anti-Japanese movement/anti-Japanese war in the late 1930s and the Occupation years.

A book written by a reporter, Tsutsui Chihiro of the *Mainichi Shimbun* newspapers provided a chart entitled "An Outline of the MCP Organisation Before and After the Outbreak of War" (Kaisen zengo ni okeru (Makyo) soshiki no gaiyo, 開戦前後に於ける(マ共)組織の概要)[5] which was apparently based on the information supplied by the Kempetai. What appears to be an original of this chart is found in a Kempeitai document held by the Library of the National Institute for Defense Studies in Tokyo.[6] Attached to it is another "Outline of MCP Organisation" (Malay Kyosanto Soshiki Gaiyo, 馬来共産党組織概要) that mentions Lai Teck (*Huang Shao-dong* 黄紹東), Chairman of the Central Executive Committee, and names of seven of its members: *Huang Guo-hun* (黄国魂, commonly known as Ng Yeh Lu, 黄耶魯, or *Huang Ya-lu*), Lim Kang Sek (*Lin Jiang-shi*, 林江石), *Chen Xi-qing* (陳錫清), (three standing members of the Central Executive Committee), *Chen Ci-we*n (陳詞文), *Chen Cang-yang* (陳滄揚), *Zeng Yu* (曽雨) and *Pan Pei-neng* (潘佩能).

It is known today that the Central Executive Committee members shown here, with the exception of Lai Teck and Lim Kang Sek, were not part of the Central Committee. It remains a mystery as to who turned this inaccurate list over to the Kempeitai, who corrected the errors and how the revised list fell into the hands of Tsutsui, who included the list — which is nearly accurate — in his book. Chin Peng, the post-war MCP Secretary General, recalled having seen the chart "during Occupation days" and also of having seen the "Cultural Society shown on the right in the chart, not on the left". "I thought", he said, "someone arrested by Japanese troops passed the information to Japanese by act of treachery. Never did I suspect Lai Teck betrayed us."[7] In the Kempeitai's "Outline", a note scribbled by the side of *Huang Shao-dong*'s name reads, "he appears to have sought asylum with his friend in Perak about a month before". Ng Yeh Lu, who accused Lai Teck publicly for the first time in the early post-war years of having betrayed the Party said, "The name *Huang Shao-dong* was an assumed name he used for liaison purpose with the Chinese Communist Party. No one except Lai Teck himself and *Zheng Ya-ning* knew of his alias."[8] Two former Kempeitai sergeants testified in an interview that prior to entering Singapore, they received from "a superior officer" a memo listing principal names such as the Secretary General (*Huang Shao-dong*) and Chairman of the Cultural Society, and that they got information about Lai Teck's hideout from a "certain Liu who was a former detective of the British Intelligence Bureau, and that Lai Teck admitted being '*Huang Shao-dong* himself' when they interrogated him by pressing on his alias *Huang Shao-dong*".[9] It is entirely possible that someone other than Lai Teck provided the information in the "Outline" to the Kempeitai.

The following pages provide brief biographical notes for the principal figures of the MCP/MPAJA for whom such information is available. Arabic numerals attached to their names correspond with numerals in parenthesis in the chart of page 68. Notations in parentheses ( ) are mine and that in square parentheses [ ] are from the original texts. The names printed in italics are Pinyin renderings of Mandarin, while those in normal type are romanised versions of such vernacular pronunciations as Hokkien for names. While the Chinese characters for these names appear in archival documents, their pronunciation is not always known.

I-1. Members of the MCP Central Committee

(1) Captured and surrendered, Lai Teck (alias *Huang Shao-dong*)

Much has been said about Lai Teck, the supreme leader of the MCP during the anti-Japanese movement. It is generally believed that he became Secretary General in 1939. According to MCP itself, "Taking advantage of the confusion within the Party in 1935, he infiltrated into the Party and in 1939 seized the post of the Secretary of the Central Committee under the false pretext of being a representative of the Third Communist International."[10] An article written in 1966 said, "In 1931, an outstanding young man emerged as a leader among longshoremen in Singapore. When the MCP Central made contact with him, he said that he was Lai Teck, dispatched by the Third Communist International. Thereafter, he rapidly seized the power of leadership in the Party." This article, however, did not overturn the established interpretation of Lai Teck's emergence as the supreme leader of the Party. Chang Ming Ching (*Zhang Ming-jin*, 張明今), a MCP Local Committee member in Perak, a cadre of the Fifth and Sixth Independent Regiment of the MPAJA and a MCP representative in Johor and Singapore (1946–early 1948), said that Lai Teck had become the supreme leader of the Party by 1937.[11]

Organisational Structure of the MCP

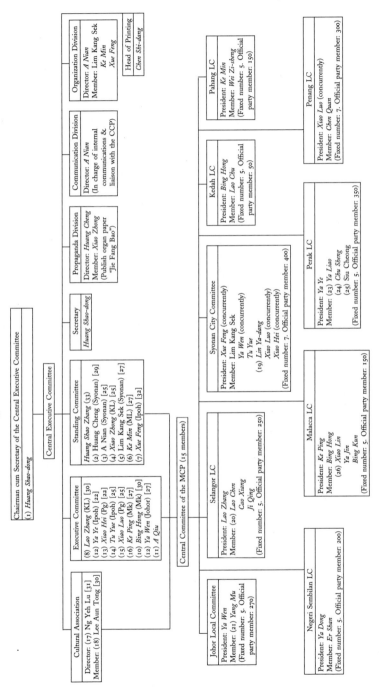

Original Notes: 1. (concurrently) means assuming plural positions.
2. Organisations placed lower than the Local Committees exclude Syonan City. Selangor Local Committee applies to each Local Committee.
3. Place names put after member names show the places where they were attached.
4. Names like *Ya Ye* and *Tu Yue* are pseudonyms that are used among the party members.

Notes by Hara: 1. Figures from (1) to (26) in front of the names are put by Hara in order to expedite analyses.
2. Figures in [ ] after the names are original data showing ages.

Source: Tsutsui Chihiro, *Nampo Gunsei Ron* (Treatise of Military Administration in the Southern Area) (Tokyo: Nihon Hoso Shuppan Kyokai, 1944), pp. 154, 155.

Japanese sources on the Occupation period note Lai Teck as *Huang Shao-dong*[12] (Hoang Thieu Dong in Vietnamese). The most authoritative study of the MCP, written by Gene Hanrahan, simply mentioned *Huang Shao-dong* as a "leader in the early 1930s" and used the name Huang Na Lu, not *Huang Shao-dong*, as Lai Teck's alias.[13] This error seems to have occurred when a Japanese translator erroneously read the second Chinese character of the name *Huang Na-lu* (黃耶魯) (see no. 17) as Na (那), based on Chinese or Japanese documents. Obviously, to presume "Lai Teck is Huang Na Lu" commits a double mistake. Lai Teck had many assumed names, including Lao Wu (老吳?), Wright, Li Teck (李德?),[14] *Ya Lie* (亞烈, 亞列 meaning "little Lenin")[15] and *Huang Jin-yu* (黃金玉).[16] His real name is unknown, but Hoang A Nhac, as he was known in the Vietnamese community in Singapore, seems most likely.[17] Chin Peng, who became MCP Secretary General shortly after Lai Teck defected from the Party in 1947, asked the Vietnamese Communist Party about Lai Teck's activities in Vietnam, and was told that Lai Teck's real name was Hoang A Nhac.[18]

According to Onishi Satoru, a former Kempeitai officer of the Second Field Kempeitai who interrogated Lai Teck about his nationality, career in the MCP, its central and local organisations as well as names of the principal members and their positions and used him as a double agent until Japan's defeat, Lai Teck was captured in early or mid-March 1942 in Syonan (Singapore), and released after being interrogated for fifteen to twenty days. Thereafter, Lai Teck served the Kempeitai.[19] He was not the only Party member to have buckled under interrogation and arrest as there were also confessions obtained from other captured Party members.[20]

The Kempeitai sergeants who arrested Lai Teck were not certain of the exact date of the arrest. The *Osaka Mainichi Shinbun*'s evening edition of 15 March 1942 (which was printed on the evening of 14 March) reported, under the headline "The MCP Destroyed", that "*Huang Shao-dong*, Chairman of the Central Committee of the Malay (sic) Communist Party [33] was captured on the eighth in Syonan (Singapore) by the Kempeitai. *Huang*, the leader was arrested, and he exposed the entire structure of the Party organisation, which put an end to their scheme."[21]

If this newspaper report was accurate, the Kempeitai prepared the above mentioned document, "Development and Activities of the Malayan Communist Party" (馬来亞共産党發展並活動狀況. See note 6) on the day Lai Teck was captured. It seems impossible for Lai Teck to have exposed the structure of the Party organisation shown in the "Outline" on the very day he was captured.[22] If some "patriotic overseas Chinese" living in Japan had been able to communicate this newspaper article to the Chinese in Malaya, the series of the tragic incidents involving Lai Teck would not have happened.

According to Onishi, the Kempeitai decided to turn Lai Teck into a double agent because "he admitted frankly that he had been an agent of the British Detective Bureau and he, resigned to his fate, obviously wanted to save his own neck". "Lai Teck gathered information so well that the Onishi unit was able to trace Communist activities on their fingertips." "He used to say, 'Apprehend this Communist but wait to arrest that Communist and we waited for the opportunity of capturing a Communist, taking his valuable advice into consideration.'"[23] Onishi however said, "Lai Teck as a Kempeitai agent served us usefully until the first half of 1943 but after late 1943, we suspected him of serving as a double agent for the British, partly because of the deteriorating war situation."[24]

It is clear from the quotations cited that Lai Teck was not only a Japanese spy but also a traitor who betrayed comrades who disagreed with him, and did not hesitate to attack his rivals, as E.F. Azev (1869–1918) did on the eve of the Russian Revolution. After the second half of 1943, Lai Teck's reports on MCP leaders fell off sharply and MCP fighting capabilities improved. Because Lai Teck did not divulge information to the Kempeitai about Lau Yew (*Liu Yao*, 劉堯), Chairman of the Central Military Committee, or Chin Peng, who, as a representative of MCP Headquarters in Perak and a prominent member rising in the Party, negotiated with Lim Bo Seng (*Lin Mou-sheng*, 林謀盛),[25] the Onishi unit was not even aware of their existence.[26] According to *Selected Sources*, Lau Yew, Administrative Officer of the First Independent Regiment, was betrayed and arrested in October 1942 and subjected to torture, but escaped while working in a suburb of Kuala Lumpur.[27] The betrayer's name is not recorded. If it was Lai Teck, *Selected Sources* would have disclosed his name. It might have been because he was unable to establish Lau Yew's identity as Lau Yew used an assumed name when he was apprehended, and Lai Teck did not dare to inform Onishi about Lau Yew's true identity. Onishi had no reason to give false information about the Lau Yew affair, which happened more than twenty years earlier.

Lai Teck developed a revolutionary road map based upon his own blueprint and strategy, which the MCP accepted. His plans were effective in the struggle against the Japanese Army and it cannot be argued that the MCP's demise and failure should be exclusively attributed to Lai Teck's betrayal, or that the party's later success was the result of efforts by dedicated Party members to overcome Lai Teck's mistakes. That Lai Teck was a double agent was irrelevant to MCP's internal strategy. Saying that the MCP's revolutionary strategy failed because Lai Teck was a spy does not answer the question of what went wrong within the MCP.

Many studies have been published about Lai Teck's career and his post-war escape from Malaya. A few facts hitherto unknown should be pointed out. Following the MPAJA surrender of arms to the British and the dissolution of the army on 1 December 1945, Lau Yew became the first President of the newly organised Ex-Service Comrades Association of the Malayan People's Anti-Japanese Army.[28] At the second conference of the Association held on 20–22 December 1946, *Zhang Hong* (張紅, one of Lai Teck's aliases) was elected its President, and Chin Peng and Lau Yew (who was serving concurrently as Secretary) were elected as vice presidents.[29] It was made public that Lai Teck was the supreme leader of Military Affairs of the Party in addition to being Secretary General. However, in early February 1947, Lau Yew, as Chairman of the Ex-Service Comrades Association, sent a letter to the British government demanding that it pay arrears of wages and compensation to wounded veterans of the wartime anti-Japanese struggle.[30] On 1 April of the same year, it was announced that Lau Yew had been President of the Association.[31] This seems to suggest that something unusual occurred around this time which affected Lai Teck's standing within the Party. Chang Ming Ching, however, has insisted that Lau Yew had been in charge of the Association, and has denied that the situation described here reflected Lai Teck's fall.[32]

(2) Arrested and executed: *Huang Cheng* (黄成, 黄誠: the latter characters normally appear in MCP documents), aliases *Huang Shi* (黄石), *Zhang Zhan* (張詹) and *Zhang Yuan-bao* (張元豹)

Born in 1913 in Xianyou Xian, Fujian (福建省仙游県), *Huang Cheng* joined the Chinese Communist Party (CCP) in 1933 and became Party Committee Secretary of Putian Zhongxin Xian, Fujian (福建省莆田中心県) in early 1934. Arrested in late April 1934 and imprisoned, he was later released after a round of highly suspected negotiations and stripped permanently of his Party membership. Shortly thereafter, he went to Malaya and dedicated himself to revolutionary activities. He joined the MCP in 1936 and was reinstated by the CCP.[33]

In September 1939, he was elected to the MCP Central Committee and was appointed within several months to its Political Bureau.[34] His unusually rapid promotion to the Political Bureau would not have been possible without his career in the CCP. In late 1939, together with Ong Yen Chee (*Wang Yan-zhi*, 王炎之, who was sent to Malaya by the CCP in 1934 to supervise the MCP), *Huang* edited the leftist newspaper *Zhonghua Chenbao* (中華晨報) in Ipoh, Perak. When he was arrested as a result of Lai Teck's betrayal in April 1942, he was a member of the Central Committee and, concurrently, Chairman of the Central Propaganda Department, as identified in *Selected Sources*. He died on 9 August 1942 in prison. His wife, *Li Ming* (李明), who was arrested with *Huang* and sentenced to 15 years of imprisonment, reportedly told her comrades in prison that someone in the highest echelon of the Party had sold out her husband. *Selected Sources* reflected, "If Party members of those days had a higher degree of self-awareness and of Marxism-Leninism, her information could have helped them establish Lai Teck's involvement." *Li Ming* was deprived of her Party membership in post-war years.[35]

In a short history of the Party compiled by the MCP, a Hoang Soong, together with Lin Jiang-shi and Li Liang, is hailed as an outstanding comrade who died in the anti-Japanese struggle. Hoang Soong must be *Huang Cheng*, Lin was Lim Kang Sek and Li was *Li Liang*, alias *Bai Yi* (白衣).[36]

(3) Arrested and executed: *A Nian* (阿年), aliases *Zheng Ya-ning* (鄭亞寧), *Lin Yi-sheng* (林義生) and *Zheng Sheng-lie* (鄭声烈)

A Nian was a Hokkien born in Muar, Johor. He graduated from Chung Ling (鐘靈) Secondary School and became a member of the MCP Central Committee in April 1939.[37] He also became a liaison officer with the CCP. His arrest came in April 1942. Ng Yeh Lu said, "After his arrest, a Japanese interrogator asked him if he knew *Huang Shao-dong*. He was flabbergasted by the question, because the name *Huang Shao-dong* was used only when Lai Teck communicated with the CCP. Only Lai Teck and *A Nian* were privy to the name." *A Nian* and Ng Yeh Lu were sentenced to ten years of imprisonment in November 1942. Released from prison on 1 April, *A Nian* was then turned over to the Onishi unit where he was kept under house arrest. In January 1944, he witnessed a secret meeting between Lai Teck and M. Sgt. Shimomura Yuhei, Lai Teck's liaison officer. When Lai Teck found out, he requested that the Kempeitai execute *A Nian*. The execution was carried out in April 1944 in Johor Bahru.[38]

An article entitled, "The Achievement of an Anti-Japanese Hero: A Reflection on Comrade *Zhang Ke-fu* (張克夫)", published on 6 July 1969 in *Zhen Xian Bao* (Battle Front Report, 陣綫報), a leftist newspaper of the Barisan Sosialis (Socialist Front) in Singapore, accused Ng Yeh Lu and *Zheng Sheng-lie* of betraying *Zhang Ke-fu* (see no. 8, *Lao Zhang*, in the chart). According to *Selected Sources*, *Zheng Ya-ning*'s two younger brothers joined the MCP. One of them died in prison in 1944 while the other one was banished from Malaya in 1949 during the anti-British struggle. *Huang Cheng* reportedly said, while being detained in prison, that "a certain Huang (Hara: *Huang Ya-lu*) and *Lin Yi-sheng* were traitors".[39] In a source published immediately after the end of war, *A Nian*'s elder brother, *Lin Yi-ping* alias *Shao Yang* (趙揚) was captured in the fall of 1942 and executed in late March 1943. His "son" (judging by the fact that *A Nian* was then 25 years old, he could be *A Nian*'s younger brother), *Zheng Dai-ming* (鄭戴明) alias *A Chuan* (阿川), was apprehended in July 1942 and died at the age of 25 in prison in the fall of 1944.[40] *Selected Sources* does not say anything about the kinship between *Lin Yi-ping* and *Lin Yi-sheng*, recording only that *Lin Yi-ping* was arrested in July 1942 and executed by hanging on 13 May 1943 when he was 22 years old.[41]

In MCP documents, *Zheng Ya-ning* is often cited as a "traitor" and his name is not recorded amongst the soldiers who died in the anti-Japanese Army.[42] Chang Ming Ching said that Lai Teck took *Zheng Ya-ning*'s widow as his second wife.[43]

(4) Arrested and executed: *Xiao Zhong* (小中, 小忠), alias *Li Zhen-zong* (李振宗)

Born in Anxi Xian, Fujian, in 1918, *Xiao Zhong* came to Singapore, accompanied by his mother, when he was eight or nine years old. He then went to Penang where his father was living and spent his childhood years there. In 1933, he joined the Malayan Communist Youth League (共產主義青年団) at Huaqiao Secondary School in Singapore, and then the MCP in 1936.

He was appointed Secretary of the MCP's Penang City Committee in 1938, and in April 1939 joined the Central Committee while concurrently serving as Secretary of the Singapore City Committee (at this period Lai Teck also demoted him to the position of Party employee because his opinions differed from Lai Teck's). In 1940, he was named Secretary of the Selangor Local Committee and on 10 December 1941, a member of the Central Standing Committee at the Second Conference of the Seventh Session of the Central Executive Committee. After Japan occupied Malaya, he moved to central and northern Malaya in order to restore relations with local organisations and establish anti-Japanese armies. On the night of 31 August 1942, when *Xiao Zhong* was presiding over a preliminary meeting (he chaired the meeting because Lai Teck failed to appear at the conference) at Batu Caves, the Japanese troops attacked the gathering. *Xiao Zhong* was killed together with many other key members of the MCP. He was the highest ranking comrade amongst the victims.[44] *Zhen Xian Bao*, 26 January 1969, cited *Xiao Zhong* as a member of the Central Military Affairs Committee.

John Cross, one of the British stay-behind agents, wrote that Ah Chong, a guerrilla leader in Johor [23 years old from Penang] was killed in the Batu Caves incident.[45] Ah Chong could be *Xiao Zhong*. A document relating to law and order prepared by the Kempeitai, "An Observation on Law and Order" (治安上の一考察), said, "Though the MCP has lost many leading members during the operations carried out in the period between late August and October 1942, such members of the MCP Standing Committee as *Xiao Ping*, *Ke Min*, *Xiao Zhong* and many other ranking members are still at large" (underline by Hara).[46] Judging from the statement, the Kempeitai was unable to ascertain whether *Xiao Zhong* was alive or dead.

(5) Arrested and executed: Lim Kang Sek, *Lin Jiang-shi* (林江石), aliases *Huang Bo-sui* (黄伯遂) and *Lao Hei* (老黑)

Born in 1916 in Zengcheng, Guangdong, Lim Kang Sek lost his father when he was a child and came to Perak with his mother. After finishing primary school, he worked in a tin mine and in 1937 (however in *Bloody Memorial*, the year was stated as 1934 or 1935),[47] joined the MCP and played a leading role in labour activities and the anti-Japanese national salvation movement. He was appointed to the Perak Local Committee and the Central Committee in April 1939, and in June also served concurrently as the Secretary of the Selangor Local Committee. In 1940, he replaced *Xiao Zhong* and served concurrently as the Secretary of the Singapore City Committee. Arrested by the British police in the fall of 1941, he was set free together with Ng Yeh Lu on 20 December. He became Chairman of the Armed Masses Department of the Singapore Chinese Anti-Enemy Mobilization Council and leader of the Singapore Overseas Chinese Volunteer Corps

(OCVC, 星洲華僑義勇軍). After the OCVC demobilised on 13 February 1942, Lim was picked up in the mass screening, but the Kempeitai released him. In early April, he was apprehended based on information divulged by Lai Teck, but he escaped the day after his arrest. Lai Teck's treachery led the Kempeitai to Lim once again, and he was captured together with *Lin Ya-dang* (李亞當) and *Ya Qiu* (亞邱) (see nos. 19 and 11 in the chart) in mid-April when he tried to leave Singapore to assume the post of the Party Representative of the Fourth Independent Regiment in Johor. He died in prison on 18 July.[48] Japanese sources said, "Lim Kang Shek was the most influential member in the MCP Executive Committee", and admitted that his arrest was the result of Lai Teck's betrayal.[49] MCP sources published in post-war years extolled Lim Kang Sek as a hero of the Malayan people.[50]

(6) Arrested and executed: *Ke Min* (客民), aliases *Cai Ke-ming* (蔡克明) and *Da Li* (大黎)

Ke Min became a member of the Central Committee in 1941, replacing *Yang Shao-ming* (楊少民), who was banished to China in September 1940.[51] *Ke Min* was Hainanese. At the start of the war, he served as the Secretary of the Eastern Pahang Local Committee. After Japanese troops had occupied Pahang, he was assigned to Party Headquarters and engaged in various tasks. In May 1942, together with *Xiao Zhong* and *Zhu Lao*, he attended a meeting of MCP cadres and military leaders of central and southern Malaya. At the conference, which was presided over by Lai Teck, the MCP Secretary General criticised the Second Independent Regiment for being too bold and demanded that it be dissolved, something that *Ke Min*, *Xiao Zhong* and *Zhu Lao* managed to prevent in June 1942. Following Lai Teck's instructions, *Ke Min* and *Zhu Lao* went to the Second Independent Regiment to conduct an inspection, and opposed Lai Teck's decision to dissolve the Second Independent Regiment. *Ke Min* barely escaped capture during the Batu Caves incident.[52]

"An Observation on Law and Order in Malaya" revealed that "*Ke Min*, a Central Standing Committee member who had been dispatched to the Malay Peninsula, secretly met with *Ya Lie*, a member of the Central Standing Committee in Syonan (Singapore) and discussed problems of damage sustained by anti-Communist operations and of restoring the strength of the Party...." This means that *Ya Lie*, alias Lai Teck, had immediately informed Onishi of this meeting.

Ke Min was arrested on 10 April 1943, and Ng Yeh Lu was taken to the place where he was being held by the Kempeitai to identify him.[53] While it is clear that Lai Teck's betrayal led to *Ke Min*'s apprehension,[54] Cross claims that it was Mee Tek's (美德?) betrayal that led in June 1943 to the arrest of a man known as Ah Chai (亞蔡?) who was an MCP Central Committee member, and that he died of torture.[55] This Ah Chai might have been *Cai Ke-ming*, but there are no MCP records to confirm this. Cross also noted that Mee Tek was killed in Kuala Lumpur in November 1943 by an anti-Japanese army soldier.[56] Neither Anti-Japanese Army nor MCP sources provide information about *Ke Min*'s early life and pre-war Party activities. In memoirs written by the wife of a former Party secretary, *Cai Bai-yun* (蔡白雲), an interesting piece of information is found. The *Cai* couple left Malaya in late 1937 and went to Yenan. Her diary entry reads:

> After having finished our studies at the Anti-Japanese Military Academy, we were preparing to go to the front. At Yenan, we were organising the Overseas Operation Group (海外工作団) mostly with overseas Chinese and engaging in the operation for overseas Chinese in Southeast Asia in order to gather their support for anti-Japanese war of the Fatherland. The leader was *Cai Ke-ming* and *Cai Bai-yun* was his deputy. There were about twenty members including me.[57]

According to a Chinese source, *Zhu De* (朱德) was the man in charge of the overseas operation. CCP Central authorities selected students (mostly overseas Chinese) from among graduates of the Anti-Japanese Military Academy and two other institutes and sent them to Southeast Asia to mobilise Chinese in support of their struggle for the Fatherland. This source cited *Cai Ke-ming* and *Cai Bai-yun* as the group leader and deputy leader respectively.[58] *Cai Bai-yun* was MCP Secretary (the highest rank of the Party at that time) in the mid-1930s and came to Yenan in early 1938. He went to Vietnam and died of illness there in 1946.[59]

Kempeitai M. Sgt. Nakayama Mitsuo, who arrested *Ke Min* and other cadres, said, "Both Ng Yeh Lu and *Ke Min* were believed to have been dispatched by the CCP to supervise [the MCP]."[60] A recently published MCP source reveals that *Cai Ke-min* studied at the Anti-Japanese Military Academy in Yenan.[61] It confirms the supposition that the CCP dispatched *Cai* to Malaya with the task of drumming up support for "the resistance movement for the Fatherland".

(7) Arrested and executed: *Xue Feng* (雪峰), aliases *Li Xue-feng* (李雪峰), *Bai Yi* (白衣, 白蟻) and *Li Liang* (李良)

Born in 1911 in Taishan, Guangdong Province,[62] *Xue Feng* was a construction worker before he joined the MCP. Elected to the Central Committee at the MCP's Sixth Enlarged Central Committee Conference in April 1939, he chaired, as Secretary of the Selangor Local Committee, the Conference of MCP Representatives in the following month. *Huang Cheng*, who attended as a representative of Central Committee, announced at the conference that *Xue Feng* had been appointed to a post at the Central Committee and that Lim Kang Sek had been designated *Xue*'s successor. On the eve of war, the British police seized *Xue* in Perak, but released him in late December 1941.[63]

The Kempeitai captured *Xue Feng* in April 1942. "The Achievement of an Anti-Japanese Hero", printed in the *Zhen Xian Bao*, said that Ng Yeh Lu and *Zheng Sheng-lie* leaked information to the Kempeitai about *Zhang Ke-fu* and *Bai Yi*, but it is more likely that Lai Teck betrayed *Xue Feng*.

Selected Sources published a letter dated November 1942 which *Bai Yi* wrote in prison and addressed to his comrades of the Singapore Overseas Chinese Volunteer Corps. In it he describes how his fellow prisoners died of torture. *Bai Yi* himself died shortly thereafter.[64]

(8) Arrested and executed: *Lao Zhang* (老張), aliases *Zhang Jin-zhang* (張錦章), *Zhang Ke-fu* (張克夫) and *Zhang Ke-zhang* (張克章)

After serving in the MCP's Selangor Local Committee, *Lao Zhang* was appointed to the Singapore City Committee in 1941 and became the Secretary early in 1942. Arrested in April 1942, he was sentenced to death in November 1942 and executed shortly after.[65]

Confusion arises over whether *Zhang Jin-zhang* and *Zhang Ke-zhang* are in fact the same person. C.F. Yong said that *Zhang Jin-zhang*, elected to the Central Committee in April 1939, was banished in 1941. His replacement is named as *Zhang Ke-zhang* (張克章),[66] but there are no documents identifying them as different men. Yong himself said that *Zhang Jin-zhang* was killed by Japanese troops in 1942.[67] The article, "Record of Eminent Anti-Japanese War Martyrs" in *Anti-Japanese Army* recorded *Zhang Jin-zhang*'s name as a Central Committee member (but not *Zhang Ke-zhang*'s name). The same book noted a *Zhang Jin-zhang* of the Central

Committee whom Lai Teck betrayed (p. 138). It is not known if they are the same man.

(9) Arrested and executed: *Xiao Luo* (小羅), aliases *Xiao Lu* (小路) and *Chen Pei-qing* (陳培青)

Japanese sources identify this MCP member as *Xiao Luo*, while MCP sources say he is *Xiao Lu* alias *Chen Pei-qing*. These two men are probably the same person, although there are no sources to establish this with certainty. He died in prison on 1 August 1942 following his arrest in April 1942.[68]

(10) Arrested and executed: *Ya Wen* (亞文), aliases *Liu Wen* (劉文) and *Zhong Bu-qing* (鍾步青)

Ya Wen was a Cantonese born in Johor.[69] Under Lim Kang Sek, *Ya Wen*, as a member of MCP's Central Military Committee,[70] helped command the Singapore Overseas Chinese Volunteer Corps. In May 1942, he attended a meeting of MCP and military leaders in central and southern Malaya. He was active in Johor. From late June to early July 1942, he was hospitalized in Singapore, when a tip-off from one of his comrades led to his arrest. He was detained in Taiping Prison until as late as October 1943. In 1944, at the age of 24, he was hanged.[71]

(11) Arrested and executed: *A Qiu* (阿邱, 阿丘), alias *Qiu Lian-jie* (邱聯傑)

Born in Muar, Johor, *A Qui* was a Yongchun Hokkien. He joined the Student National Salvation Society in 1938. In 1940, he became a member of the Standing Committees of the General Labour Union and of the Chinese National Liberation Vanguard Corps, and in 1941, a Standing Committee member of the Singapore City Committee of the MCP.[72] Together with Lim Kang Sek and *Lin Ya-dang*, he was arrested in mid-April 1942 as a result of Lai Teck's betrayal when the three men tried to cross the Johor Straits to take up new missions. On 1 August of the same year, he died in prison.[73]

I-2. Other MCP Central Committee Members

According to MCP sources, the eleven men mentioned above were members of the Central Committee while the other five men (nos. 12 to 16 of the chart) were not recorded as its members. On the other hand, though MCP sources recorded *Zhu Lao*, *Xiao Ping* and *Ya Zhong* as its members, they were omitted from the Chart. Brief biographical sketches of these three men are as follows:

(27) Arrested and executed: *Zhu Lao* (朱老), alias *Zhu Ri-guang* (朱日光)

Zhu Lao was a Hainanese, and a member of the Central Committee in April 1939.[74] He attended a meeting held on 4 January 1942 in northern Selangor to establish the First Independent Regiment. Thereafter until April, he acted as the liaison between local organisations and MCP's Central Committee, travelling by bicycle around central and northern Malaya. He became Party Representative of the Fourth Independent Regiment in April 1942, and together with *Ke Min*, was dispatched to the Second Independent Regiment in June. On 1 September 1942, he was killed while attending the ill-fated MCP meeting at Batu Caves.[75]

(28) Arrested and executed: *Xiao Ping* (小平), alias *Lin Wang-sheng* (林旺生)

Born in Ipoh, Perak, *Xiao Ping* was a Cantonese from Guangzhou province.[76] He became a Central Committee member in 1941 and attended a conference of cadres of central and southern Malaya held in north Johor in mid-May 1942.[77] While concurrently serving as the Secretary for the Selangor Local Committee, he barely survived the Batu Caves incident. He was apprehended in April 1943 in Selangor.[78]

The treatment of *Xiao Ping* in the two books published by the Friendship Society of Returned Chinese from Singapore and Malaya is somewhat strange. In one publication, *Xiao Ping* is mentioned as a Central Committee member who was victimized by Lai Teck, but in the other, *Anti-Japanese Army*, the "Record of Eminent Anti-Japanese War Martyrs" does not even record his name. According to Chang Ming Ching, while *Xiao Ping* was incarcerated in late 1943, the Kempeitai showed him a classified report he had earlier prepared and presented to Lai Teck. When he saw it, he thought the Kempeitai had apprehended Lai Teck and seized the report. Later, *Xiao Ping* broke out of prison and reported this incident to Chin Peng. The latter immediately informed Lai Teck. On orders from Lai Teck, *Xiao Ping* was shot to death after having been sent to eastern Pahang.[79] Chin Peng, who was at that time Secretary of Perak Local Committee tells a different and much more detailed story. His explanation is as follows:

We were holding the Eighth Enlarged Central Committee conference on
1 September 1942 when Japanese troops attacked us at the Batu Caves,
delivering a crushing blow. We planned to hold a meeting of the new
Eighth Enlarged Central Committee at Bidor, Perak, which was close to
our operation base in the jungle. In March 1943, when we held a meeting
of the Perak Local Committee to elect two members representing the
Local Committee, two high ranking members of the State, Secretary *Liang
You-ming* (梁友明) [alias *Liang You-min* (梁友民)] and Deputy Secretary
Chang Ming Ching were arrested. As a result, I became automatically the
highest ranking member of the State, though I was then the third ranking
member of the Local Committee. *Xiao Ping*, dispatched by *Cai Ke-ming*,
a Hainanese, came to inspect the situation in Perak. *Xiao Ping* said he, as
the appointed Secretary of the Local Committee, had to present a report to
Cai in Singapore, as the latter had instructed *Xiao Ping*. Lai Teck tipped
off the Kempeitai of *Xiao Ping*'s train schedule passing Kuala Lumpur.
The Kempeitai arrested *Xiao Ping* without difficulty at Kuala Lumpur
railway station, because trains ran very infrequently in those days. It was
early April or May. Only a few days later the Kempeitai set *Xiao Ping* free
and he showed up to report to Yeung Kuo (*Yang Guo*, 楊果), Secretary of
the Selangor Local Committee. In a few days, the Kempeitai surrounded
a meeting place of the Selangor Local Committee. Those of us inside the
house luckily noticed a strange noise and dashed out of the house, barely
escaping arrest. *Xiao Ping* was suspected of having leaked the information
to the Kempeitai. Pressed on the matter, he retorted by saying, "It is a
matter of principle that you should not gather at the house knowing any of
the relevant persons has been arrested. Why did you go there?" Lai Teck
relieved *Xiao Ping* of his post in the Central Committee and sent him to
eastern Pahang and downgraded him to a Party employee. In September
1944, when a conference of cadres of Selangor was held, Yeung Kuo
protested in anger at Lai Teck's decision about *Xiao Ping*, and all of us
attending the meeting supported Yeung Kuo. When Lai Teck proposed
that *Xiao Ping* be executed by shooting, all of us unanimously voted for it.
In a short while, Lai Teck ordered commander *Ya Zhong* of the Seventh
Independent Regiment to carry out *Xiao Ping*'s execution at once.[80]

I do not have any evidence to corroborate either Chang's or Chin's testimonies.
In any case, *Xiao Ping*'s execution is yet another tragic incident in which
Lai Teck was implicated.

(29) *Ya Zhong* (亞仲), alias *Wu Tien* (呉田)

Ya Zhong, who was born in Hainan, became a candidate member of the
Central Committee in April 1939.[81] In the first half of 1942, he also held
the post of Secretary of the Eastern Pahang Local Committee. After
April 1943, he was the only member of the Central Committee except

Lai Teck. Of the 13 members (excluding Lai Teck) of the Central Committee identified by the Friendship Society of Returned Chinese from Singapore and Malaya, only *Ya Zhong* survived the Occupation years, partly because Lai Teck did not disclose his name to the Kempeitai and partly because he operated in a remote area. The other twelve members were betrayed by Lai Teck and had been executed by April 1943. The MCP Central Committee was wiped out and after that Lai Teck himself carried out its functions.[82]

It is not known why Lai Teck did not inform the Kempeitai about *Ya Zhong*, *Zhu Lao*, and *Xiao Ping* when the Kempeitai prepared the "Outline of the MCP Organisations" and why he included non-Central Committee members in the list of the Central Committee. According to Chin Peng's memoir, *Ya Zhong* (called Ah Chong in Chin Peng's book) was charged with betraying the Party and was arrested and killed by his comrades in Betong East (Southern Thailand) in 1971. Years later, towards the end of 1989, Chin Peng restored *Ya Zhong*'s honour after he reached a peace accord with the Malaysian government.[83]

II. Cadres of MCP Local Committees and of the MPAJA

(12) Captured and surrendered: Ya Ye (亞業), alias Ye Ya-ye (葉亞業) and Lao Ye (老葉)

Ya Ye, who was a Hakka, graduated from a secondary school in Kuala Lumpur. In 1940, he visited various places in Perak on his bicycle and supervised the anti-colonial struggle. He was a candidate for the MCP Central Committee when war broke out in December 1941.

Following a sweeping arrest of leaders of the Singapore City Committee in August 1942, he assumed the position of its Secretary and strove to reconstruct the organisation. The Kempeitai apprehended *Ya Ye* in April 1943. He was suspected of having betrayed the Party and his comrades.[84]

(13) Arrested and executed: *Xiao Hei* (小黑), alias *Wang Xiao-hei* (王小黑)

In Onishi's *An Untold Record of the Syonan (Singapore) Sook Ching* there are two men named *Xiao Hei*. Tipped off by Lai Teck, the Kempeitai "shot *Xiao Hei* to death in April 1942 in an attempt to arrest him",[85] and captured the other *Xiao Hei* on 27 August 1942 when he and fourteen other leaders were "holding a meeting in Syonan".[86] Onishi surmised that the first *Xiao Hei* was the real *Xiao Hei,* and that upon his death, another man assumed his name.[87] Ng Yeh Lu said that *Xiao Hei* was captured on 30 June 1942, and another post-war account written by a man who knew about *Xiao Hei*'s fate said the latter was apprehended in June 1942, shortly after becoming City Committee Secretary, and was executed on 20 November 1942.[88] *Zhen Xian Bao* (14 September 1969) reported that *Xiao Hei* escaped the Batu Caves incident but was seized by the Kempeitai and executed in November 1942. Then, four men assumed *Xiao Hei*'s name, appearing one after another.

On the other hand, a Kempeitai Sergeant Major wrote in his memoirs:

> About October 1942, when I was on guard duty watching *Xiao Hei,* he escaped from detention while I was intoxicated with *sake* and asleep. It was a very grave act of disciplinary negligence. In January 1943, my fellow senior officer told me, "I arrested *Xiao Hei* when he tried to escape from Syonan to Johor (the Kempeitai captured him based on information from Lai Teck's tip-off).[89] Don't worry about your negligence. I shot him to death while he was attempting to escape." I appreciated the comradeship of my fellow officer.[90]

There may be some relationship between covering up *Xiao Hei*'s escape and the appearance of more than one individual named *Xiao Hei.* Looking at how disciplinary negligence was given much greater importance than the life of an enemy, one cannot help thinking of the absurdity of war. Strangely, *Xiao Hei*'s name does not appear in *Anti-Japanese War* or in *Selected Sources.* Nor is his name found in the roll of wartime victims that is included in *Anti-Japanese War.*

(14) Arrested and executed: *Tu Yue* (土月) or *Shi Yue* (土月), alias *Huang Shi-rui* (黃式鋭)

Huang Shi-rui came from Dafu, Guangdong province. Thus, he is a Hakka. Ng Yeh Lu said that *Huang Shi-rui*'s alias was *Shi Yue.* So, *Tu* (土) might be the wrong Chinese character used by the Japanese Kempeitai. In the pre-war days, *Shi* was a student at Huaqiao Secondary School, and was the highest ranking leader of the Pan Malayan Student Anti-Japanese Standing Committee. In 1940, he was active in the Batu Arang Coal Mine labour strike in Selangor and became Chairman of the Propaganda Department of MCP's Selangor Local Committee. The British police apprehended him when he was Secretary of the Perak Local Committee. In April 1942, the Kempeitai arrested him and he died in prison on 19 July 1942.[91]

(15) Captured and collaborated: *Ke Ping* (客平), alias *Gao Ke-ping* (高克平)

Until 1940, *Ke Ping* was Propaganda Chief of the MCP's Selangor Local Committee. He was *Shi Yue's* predecessor. When war broke out, he was the Secretary of the Malacca Local Committee. Shortly afterwards, the Kempeitai captured him. Together with *Huang Guo-ping* (黃国平), a Party Representative of the Second Independent Regiment who was arrested in the Batu Caves incident, *Ke Ping* collaborated with the Japanese Army in organising a bogus central committee in order to appeal to MPAJA soldiers to surrender. In late 1942, he organised Syonan Corps (昭南隊), based in Perak, to fight Britain and cooperate with Japan. It ended in failure.[92] Nothing is known about his activities thereafter.

In a post-war memoir written by a former Kempeitai Sergeant who fought anti-Japanese operatives in Perak, it is recorded, "*Huang Ji-qiang* (黃自強), a ranking member of the MCP who surrendered to us, served the Kempeitai as an efficient secret agent. After the war was over, I gave him a large sum of Straits Dollars, gold bullion and a pistol for self-defence when I bid him a tearful farewell."[93] *Huang Ji-qiang* could be *Ke Ping* or *Huang Guo-ping*.

(16) Arrested and executed: *Bing Hong* (炳紅), alias *Chen Bing-hong* (陳炳紅, 陳炳宏)

He attended the Batu Caves Conference as the Secretary of MCP's Kedah Local Committee and died in action there.[94]

(17) Captured and said to have collaborated: Ng Yeh Lu or *Huang Ya-lu* (黃耶魯), alias Wee Mong Chen or *Huang Wang-qing* (黃望青)

Ng Yeh Lu was born in Amoy, Fujian Province, in 1913. In 1931, the year Ng, a self-supporting student, entered Amoy University, the Manchurian incident (9/18 incident) occurred, and he dedicated himself to the cause of national salvation. Ng and MCP sources never said that he was a CCP member, but they made it known publicly that he joined the Anti-Imperialist League, and that he escaped from China in 1935 to evade the Kuomintang police. Travelling via Burma and Miri (Sarawak), he came in 1936 to Singapore where he taught in schools and participated in a Leftist movement, for the most part taking charge of cultural activities. In 1938, he joined the MCP, and in July of that year became one of five members of the Standing Committee of the Malayan Chinese Anti-Enemy Backing-Up

Society (馬來亞華僑抗敵後援会) at its inaugural assembly. The first Backing-Up Society was established in August 1937, and until July 1938 that seemed to have remained a local organisation in each state. In autumn of the same year, he became a reporter with the *Kwong Wah Yit Poh* (光華日報), a newspaper in Penang and supervised the Anti-Enemy Backing-Up Society in northern Malaya. The British police apprehended him in May 1941 but set him free on 20 December as Japanese Forces advanced southward through the Malay Peninsula, and put him in charge of organising the Singapore Overseas Chinese Volunteer Corps.[95] Japanese sources describe him as a "contributor to newspapers and magazines", "very active operative in cultural circles",[96] and the "most intellectual among ranking members of the MCP".[97]

He continued his underground activities during the Japanese Occupation. Acting on Lai Teck's tip-off, the Kempeitai arrested him on 8 April 1942, just before he was going to escape to Johor. On 20 November, he was sentenced by a military court to ten years of imprisonment. Six MCP members were tried before at the same court: *Lao Zhang*, *Bai Yi*, and *Chen Li-fen* (陳力奮) were sentenced to death and Ng and *Zheng Ya-nian* to ten years of imprisonment. The sixth person was pronounced innocent (he was known as *Xiao Di-di*, meaning little younger brother, and was probably a young boy).

It was extremely unusual for Ng Yeh Lu, a high-ranking cadre, not to be given the death sentence. The verdict was an attempt to frame Ng and *Zheng* as traitors who fed information to the Kempeitai. Ng maintained that it was a mock trial, planned by the Kempeitai and Lai Teck, to blame Ng and *Zheng* for a series of arrests of Party leaders, thereby diverting suspicion from Lai Teck.[98]

According to Onishi, the Kempeitai "put Ng under house arrest after having released him on parole and used his knowledge for the study of the Communist Party and sifting its information", but the Kempeitai was hardly able to obtain any information about individual cadres.[99] The MCP sentenced Ng to death, and Lai Teck, afraid of being revealed as the spy that he was, asked the Onishi Kempeitai to execute Ng. However, Ng managed to escape execution by either party. In October 1945, he sent an apology/indictment to persons in the MCP who were concerned with the anti-Japanese struggle, based on information he collected during his detention and house arrest. In those days, however, Lai Teck's position in the Party was so unassailable that the Party ignored Ng's plea of innocence. *Selected Sources* refers to Ng's real name when discussing his pre-war activities, but conceals his given name (shown as *"Huang* [Ng] XX") when talking about his wartime activities.[100]

The *Osaka Mainichi Shimbun* for 24 February 1942, published an interesting article under the headline, "Anti-Japanese Overseas Chinese Arrested"[101] which read:

> The arrest of overseas Chinese anti-Japanese leaders has been underway. As of the twenty-second, numbers of them have been apprehended and severely punished. Among the arrested principal leaders were *Chen Lan-jia* (陳蘭嘉), the representative of the Cultural Society and the Federation of Anti-Enemy Societies (抗敵聯合会); *Huang Liao-lu* (黃聊魯); *Chen Jin-yao* (陳錦耀); *Chen Gu-zhou* (陳谷州) — the latter three are standing members of the Singapore Chinese Anti-Enemy Committee (華僑抗敵委員会) — *Chen Xi-yao* (陳錫耀), the representative of the Youth Anti-Japanese Corps Anti-Cannon [sic] League (青年抗日団反砲逍同盟); *Li Yun* (李雲), the representative of Women's Wartime Service Corps (婦女戰時服務団); *Lin Ya-dang* (林亞當), the representative of the MCP Singapore City Committee; and Yeung Kuo (楊果).

This is a puzzling newspaper story. Several of the names are otherwise unknown. The names *Huang Liao-lu* (黃聊魯) and *Chen Xi-yao* (陳錫耀) seem to be incorrect. *Huang Liao-lu* (黃聊魯) could be *Huang Ya-lu* (黃耶魯) and *Chen Xi-yao* (陳錫耀) could be *Chen Xi-qing* (陳錫清, alias *Yang Li* 楊励), an MCP cadre. *Lin Ya-Tang* and Yeung Kuo were ranking MCP members, as will be discussed later. MCP sources have no records of any of the four having been arrested in the early stages of the Japanese Occupation. "Severe punishment" was a military jargon that meant execution in those days. It is not known who was actually captured in this early period or whether the Kempeitai apprehended some but released them for whatever the reason.

According to a recently published memoir, *Chen Lan-jia* was born in Chenghai, Guangdong (meaning he was Teochew). He was a wood engraver before he joined the CCP in 1932. In 1936, he came to Malaya to evade arrest by the Koumintang government. He joined the MCP in 1937. He participated both in anti-Japanese and anti-British armed struggles and died in action in 1950 at the age of 39.[102]

Changing his name to Wee Mong Chen (黃望青), Ng later became a successful businessman and served as Singapore's ambassador to Japan from 1973 to 1980. In that capacity he established a good reputation. In the 1980s, it is thought he ran into trouble with the Singapore government, and he settled down in Hong Kong. His biography was published in Amoy, his native city.[103] Publication of this book represents official recognition that his activities while in detention were not traitorous. He passed away in Hong Kong in 2003.

(18) Lee Aun Tong, Lee An Tung, *Li An-dong* (李安東)

Lee Aun Tong was a Teochew born in Swatow (Shantou) in 1917.[104] He came to Singapore in 1922,[105] and became the leader of the Armed Masses Department of the Singapore Chinese Anti-Enemy Mobilisation Council.[106] Ng Leong Meng (*Wu Liang-ming*, 吳亮明), the former Party Representative of the First Independent Regiment, said about Lee, "He was a member of the Propaganda Department, MCP Central Committee. He was on such good terms with Lai Teck that he felt free to talk to him, and he was well known second to Lai Teck in the Anti-Japanese Army."[107] His elder sister, *Li Qiong* (李瓊), was the wife of *Wang Qing* (汪清),[108] Commander of the Overt Sixth Independent Regiment. Lee became Deputy Secretary General of the MCP in 1955 and travelled to Beijing in December 1961 after having left Malaya in January 1961 to go into hiding in Bangkok. Together with Chin Peng, who also went to Beijing in mid 1961, Lee directed MCP activities in Malaya from there. According to Thai police sources, his wife, Tan Leng (陳玲?) alias Lim Chan (林珍?) had been in Beijing since 1951.[109] Her pseudonym commonly known among the Party members was *Lin Rui* (林鋭). In the late 1960s, his wife was executed by the MCP's North Malaya Bureau (its Director-cum-Secretary was *Zhang Feng-yun* 張峰雲 alias Ah Soo 阿蘇),[110] and Lee himself was demoted by Chin Peng.[111] According to former guerrilla members, the real name of his wife was Ling Ying Ting (林英婷) who was born in 1924 and died in 1970.[112] After the conclusion of the 1989 armistice agreement, Lee lived in a "Peace Village" in southern Thailand until his death in July 1999.[113] He retained the status of Deputy Secretary General, and the Party buried him ceremoniously in the Heroes' Cemetery, where *Chen Tian* and Ah Soo were also buried.[114]

(19) Arrested and executed: *Lin Ya-dang* (李亞當) alias *Jin Hui-yu* (金惠余)

Born in Singapore in 1916 or 1917, *Lin Ya-dang*, a Hokkien, was a longshoreman before he joined the MCP. As a member of the MCP's Singapore City Committee, he led the Anti-Enemy Backing-Up Society and was arrested by the British police. On 20 December 1941, he was released from prison, together with Lim Kang Sek and Ng Yeh Lu, and was asked to take charge of the Singapore Overseas Chinese Volunteer Corps. Like Lim Kang Sek, *Lin* dodged the "Screening", but the Kempeitai arrested him on 14 April 1942, as he was attempting to cross the Johor Straits together with Lim Kang Sek. He remained silent throughout interrogation despite being tortured, and on 31 July 1942 committed suicide by slashing his wrist with broken glass.[115]

(20) *Lao Chen* (老陳)

There is no hard evidence that verifies *Lao Chen*'s true identity. He could be either Tan Thian Kheng (*Chen Tian-qing*, 陳天慶)[116] or *Chen Da-zhi* (陳大智).[117] Tan Thian Kheng was First Commander of the First Independent Regiment. Japanese troops, acting on a tip-off from an informer, surrounded him and shot him to death outside Kuala Lumpur, where he was working in early 1943. *Chen Da-zhi* was Deputy Commander of the Overt First Independent Regiment. He was captured by the British in the post-war anti-British struggle and deported to China in 1959.

(21) *Yang Mu* (楊木), aliases *Yang Ke* (楊科), *Ya Ke* (亞科) and *Ya Shen* (亞森)

According to a recently published memoir referred to earlier (see note 102), *Yang Mu*'s real name was *Yang Jing-yuan* (楊鏡圓). He was born in Dapu (大埔), Guangdong, in 1907 and was a Hakka. He came to Malaya in the early 1930s and joined the MCP in 1933, becoming a member of the Selangor Local Committee in 1935 and Secretary of the Southern Johor Local Committee in 1937.[118] He also became a leader of the Anti-Japanese General Association in Tengkil, Johor. In October 1944, he attended a meeting of the MCP and military leaders held in a suburb of Kuala Lumpur, and at about this time, was transferred to the Selangor Local Committee.[119] Soon after the end of the anti-Japanese war, he was appointed Deputy Secretary of the Selangor State Committee, and in May 1947, became the Secretary of the Kedah State Committee cum member of the Central Committee. In September 1948, he was assigned the post of Secretary of the Kedah-Penang Liaison Committee. He died in action in June 1961, during the anti-British struggle.[120]

(22) Arrested and executed: *Chen Quan* (陳全)

He could be *Chen Wen-yan* (陳文燕),[121] Secretary of the Penang Local Committee, who was killed in the Batu Caves incident. In the chart, *Xiao Luo*, Penang Local Committee's President, is listed on *Chen Quan*'s right. At the time, the post of committee president did not exist in the central as well as local organisations of the MCP. The secretary of a local committee played the role of committee president. Therefore, one could assume that *Xiao Luo* was an anonym of *Chen Pei-qing* (陳培青) (see no. 9) and that *Chen Pei-qing* and *Chen Wen-yan* were the same person. However, according to the roll of victims listed in *Anti-Japanese Army*, they were different people. *Chen Pei-qing* is cited as a member of the Central Committee and *Chen Wen-yan* as a martyr of Kedah-Penang.[122]

(23) *Ya Liao* (亞廖)

This name might refer to *Liao Wei-zhong* (廖偉中) alias Itu,[123] who became Party Representative of the Fifth Independent Regiment, succeeding *Zhang Qi-sheng* (*Xu Qing* 徐清). *Liao Wei-zhong* became President of the Perak Ex-Service Comrades Association. The British captured him in July 1948, shortly after the commencement of the armed struggle.

(24) Arrested and executed: *Chu Sheng* (除生)

The character *Chu* 除 is not a Chinese surname. The Japanese who interrogated this person or who wrote the report on him made an error or else misprinted the name. Judging from the Japanese pronunciation of Jo Sei which is similar both to *Chu Sheng* (除生) and *Xu Qing* (徐清), and the position this MCP member held in Perak, *Chu Sheng* (除生) could be *Xu Qing* (徐清). *Xu Qing*'s other names were *Zhang Qi-sheng* (張奇生) and *Zhang Lang-ping* (張浪萍) who died in the Batu Caves incident.[124] *Xu Qing* (許青) mentioned in *Zhen Xian Bao* (26 January 1969) could be *Xu Qing* (徐清).

(25) Siu Cheong, Siao Chang (*Xiao Zhang*, 小張), aliases *Zhang Chuan-qing* (章伝慶), *Zhang Feng-yun* (張峰雲), Ah Soo (*A Su* 阿蘇), *Lin Wen* (林文) and Chang Ling Yun (*Zhang Ling-yun*, 章凌雲)

Born in Pahang in March 1921, Siu Cheong was a Hokkien who joined the Malayan Student Union (馬来亞学生聯合会) in 1936, and the MCP in 1938. Appointed Secretary of the Western Pahang Special Regional Committee in January 1941, he was arrested in September and released on 31 December that same year. Upon his release, he immediately returned to western Pahang (or upper Pahang) with *Wang Qing* (汪清), who was to become Commander of the Overt Sixth Independent Regiment. There Siu organised a guerrilla force. In February 1942, the Upper Pahang People's

Anti-Japanese Army was organised and he became a senior political officer (*Huang Chun*, 黃春, the Party Representative of the same Army was arrested sometime in 1943). He assumed the position of Secretary of the Western Pahang Local Committee in May 1942. Siu sustained a leg wound during the Batu Caves incident but returned, assisted by his comrades, to upper Pahang. He remained Party Representative of the reorganised Sixth Independent Regiment until the war ended.

In January 1946, at the 8th Enlarged Plenum of the MCP Central Committee, he was elected a member of the Central Committee. At the 9th Enlarged Plenum of the Central Committee held in June 1947, he was appointed a Politburo member.[125]

There are some discrepancies over the identity of Siu Cheong. On the one hand, in the inside story of the MCP written by Aloysius Chin, an officer of the former Special Branch (similar to the Japanese Tokko, or thought control police), a man named Siu Cheong, aliases Ah Soo, Chang Ling Yun and Lin Wen (Chinese characters are not given in this publication), appears quite frequently. On the other hand, Chang Ming Ching pointed out in an interview with the author that the men named above in Chinese characters were one individual. Though Romanised Chinese spelling in Malaysia is slightly different from Pinyin, there is little doubt that the man bearing the different pseudonyms pointed out by Chang and Chin is the same person. According to two government sources, his post-war activities are as follows:

In April 1953, he arrived in Beijing and became the representative of the MCP's Beijing office. In 1955, at a meeting of the Enlarged MCP Central Committee held at Baling prior to the peace negotiations with the Malayan Government, he was elected *in absentia* to be a member of the Central Committee. At the November 1956 Conference held in Beijing, he was elected a member of the MCP Political Bureau, ranking third in the Party after Chin Peng and Lee Aun Tong. Representing the MCP together with Musa Ahmad, then MCP Chairman, he attended the Twentieth Communist Party Congress of the Soviet Union in June 1956, the Eighth CCP General Congress in August 1956, the World Communist Party Conference held in Moscow in 1957, and the Twenty-first Soviet Communist Party Congress in 1958. He stayed in Hanoi under the name of *Lin Wen* in 1961–63, before returning to the Malaysian-Thai border area to command the Twelfth Regiment of the National Liberation Army. In the 1960s and 1970s, he was the Secretary of the North Malayan Bureau, the highest-ranking officer in the organisation, and directed mass purges of soldiers in the Eighth and the Twelfth Regiments. This incident split the Party and the National Liberation Army into three rival factions. At the Peace Conferences held at Phuket, Thailand, from February 1989, between the MCP and the Malaysian and Thai governments, Siu was present as the chief delegate of the MCP (he was Deputy Secretary General or Acting Secretary General). Stricken with illness in May of the same year, he died in a hospital in Guangzhou.[126]

In anti-Chin Peng sources, Siu Cheong, along with Chin Peng, has been accused of having betrayed and murdered many comrades of the Eighth Regiment.[127] Nevertheless, among Party leaders of the anti-Japanese war years, Siu Cheong left a splendid legacy, second only to that of Chin Peng.

(26) *Xiao Lin* (小林), alias *Wu Mong-chao* (呉夢超)

Xiao Lin was one of the five members of the Standing Committee of the Penang Anti-Enemy Backing-Up Society, and became a member of the Northern Johor Local Committee of the MCP. From late 1942, he was the MCP representative of the Third Independent Regiment and attended the meeting of MCP and military leaders held in the outskirts of Kuala Lumpur in October 1944.[128] After the war, prior to the commencement of the armed rebellion, he withdrew from the Party and left for China where he joined the Zhigong Dang (致公党).[129]

The Japanese killed 18 to 19 of the 28 (excluding Lai Teck) MCP Central Committee and local committee leaders discussed in preceding pages. Four collaborated with the Japanese and only six or seven survived.

Malayans were not the only victims of Lai Teck's betrayal. According to Chang Ming Ching, a number of surrendered Japanese who joined the Japan Anti-War League (日本反戦同盟) were executed on orders from Lai Teck during the war. Lai Teck must have been afraid that these Japanese soldiers might have known that he was a spy.[130] Chin Peng has said that about 200 Japanese joined the MCP's anti-British struggle, but Lai Teck ordered their execution because they became an obstacle to the MCP's early post-war policy of peaceful struggle. About 100 men were executed.[131]

III. Five Other Important Party Cadres

Five other individuals were influential local (state) committee members (a few of them were believed to be Lai Teck's protégées), or distinguished military leaders serving as Party Representatives of Independent Regiments. They were hardly known to the Kempeitai.

(30) Chin Peng, *Chen Ping* (陳平), real name Ong Boon Hua, *Wang Wen-hua* (王文華)

Born in Sitiawan, Perak in 1924,[132] Chin Peng is a Hockchia (Fujian) Hakka. He joined the MCP in 1940, and served as a Perak Local Committee member, Secretary of a Local Committee and MPAJA Central Military Committee member during the Occupation years. He was also a liaison officer with Force 136. In May 1947, he became MCP's Secretary General.[133] From 1961, he directed the Party from China.[134]

During the Occupation, the Kempeitai had no information about Chin Peng. He was reportedly not arrested but was actually captured twice. On one occasion, he was seized with two other Party members including Lai Teck. At that time, the Kempeitai let him go without suspecting him of being an anti-Japanese operative, because an interrogator who noticed calluses on Chin Peng's palms thought he was a farmer. Chin Peng thought that Lai Teck managed to escape arrest on this occasion by eluding police interrogation.[135]

Chin Peng, alias *Lai Wen-ming* (賴文明),[136] third Political Commissar of the Sixth Independent Regiment established in 1943, was a different person with the same name.[137] He was the fourth most high ranking officer in the Regiment, after the Party Representative, Commander and Deputy Commander.

(31) Arrested and executed: Lai Lai Fook, *Lai Lai-fu* (賴来福) alias *Du Long-shan* (杜龍山)

Lai Lai Fook was born in Sitiawan, Perak, in 1922. In 1937, while still a student at Nan Hwa Secondary School, he joined the anti-Japanese national salvation movement as a leader of the Sitiawan Anti-Enemy Backing-Up Society. After graduating, he became a newspaper reporter. He joined the MCP in 1939 and served in the South Section Committee of Perak in the following year. In 1941, he led a labour movement of tin miners and helped train Rashid Maidin, who became one of the highest ranking Malays in the MCP. He was arrested in 1941 but released on 20 December that same year. In that month, he was selected by MCP's Central Committee to join the 101 Special Training School and became Commander of the Second Independent Regiment, and in January 1942, a Party Representative of the same Regiment. He was appointed Commander of the Fifth Independent Regiment in July 1942. Betrayed by an informer, he was apprehended in 1943 and beheaded.[138]

(32) Lau Yew, *Liu Yau* (劉堯), real name *Liu Chang-biao* (劉昌標)

Born in Hainan Island in 1915, Lau Yew joined the CCP in 1931. In 1936, he travelled to Singapore to escape the nationalist government police. In July 1937, he joined the Anti-Enemy Backing-Up Society and directed one of its departments organised by shop clerks. He joined the MCP in February 1940 and received training at 101 Special Training School in December 1941. With the establishment of the First Independent Regiment in January 1942, he was appointed senior staff of the headquarters' Administrative Department. He escaped from prison after being captured in October 1942, and became Commander of the First Independent Regiment in early 1943 and the Party Representative of the same Regiment in early 1944. In the meantime, he also served as Chairman of the Central Military Committee of the Anti-Japanese Army, established in May 1942.

After the war, he held the offices of Vice President, Chairman and President of the MPAJA Ex-Service Comrades Association, established on 1 December 1945, immediately after the MPAJA dissolved. He died in action in July 1948, only a month after the anti-British war broke out.[139]

(33) *Chen Tian* (陳田), real name *Gao Cai-jie* (高才傑)

Chen Tian was born in Singapore in 1923. He returned to his ancestral home in Denghai, Guangdong Province, with his grandmother as a child and came back to Singapore at the age of twelve. In 1941, he joined the MCP and became Commander of the Fourth Independent Regiment in early 1944. After the war, he became the Chief Editor of *Combatants' Friend*, a newspaper published by the MPAJA Ex-Service Comrades Association. He became a member of the MCP's Political Bureau, was concurrently Chairman of its Propaganda Department in 1952 and participated in the Baling Conference of 1955.[140] In 1961[141] he went to China where he died in 1990.[142]

(34) Arrested and executed: *Ye Li-tian* (葉立天) alias Ye John (葉約翰)

Born in 1921 (probably in Guangdong), he came to Singapore with his mother to seek refuge here following the failure of the 1927 Revolution.

His father was the owner of a shoe shop. After the Sino-Japanese War broke out in 1937, he participated in the anti-Japanese movement through a chorus group named Gong Chorus Troop (銅鑼合唱団) and performed in musical activities. He became known as a composer of revolutionary songs. He participated in 101 Special Training School as a member of the MCP's Singapore City Committee and served as an interpreter there. Living dangerously, he studied Japanese and infiltrated the Japanese Military Administration Department, passing information he learned there to the MPAJA. Arrested on 11 April 1943, he was executed on 18 June of the same year at the age of 22.[143]

Conclusion

In the early stages of the struggle, the MCP's anti-Japanese resistance suffered a serious blow as a result of Lai Teck's betrayal. Nearly all of its ranking officers were arrested or killed. After mid-1943, however, the anti-Japanese struggle gained widespread popular support from the masses and steadily expanded its activities. If Lai Teck had not betrayed his comrades, the anti-Japanese struggle could have been much stronger. Nevertheless, it is too hasty and too simplistic to conclude that Lai Teck simply strove to protect the Japanese Army and to wreck the MPAJA. In fact, as the Kempeitai complained, Lai Teck was "really useful only until the first half of 1943.... After 1943, partly due to the deteriorating war situation, he was seriously suspected of being a double agent."

The MCP is believed to have failed to convert its powerful anti-Japanese struggle into a struggle against the British because Lai Teck once again cooperated with the enemy. An established theory says that the MCP and the MPAJA were eager to take up arms against the British, but Lai Teck used his position of authority to change the anti-British struggle into a peaceful one — which did not reflect the reality of the situation. *Anti-Japanese Army* analysed this claim as follows:

> Lai Teck's criminal acts were really horrible. It is wrong, however, to say that this spy was capable of changing the course of history. An elfish devil (鬼魅) would not be able to see the sun. By camouflaging the revolution, Lai Teck was able to cover up the real state of his being a spy and to perpetuate the destructive conspiracy. He was only able to destroy it surreptitiously but unable to stop the massive tide of the revolution.[144]

No matter which way the revolution turned, it was not Lai Teck but the masses who created its main stream. *Anti-Japanese Army* further argued:

There were three fundamental causes why the anti-Japanese resistance was not able to achieve its strategic objective. First, the conditions in Malaya itself were not ready yet for achieving independence. Second, there were serious problems within the MCP as the nucleus of leading the anti-Japanese struggle and it committed errors in directing the war. Third, the British government firmly maintained its colonial policy and forcefully suppressed the national independent movement.

All sorts of conditions had to be satisfied after the Japanese surrender in order to establish a democratic republic. There had to be a united organisation, a government that was capable of mobilizing the three ethnic groups (三族人民), of unifying them, and of leading the masses and transforming the anti-Japanese struggle into an independence movement. Due to restraints derived from the different historical backgrounds of the three ethnic groups and from the reality of the subjective and objective conditions, the conducive conditions for the movement had not been created yet at that time.

The majority of the Chinese in those days maintained close ties with China. As a result of Japan's aggression in China, their anti-Japanese feelings heightened, generating a powerful anti-Japanese patriotic movement. Anti-Japanese sentiment had also begun to sprout among the Malays. However, except for a minority of Malays who sympathised with the Chinese, most Malays did not support the MPAJA or were sitting on the fence at best.

The sojourner attitude of the Indians was much stronger than that of the Chinese; they hated the British colonial government and were zealous for India's independence. The MCP and the MPAJA failed to understand the situation of the Indians and to formulate a united front policy with these three ethnic groups.[145]

Meanwhile, in an interview published in the *Sin Chew Jit Poh* (星洲日報) on 15 August 1998, Secretary General Chin Peng himself said about Lai Teck's insistence that the MCP should not fight the British, "we were convinced by Lai Teck's analysis". The MCP and Chin Peng himself asserted that it was not Lai Teck's treachery but the objective conditions of the time that did not permit the MCP to immediately launch the anti-British war.

Sources recorded by the MCP members concerned reveal the birthplaces of MCP leaders as follows:

Apart from Lai Teck, of the 13 members of the Central Committee (nos. 2–11, 27–29), 6 were known to be born in China: they were *Huang Cheng, Xiao Zhong,* Lim Kang Sek, *Ke Min, Xue Feng* and *Ya Zhong.* Among the 15 non-Central Committee members (nos. 12–26), Ng Yeh Lu, Lee Aun Tong and *Yang Mu* were born in China. In short, 9 out of the 28 leaders recorded above were China-born. Malaya-born leaders numbered only 6 out of the 28 cadres: *A Nian, Ya Wen, A Qiu, Lin Ya-dang, Xiao Ping* and Siu Cheong.

Apart from this group of leaders, out of the eight MPAJA leaders whose birthplaces have been identified, four were Malaya-born, and four China-born. The Malaya-born leaders were: Lai Lai Fook; Chin Peng; *Chen Tian*; *Chen Lu* (陳路) alias *Hu Tian-bao* (胡天保),[146] Party Representative of the Fourth Independent Regiment. The China-born leaders were Lau Yew; Ng Leong Meng, Party Representative of the First Independent Regiment; *Zeng Guang-biao* (曾冠彪); and *Zhuang Qing* (莊清), Party Representative of the Seventh Independent Regiment.

Of the martyrs (who comprised MCP Central Committee members, MPAJA cadres and its members) listed in *Malayan People's Anti-Japanese Army* edited by the Friendship Society of Returned Chinese from Singapore and Malaya, ten persons including *Xiao Zhong* and *Lim Kang Sek* were China-born and only two (Lai Lai Fook and *Lei Yin* (雷英) alias *Fang Qiong-sheng* (方瓊生)) were Malayan-born.[147] After removing the men whose names appeared twice, out of the 31 MCP and MPAJA leaders whose birthplaces have been identified, 20 were China-born and 11 were Malayan-born.

Besides them, Chang Ming Ching, staff of the Fifth and Sixth Independent Regiments and the MCP representative in Singapore in early post-war years, was born in Guangdong in 1920 and came to Malaya in 1936.[148] Phang Sau Shoong, or *Peng Shao-xiong* (彭少雄), cadre of the First Independent Regiment and the MCP's Selangor representative in 1945, was born in Kuala Kubu Baru, Selangor, and died on 21 May 1946. In short, Phang Sau Shoong was locally born (*qiao-sheng*, 僑生). In 1939, he returned to China after joining the Dongjiang Overseas Chinese Returning Home Service Troop (Dongjiang Huaqiao Huixiang Fuwutuan, 東江華僑回鄉服務団), organised by the Fui Chiu Association (Huizhou Huiguan, 惠州会館) for the purpose of recruiting volunteers to fight the anti-Japanese war at home.[149]

Judging by this information, the majority of MCP and MPAJA leaders were China-born, and had a strong sense of spiritual unity, solidarity and belonging with China. One of the driving forces that inspired their anti-Japanese resistance movement in the second half of the 1930s was their spiritual affinity with China. *Ke Min*, an MCP Central Committee member, was directly dispatched by CCP's Central Committee. *Huang Cheng*, a Standing Committee member ranking only second to Lai Teck, and Lau Yew, Chairman of the MPAJA Central Military Committee, had both been CCP members before coming to Malaya. The same can be said of various rank and file MCP members and MPAJA soldiers. According to the MPAJA Ex-Service Comrades Association, of the 1,225 soldiers who died in the anti-Japanese struggle, 661 had homes in China or the whereabouts of their homes were unknown.[150] Only 564 had homes in Malaya.

Out of the 49 highest-ranking staff of the 8 Independent Regiments during the Japanese Occupation, including Party Representatives, Commanders and Deputy Commanders, ten died in action or in prison and two defected. Of the 37 survivors, 10 are known to have returned to China (most of them deported by British authorities).[151]

These observations prove that a close relationship existed between the MCP's anti-Japanese struggle and China, a position I have maintained for years.[152] Most pre-war MCP ranking leaders came from China where they grew up and became CCP members. In contrast, (1) CCP members were few among war-time MCP leaders; (2) the war-time party leaders came to Malaya when they were children; and (3) Malaya-born Chinese were increasing in number. The MCP appeared to be in a transitional stage, in which it was letting go of its ties with and control by the CCP. However, history shows that it did not move straight towards that direction. Because Chin Peng and other high-ranking leaders had sought refuge in China, the MCP had to depend on the CCP after the outbreak of the anti-British armed struggle in 1948.

Another important factor, though not related to the anti-Japanese war itself, is that influential leaders such as Chin Peng, Siu Cheong and *Chen Tian* remained in power and held high-ranking positions until the conclusion of the armistice agreement in 1989. This does not mean that the Party remained stable during these years, but rather it shows that the Party discouraged criticism and democratic processes, and stagnated. These factors might have contributed to the MCP's failure to take advantage of its victory in the anti-Japanese war and thus to go on to victory in the Malayan liberation struggle.

Notes

1. Stephen Leong, "Sources, Agencies and Manifestations of Overseas Chinese Nationalism in Malaya", Ph.D. diss., University of California, Los Angeles, 1976; Yoji Akashi, *The Nanyang Chinese National Salvation Movement 1937–1941* (Lawrence: University of Kansas, 1970); G.Z. Hanrahan, *The Communist Struggle in Malaya* (Kuala Lumpur: University of Malaya Press, 1971, first edition in 1954); F.S. Chapman, *The Jungle is Neutral* (London: Chatto and Windus, 1957); Cheah Boon Kheng, *Red Star over Malaya:*

Resistance and Social Conflict During and After the Japanese Occupation of Malaya, 1941–1946 (Singapore: Singapore University Press, 1983); Hai Shang-ou (海上鷗), *Malayan People's Anti-Japanese Army* (馬來亞人民抗日軍) (Singapore: 華僑出版社, 1945); Shu Yun-tsiao (許雲樵) and Chua Ser-Koon (蔡史君), eds., *Malayan Chinese Resistance to Japan 1937–1945: Selected Source Materials* (新馬華人抗日史, 1937–1945) (Singapore: 文史出版, 1984).

2. Friendship Society of Returned Chinese from Singapore and Malaya, ed., *Malayan People's Anti-Japanese Army* (Hong Kong: Witness Publishing 見証出版, 1992).

3. Friendship Society of Returned Chinese from Singapore and Malaya, ed., *Selected Sources of the Malayan People's Anti-Japanese Struggle* (Hong Kong: Witness Publishing, 1992).

4. Yong Chin Fatt, *The Origins of Malayan Communism* (Singapore: South Seas Society, 1997) is an outstanding study based on sources of and interviews with persons concerned.

5. Tsutsui Chihiro (筒井千尋), *Treatise of Military Administration in the Southern Area* (Nampogunsei-ron, 南方軍政論) (Tokyo: 日本放送出版協会, 1944). This chart is shown on pp. 154–5.

6. The Second Field Military Police Force (第二野戦憲兵隊), "Development of the Malayan Communist Party and its Activities" (馬來亞共産党發展並活動状況). The date on the document is 8 Mar. 1942. The Japanese used to refer to the Malayan Communist Party (hereafter MCP) as the Malay Communist Party, and after Dec. 1942 the Malai Communist Party. This document, which was provided to me by Professor Yoji Akashi, is exceptional in that the title uses the correct name.

7. The Malayan Emergency Workshop was organised by the Australian National University and took place from 22 to 23 Feb. 1999 at Canberra.

8. Ng Yeh Lu, "MCP Secretary General Lai Teck. How He Killed Cadres of the Nationalist and Communist Parties and the Allied Powers" (馬共中央總書記萊特、如何殺害国共両党及聯軍幹部), Oct. 1945, in *International Times* (国際時報), Singapore, Aug. 1968.

9. Nakayama Mitsuo (中山三男) and Ishibe Toshiro (石部藤四郎), "Special Policemen who Fought the Malayan People's Anti-Japanese Army (MPAJA)" (マラヤ人民抗日軍と戦った特警隊員として) in Forum for the Study of Sources Related to the Japanese Occupation of Malaya and Singapore (「日本の英領マラヤ・シンガポール占領期史料調査」フォーラム), ed., *Japanese Occupation of Malaya and Singapore* (日本のマラヤ・シンガポール占領) (Tokyo: 龍渓書舎, 1998), pp. 464–7.

10. "A Short History of the MCP" (マラヤ共産党略史) in *A Collection of Important Statements Made by Communist Parties in Southeast Asian Countries* (東南アジア諸国共産党の重要声明集) [Tokyo: Institute of Developing Economies (アジア経済研究所), 1975], p. 3. Hereafter *MCP Short History*.

11. Letter to Hara from Chang Ming Ching, 28 Mar. 1993. For further information about Chang, see my article, "Interview with the Former Leaders of the MCP" (マラヤ共産党元幹部会見記), *Ajia Keizai* (アジア経済), vol. 33, no. 7 (July 1992).

12. Tsutsui Chihiro, *Treatise of the Military Administration in the Southern Area*, pp. 150, 154–5.

13. Hanrahan, *The Communist Struggle in Malaya*, p. 231.

14. John Cross, *Red Jungle* (London: Robert Hale, 1957), p. 94.

15. Interview with Onishi, 31 May 1978.

16. Shinozaki Mamoru (篠崎護), *An Untold Record of Occupied Singapore* (シンガポール占領秘録) (Tokyo: 原書房, 1976), p. 168.

17. Hara, "Interview with the Former Leaders of the MCP".

18. Interview with Chin Peng in Canberra, 24 Feb. 1999.

19. *Cultural Conflict D: Japanese Military Administration 6, Interview Record* (特定研究「文化摩擦」D: 日本の軍政6インタヴュー記録) (Tokyo: 東京大学教養学部国際関係研究室, 1980), p. 42. M. Sgt. Nakayama Mitsuo stated that he arrested Lai Teck "on or about 10 March 1942", Onishi Satoru (大西覚) said that his interrogation lasted 15 to 20 days and he released Lai Teck "before 10 March", and Shinozaki Mamoru (who took part in forming the Syonan Oversea Chinese Association) recalled that "Lai Teck voluntarily surrendered on 16 February". Evaluating these three pieces of information, Professor Akashi concluded that the Kempeitai "arrested Lai Teck in early or mid March and released him no later than late April". Akashi, "Lai Teck, Secretary General of the Malayan Communist Party, 1939–1947", *Journal of South Seas Society* 49 (1994): 70–1. It is highly unlikely that Lai Teck went to the Kempeitai on 16 Feb., the day after the fall of Singapore.

20. Onishi Satoru, *An Untold Story of the Syonan Chinese Massacre Incident* (秘録昭南華僑粛清事件) (Tokyo: 金剛出版, 1977), p. 157; interview with Onishi.

21. Professor Akashi called my attention to this article.

22. The Kempeitai also produced another document on 8 Mar., "Anti-Japanese Communist Party (including conspiracy) Activities Table: From Jan. to 28 Feb. 1942" (抗日共産党[含謀略的]事案状況表: 昭和17年自1月至2月28日). It is highly likely that the period covered in "Activities" corresponds to that of the table.

23. Onishi, *Syonan Chinese Massacre*, pp. 177–9.

24. Ibid. p. 187.

25. Sent by the British as Commander of the Force 136, together with John Davis.

26. Interview with Onishi.

27. *Selected Sources*, pp. 386–7.

28. *Nan Chiau Jit Pao* (南僑日報), 3 Dec. 1946.

29. *Nan Chiau Jit Pao*, 27 Dec. 1946.

30. *Min Sheng Bao* (民声報), 5 Feb. 1947; *Nan Chiau Jit Pao*, 8 Feb. 1947.

31. *Nan Chiau Jit Pao*, 1 April 1947; *Min Sheng Bao*, 10 May 1947.

32. Chang Ming Ching's letter to Hara, 16 May 1995.

33. Editorial Committee of the Expanded *Bloody Memorial* (『血碑』増補本編輯委員会), ed., *Bloody Memorial: Expanded Edition* (血碑: 増補本) (Guangdong: Editorial Committee, 1997), pp. 7–8; *Chen Kai* (陳凱), *Memoirs of Penang, Kedah and Perlis People's Anti-Japanese Struggle* (回憶枳吉坡人民抗日鬪爭) (Hong Kong: Nan Dao Publisher 南島出版社, 1999), pp. 90–2. The original *Bloody Memorial* was edited by The Friendship Union of Former Imprisoned

Anti-Japanese Comrades of Singapore (星洲出獄抗日同志聯誼会) and published in Singapore in Feb. 1946. Tan Kim Hong (陳劍虹), a historian in Penang, showed me a copy of the expanded edition. M. Sgt. Nakayama Mitsuo of the Second Field Kempeitai Force (Syonan Kempeitai) said that the CCP dispatched *Huang Cheng*, together with Ng Yeh Lu and *Ke Min*, as MCP leaders. Nakayama's letter to Hara, 17 Sept. 1997.

34. Yong, *The Origins of Malayan Communism*, p. 181.
35. *Anti-Japanese Army*, p. 379; *Selected Sources*, pp. 286, 296, 323–4, 335, 464. According to *Anti-Japanese Army*, Li Ming (李明) alias *Li Jing-ming* (李鏡明) was a senior officer of the Administration Department of the Third Independent Regiment Headquarters when it was established in Jan. 1942 (p. 213). But this *Li Ming* was a male and obviously not the same person as Mrs. *Huang Cheng*. During the Emergency period, an activist named *Li Ming*, was deported to China, where she married *Chen Tian*. But this *Li Ming* seems to be a different person too.
36. "A Short History of the MCP", p. 6.
37. Yong Chin Fatt, "An Investigation into the Leadership, Ideology and Organisation of the Malayan Communist Movement 1936–1941", *Journal of Malaysian Chinese Studies* 1 (1997): 135.
38. Ng Yeh Lu, "MCP Secretary General Lai Teck".
39. *Anti-Japanese Army*, p. 138; *Selected Sources*, pp. 324, 329–30.
40. *Bloody Memorial*, pp. 66–76, 116, 117.
41. *Selected Sources*, pp. 325–6.
42. *Anti-Japanese Army*, pp. 379–82.
43. Interview with Chang Ming Ching, 3 and 5 Sept. 1993.
44. *Selected Sources*, pp. 54, 282–96.
45. Cross, *Red Jungle*, p. 91.
46. Police Department, Military Government Superintendency (軍政監部警察部), "An Observation on Law and Order in Malay" (馬來ニ於ケル治安上ノ一考察), top secret, 27 Nov. 1942, The Tokugawa Yoshichika Collection, War History Department, National Institute of Defense Studies, Self Defense Agency (防衛庁防衛研究所戦史部徳川義親資料).
47. *Bloody Memorial*, p. 38.
48. *Selected Sources*, pp. 296–312, 335.
49. Onishi, *Syonan Chinese Massacre*, p. 154.
50. "A Short History of the MCP", p. 6; The Central Propaganda Committee of the Barisan Sosialis Malaya (馬來亞社会主義陣綫中央宣教委), ed., *Sources of Malayan History 2* (馬來亞歴史資料二) (Singapore: Barisan Sosialis, 1966), pp. 13–19; Lin Fang-sheng (林芳声), *Malaya* (馬來亞) (Beijing: 世界知識出版社, 1957), p. 94. Neither of the sources mentioned Lai Teck's involvement in Lim Kang Sek's arrest, but they said Lim "met heroic death in the anti-Japanese war".
51. Yong, *The Origins of Malayan Communism*, p. 185.
52. *Anti-Japanese Army*, pp. 197–200, 338; *Selected Sources*, pp. 54, 58, 286.
53. Ng Yeh Lu, "MCP Secretary General Lai Teck".
54. *Cultural Conflict D: Japanese Military Administration 2, Interview Record*, p. 42.

55. Cross, *Red Jungle*, pp. 121–2.

56. Ibid., p. 134.

57. *Cai Bai-yun* and *Zhong Ping* (鐘萍), "Ran to the Holy Place with Sincere Heart" (拳拳赤心子迢迢奔聖地) in People's Political Consultative Conference of China (全国政協文史資料研究委員会華僑組), ed., *Turbulent Years: A True Record of Overseas Chinese Youths who Returned to China and Participated in Anti-Japanese War* (峥嵘歲月—華僑青年回国参加抗戰記實) (Beijing: 中国文史出版社, 1988), p. 137. Hereafter *Turbulent Years*.

58. The Association of Chinese Anti-Japanese War History and The War Memorial Museum of Chinese People's Anti-Japanese War (中国抗日戦争史学会,中国人民抗日戦争紀念館編), eds., *Overseas Chinese Compatriots and Anti-Japanese War* (海外僑胞与抗日戦争) (Beijing: Beijing Publishing House, 北京出版社, 1995), p. 325.

59. Yong Chin Fatt, *Chinese Leadership and Power in Colonial Singapore* (Singapore: Times Academic Press, 1992), p. 242; *Zhou Nan-jing* (周南京主編) ed., *Dictionary of Overseas Chinese* (世界華僑華人詞典) (Beijing: 北京大学出版社, 1993), p. 851; *Cai Bai-yun* and *Zhong Ping*, "Ran to the Holy Place with Sincere Heart", pp. 132–8; Chang Ming Ching's letter to Hara, 28 Mar. 1993.

60. *Cultural Conflict D: Japanese Military Administration 2, Interview Record,* pp. 12, 14.

61. *Shan Ru-hong* (單汝洪), *Memories of Anti-Japanese Guerrilla War in Negeri Sembilan* (森美蘭抗日遊撃戦争回憶録) (Hong Kong: 南島出版社, 1999), pp. 40, 189.

62. *Bloody Memorial*, pp. 30–5.

63. *Selected Sources*, pp. 296, 299–300, 489.

64. Ibid., pp. 334–9.

65. Ng Yeh Lu, "MCP Secretary General Lai Teck"; *Zhen Xian Bao* (陣綫報), "Battle Front Report", 6 July 1969; *Anti-Japanese Army*, p. 138.

66. Yong, *The Origins of Malayan Communism*, p. 186.

67. Ibid., p. 188.

68. *Selected Sources*, pp. 286, 296, 335.

69. Yong, "An Investigation into the Malayan Communist Movement", p. 135.

70. The MCP Central Military Committee is different from the Anti-Japanese Army Central Military Committee, established in May 1942 (*Hai Shang-ou, Malayan People's Anti-Japanese Army*, p. 45). The former was organised in Dec. 1941, immediately after the Japanese invasion (*Selected Sources*, p. 30). Lau Yew was Chairman of the Anti-Japanese Army Central Military Committee (馬來亞人民抗日軍退伍同志会機関紙, *Combatants' Friend* (戦友報), 28 Nov. 1947.

71. *Selected Sources*, pp. 20, 22, 27, 54, 324–5, 331; *Bloody Memorial*, p. 102.

72. Chen Kai, *Memoirs of Penang, Kedah and Perlis People's Anti-Japanese Struggle,* pp. 93–5.

73. *Selected Sources*, pp. 296, 299, 322, 335, 483.

74. Yong, *The Origins of Malayan Communism*, p. 185.

75. *Anti-Japanese Army*, p. 138, 150, 156, 198, 245; *Selected Sources*, pp. 53–9, 286.

76. Guo Ren-de (郭仁德), *Malaya and Singapore Anti-Japanese Sources: Mysterious Lai Teck* (馬新抗日史料: 神秘莱特) (Johor Baru: Penerbitan Pelangi, 1999), pp. 208, 218.
77. Yong, *The Origins of Malayan Communism*, p. 186.
78. *Anti-Japanese Army*, p. 138; *Selected Sources*, pp. 54–9.
79. Interview with Chang Ming Ching, 5 Sept. 1993.
80. Interview with Chin Peng, 24 Feb. 1999 in Canberra.
81. Yong, *The Origins of Malayan Communism*, p. 186.
82. *Anti-Japanese Army*, pp. 38, 138, 339.
83. Chin Peng, alias *Chin Peng: My Side of History* (Singapore: Media Masters, 2003), pp. 468–9, 499.
84. *Bloody Memorial*, pp. 16, 118, 126, 196.
85. Onishi, *Syonan Chinese Massacre*, p. 154.
86. Ibid., p. 254.
87. Interview with Onishi.
88. *Bloody Memorial*, pp. 46–50, 287.
89. Nakayama and Ishibe, "Special Policemen who Fought the MPAJA", p. 480.
90. Ishibe, *My Youth: Kempei NCO Ishibe Memo* (青春: 憲兵・下士官石部メモ) (Private Publication, 1990), pp. 62–4.
91. *Selected Sources*, pp. 314, 335, 404, 441–2.
92. *Anti-Japanese Army*, pp. 45, 50, 287; *Selected Sources*, p. 441.
93. Ishibe, *My Youth*, pp. 110–1.
94. *Anti-Japanese Army*, pp. 156, 351, 381; *Selected Sources*, p. 58.
95. Ng Yeh Lu, "MCP Secretary General Lai Teck"; *Li Li-wen* (李立文編), ed., *From Gulangyu to Singapore: Travelling of a Foreign Chinese* (從鼓浪嶼到新加坡: 一位外籍華人的歷程) (Amoy: 廈門大学出版社, 1995), pp. 35–78; *Dictionary of Overseas Chinese*, p. 724.
96. *Hu Mai* (胡邁), Translated by Ida Keishou (井田啓勝訳), *Overseas Chinese Born Again* (華僑新生記) (Tokyo: 新紀元社, 1944), p. 107.
97. Onishi, *Syonan Chinese Massacre*, pp. 187–8.
98. Ng Yeh Lu, "MCP Secretary General Lai Teck"; according to *Guo Ren-de*, *Mysterious Lai Teck*, p. 181, *Xiao Di-di* (小弟々) was executed by the MCP's Eradicating Traitor Corps (鋤奸隊) soon after his release. Guo did not cite the source. On the other hand, *Bloody Memorial* states that *Xiao Di-di*, whose original name was *A Fang* (阿芳) and who was less than 20 years old, was rearrested in May 1943 by the Japanese police and executed on 25 July of the same year.
99. Onishi, *Syonan Chinese Massacre*, pp.187–8.
100. *Selected Sources*, pp. 19, 303, 329.
101. Professor Akashi called my attention to this article.
102. Witness Series Editing Committee (見証叢書編委会編), ed., *Manman Linhai Lu* (漫漫林海路, Trails in a Boundless Ocean of Trees) (Hong Kong: Witness Publish Co., 見証出版社, 2003), pp. xii, 237–41.
103. Li Li-wen, *From Gulangyu to Singapore*.
104. Interview with Chang Ming Ching, 3 and 5 Sept. 1993.

105. *Fang Shan* (方山), ed., *Witnessing the Reconciliation and Return to Malaya: Commemorating the Tenth Anniversary of Return to Malaya* (見証和解与回馬: 紀念回馬10周年) (Kuala Lumpur: *Fang Shan*, 2002), pp. 179, 184.

106. *Selected Sources*, p. 20.

107. Interview with Ng Leong Meng, former Party Representative of the First Independent Regiment, 4 Sept. 1994, Singapore.

108. Interview with Chang Ming Ching, 3 and 5 Sept. 1993.

109. Aloysius Chin, *The Communist Party of Malaya: The Inside Story* (Kuala Lumpur: Vinpress, 1994), pp. 46, 69, 90–2.

110. Chin Peng, op. cit., pp. 469, 470. *Fang Shan* (方山), ed., *Record of Convulsion at the Malaysia-Thai Border*, Volume 2 (馬泰邊區風雲録 第二集 万水千山密林情), Kuala Lumpur, Penerbitan Abad 21, p. 124.

111. Interview with Chang Ming Ching, 3 and 5 Sept. 1993.

112. *Fang Shan, Witnessing the Reconciliation and Return to Malaya*, p. 179.

113. C.C. Chin provided me with this information.

114. *Fang Shan, Witnessing the Reconciliation and Return to Malaya*, pp. 184–8.

115. *Jin Xing-zhong* (金星衆), "Singapore Overseas Chinese Volunteer Corps in World War II" (第二次世界大戰時期的星洲華僑義勇軍), *Historical Sources of Guangzhou* (広州市文史資料) 19 (1980): 71, 72, 82, 86; *Selected Sources*, pp. 19, 296–9, 306, 310, 322, 335; *Bloody Memorial*, p. 52.

116. *Anti-Japanese Army*, pp. 150, 157–8.

117. Ibid., pp. 149, 173.

118. *Trails in a Boundless Ocean of Trees*, pp. 191–203.

119. *Anti-Japanese Army*, p. 247; *Selected Sources*, pp. 261–3; *Ya Zhu* (亞竹), ed., *MPAJA First Regiment* (馬來亞人民抗日軍第一独立隊) (Hong Kong [?], 1992), p. 64. C.C. Chin kindly presented a copy of this book to me.

120. *Trails in a Boundless Ocean of Trees*, pp. 191–203; Shan, *Memories of Anti-Japanese Guerrilla War in Negeri Sembilan*, pp. 45, 47, 173, 190.

121. *Anti-Japanese Army*, pp. 156, 381; *Selected Sources*, p. 371.

122. *Anti-Japanese Army*, pp. 379, 381.

123. *Anti-Japanese Army*, p. 285; *Selected Sources*, p. 6.

124. *Anti-Japanese Army*, pp. 281, 285; *Selected Sources*, pp. 5, 58, 315.

125. *Anti-Japanese Army*, pp. 34, 311, 314, 316, 331; *Selected Sources*, pp. 6, 55, 188, 489; Editorial Committee of the Nandao Serial Books (南島叢書編輯委員会編), *70 Years of Vicissitudinous in Malaya 1930–2000* (馬來亞風雲70年 1930–2000) (Hong Kong: 南島出版社, 2000), pp. 47–56.

126. Chin, *The Communist Party of Malaya*, pp. 17, 46, 49, 64, 94, 131,190–6, 206–27, 241; Ratanachaya Kitti, *The Communist Party of Malaya, Malaysia and Thailand: Truce Talks Ending the Armed Struggle of the Communist Party of Malaya* (Bangkok: Duangkaew Publishing House, 1996), pp. 34, 51, 58, 108, 143, 182, 221.

127. *Qing Lang* (晴朗), ed., *Camouflage Must Be Removed: A Thorough Exposure of Chin Peng Clique's Anti-Revolutionary Crimes* (偽裝必須剥去—徹底掲露陳平一伙的反革命罪行) (Macau, 1987), pp. 54–61.

128. *Turbulent Years*, p. 222; *Anti-Japanese Army*, p. 220; *Selected Sources* pp. 261–4.

129. Shan, *Memories of Anti-Japanese Guerrilla War in Negeri Sembilan*, pp. 191–2.

130. Chang Ming Ching's letter to Hara, 25 Feb. 1996; Ishibe in his book said that Kempei S. Sgt. Maeda Mitsuo of the Taiping (Perak) Kempeitai squad deserted and joined the MCP's Fifth Independent Regiment, but he had been missing since the end of war (Ishibe, *My Youth*, pp. 124–7). S. Sgt. Maeda might have been executed by Lai Teck's order.

131. Chin Peng's testimony at Malayan Emergency Workshop held at the Australian National University in Canberra, 22–23 Feb. 1999. In a recently published memoir, Chin Peng says that some 400 individual Japanese were accepted into the MPAJA. Chin Peng, *My Side of History*, p. 124.

132. Some sources have reported that Chin Peng was born in 1922, but he said the correct date is 1924 (*Sin Chew Jit Poh*, 20 June 1998).

133. *Dictionary of Overseas Chinese*, pp. 432–3; *Bloody Memorial*, p. 219.

134. Chin, *The Communist Party of Malaya*, pp. 68–70, 90.

135. Chin Peng's testimony at the Malayan Emergency Workshop.

136. *Anti-Japanese Army*, pp. 316, 334; Ng Leong Meng's letter to Hara, 19 June 1999.

137. Interview with *Chen Rui-yao* (陳瑞瑤), 4 Sept. 1999, Singapore. *Chen Rui-yao* was a cadre of a company of the Sixth Independent Regiment; Ng Leong Meng's letter to Hara, 9 Dec. 1997. Ng Leong Meng, as a senior political officer, was a predecessor of Chin Peng (*Lai Wen-ming*) of the Sixth Independent Regiment. Lai Wen-ming is living in Singapore. Ng Leong Meng and *Chen Rui-yao* said that during wartime they never heard of Chin Peng (Ong Boon Hua, who was to become the Secretary General). According to Chang Ming Ching's letter to Hara, 13 Dec. 1997, *Lai Wen-ming* was arrested in Penang while working as an underground agent and engaged in party activities in Pahang after escaping from captivity.

138. *Selected Sources*, pp. 312–7; *Bloody Memorial* said his arrest was made in Nov. 1943, p. 65. Concerning Lai Lai Fook's arrest, see Akashi, "The Anti-Japanese Movement in Perak during the Japanese Occupation 1941–45", in *Malaya and Singapore during the Japanese Occupation*, ed. Paul H. Kratoska (Singapore: Singapore University Press, 1995), pp. 97–8, 115; and Tamura Hideyuki (田村秀行), *The Perak State Police: A Record of the Pacific War* (軍政下のペラ州警察—太平洋戦争の記録) (Private Publication, 1980), pp. 94–6. Tamura did not mention Lai Lai Fook's execution. Sybil Kathigasu, a female medical doctor who was incarcerated in Ipoh Prison, said the Police Chief (Nagayasu Mamoru, 長安守) led Lai out of the prison and decapitated him. A tip-off led to Kathigasu being apprehended for having treated guerrillas (she died in 1949 as a result of torture she sustained in detention). Sybil Kathigasu, *No Dram of Mercy* (Singapore: Oxford University Press, 1983), pp. 151–2. The Ipoh Police Chief was given the death sentence in a post-war war crime trial (Tamura, *The Perak State Police*, pp. 57, 234–5).

About the torture inflicted on Mr. and Mrs. Kathigasu and their small daughter, see Ahmad Murad Nasaruddin's famous Malay novel, *Nyawa di Hujung Pedang* (Life on Edge of a Sword, 剣の先の生命) , in *Selected Anti-Japanese Novels of Malaysia* (マレーシア抗日文学選), ed. and trans. Hara (Tokyo: Keiso Shobo, 1994). This Malay novel was translated by Imani

Naomi. It revealed that the Kempeitai set up its headquarters by confiscating the home of Leong Sin Nam (*Liang Shen-nan*, 梁燊南), businessman and leader of the anti-Japanese movement, and that S. Sgt. Yoshimura Ekio, the Kempeitai officer most notorious for his cruelty, was executed in a war crimes trial.

139. *Selected Sources*, pp. 385–8; see section on Lai Teck and note 69.
140. *Dictionary of Overseas Chinese*, p. 433.
141. Chin, *The Communist Party of Malaya*, p. 90.
142. Interview with Chang Ming Ching, 3 and 5 Sept. 1993.
143. *Selected Sources*, pp. 331–2, 360–3.
144. *Anti-Japanese Army*, p. 140.
145. Ibid., pp. 134–6.
146. Concerning *Chen Lu*, see *Shan Ru-hong, Recollection of the Past* (回憶往事) (Hong Kong: 南島出版社, 2002), p. 216.
147. *Selected Sources*, pp. 282–395; Chang Ming Ching's letter to Hara, 24 July 1993.
148. *Combatants' Friend*, 17 Oct. 1947.
149. *Min Sheng* Bao, 23–25 May 1946; *Selected Sources*, pp. 40, 359.
150. *Nan Chiau Jit Pao*, 8 Sept. 1947.
151. Hara, "The Japanese Occupation of Malaya and the Chinese Community" (日本のマラヤ占領と華人社会) in *Japanese Occupation in Southeast Asian History* (東南アジア史の中の日本占領), ed. Kurasawa Aiko (倉沢愛子) (Tokyo: 早稲田大学出版部, 1997), pp. 339–40.
152. Hara, "The Malayan Communist Party and its Anti-Japanese War: An Interplay of 'Supporting the Fatherland' and 'the National Liberation of Malaya'" (マラヤ共産党と抗日戦争: "祖国救援", "マラヤ民族解放" の交錯), *Asia Keizai* (アジア経済) 19, 8 (1978): 2–27.

General Yamashita Tomoyuki, C-in-C of the 25th Army pictured with Sultans of Malaya (June 1942). Tokugawa Yoshichika, advisor of Military Administration (left in front row), Colonel Watanabe Wataru, chief of Military Administration Department (centre in second row)

Major General Fujimura Masuzo, superintendent of Military Administration (1943–44)

General Itagaki Seishiro, C-in-C of the 7th Area Army surrendering to the British, Singapore

Subhas Chandra Bose, commander of the INA pictured with Lt. Gen. Isoda Saburo and his staff officers (January 1944)

Odachi, Mayor of Syonan, with sultans of Malaya and Sumatra, January 1943

Japanese staff personnel of the Perak State Government, 1944. Shuchokan Mawamura Naooka is in the centre of the front row.

Maj. Gen. Tatsumi Hiroshi (third from left), who commanded his troops for landing operations at Kota Bahru, with the sultan of Kelantan

War memorial at Bukit Timah commemorating battle at Bukit Timah
fought by the 18th Division

Syonan Jinja

A Japanese officer instructing a Malay on making rope with rice straw

4

Japan's Economic Policy for Occupied Malaya

YOSHIMURA MAKO

Introduction

The Japanese invasion of Southeast Asia aimed at obtaining the natural resources and goods to wage the war against China, and to cut off lines of communication and supply route that allowed the Allied Powers to send supplies to Chinese forces. Japan's violent exploitation of the region brought chaos to local economies and made it difficult for the local population to earn living. Although the Occupation lasted for only three-and-a-half years, it had an enormous long-term impact on local economies and societies. This chapter examines Japan's economic policies in the Malay Peninsula (called *Malai* by the Malai Gunsei Kambu or Military Administration in Malaya) and Singapore (Syonan). In this chapter, $ means Straits Dollars.

The Japanese Occupation and Economic Policy in Southeast Asia

Invasion in the South and the Economic Policy

Before invading Southeast Asia, the Japanese military government started studying economic plans for the region. An initial proposal was submitted in November 1941 shortly prior to the invasion of Kota Bahru, Malaya, on 8 December 1941.

In early 1941, the Japanese General staff set up a research group to start making plans[1] for controlling the Southern territories such as the Netherlands Indies (currently Indonesia), rich in natural resources such as crude oil, which were indispensable in waging war. The main purpose of invading the South was to obtain natural resources and goods and thus reduce the burden of war expenditures for the home country.[2] The general headquarters of the Southern Army prepared "The Implementation Plan of Military Administration of Southern Army (Draft) [Nanpogun Gunsei shiko

Keikaku (An)]" dated 3 November 1941, which included policies for finance, currency, trade, development and acquisition of resources, transport, as well as administration. It shows that the Japanese military had already developed concrete economic policies for the occupation at that point.[3]

At a council meeting in the presence of the Emperor on 5 November 1941, a session that ended the negotiations with the United States of America and made the decision to attack the South, Suzuki Teiichi, Director of Planning Board (Kikakuin Sosai), reported on the raw materials and goods that Japan could expect to obtain from the Southern region. In addition to crude oil in the Netherlands Indies and rice in Thailand and French Indochina, he stated that the natural rubber, tin, bauxite and other materials in Malaya would not only fulfill the demand created by the Southern operation, but would also inflict damage on the United States.

"The Principles of Implementation of Military Administration in the Occupied Southern Area (Nanpo Senryochi Gyosei Jisshi Yoryo)"[4] approved at the Imperial Headquarters-Government Liaison Conference on 20 November 1941, provided the three *gunsei* principles: acquisition of strategic materials, establishment of the self-sufficiency of the occupying army, and restoration of law and order. It mentioned the importance of denying special materials such as crude oil, rubber, tin, tungsten and quinine, from the enemy. "The Administrative Principles for Occupied Region in the Operation of the Southern Area (Nanpo Sakusen ni tomonau Senryo chi Tochi Yoko)" (25 November 1941)[5] issued by the Army Division of Imperial Head-quarters, also instructed the Military Administration to take measures for obtaining important national defence materials to achieve war aims and to sustain the Empire's military capability.

"The Principles of Economic Policy in the Southern Region (Nanpo Keizai Taisaku Yoko)",[6] issued on 12 December 1941 (after the outbreak of war) first used the term, "Greater East Asian Co-Prosperity Sphere", in reference to the territories to be occupied by Japan in the South and called for the acquisition of important materials to conduct the war by establishing self-sufficiency within the Greater East Asian Co-Prosperity Sphere in order to reinforce and strengthen the imperial economy.

The Japanese military did not intend to grant independence of the people of Southeast Asia when it planned the invasion and occupation of the Southern territories. In fact, "The Principles of Implementation of Military Administration in the Occupied Southern Area", released one month before the invasion, stated that Japan should not encourage independence movements in the territories.[7] Even today, several right-wing groups in Japan point to the slogans of the Greater East Asian Co-Prosperity Sphere and claim that the Japanese military administration ultimately intended to liberate Asian nations and encourage their independence. In reality, the Japanese military administration in Malaya had no intention of granting independence. It is clear that from the outset, the Japanese government planned that Malaya would be a permanent colony of Japan, a decision reaffirmed by the Ministry of Foreign Affairs in February 1945, and by the Ministry of Greater East Asia Affairs in June 1945.[8]

Exploitation of Raw Materials from Malaya

Japan expected to exploit iron ore, bauxite, manganese, tin, natural rubber and tannin in Malaya[9] as well as crude oil in the Netherlands Indies (Indonesia), and rice in Thailand and French Indochina (Vietnam). Also, the Malay Peninsula and Singapore were to have a central function for economy and transport in Southeast Asia.

According to the "Principles for the Implementation of Military Administration of the 25th Army (Dai 25gun Gunsei Jisshi Yoko)",[10] the priority placed on resources in Malaya was firstly bauxite and manganese, secondly iron ore, tin and rubber, and thirdly tannin.

Japan, however, considered that the production of rubber and tin in Malaya exceeded the demands of domestic industries in Japan. According to "The Principles of Army Management of the Southern Economy (Nanpo Keizai Rikugun Shori Yoko)",[11] the production of rubber and tin was to be reduced as it exceeded the demand of the Empire of Japan.

In the 1930s, Malayan rubber accounted for about half to two-thirds of total world production and Malayan tin made up one-third of world output. Malaya exported 57 per cent of its rubber and 74 per cent of its tin mainly to the U.S.[12] Japan considered it important to prevent these commodities from reaching enemy states.

In August 1942, six months after the Japanese occupation began, "Instructions of the Superintendent-General of Military Administration (Gunsei Sokan Shiji)"[13] directed that since rubber and tin were world-wide special materials, Southeast Asian production should not only meet the demand in the Greater East Asian Co-Prosperity Sphere, but should also respond to meet global demand so that in post-war economic competition, Japan would retain world control of these resources.

Trade of Malaya

The distinguishing feature of pre-war Malayan trade was the high proportion of exports to the U.S.A. Unlike India which had close trade
relations with the United Kingdom (U.K.), 53 per cent of Malayan
products were exported to the U.S.A., and only 15 per cent to the U.K.
in 1940.[14]

The profile for Malayan imports was also different. The Netherlands
Indies was the major source of supplies (35 per cent) and Thailand was
the second (15 per cent), while the U.K.'s share was only 14 per cent and
the U.S.A. 5 per cent. About a half of the imports from the Netherlands
Indies were rubber and tin, but they were re-exported from Malaya as
entrepot trading.[15]

About 70 per cent of Malayan imports were raw materials. The biggest
item was rice, which came mainly from Thailand and Burma (Figure 1).
Domestic rice production supplied only 21 to 43 per cent (for an average of
35 per cent) of consumption in Malaya, so one-third of domestic consumption
relied on imports.[16]

Figure 1: Import of Rice in Malaya, 1938–45

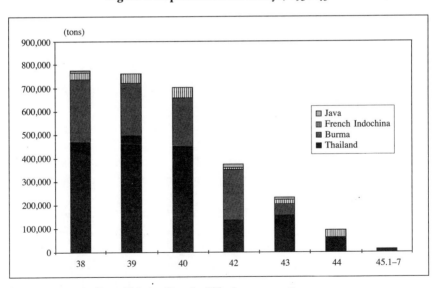

Source: 1937–38: Great Britain, Board of Trade, 1939: 158.
    1939–40: Great Britain, Board of Trade, 1947: 164.
    1942–45: Marai-wo Kataru-kai. 1976: 113.

Thus, the Malayan economy, which depended on trading, was badly damaged when it largely lost its trade market.[17] During the Japanese Occupation, Malaya exported only to Japan, occupied territories in the Southern regions, and the Axis powers.

Before the war, Malaya exported rubber, tin and iron ore to Japan, and Japan exported manufactured goods to Malaya. While the U.K. dominated the market in manufactured goods imported into Malaya, Japanese exports increased in Malaya during the 1930s, and the U.K. began to consider Japan a trade threat. The Japanese share of the Malayan trade market was only 2 per cent of overall imports and 5 per cent of exports. The U.K., however, introduced a quota system in 1934 for cotton thread and limited the Japanese imports.

Figure 2 shows export-import trade between Malaya and Japan. By 1940, Japan had accounted for just 5 per cent of Malaya's total trade, and it was obvious that Japan and the Japanese Empire would not be able to maintain Malayan trade at anything like pre-war levels.

In 1941, as Japan-U.K. relations worsened, trade between Japan and Malaya shrank by more than 50 per cent, and, in 1942, just after the war broke out,

Figure 2: Trade between Malaya and Japan, 1937–45

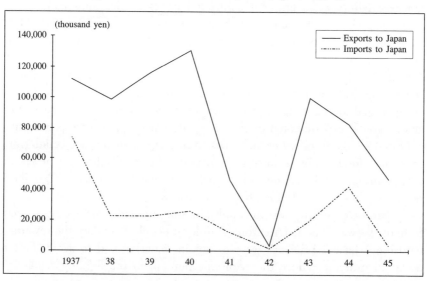

Source: Compiled from Ministry of Finance. *Annual Report of Japanese Foreign Trade, various issues:* Iwatake 1995b: Appendix 2-18: 498 and *Nanyo-Nenkan (Yearbook of South Seas)*, 1218–1220 (Iwatake 1995b: Appendix 2-7, 475).

it dropped even more precipitously and exports to Japan dropped to 2–3 per cent and imports from Japan dropped to 6–7 per cent of the level of 1940. However, even if it was only 5 per cent of total trade of pre-war Malaya (so it was obvious that Japan could not take over the whole volume of Malayan trade), trade recovered to the level of 1940 under the Japanese Occupation.

Malaya was highly dependent on imports in the 1930s — domestic rice production supplied only one-third of local demand, and Malaya depended on the import of rice from Thailand and Burma before the war. After the autumn of 1942, rice supplies fell well below the level of pre-war imports because of the deteriorating war situation, irregular railway and marine transport services, and damage to Thailand's rice crop as a result of flooding.

The supply of food and basic necessities to the local people was a major issue as there were not many manufacturers in Malaya.[18] However, the Japanese themselves faced serious shortages of food and commodities at home, and could not supply food to the occupied areas. As Figure 1 shows, Malayan rice imports shrank to 375 thousand tons in 1942, about one half of what was imported in 1940, and further decreased to 229 thousand tons in 1943 and to 94 thousand tons in 1944. By 1945, between January and July, its import plummeted to 12 thousand tons of rice. The Japanese Military Government controlled prices of rice and reduced the ration supplies distributed through the *kumiai* (association) system. For instance, the Selangor government reduced the ration from a generous 36 *katis* per month (about 48 pounds) for males over twelve years old to just 17 *katis* by late January 1943. In early 1944, the Military Government (JMA) stated that Malaya needed to become self-sufficient in food production,[19] and it urged local people to grow their own food crops by utilising empty land. Later it experimented in cultivating double-cropping rice plants, and relocated people from towns and cities to rural areas where they could grow their own food.[20] The death rate increased substantially because of severe food shortages and malnutrition, which also worsened illness.[21] No food relief was in sight until after the end of the war.

Japan's top priority was to supply the military with whatever it needed to fight the war. The JMA enforced on local people to endure the resulting hardship.[22] Japan's priorities were to obtain materials and to avoid "barter trade" in order to reduce the economic burden on the fighting capability of the empire.[23]

The bottleneck for sending materials to Japan was shipping. Under the Occupation administration, the army controlled transport and shipping.

According to the 25th Army, the allocation of ships for September 1942 was only 80 thousand tons, just 60 per cent of the requested 134 thousand tons. Actually it assigned only 53 thousand tons, 40 per cent of the tonnage requested.[24] Moreover, from late 1943 to early 1944, many vessels were damaged or sunk by Allied attacks, and it became difficult to allocate ships to the South.[25]

Transport and freight services were not well organised. Shipping arrangements were not well coordinated with the orders and requests because of enemy airplane and submarine attacks sinking freighters. Furthermore, reliable information about supplies was lacking. Despite vessel shortage and overstocking, the Army General Staff demanded more materials and the local military administration authorities planned transport accordingly (Table 1).

Since Malayan export goods could not be transported easily due to vessel shortages, stockpiles increased. The Army General Staff decided to buy the excess stocks on paper to settle the problem; however, the excess stocks piled up at harbours, estates, and factories.

In 1942 only 415,000 tons, 15 per cent of the export target of 2,814,000 tons, were sent from Malaya to Japan. The total volume of freight between 1942 and 1945 was 2,902,000 tons, 33 per cent of the 8,543,000 ton targeted for 1944 (Table 1).

Figure 3: Production of Tin in Malaya, 1937–45

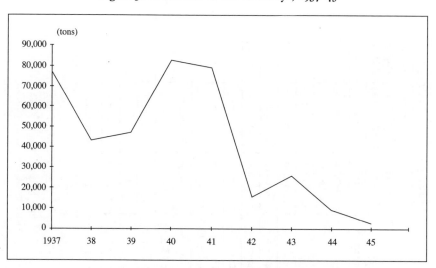

Source: Department of Mines, Federation of Malaya 1949: Appendix IV, 62.

Table 1: Japanese Target and Achievement of Major Materials in Malaya (tons)

Materials	End of 1941 Actual Production (1)	1942 Target of Acquisition (End of 1941) (1)	1942 Actual Import of Japan (2)	1943 Actual Import of Japan (2)	1944 Target of Development (End of 1941) (1)	1944 Plan of Sending Materials to Japan (3)	1944 Actual Import of Japan (2)	1944 Actual Import Japan/Target of Sending (%)	1945 Actual Import of Japan (2)	1942–45 Total of Actual Import of Japan (2)
Raw Rubber	650,000 (600,000a)	100,000	— (158,517b)	20,461	(C) 300,000	110,000	18,750	17	17,541	56,752
Tin	80,000	10,000	—	7,934	(C) 20,000	18,000	6,132	34	3,077	17,143
Iron Ore	2,000,000	500,000	76,887	37,700	2,500,000	—	—	0	—	114,587
Bauxite	150,000	100,000	2,032	251,645	200,000	1,200,000	268,057	22	21,414	543,148
Manganese	25,000	30,000	—	—	40,000	14,000	400	3	400	400
Tungsten	—	—	—	—	—	300	169	56	112	281
Palm Oil (& Coconut Oil)	—	—	—	32,038	—	20,000	—	0	—	32,038
Copra Oil	160,000a	50,000	—	—	(M) 160,000	35,000	7,798	22	497	8,295
Tannin Material	NA	5,000	—	559	10,000		323	—	—	882
Tannin Extract	—	—	—	130	—		242	—	—	372
Resin	—	—	—	1,752	—	1,000	54	5	—	1,806
Derisu Root	100a	100	23	262	1,000	800	142	18	—	427

Notes: M — Maintain the present level
C — Control and reduce the production level
a — Actual Export
b — Senji Geppo (Wartime Monthly Report), May 1942.

Sources: (1) Nanpo Keizai Taisaku Yoko (Principles of Policy for the Southern Economy). Attached Sheet 1 (12 December 1941).
(2) Ministry of Finance, Japan. Annual Report of Japan Foreign Trade, various issues.
(3) Naichi Kanso Keikaku Kiso an (Basis Proposal for Plan of Sending to Japan), 1944. Nanpo Gunsei Sokanbu Somu Bucho Kaigi Haifu Shiryo Besshi Dai-2.

Rubber Estates under the Japanese Occupation

Control of Rubber Estates

Rubber was the most important export commodity apart from tin for Malaya. Rubber was a strategic material needed by the Japanese military administration. In 1938, over 3,278,000 acres in Malaya were planted with rubber trees. Major producing states were Johor (27 per cent), Perak (17 per cent), Selangor (15 per cent), and Negri Sembilan (12 per cent) (Table 2). The rubber industry rapidly developed after the "rubber boom" of 1909–11[26] in Malaya. Nearly one-quarter of Malaya's rubber industry was controlled by Japanese planters whose smallholdings and estates totalled 800,000 acres. With the assurance of the 999-year lease of land, Japanese plantation owners were able to expand rubber estate operations (in Johor) which became the major industry in the state.

The 25th Army Administration created an "Implementation Plans for Important Industries" shortly after setting up the military administration. The JMA organised "an association (*kumiai*) with private companies as a body to enforce and to entrust the management" of every important industry in Malaya "under the military administration supervision (control)".[27]

Table 2: Rubber Area in Malaya, 1938

State	Area (acres)	%
Johor	890,000	27.2
Kedah	302,000	9.2
Trengganu	43,000	1.3
Kelantan	92,000	2.8
Perlis	5,500	0.2
Perak	563,000	17.2
Selangor	496,000	15.1
Negri Sembilan	381,000	11.6
Pahang	173,000	5.3
Singapore	53,000	1.6
Malacca	194,000	5.9
Penang	18,000	0.6
Province Wellesley	68,000	2.1
Total	3,278,000	100.0

Source: Malaya, Department of Agriculture 1938: 3.

In accordance with this plan, the JMA directed the association to put the rubber estates management under unified control in Malaya. Before the arrival of necessary personnel in Malaya, the military administration had restored and managed enemy rubber estates. It also decided to buy the output of rubber estates belonging to third nations, with a provisional military budget set up to maintain operations and to send the products to Japan, and to provide employment for workers in producing estates.

In May 1942, the 25th Army set up "the Syonan Rubber Association (Syonan Gomu Kumiai)" with its headquarters in Singapore (Syonan). According to "The Principles of Syonan Rubber Association", it was "to control and manage the production, collection, delivery, export and related work of rubber of Japanese estates and enemy estates under the military control in Malaya and Sumatra".[28] The Association was comprised of representatives of 16 companies, which had managed rubber estates since pre-war years.

The Association set prices and production allocations for each area. The price for raw rubber was 20 cents per pound for the first grade sheet, 20–25 cents per pound for the first grade pale crepe, and 26 cents per pound for the dry latex. "The minimum production" was 100,000 tons for Malaya (excluding Penang and Syonan) and 70,000 tons for Sumatra. The companies that arranged to purchase the raw rubber were Mitsui Bussan, Nomura (Higashi-Indo) Shokusan, Senda & Co., Koei Shokai, Kasho, and Mitsubishi Shoji.

In September 1942, 1,239 estates were managed under the Syonan Rubber Association. The Association's total planted area was 1,981,000 acres and the workers numbered 237,000. The monthly production was 6,800 tons and 30,000 tons were stocked at estates.[29]

A plan of Rubber Public Corps (Gomu Koei-dan) was considered for the management of rubber estates. The idea was to assess these rubber estates and to issue shares to Japanese nationals in exchange for war loans (wartime bonds) and to guarantee the dividend equal to the interest of national bonds. This plan was ultimately considered to be impractical and was not carried out.

In October 1942, the Military Administration of the 25th Army drafted the "Principles of 25th Army's Agriculture-Related Companies Management" as a basic policy for management and control of enemy estates. Under the Principles, government-designated companies were assigned areas to manage estates under the guidance of the Syonan Rubber Association.

The Planning Section of the Military Administration drew up the "Principles of Policies Dealing with Rubber (Draft)" on 19 December 1942[30] and set up production levels for the next three years (until the end of 1945) analysing world rubber demand. The Principles estimated that the post-war world demand for rubber would be 1,200,000 tons in addition to the stockpile of 300,000 tons. Since Britain and the U.S. could supply 500,000 tons out of the total 1,500,000 tons, Japan and Japanese territories would potentially supply 1,000,000 tons. So the Planning Section instructed rubber plantations to set levels of production at 1,000,000 tons and the production and allocation in Malaya, Sumatra and so on. The rubber industry was directed to maintain about 70 per cent of their pre-war production level and to regulate production in 1943 so as to increase quality and reduce the cost. The policies also provided for reduction in production by smallholders to 8 per cent of pre-war levels so that land and labour forces could instead be used to increase food production.[31]

The Malay Military Administration discussed ways to improve local self-sufficiency and to increase food production, major concerns since the first half of 1943. The "Policy Principles Dealing With Rubber (Draft)", formulated on 19 December 1942, reviewed estates with the goal of reclaiming land that might be better used for food production.

On 15 February 1943, the "Principle of Enemy Rubber Estate Allotment (Tekisan Gomu Noen Haito Hoshin)", drafted by the Planning Section of the Military Administration,[32] decided that "productive enemy estates should be assigned to companies one by one for limited production" and that non-producing estates should be under the control of state officials. Forty per cent of the 1,628,000 acres of enemy estates were divided among Japanese plantation companies and the remaining 60 per cent were retained by state governments under the direct management of the Military Administration.

The appendix to this Principle stated that the "Rubber Control Association (Gomu Tosei-kai)" was to replace the Syonan Rubber Association and the Estate Supervision Bureau to supervise re-allotments and provide technical advice and inspection.

The Administration allotted to Japanese plantation companies the areas for the rubber production and appointed their buyers as well (Table 3) (see the case of Showa Gomu K.K. in the next section). It included Japanese companies who had been operating in Malaya before the war. Johor, with 27 per cent of the rubber plantations in Malaya and many Japanese planters, was allotted to Mitsubishi Shoji Co.

Rubber prices were to be controlled under the Malaya Rubber Management Association (Marai Gomu Kanri Kumiai) after October 1943. However, prices set at 20 cents per pound in May 1942 had increased to 40 cents per pound by April 1944 and doubled or tripled again in October. This price fluctuation happened because Japanese troops purchased rubber disregarding the controlled price. Also, illegal trading occurred; Chinese black marketeers illegally sold 3,000 tons of rubber in the black market in Singapore according to a November 1943 survey by Okamoto of the Malaya Rubber Management Association.[33]

Unlike other agricultural and forestry products, there were no instructions until 1943 for the rubber industry with long-term perspectives from the Central Administration of Japanese Army in Japan. So, the 25th Army decided to regulate the surplus rubber production and to switch the land for increasing food production in the "Policies Dealing With Rubber". This kind of planning would normally have

Table 3: Japanese Planters and the Allotted Areas and the Exporters under the Japanese Occupation

Planters	Allotted Area	Exporter
Shonan Saibai Kumiai (Association of Japanese small holders)	Singapore including Riau Island	Mitsui Bussan K.K.
Sango Kongsi	Most parts of Johor	Mitsubishi Shoji K.K.
Nanai Gomu K.K.	Muar and a part of Tangkat district in Johor	Kasho K.K.
Nanyo Gomu Takushoku K.K.	Most parts of Kluang districts in Johor	Kasho K.K.
Nettai Sangyo K.K.	Malacca, South parts of Negri Sembilan	Mitsui Bussan K.K.
Malay Gomu K.K.	North parts of Negri Sembilan	—
Toyo Takushoku K.K.	Pahang	—
Nanyo Gomu K.K.	South parts of Selangor	Nikka Kongsi
Nissan Norin K.K.	North parts of Selangor	Koyei Shokai
Showa Gomu K.K.	Perak	Nomura Tohindo Shokusan K.K. (south parts), Senda & Co. (north parts)
Senda Gomu	Penang and Province Wellesley	Senda & Co.

Source: Malaya: Japanese Penetration of the Rubber Manufacturing Industry, NARA RG226 XL23029.

Figure 4: Production and Export of Rubber, 1937–45

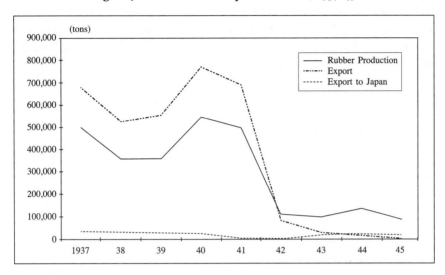

Note: The export of 1937–41 exceeded over the import because it includes re-export, which came from other countries.

Source: Compiled from Data of Table 1 and Dept. of Agriculture, Federation of Malaya 1947: Table 11, 12 and 13.

come directly from the headquarters in Japan, but the local military authorities developed long-term plans for the Malayan rubber industry. Iwatake believed that the local staff had high-level planning capabilities but he considered the idea to allocate surplus labour force to increase food production was rather impracticable.[34]

In June 1943, the Central Administration of the Japanese Army sent a telegram communicating the basics of a new long-term rubber production policy. This new policy indicated that the local military authority should secure pre-war rubber production level, banning the further reduction of planting areas or felling rubber trees, and gave priority to local smallholders in purchasing their products.[35] The Malay Military Administration released the "Matter on Revising the Purchase Target of Rubber" on 13 August 1943, which increased the purchase of rubber from smallholders from 18,000 tons to 100,000 tons.

The Malay Military Administration indicated a revised purchasing target in mid-November 1943. Rubber overstock was paid for with the provisional army budget and stored in the area designated warehouses, according to the "Principles of Purchase and Storage of Overproduction of Rubber".[36]

Thus, even in 1944 when the food production crisis was most severe, reclamation of land was limited and rubber felling was restricted to about 3,000 acres. Records indicate that the rubber productive capacity in Malaya was 86,000 tons with 890,000 acres managed by Japanese companies; the amount of raw rubber in local storage was 57,000 tons at the end of war.[37]

Case of a Japanese Rubber Company and its Estates

(a) *Showa Gomu K.K. and the Rubber Estate*[38]

Japanese planters opened numerous estates in Johor in the 1910s and 1920s. In 1911, the company Nan'a Kabushiki Kaisha (K.K or Company) opened the 13,000 acres as Telok Sengat Estate in Kota Tinggi, Johor. In 1937, Showa Gomu K.K. merged with Nan'a K.K., Sumatra Kogyo K.K., Tokyo Gomu Kogyo K.K., and Meiji Gomu Kogyo K.K. As a result, the Telok Sengat Estate became part of the Johor estates of Showa Gomu K.K. when the war broke out.

The British colonial government froze Japanese property in Malaya on 26 July 1940. After Japan's invasion of southern French Indochina in July 1941 (Japan had invaded northern French Indochina in September 1940), the 18 Japanese staff still employed at the Telok Sengat Estate were ordered by the National Defence Ordinance of 16 August 1941 to leave the designated defence areas within two weeks. When the Asia-Pacific War broke out, the estate was requisitioned by Britain, and the employees were arrested by the army and detained in a suburb of New Delhi, India, and other locations.

When the Syonan Rubber Association was established in Syonan (Singapore) under the Japanese Military Administration in February 1942, Matsumoto Saburo, Executive Director of Showa Rubber K.K., became a director of the Association. He was installed as the chairman in May 1942.

About 700 Japanese, approximately one-fourth of the 3,000 Japanese detainees in India, were exchanged for British detainees. Yet, the rest were compelled to stay in the internment camps until the end of the war. The Japanese staff of Showa estates, interned in India and Australia, were included in the exchange and arrived in Singapore in September 1942. By this time, the estate had been managed by the Syonan Rubber Association under the supervision of the Japanese army, and the repatriated workers joined the Japanese staff who had arrived from Japan to work at the estate.

The Military Administration organised the Malaya Rubber Management Association (Marai Gomu Kanri Kumiai) to replace the Syonan Rubber

Association as the controlling body in October 1943, naming Matsumoto its chairman.

The Showa Gomu K.K. was allotted 253,000 acres in Perak. The company's estates in Perak were managed by Yoshihara, who served as the manager and 17 other staff members who stayed at the company's headquarters located in Ipoh.

The southern estate area was secure and well managed. In some parts of Malaya and Sumatra, however, production facilities were destroyed and workers dispersed. Moreover, transportation was limited and food and clothing shortages reached critical levels. Shortages in capital and labour forces caused a sharp production decrease and the estates estimated their production to be about 20 to 30 per cent lower than pre-war time.

In 1944, Japan lost command of the seas and warship and vessel damage increased. And the military administration mobilised even wooden sailing boats to ship rubber. But, they were attacked and sunk by airplanes and submarines. The supply of food and other materials decreased. As the rubber production reduced, states and staff increasingly concentrated on food production.

Since January 1945 when the US Army landed in Luzon Island, the Philippines, the Japanese had been unable to manage the rubber estates in the Southern territories and after Japan surrendered, Japanese in Malaya were repatriated beginning in March 1946.

(b) *Villagers in or near the Estate: Interviews*

This section examines villagers' experiences and their memories of the Japanese Occupation in or near the Telok Sengat Estate, in Kota Tinggi, Johor. Interviews were conducted by the author in 1995 and 1996. The interviewees were 22 villagers who had experienced the Japanese Occupation; they were 15 Malays, 5 Chinese and 2 Orang Asli.[39]

The villagers who worked at the Telok Sengat Estate before the war made their living as tappers. They usually tapped rubber from 6 a.m. to 11 a.m. daily and their daily wage was 55 cents for male tappers and 45 cents for female tappers. This provided them with a subsistence level of income.

None of the villagers received much formal education and some cannot read or write. Most of their parents worked in the estate, so they naturally started working as tappers in the same estate. There were no other local jobs available at the time.

The workers and villagers in or near the estate knew about the outbreak of the war when Japanese airplanes bombed Singapore in December 1941. In the morning of the invasion, the estate workers in their fields saw Japanese airplanes flying to Singapore and bombing it.

At that time, the Japanese army had already landed in the Malay peninsula and the Japanese staff at the rubber estates told the workers that war would soon come to the village. The estates were closed when airplanes bombed Singapore. Workers said that the Japanese administrative staff of the estates returned to Japan without saying anything to the workers. But, according to the record of Showa Gomu K.K., the Japanese staff were ordered to leave for Japan in August 1941. They were arrested when the war started on 8 December 1941. The workers misunderstood that the Japanese staff had left for Japan, not knowing that they had been detained by the British police.

The Japanese staff at the Telok Sengat Estate gave a letter written in Japanese to each worker stating that he or she was a worker of the estate and asking the authority to allow the workers to remain in their quarters. The workers showed these letters to the Japanese military authorities when the officers came to the estate. In this estate there were no cruel actions taken against the workers by the Japanese army.

Most of the workers lost their jobs as tappers when the war started. Yet, there were some who continued to work on the estates when they were re-opened under the Japanese management. The wage system was changed from a daily system to a contract system and the wage was $3.50 per day.

Neighbours of the estate recalled in their interviews the severe hardships and food shortages of the local people during the Japanese Occupation. All the interviewees suffered from food shortage during the war; they planted tapioca and sweet potatoes, and saw people dying of diseases and malnutrition because of a shortage of food and medicine.

Interviewees reported hearing about brutal acts committed by the Japanese soldiers. They killed Chinese villagers particularly in the Chinese neighbourhoods of Lamping, Timon, and Sungai Sembilan. In the Chinese village in Lamping, 10 to 20 Japanese soldiers came into the village, massacred about 200 Chinese villagers and burned all the houses. In a Chinese village in Timon, 50 to 60 Japanese soldiers came into the village and killed the villagers.

Interviewees reported witnessing different treatments meted out to different ethnic groups during the Occupation. The Chinese were regarded as potential activists and spies for anti-Japanese movements. So even if the Chinese villagers themselves had no direct experience of such brutal acts by the Japanese army, they ran away into the jungles when they heard that the Japanese army was coming.

Kota Tinggi in Johor was the place where massacres took place in which the Chinese were victimised most in the Malay peninsula. The interviews included those who survived and witnessed these massacres. The testimonies of the survivors of these massacres were similar. Usually the Japanese soldiers suddenly came to their villages and gathered the villagers to be killed without any explanation or official procedures. There was no evidence of the presence of communists, subversive elements or saboteurs. The villagers assumed that the Japanese army had obtained some information of communists, guns, thieves and so on. In any case, however, Japanese soldiers did not follow any kind of legal procedures (to investigate, to arrest, to review the case) and killed unarmed and unresisting villagers. The massacres were brutal and the victims included women, children and babies.

On the other hand, Malays often received favourable treatment from the Japanese army. Young Malay men were recruited to join the army through village heads in some villages (i.e. Kampung Tanjung Buai). Some Malay men were drawn to Japanese slogans believing that Japan was wonderful and Malaya would develop with Japan. Yet, Malays were also terrified to see the Japanese soldiers' brutal acts such as killing villagers without reasons and showing the victims' bodies and heads to the public.

The interviews with Orang Asli were also impressive. They lived on the opposite shore of Johor River in Kampung Telok Sengat. They lived in boats before the war, but during the Occupation were ordered to relocate to the land by the Japanese army. They suffered from food shortage and planted tapioca. Their family members died of malnutrition. Although the Japanese army and the war brought all these hardships, they offered their food to Japanese soldiers when they came to ask for food and they bid farewell to them when they left.

All the interviewees lived in the same area. Malay villagers in Kampung Tanjung Buai frequented Chinese shops in Kampung Lamping and witnessed the Japanese army's massacre. The only Chinese survivor who escaped and rescued by a Malay fisherman, was taken to Kampung Tanjung Buai. Yet, in general, the relations between the Chinese and Malay communities were not close. Their impressions and feelings about the Japanese army were different.

In addition to ethnicity, gender also made a difference in the villagers' experiences of the Japanese Occupation. For example, Malay girls stayed at home and had little contact with the Japanese. Thus, even for people of the same generation who lived in the same area, experiences were quite different and varied by ethnicity and gender.

(c) *Reparations and Rubber Estates*

When Japan surrendered, Malaya came under the administration of the British Military Government. The British government prepared a scheme to rehabilitate industries as well as public facilities in Malaya. The estate sector got assistance from the government and was responsible for its own rehabilitation. Just after the war ended, individual estate owners formed a company to ensure "a fair distribution" of equipment and services which were in short supply. Smallholders were provided with equipment by a unit of the Ministry of Supply. The tin industry required capital for equipment and the Malayan Chamber of Mines, representing English company owners, set up a Rehabilitation Committee and insisted on some financial assistance required for resuming production.[40]

In early 1945, before the surrender of Japan, the Malayan Planning Unit had planned a proposal for the Malaya Reconstruction Finance (Table 4). A sum of £43 million (approximately $367 million) was allotted for industrial rehabilitation. It proposed £12 million (approximately $102 million) for rubber estates and £26 million (approximately $222 million) for tin mines. The allotment consisted of 9.5 per cent (for rubber estates) and 20.5 per cent (for tin mines) of the total budget of this finance plan. Later, however, the government gave financial assistance of $50 million to the rubber industry as a bank loan with government guarantee through mid-1949 and $78.5 million to the tin industry as a reconstruction loan up to the end of 1949.

Table 4: Proposal of Finance for Reconstruction in Malaya, March 1945

	(thousand pounds)
Reconstruction and repair of public facilities (Trains, electricity, water supply, communication, roads, etc.)	3,715.0
Public expenditure exceeded over the local revenue (First two years/including wages)	2,400.0
Treatment for Initial Emergency	2,282.5
Rehabilitation of Industries	
(1) Tin mines	2,600.0
(2) Rubber estates	1,200.0
(3) Other industries	500.0
Total	12,697.5

Source: A Letter from S. Caine to Lord Keynes, 29 March 1945 (T220/52).

After the war, the British authorities in Malaya and Singapore set up the War Damage Claims Commission,[41] which provided an opportunity from early 1947 through November 1950 for people to file War Damage Claims against Japan.

The colonial government discussed appropriate compensation for war damage,[42] inflicted primarily on equipment, plants, and machinery of the rubber and tin industries.[43] Damage compensation for other nationalities other than the British (American, Chinese, Australian, Canadian, etc.) was also discussed.[44] However, the compensation for Malayan people was not an issue in the negotiations.

The British government formulated September 1948 the Malayan War Damage Compensation Scheme with $475 million (Table 5). However, the plan was criticised because Malayan taxpayers were saddled with a disproportionate percentage; as much as 50.4 per cent of the budget was to come from the local government. In 1949, a revised scheme was announced (Table 5). In this scheme, compensation from Japan was reduced from $85.7 million to $60 million because the U.S. government was opposed to the compensation demanded from Japan. This new proposal was also criticised, though it reduced the Malayan burden to 33.8 per cent, but despite these concerns, the plan was ultimately approved in order to avoid further delay of compensation payment.[45]

However, the U.S. insisted that Japan should not be saddled with paying damage claims as it would affect its economic reconstruction and recovery in the Cold War years. Britain officially renounced the right to claim reparations at the Peace Conference in San Francisco in September 1951. The Peace

Table 5: Malayan War Damage Fund ($ million)

	Sept. 1948	July 1949	Dec. 1952
(1) Free gift from British government	8,570	17,140	17,140
(2) Japanese reparations	8,570	6,000	—
(3) Japanese property in Malaya	—	—	6,000
(4) War Risks Insurance Fund	1,200	−1,160	−1,940
(5) Assets held by Malayan CEP	5,200	8,100	7,330
(6) Malayan government contribution	23,960	—	—
(7) Interest-free loan from British government	—	15,360	14,970
Total	47,500	45,440	43,500

Source: Hara Fujio 1994, Tables 2, 4 and 5, pp. 160–3.

Treaty freed Japan from paying reparations, but granted the Allied Powers the right to confiscate Japanese properties in their occupying territories. All of the properties owned by Japanese companies in Malaya were forfeited to the British authorities in Malaya and were sold at auctions. By the end of 1952, although the War Damage Fund had received no direct compensation from Japan, it had amassed $60 million dollars from the sale of Japanese properties in Malaya (Table 5). The assets still held by the Custodian of Enemy Property (CEP) were the properties of nationalities of third nations looted by the Japanese and their original owners untraceable. The value of these assets was estimated at $73.3 million in 1952, but their auction sales total had reached $70.5 million by the end of 1958.

Thus, the fund of the War Damage Compensation included proceeds of the sale of Japanese assets left in Malaya. *The Straits Times*, however, noted on 14 May 1948 that of the CEP-held assets, some 80,000 acres of Japanese rubber estates should not be disposed as trophies of war, but should be considered the permanent property of peacetime economy in Malaya. And a Chinese newspaper on 9 September and 11 September 1951 argued that the $60 million from the sale of Japanese assets were not enough to compensate for the damages and terrible losses suffered during the war. It also highlighted that the War Damage Compensation ignored the sufferings and property losses of the people in Malaya.[46]

Japanese assets were primarily made up of rubber estates and iron ore mines, including 11 Japanese-company owned rubber estates covering 88,068 acres and individual-planter-owned estates covering 10,137 acres in 1941. The lease period was 99 years or 999 years and many Japanese estates were concentrated in Johor where they were offered a 999-year lease.[47] According to the "Table of Record of Japanese businesses in the Southern Army Territories at the End of the War", Japanese managed 29 mines and 98 factories when Japan surrendered: 10 steel manufacturers, 14 chemical, 17 automobile and related industries (including repairs), 4 paper and print, 9 ceramics, 22 general machine, 3 textiles, 2 medicine and hygiene factories, and 17 lumber factories.[48]

After the war, the former Japanese-owned rubber estates were under new management assigned by the Malaya and Singapore governments, and the smallholdings were rented out to local residents until the Peace Treaty resolved the issue of dealing with ex-Japanese assets. The Telok Sengat. Estate in Johor was one of those requisitioned by the state government of Johor after the war, and was later re-opened by the British.

Japanese estates went to the block from June 1951 through 1955. The auctions were set up to sell large lots at a relatively low price. Due to the size of the lots, most Malayan planters could not afford to bid. In addition, the low price per acre benefited British planting companies bidding the large lots.[49] Telok Sengat Estate was purchased by a Chinese businessman, Heah Joo Seang. He bought rubber estates totalling 26,000 acres for about $6 million and kept the estate until 1977, when he sold Boustead Company.

At the end of 1958, the CEP finished its work and the War Damage Committee, which was set up in 1950, also completed its assigned task. At that time, $46.2 million of the $49 million raised by selling formerly-Japanese-held assets in Malaya was in the coffers of the War Damage Compensation Fund and $21 million out of $23 million raised by selling formerly-Japanese-held assets in Singapore was turned over to the Malaya War Damage Compensation Fund at the end of 1954. The assets owned by nationalities of third nations were sold up to the end of 1958 and $70.5 million earned from those sales was incorporated into the Fund. $67.2 million from the sale of Japanese assets accounted for 15 per cent of the Fund. There was no information available about the final allotment for compensation, but the payment and allotment through 1952 can be seen in Table 6.

Many Malayan people believed that the compensation fund should be used for the social welfare and aiding victims and bereaved families. The

Table 6: Claims submitted to Commission for War Damage Compensation, 1952

Claims in respect of:	Amount ($ million)
Tin	19,075
Rubber	37,925
Industrial/commercial	19,100
Dwelling houses	5,875
Private chattels	16,350
Stock-in-trade	12,675
Livestock/crops	2,450
Other	17,375
Total	130,325

Source: Memorandum on Proposals for a Malayan War Damage Compensation Scheme, p. 7 (quoted from Kratoska 1998: Table 11.9, 337).

Table 7: Allocation and Payment from the
War Damage Compensation Fund ($ million)

	Allocation (Sept. 1948)	Payment (Dec. 1952)
(1) Rubber planting	8,500	4,110
(2) Tin mining	8,500	5,660
(3) Private chattels	5,000	1,960
(4) Requisition	—	3,650
(5) Other businesses	15,500	—
(6) Other claims	—	3,880
(7) War Risks (Goods) Insurance Scheme	10,000	1,940
Total	47,500	21,200

Source: Hara Fujio 1994, Tables 2, 4 and 5, pp. 160–3.

fund, however, was used for the reconstruction of industries, especially British rubber and tin companies. It primarily benefited the British and the fund was allotted for big British companies.[50]

Conclusion

Japan invaded Malaya to obtain strategic materials. As the production of rubber and tin in Malaya exceeded Japanese demand, the JMA initially planned to restrain production to prevent outflow into enemy countries. Malaya was considered to have a geographically important position and to serve strategic military purposes for the JMA. Japan, however, did not have the capability to provide enough food and basic necessities such as clothes, paper, and medicine to local communities. And Japan merely exploited materials to send to the homeland. The Japanese army requisitioned estates, mines and factories and assigned their management to private companies under the military administration. However, rubber estates and tin mines could not maintain their pre-war production levels and difficulties in shipping resulting from lack of vessels caused pile-up of materials at ports and estates.

After Japan surrendered, the British colonial government confiscated the Japanese estates and other properties that Japanese owned during the pre-war time. The Japanese assets were sold in auctions and the money was incorporated into the War Damage Compensation Fund.

The U.K. renounced the right for reparations from Japan when the U.S. decided not to claim reparations from Japan in the San Francisco

Peace Treaty of 1951 and requested other countries follow its lead due to the intensified Cold War. Hara Fujio (1994) has noted that it is necessary to include the U.K. government's War Damage Compensation scheme and the Friendship Treaty with Japan when discussing Japanese reparations.

The War Damage Compensation scheme whose funds included the sale of pre-war Japanese-owned private property primarily benefited larger companies. These British-owned big estate and tin companies largely recovered under the rehabilitation programmes by the U.K. government and ultimately profited from the Korean War as well. However, the local Malayan communities who suffered from the war did not receive compensation from either the Japanese or the U.K. government. While the U.K. government settled the issue for reconstructing the Japanese economy in the wake of the Cold War, Malayan/Malaysian nationals have continued discussing the issues on the Japanese compensation for war damages, including the forced "¥50 million contribution" extorted from the Chinese community in Malaya and Singapore during the Japanese Occupation.

Notes

In preparing this study, I have received generous help from Akashi Yoji, Hara Fujio, Nakahara Michiko and Yamada Hideo, all of whom supported this research topic and suggested useful references.

1. The group submitted the proposal, "Draft of Principles for the Administration of Occupied Areas Following Southern Operations" (Nanpo Sakusen ni okeru Senryo chi Tochi Yoko An). In November it became the basis for the Occupation policy. The section concerning policies for industries and trade said, "the main focus is obtaining natural resources in order to sustain a minimum level of self-sufficiency in the occupied territories". "Nanpo Gunsei ni Tomonau Senryo chi Tochi Yoko" (Tairiku Shi No. 993, Appendix No. 1, 25 Nov. 1941) is similar to the proposal's content and ideas and it is surmised that the proposal was used for the November plan. Iwatake Teruhiko, *Nanpo Gunsei ka no Keizai Shisaku*, vol. 1 (Tokyo: Ryukei Shosha, 1995), pp. 24–5.
2. "Nanpo Sakusen ni okeru Senryo chi Tochi Yoko-An".
3. Iwatake, *Nanpo Gunsei ka no Keizai Shisaku*, vol. 1, pp. 34–5.
4. Daihon'ei Seifu Renraku Kaigi Kettei tuzuri, No. 2, Defence Agency, Department of War History, p. 118.
5. "Shi" vol. 5, "Tairiku Shi" No. 993, Supplement No. 1118, Defence Agency, Department of War History.
6. Dai Toa Sho, ed., *Nanpo Keizai Taisaku*, p. 20.
7. Nanpo Senryo chi Gyosei Jisshi Yoryo, decided at the Daihonei Seifu Renraku Kaigi on 20 Nov. 1941.
8. Ministry of Foreign Affairs, "Maraya no Dokuritsu Mondai", 20 Feb. 1945 and Document of Dai Toa Sho Kankei, June 1945, Ministry of Foreign Affairs.

9. Nonpo Sakusen ni Tomonau Senryo chi Tochi Yoko, 25 Nov. 1941 (Section of War History, Shi, vol. 5, Tairiku Shi No. 933 Supplement No.1).
10. Document without date, Dai-25-Gun Shirei-bu, Gunsei Shiryo Document, No. 19.
11. "Section 8 Tai-Teki-sei-Koku Keizai Appaku" in Riku A Mitsu No. 3393 Supplement, Gunsei Shiryo Document No. 46.
12. Great Britain, Board of Trade, *Statistical Abstract for the British Commonwealth for each year from 1936 to 1945*, 1947, pp. 168–9.
13. Gunsei-Shiryo Document No. 20.
14. Yoshimura Mako "Shokuminchi to shite no Malaya Keizai to Igirisu: Maraya no Gomu to GB-US Boeki (Malayan Economy under the British Colonial System: Malayan Rubber and the G.B.-U.S. Trade Structure)", *The Journal of Economic Studies* (The University of Tokyo), no. 34 (Dec. 1991): 10–20. This paper discusses the Malayan trade structure in the 1930s.
15. Ibid., pp. 12–3.
16. Ibid., p. 12; Cheng Siok Hwa , *The Rice Trade of Malaya* (Singapore: University Education Press, 1973), Appendix IX, p. 42. The import of rice increased with an influx of labour immigrants for the rubber and tin industries. Although the British colonial government encouraged the increase of rice production, it was not successful since Malay smallholders preferred planting rubber as cash crop. Moreover, it was relatively easy to import rice from Thailand and Burma which were under the British influence.
17. Dai 25gun Gunsei Jisshi Yoko, in Gunsei Shiryo Document No. 19, undated.
18. Necessities of life were controlled by "Seikatsu Hitsuju Busshi no Rinji Sochi ni kansuru ken", in *Marai Kanrei*, no. 10; *Marai Koho*, no. 22, 20 Aug. 1943, which required merchants to obtain a sales licence, "Seikatsu Hitsuju Busshi no Hanbai Seigen ni kansuru ken", in *Marai Kanrei*, no. 12, *Marai Koho*, no. 30 (10 Sept. 1943), which prohibited sales except designated sellers. Simultaneously, "Bukka Toseirei" in *Nan Sokan rei*, no. 16; *Marai Koho*, no. 31, regulated the prices.
19. The Military Administration ordered the establishment of the production system by 1945 in Jan. 1944 and the Malayan Military complemented it in March 1944.
20. The military government enforced the semi-annual production of crops and conversion of land-use, relocation of urban residents to rural areas, compulsory delivery of rice to the government in Malaya. See Iwatake, *Nanpo Gunsei ka no Keizai Shisaku*, Volume 1, pp. 241–9; Chin Kee Onn, *Malaya Upside Down* (Kuala Lumpur: Federal Publications, 1976), pp. 46–7 and 57–8; Paul H. Kratoska, *The Japanese Occupation of Malaya 1941–1945* (London: Allen & Unwin, 1998), Ch. 9.
21. The annual number of deaths increased from 16,000 in 1940–41 to 30,000 in 1942 and 43,000 in 1944 in Singapore. For Malaya it grew from 92,000 in 1940 to 123,000 in 1943 and 146,000 in 1944. See Kratoska, *The Japanese Occupation of Malaya*, pp. 276–7.
22. "Nonpo Senryo chi Gyosei Jishi Yoryo", 20 Nov. 1941.
23. "Nonpo-Keizai Rikugun Shori Yoryo", 30 Dec. 1941 (Riku A Mitsu, No. 3392 Supplement, Gunsei-Shiryo Document, No. 46).

24. *Gunsei Junpo* by the 25th Army Military Administration, early Oct. 1942.
25. Iwatake, *Nanpo Gunsei ka no Keizai Shisaku*, vol. 1, pp. 117–8.
26. G.B. Colonial Office 1911, p. 38.
27. "Juyo Sangyo no Jisshi Keikaku", Gunsei Shikko jo no Kitei, Seirei, Fukoku, Hoshin, Keikaku Yoryo Tuzuri (Gunsei Shiryo Document, No. 46, no date).
28. "Syonan Gomu Kumiai Zantei Yoryo", 17 May 1942.
29. "Senji Geppo", Marai Gunsei Kambu, Sept. 1942.
30. Gomu-Kankei Shorui, Gunsei Shiryo Document, No. 22.
31. Iwatake, *Nanpo Gunsei ka no Keizai Shisaku*, p. 229.
32. Gomu Kankei Shorui, Gunsei Shiryo Document, No. 22.
33. "Malaya: Japanese Penetration of the Rubber Manufacturing Industry", NARA RG226 XL23029.
34. Iwatake, *Nanpo Gunsei ka no Keizai Shisaku*, p. 229.
35. Riku A Mitsu No. 3607, 15 June 1943. Iwatake pointed out that the Japanese Army Ministry sent the telegram without the official examination and permission by the Sixth Committee or other authorities in Tokyo. He supposed it was because the Ministry tried to stop felling rubber trees for increasing food production projects in Malaya and to smooth things out by indicating some policies on rubber to local military authorities before the Prime Minister and Army Minister Tojo came to inspect the Southern territories as he was said to be interested in rubber, see Iwatake, *Nanpo Gunsei ka no Keizai Shisaku*, p. 231.
36. "*Senji Geppo*", Marai Gunsei Kambu, Nov. 1943, Gunsei Shiryo Document, No. 7.
37. Marai wo Kataru-kai, Marai no Kaiso, 1978, pp. 116–8; memo; Iwatake, *Nanpo Gunse ka no Keizai Shisaku*, vol. 1, p. 126.
38. The section is based mainly from information obtained from Showa Gomu Company History Editorial Board, ed., 1969, pp. 25–6 and pp. 118–25.
39. The interviews were held by the author mainly in Malay (Bahasa Melayu). The record of the interviews is in Yoshimura Mako, "Nihon Gunsei ki no Malaya no Estate no Sonmin (Malayan Villagers in an Estate under the Japanese Occupation: Interviews in Johor) (1)–(4)", *Society and Labour* 43(1–2) (November); 43 (3–4) (March); 44 (1) (September); 44 (3–4) (March), 1996–98.
40. Reoccupation of Malaya and Sumatra, 1945 (FO371/46340).
41. Regarding War Damage Claims Commission, see public records; Ministry of Finance, Claims Commission: Malayan Progress Reports, 1947 (CO825/62/1); Malayan War Damage Compensation; Note of Meeting held at Treasury on 5 February 1948 memo (CO825/62/2); CO825/62/4; War Damage Claims Commission, Report by Labour Party of Singapore (CO825/64/3).
42. The U.K. government had discussed on the compensation since early 1945. It considered that it might be difficult to prove and assess the war losses and damages and to pay immediately, especially for private losses (Registration of War Losses and Damage in Far East, 1945, CO825/44/10).
43. Conversation with Rubber Growers' Association and Malayan Chamber of Mines, memo, 12 July 1946 (CO825/59/4).

44. Ministry of Finance, Compensation/Registration of Losses, Damage: Questions of Principle 1945 (CO825/44/11; CO825/45/5). Mining Industry in Malaya (Rehabilitation), 1945 (FO371/45727).
45. Hara Fujio, "Nihon to Malaysia Keizai", in *Malaysia ni oketu Kigyo group no Keisei to Saihen*, ed. Hara Fujio (Tokyo: Institute of Developing Economies, 1994), pp. 159–7.
46. Ibid., pp. 167–8 and 171.
47. Hara Fujio, *Eiryo Malaya no Nihonjin* (Tokyo: Institute of Developing Economies, 1986), Table 4, p. 222 and Table 7, p. 224.
48. Iwatake, *Nanpo Gunsei ka no Keizai Shisaku*, vol. 2, App. Table 4–3, 628.
49. Hara, "Nihon to Malaysia Keizai", p. 176.
50. Ibid., p. 174.

5

Railway Operations in Japanese-occupied Malaya

OTA KOKI

This chapter studies the management and operation of the railway in Japanese-occupied Malaya. The Japanese Army occupied British Malaya and Singapore during the Pacific War and established a military administration there.

The 25th Army occupied and administered both Malaya and Sumatra at first, but in April 1943, the 25th Army was deployed to Sumatra, and in January 1944, a newly organised 29th Army took over the administration of Malaya, with the exception of Johor State, while the 7th Area Army Military Administration retained the administrative control of Syonan (Singapore) because of its strategic importance as the centre of defence and transportation. A discussion of the management and operation of the railway during the administrative period of the 25th Army ideally should treat both the Malayan and Sumatran railways together, but the Sumatran railway is itself an enormous subject and beyond the scope of this chapter.

There are other reasons for excluding the Sumatran railway from this study. Sumatra is separated from the Malay Peninsula by the Straits of Malacca. Its railway, administered by the Dutch, was thus never linked to the Malayan railway, and the two operations were dissimilar even though they came to be administered by the same military government during the Japanese Occupation. This study, therefore, focuses only on the management and operation of the railway in Malaya.

The Malayan railway was linked with the railway network of Thailand (an independent state cooperating with Japan under an alliance) just north of the Malayan border. The Thailand-Burma railway, completed in October 1943, joined these railways with that of Burma (under the administration of the 15th Army). The 25th Army, the Garrison Army in Thailand and the 15th Army used this railway network jointly to transport military supplies.

There are very few historical materials available for the study of the railway in occupied Malaya. Two official sources, 昭和17年度富軍政年報 (*Annual Report of the Tomi Military Administration 1942*),[1] here-after referred to as Annual Report 1942, and 川原資料綴 (*The Kawahara File*),[2] help elucidate the management and operation of the railway in Malaya.

The Kawahara File is a collection of materials accumulated by Kawahara Michimasa, who was appointed on 27 February 1943 to General Superintendent Office of Military Administration, Southern Army, with responsibility for railway affairs. He was thoroughly familiar with railway administration and policy implementation. *The Kawahara File* includes official papers relaing to railway affairs prepared by the military administrations of the armies of Malaya, Sumatra, Indonesia, Burma and the Philippines, along with Kawahara's own memoranda and notes, graphs, diagrams and tables. This File is an extremely important and reliable source for the study of railway affairs in the Southern region. Judging from Kawahara's career record and the position he held during the Japanese Occupation, the authenticity and reliability of *The Kawahara File* as a primary source is impeccable.

The Railway Network of Malaya under the Military Government (as of February 1943)

The railway network of Malaya under the military administration is shown in Figure 1 and Table 1. It was divided into the West Coast Line and the East Coast line. The West Coast Line ran through the length of the Peninsula connecting Syonan (Singapore) with Padang Besar on the Malayan-Thai border by way of Kuala Lumpur, and was the principal trunk line. The East Coast Line ran from Tumpat to Sungei Golok, to Pasir Mas. During the Occupation, service from Sungei Kusial to Kuala Lipis was suspended. From Kuala Lipis, the East Coast Line went southwards to Gemas, where it joined the West Coast Line. Following the transfer of the four northern Malay states to Thailand in October 1943, the affected train service in the territories, the track between Sungei Golok and Tumpat and between Pasir Mas and Kuala Krai on the east coast, and between Sungei Patani and Padang Besar on the west, were transferred to the Thai railway administration.

The *Annual Report 1942* recorded the state of reconstructing the destroyed railway and the progress of restoring railway bridges from October 1942 to late March 1943 as follows:

> A heavy rainfall that hit the Malay Peninsula inflicted extraordinary damages to the Malayan railway and compelled it to temporarily suspend its operation. On 17 December, all railway services resumed their operations. As for the reconstruction of the railway facilities of the West Line damaged by war, 54 out of 79 damaged bridges have been completely restored, 19 have been under construction, and 6 have been left untouched. By late February 1943, reconstruction of all bridges of the West Line will be expected to be completed. As for the East Line, the railway running from Gemas, Kuala Lipis, Sungei Kusial, and to the

Table 1: Railway Distances of Malayan Railway

Name of Line		Route	Distance (km)
West Line		Padang Besar – Syonan	926.4
Branches of West Line	Prai Branch	Bukit Mertajam – Prai	10.5
	Port Weld Branch	Taiping – Port Weld	12.1
	Tronoh Branch	Ipoh – Tronoh	24.1
	Telok Anson Branch	Tapah Road – Telok Anson	29.0
	Sungei Tambuan Branch	Kwang – Sungei Tambuan	11.4
	Batu Caves Branch	Kuala Lumpur – Batu Caves	5.4
	Port Swettenham Branch	Kuala Lumpur – Port Swettenham	43.5
	Ampang Branch	Sultan Street – Ampang	9.6
	Port Dickson Branch	Seremban – Port Dickson	40.2
	Malacca Branch	Tampin – Malacca	40.0
East Line North		Sungei Kusial – Sungei Golok	65.3
East Line South		Gemas – Kuala Lipis	229.6
East Line Tumpat		Pasir Mas – Tumpat	20.9
Total			468.0

Note: The sections between Sungei Kusial and Sungei Golok, and between Pasir Mas and Tumpat of the East Line were transferred to Thailand, and the section between Padang Besar and Patani to Thailand (124 kilometres).

Source: "A Table of Railway Mileage of the Southern Region (French Indochina, Thailand, Malaya, Sumatra)", *The Kawahara File*, p. 158. Prepared by the Third Field Railway Command, Feb. 1943.

Figure 1: The Malayan Railway

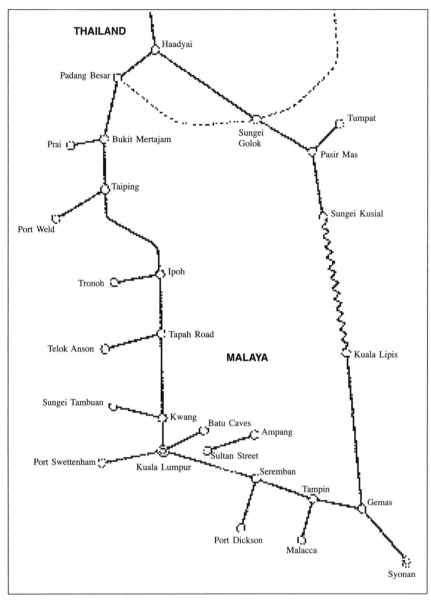

Note: At Padang Besar, the Malayan railway joined the Southern Line (Padang Besar-Haadyai) of the Thai railway system. At Sungei Golok, it linked with the South Line (Sungei Golok-Bangkok) of the Thai railway. A wavy line between Sungei Kusial and Kuala Lipis indicates suspended service.

Source: "A Table of Railway Mileage of the Southern Region (French Indochina, Thailand, Malaya, Sumatra)", *The Kawahara File*.

Thai border has been temporarily restored. Because the railway between Sungei Kusial and Kuala Lipis has not been in operation, the entire East Line has not been opened yet. At the same time, the reconstruction of the largest bridge, Gilmard, will be undertaken.[3]

Comparing the reconstruction of the West Line with that of the East Line, the latter was falling behind. The *Annual Report 1942* explains the reasons for the delay in the reconstruction of the East Line:

> The East Line is divided into the south sector between Gemas and Kuala Lipis and the north sector between Sungei Kusial and the Thai border. The south sector is administered by the Syonan Transportation Office and the north sector by the Tumpat Transportation Office. Since there is no direct transportation going to the northern part of the East Line, it is necessary to go there via the Thai railway [Ed. Note: that is, via Haadyai].[4]

As of late March 1943, the northern sector of the East Line (north) had not been transferred to Thailand. Yet, it was "necessary to detour" via the Thai railway to reach the northern sector. Later, when the East Line was transferred to Thailand, the administration and operation of the East Line came under the Thai railway authorities.

The military administration gave priority to restoring the operation of the West Line in view of its importance as a trunk line and a link with the Thai railway system in the northern part of Malaya (see Figure 2). The Malayan railway was in turn to be connected with the Thailand-Burma railway, which was expected to be constructed in the near future. This railway transportation network was vital for the Japanese forces.

History of the Railway of the Southern Region Recorded in *The Kawahara File*

The Kawahara File is the best source of information about the Malayan railway. Kawahara himself wrote the following summary of railway affairs in the Southern Region based on official papers that came into his possession while working at the General Headquarters of the Southern Army.

> Landed Malaya and southern Thailand at four locations.
> Three battalions of the 9th Railway Regiment.
> The West Line of Malaya: Opened to Syonan, 21 February.
> At the speed of 16 kilometres per day.
> Order of the operations, the 5th and the 9th Railway Regiments, the 5th Special and the 4th ad hoc Railway Battalion

Figure 2: Railway Network of Thailand

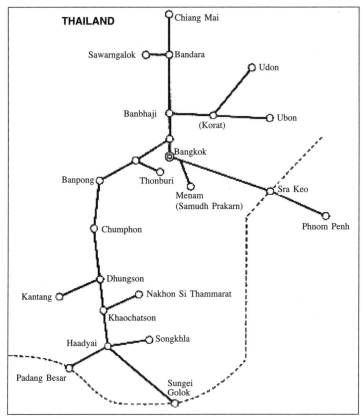

Note: A few words of explanation are in order about the Thai railway network. Padang Besar was linked with the West Line of the Malayan railway, and the Thai railway was linked with the northern section of the East Line at Sungei Golok.

Source: "A Table of Railway Mileage of the Southern Region (French Indochina, Thailand, Malaya, Sumatra)", *The Kawahara File*, p. 159.

Table 2: Distance of Sections of Malayan Railway Transferred to Thailand

Section	Distance (km)
Padang Besar – Sungei Patani (West Line)	124
Sungei Golok–Tumpat (East Line)	46
Pasir Mas–Kuala Krai (East Line)	59
Total	229

Source: "Various Original Tables of Railways, Oct. 1944", *The Kawahara File*. Prepared by General Headquarters of the Southern Area Army, Oct. 1944.

The management of the West Line: The 4th ad hoc Railway Battalion took charge of the West Line, effective 1 April. The 5th ad hoc Battalion took over the operation of the East Line.

15 November, Malayan Railway General Bureau established. Railway bureaus established and administered by the state governors, assuming their offices beginning April to June.

August to late 1942: Principles for the operation of the railway in the Southern Region.

State of the operation during the period.

Passengers: 50 per cent to 100 per cent increase from pre-war level

Freight: 30 per cent to 50 per cent decrease from pre-war level

April 1943, cancellation of one of two express services in Malaya

Late March, delivery of 20 engine locomotives and 920 freighters from Java decided.

April 1943, the 25th Army transferred to Sumatra.

Malaya and Sumatra separated.

1944, the Malayan Railway General Bureau came under the Command of the Field Railway Headquarters of the Southern Army.

20 October 1944, the management of railways in the Southern Region fundamentally reorganised.

15 April 1945, Transportation Command, Southern Army established.

20 August, dissolved.[5]

The Field Railway Headquarters, established in March 1944, commanded the operation of the Malay, Thai, Kra and French Indochinese (Cambodian) railways. (Railways in Burma, Sumatra, Java, Borneo and the Philippines were excluded from its command.) In October of the same year, it took charge of operating these four railways in order to establish a southern railway network in readiness for decisive combat. The Transportation Command of the Southern Army was established in April 1945, and administered the railways in Malaya, Thailand, French Indochina and the Thai-Burma railway.

Railway Operations in Malaya During the Reactivation Period

The *Annual Report 1942* states that, "by 20 February, the entire West Line had been opened after being repaired by railway regiments of the field army. The military has allocated extra transportation service to the public, free of charge, for people who possess a certificate issued by the military."[6] It also said, "In the second half of 1942, the railway operation is in full swing. We are extremely proud of having accomplished the expanded passenger and freight services and having increased the speed and frequency of train operation."[7]

Concerning the railway administration between December 1942 and March 1943, The *Annual Report 1942* recorded:

> A Japanese railway corps after landing at Singora (Songkhla) on 13 December occupied Alor Star, and another railway corps after landing at Kota Bahru captured Tanah Merah, thus securing the strategic points of the West and East Lines of the 'Malai' [the Japanese rendering of Malaya] railway. Responding to a request from the armies fighting in the field, the railway regiment took on the task of repairing the railways destroyed by the retreating enemy and administering them. By mid-January 1942, the Line was open as far as Gemas.[8]

In view of the importance of the West Line as a trunk line, its restoration was the most urgent task, and Gemas Station, close to Singapore, served as a key junction leading to the southern section of the East Line.

With the fall of Singapore, the entire railway system was placed under the Japanese army. The *Annual Report 1942* describes the situation as follows:

> The area north of Ipoh was administered by the Kamata ad hoc Railway Command and the area south of Ipoh by the Iwakura ad hoc Command. A transportation policy drafted by the Military Administration was to urge railway workers to return to their former positions and to gain public peace by restoring the railway operation, in some sections, for transporting goods for civilian needs and opening passenger services. After the fall of Singapore on 15 February, the army railway corps took charge of administering and operating all of the Malai railways. The Malay military administration began its activities on 22 February, the entire West Line opened its operation and an express train began its service all the way to Syonan.[9]

Iwai Takeshi, the author of *C56 Going to Battle Front of the Southern Region: Memoirs of a Railway Company Commander*, describes the opening ceremony at the Singapore station after restoration works were completed:

> On 22 February, the opening ceremony of Singapore Station was observed. Efforts of the 9th Railway Regiment bore fruit. Of course, the 5th ad hoc Railway Regiment and other units should be given credit for their contributions to the opening of the entire West Line.[10]

The Railway Regiment began to undertake the restoration of the East Line, but its reconstruction was abandoned when the Japanese government decided to transfer the four northern Malay States to Thailand, and the army stripped the railway track of the East Line for the construction of the Burma-Thai railway.

From late February through March, the army railway corps concentrated on repairing track and rolling stock, an effort described in the *Annual Report 1942* as follows:

(1) Opening of the entire West Line and authorising people who possess a permit issued by the military to take the trains.

(2) Successfully salvaging locomotive parts and main rods abandoned in Syonan Island in late February.

(3) By operating 24 trains, transporting 7,735 (Chinese, Malays, and Indians), who sought refuge in Syonan, to Gemas, Kuala Lumpur and Ipoh during the period 5–14 March.

(4) Transporting and distributing 13,000 tons of Thai rice to the Malay states for a week, beginning 17 March.

(5) Starting the transportation of semi-military and civilian supplies (after mid- March).

(6) Adapting Principles of Emergency Measures for Land Transportation.[11]

The military gave priority to repairing railways and locomotives. According to Iwai, "Coupling rods on both sides of every locomotive were removed and hidden in the sea near the Empire Dock in Keppel Harbour" where "divers found them at the bottom of the sea covered heavily with grease, and salvaged them."[12]

The *Annual Report 1942* notes the operation of an express train service in the West Line and the state of restored railway service between April and October. Effective on 1 March, the train time table called for express trains to run from Syonan to Padang Besar on the Thai border in 29 hours and 19 minutes. Plans called for further reductions in travelling time, and an increase in freight volume to about 190,000 tons per month. The *Annual Report 1942* notes:

At present, the following railways were in operation:
The entire West Line running 938 kilometres
The East Line:
227 kilometres between Gemas and Kuala Lipis
56 kilometres between Tumpat and Sungei Kusial
21 kilometres between Pasir Mas and Sungei Golok
No train running between Sungei Kusial and Kuala Lipis
Other branch lines 208 kilometres
Total: 1,450 kilometres[13]

Establishment of the Railway General Bureau: Management of Railways by the Military Administration

Passenger and freight services resumed on 1 May 1942, with passengers charged the same fares as before the war.[14] It is assumed that the Gunsei kambu decided to charge passengers to defray the operational costs of the railway services.

At this point the Malayan railway system moved from reconstruction to a resumption of normal operations. The *Annual Report 1942* explains this transition as follows:

> After several negotiations among military officials concerned, they reached a final decision on the fundamental policy for the direct management of the Malai railways in late June. It is absolutely necessary to integrate the Malai and Sumatra railways under a unified administration of the Railway General Bureau [established on 1 October]. With the deployment of the Iwakura command to Burma on 1 June, the Kamata corps is solely responsible for the administration of the Malai railway.[15]

The Railway General Bureau inaugurated its business on 15 November 1942 in Kuala Lumpur, and took over the general administration of the Malayan railway from the Kamata command. After the Kamata command was deployed to Burma on 1 March 1943, the Railway General Bureau took charge of engineering works and bridge repairing as well.[16] The General Bureau began with a staff of 345 Japanese assisted by 10,200 local employees. The number of Japanese staff was later augmented with the arrival of engineers from the Ministry of Transportation in Japan, and in July 1944, 377 Japanese and 14,551 local employees were working under the General Bureau compared with pre-war figures of 107 Europeans and 11,878 local employees working for the British.[17] The General Bureau administered the Malayan railway directly, and its regional bureaus at Medan, Padang and Palembang administered the north Sumatran, central Sumatran and south Sumatran railways, respectively.[18]

Transfer of Four Malayan States to Thailand and Removal of the Southern Sector of the Railway Track of the East Line

The Imperial Headquarters/Government Liaison Conference of 26 June 1943 made the decision to transfer the four Malay states (Perlis, Kedah, Kelantan and Trengganu), acquired by the British under a 1909 treaty with Siam, back to Thai control.[19] Upon the signing of the formal treaty on 31 July 1943, the railways in these states were transferred from the Malayan to the Thai railway system (see Figure 3).[20] The transfer completed in late September.

Figure 3: Sections of the Malayan Railway Transferred to Thailand

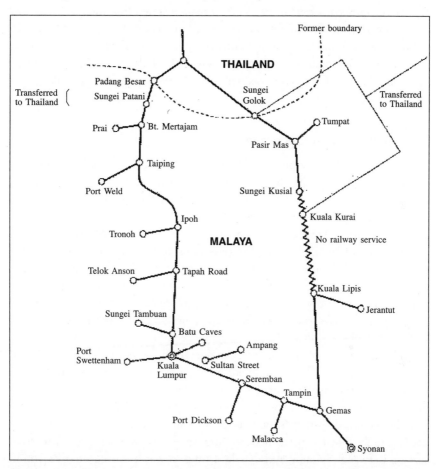

Notes:

1. Ipoh–Tronoh Railway service discontinued 9 June 1943. *Malai Koho Gogai* (馬來軍政監部) 4 June 1943. Malai Gunsei ambu (馬來軍政監部)

2. Telok Anson Railway service discontinued 10 July 1943. *Malai Koho* No. 12 (28 June 1943)

3. Tumpat–Sungei Kusial Railway service discontinued 19 October 1943. *Malai Koho* No. 44 (12 October 1943)

4. Tampin–Malacca Railway service discontinued 31 October 1943. *Malai Koho* No. 48 (22 October 1943)

5. Kuala Lipis–Jerantut Railway service discontinued 15 November 1943. *Malai Koho* No. 53 (2 November 1943)

Source: "A Table of Railway Mileage of the Southern Region (French Indochina, Thailand, Malaya, Sumatra)", *The Kawahara File*, p. 171. As of February 1943.

The southern sector of the East Line was to be stripped of its track. *C56 Going to Battle Front of the Southern Region* stated that the 4th Company of the 9th Railway Regiment was assigned the task in the spring of 1942 to remove the rails for the planned construction of the Thai-Burma Railway, and for the construction of a railway across the Isthmus of Kra.[21] For this purpose, the 4th Company was sent to Mentakab, about 140 kilometres from Gemas.[22]

Frequency of Train Operations

In the "General Principles of Operation" adopted for the operation of the Malayan railway in the early stages of the Military Administration, the plan was to run six round trips per day on the West Coast Line and one round trip per day on the East Coast Line. Based on operating conditions from April to October 1942, the operating speed was set at a maximum of 60 kilometres for passenger trains and 50 kilometres for passenger-freight trains per hour. As a result, travelling time for passenger trains running between Syonan and Kuala Lumpur was reduced from 19 hours and 45 minutes to 14 hours and 5 minutes and for mixed passenger/ freight trains it was shortened from 20 hours and 25 minutes to 17 hours and 45 minutes.[23]

The frequency of inter-city train operations began to decrease in late 1943, as indicated in Table 3. There was one express passenger train service running between Syonan and Padang Besar until March 1943.[24] Beginning in August 1944, the frequency of inter-city passenger-freight train services sharply decreased from 7.6 train services to an average of 3.6 trains running daily, largely due to intensified air attacks. In September 1944, the train service between Syonan and Kuala Lumpur was restored to five round trips per day. Figure 5 shows an increase in air raids after September 1944 on the Thai railway and the Thailand-Burma railway, as well as on other railways. The railway in Malaya also sustained damages, beginning in mid-November, when the Allied Powers commenced air attacks. Allied air raids against Malayan railway began in November 1944, Syonan being attacked on 5 November for the first time. Thereafter, Allied bombers air raided, primarily targeting the Malaysian railway until April 1945.

They caused heavy damages of railways, libraries and museums. Kuala Lumpur railway yards, where the General Headquarters of the Malai Gunsei Kambu Railway Bureau was located, were heavily attacked. In one of the air raids on Kuala Lumpur railway yards, at least one bomb struck the grounds

Table 3: Frequency of Inter-city Train Service (1942–44)

Section	June 1942	December 1943	August 1944
Syonan – Gemas	8	5	3
Gemas – Kuala Lumpur	9	5	3
Kuala Lumpur – Ipoh	9	7	5
Ipoh – Prai	7	7	4
Prai – Padang Besar	5	4	3

Source: *The Kawahara File.*

Figure 4: Northern Section of the East Line Transferred to Thailand

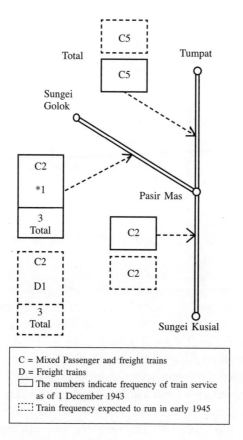

C = Mixed Passenger and freight trains
D = Freight trains
☐ The numbers indicate frequency of train service as of 1 December 1943
⌐⌐⌐ Train frequency expected to run in early 1945

Source: "Train Service Frequency of Railways in the Southern Region"(南方鉄道列車回数), dated Sept. 1944, *The Kawahara File.*

Figure 5: Allied Forces Air Attacks on Railways

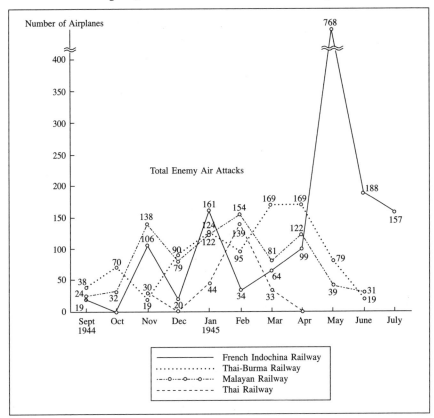

Source: "Total Enemy Air Attacks" (敵機来襲延機数), *The Kawahara File*.

of the Selangor State Museum across the road and it completely destroyed it and also killed the young daughter of the caretaker. In an Allied bombing on Penang Harbour facilities, "the Penang Library was hit by bombs in February 1945 and looted thereafter, and losing over 100 valuable historical books and practically all its newspapers files".[25]

Figure 6 shows the frequency of train services as of 1 December 1943. The figure remained about the same in September 1944, as shown in the table "Train Frequency of the Southern Region, the State of Maintenance of Locomotives, and Operation Volume" (see note 24). Figure 7 shows the transportation capability for September 1944, indicating the frequency of trains per day. It also reflects the importance of linking the Thai railway

Figure 6: Frequency of Inter-city Train Service (1 Dec. 1943)

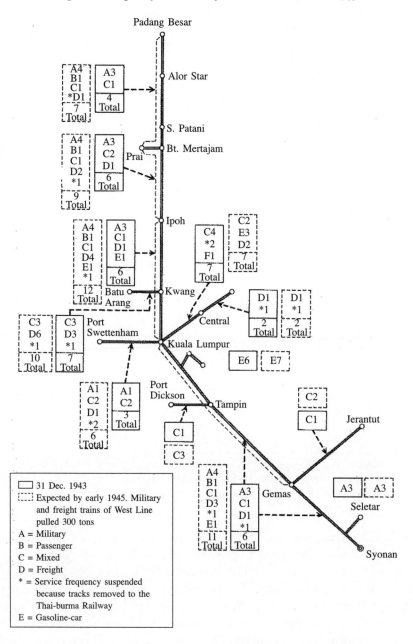

Source: "Train Service Frequency of Malai Railway", *The Kawahara File*.

Figure 7: Transportation Capability of Trunk Lines (Sept. 1944)

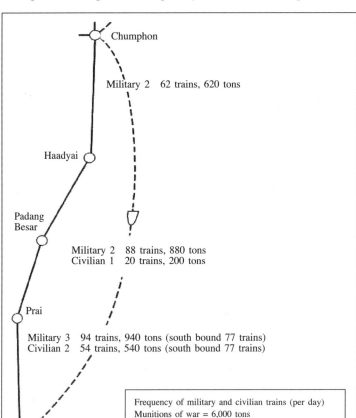

Source: "The Transportation Capability of Principal Trunk Lines in the Continent", dated Sept. 1944, *The Kawahara File.*
Figures after military or civilian indicate the number of rolling stocks.

with the Malayan railway. Figure 8 is an operational diagram believed to be that of June 1945. According to this table, the Malayan railway maintained four train services every day (1.5 express train services per day and 2.5 inter-city train services) between Syonan and Padang Besar. The Military Administration was able to maintain these services largely because Malaya was not affected by Allied counter offensive operations between 1944 and 1945. It is to be noted, however, that trains going to Thailand decreased in number.

Figure 8: Railway Operations (June 1945)

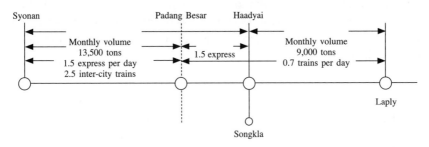

Source: "Estimate of Rotary Materials and Railway Transportation Capability" (推定輪 転材料並二鉄道運送力), *The Kawahara File.*

Conclusion

Of all railway networks in the Southern region, the Malayan railway operated rather smoothly until the end of war because Malaya was relatively free from security risks. The Japanese army regarded the Malay railway system strategically vital for maintaining supply lines connecting with Thailand and French Indochina. Under the supervision of the Southern Army, the railways in the Southern region continued to operate despite enemy air attacks. Because Japan's Southern Army lost its air and sea supremacy later in the war, it had to rely on land transport to carry troops and military supplies and was very anxious to build a broad railway network covering continental Southeast Asia. This was in line with the Japanese military's original plan to establish a unified operation integrating the railway networks of Malaya, Thailand, French Indochina, and Burma under a unified railway administration of the Southern region. In May through December 1944, Japanese armies in China launched major operations in the south and south west. They aimed at controlling the railways between Beijing and Hankou (Hunan province); Hankou and Guiling, Liuzhou and Nanning (Guanxi province); and Henyang (Hunan province) and Guangdong province. The operations had been successfully completed by December 1944 in controlling the railways in the south and the south west linking Beijing to Nanning and Canton through Henyang.

At the same time, coordinating with the China operations, the Southern Army deployed its troops in French Indochina from Lang Son to China crossing over the border. They joined on 10 December the Japanese China Army at Suilu, linking Southeast Asia to the rail network in China.[26]

The Council for the Construction of Greater East Asia of the government envisaged a grand design for constructing a Greater East Asia railway network by linking Southeast Asian railways to the Chinese railway network and through it, to Manchuguo and Korea, and eventually to the railway network in Japan.[27]

Notes

1. Tomi Military Administration, *Annual Report of the Tomi Military Administration 1942* (hereafter *Annual Report 1942*), June 1943. *"Tomi"* was the code name for the 25th Army.
2. *The Kawahara File* is in the possession of the author. It originally consisted of three volumes, but the second volume is missing.
3. *Annual Report 1942*, p. 164.
4. Ibid., pp. 164–5.
5. "A History of Railway in the Southern Region", *The Kawahara File*.
6. *Annual Report 1942*, p. 51.
7. Ibid., p. 63.
8. Ibid., pp. 152–3.
9. Ibid., p. 53. The commander was Maj. Gen. Kamata Sen'ichi. This was given the abbreviated name of 4th ad hoc Command. An ad hoc railway command is a "mini ministry of transportation, capable of operating transportation and constructing new railways". Its members were drafted from employees of the National Railway Corporation. Kenmochi Yasuji (剣持保治編), ed., *A Desperately Struggling Civilian Railway Regiment: Escape from Hell* (死闘軍属鉄道隊―地獄から脱出) (Association of the 5th ad hoc Railway Regiment, 27th Engineering Unit, 1983), p. 4. See also Hiroike Toshio (広池俊雄), *The Thai–Burma Railway: The Bridge Still Standing in Battle Field* (泰緬鉄道―戦場に残る橋) (Tokyo: Yomiuri Shimbunsha, 1971), p. 47. The *Annual Report 1942* says the commander was named Iwakura (p. 7), but its editor apparently made a mistake. The commander was Maj. Gen. Chiba Kumaji. See Toyama Misao, ed., *Biography of Army Generals and Naval Admirals* (外山操編 「陸海軍将官人事総覧 陸軍編) (Tokyo: Fuyoshobo, 1981).

    According to "A Brief History of Railway Bridge Unit, the Fifth ad hoc Command" (第五特設鉄道橋梁部隊略歴) in *A Brief History of the Forces Deployed in Malai and Boruneo (Railway)* (マライ・ボルネオ方面部隊略歴 [鉄道部隊略歴]), (Tokyo: Koseisho Engokyoku, 1961), p. 481, the 5th ad hoc Railway Command was deployed to Malaya in Jan. 1942 and was engaged in the operation of the Malayan railway and its restoration and maintenance from 21 Jan. to 8 June. It was then deployed to Burma.

10. Iwai Takeshi (岩井健), *C56 Going to Battle Front of the Southern Region: Memoirs of a Railway Company Commander* (C56南方戦線を行く―或る鉄道隊長の記録) (Tokyo: Jiji Tsushinsha, 1978), p. 79.
11. *Annual Report 1942*, p. 153.
12. Iwai, *C56 Going to Battle Front of the Southern Region*, pp. 78–9.

13. *Annual Report 1942*, p. 159.
14. Ibid., pp. 154–5.
15. Ibid., p. 155.
16. Ibid., pp. 75–165.
17. Ibid., pp. 161–2. Japanese employees included soldiers, administrators and engineers. See also "Various Original Tables of Railways of the Southern Region (南方鉄道諸元表), October 1944", *The Kawahara File*.
18. *Annual Report 1942*, p. 162.
19. Kajima Peace Research Institute (鹿島平和研究所編), ed., *History of Japanese Foreign Relations* (日本外交史), vol. 24 (Tokyo: Kajima Peace Research Institute, 1971), p. 175.
20. "Various Original Tables of Railways, October 1944", *The Kawahara File*.
21. Iwai, *C56 Going to Battle Front of the Southern Region*, p. 81.
22. Ibid., Shimizu Ryoto (清水寥人), *The Thai-Burma Railway* (小説泰緬鉄道) (Tokyo: Mainichi Shimbunsha, 1968), p. 156. "The corps [a contingent of the 4th ad hoc Railway Command] was deployed to remove 200 kilometres of the railway tracks between Merbok and Gemas and the turnouts incidental to the railway, which was the only means of transportation in the eastern part of Malaya. Upon completing the removal, our corps departed in mid-July [1943] to join the 4th ad hoc Railway Command."
23. *Annual Report 1942*, pp. 155–6.
24. "Train Service Frequency of Railways in the Southern Region", *The Kawahara File*.
25. Donnison, F.S.V., *British Military Administration in the Far East 1943–46* (London: HMSO, 1957), p. 166. Information provided by Paul Kratoska.
26. Hattori Takushiro. *Daitoa Senso Zenshi* (Tokyo: Asagumo Shimbun, 1965), pp. 616–30. Attached Map No. 7.
27. Kikakuin/Daitoa Kensetsu Shinjikai. ed., *Daitoa Kensetsu Shinjikai Kankei Shiryo*, vol. 4 (Tokyo: Ryukei Shosha, 1995), pp. 122–3. The idea was suggested by the 8th Section (Transportation) of the Council.

6

Japanese Research Activities in Occupied Malaya/Syonan, 1943-45

AKASHI YOJI

During the Occupation of Malaya and Singapore, the Japanese Army operated a chosabu, or research department, that provided field reports needed for policy planning. The chosabu compiled numerous studies on various topics, but no study of the chosabu activities and the reports has been attempted apart from an article in Japanese by Fukami Sumio about chosabu activities in the Southern region.[1] This is partly because many chosabu documents were destroyed by a military order immediately after Japan's surrender, and those that survived were kept in the archives of the War History Department of the National Institute of Defence Studies under restricted access until the late 1970s. This chapter focuses on the chosabu's activities in Malaya and Singapore under the 25th Army and, later, the 29th Army of the 7th Area Army.

Organisation and Activities

When the 25th Army started its *gunsei*, it lacked information about the occupied people and their language, religion, society, customs, and political and economic systems. The majority of the *gunsei*'s 70 administrative staff were critically deployed to occupied states in peninsular Malaya, while some 20 men were assigned to the Gunseibu in Singapore. They were the elite of the elites among the bureaucrats drafted from the Ministry of Internal Affairs.[2] Until a chosabu team arrived to carry out fresh research, they scoured *Nanyo keizai sosho* (a series of South Seas economies) for relevant articles for reprinting them,[3] and reproduced articles from *Shingaporu Nippo* and *Nanyo Nichi Nichi Shinbun*, Japanese language newspapers published in prewar years in Singapore. With the arrival in June of more personnel, they tapped stores of documents seized from the previous colonial administration and disseminate information about the overseas Chinese, the Islamic religion and its customs as well as statistics and ordinances of the British colonial government. The Gunseibu made these reports available as *chosahan* reference materials.

Nanpogun Sokambu Chosabu: July 1942–April 1944

On 31 July 1942, the vice war minister notified the Southern Army (Nanpogun) that a decision had been made to organise chosabus attached to Southern Army headquarters to serve its newly established Gunsei Superintendent General's Office (*Gunsei Sokambu*) and Gunsei Kambu in the occupied southern territories.[4] The purpose was to reap the fruit of Japan's victory and solidify the military administrations which were then reconstructing the occupied territories. The role of the chosabu was to provide the Gunsei Kambu with information necessary for planning *gunsei* policy in this second stage.

The War Ministry's decision was based on a proposal by the *ad hoc* Department of Political Affairs for the Southern Region (Nanpo seimubu), which was created in May and was responsible for supervising the chosabu. The Department of Political Affairs laid out a set of seven priorities for study in support of three *gunsei* objectives (restore public order, expedite acquisition of resources vital for national defence, and ensure the economic self-sufficiency for military personnel) and the implementation of national policy. These priorities were:

1. to study the production and utilization of resources vital to national defence such as fuel, copper, nickel, cobalt, tungsten, vanadium, zinc, lead, quicksilver, manganese, chrome, mica, bauxite, tannin and cow hide;
2. to study the production of everyday necessities such as cotton, coal and rice;
3. to study the disposition of native products such as rubber, tin, teak, sugar, quinine, Manila hemp, copra and palm oil;
4. to study the guidance of ethnic groups;
5. to study the maintenance of tropical hygiene, focusing especially on the adaptability of the Japanese to a tropical climate;
6. to study the development of transportation and railway networks;
7. to study currency and finance and the exchange of materials within the sphere of greater East Asia, especially within the occupied intra-regional area.[5]

The Southern Army, which had transferred its headquarters from Saigon to Syonan in July 1942, drew up plans on 27 August specifying the chosabu's organisational structure and research plans, and the procedure for making reports available to Southern Army Gunsei Sokambu (Superintendent General's Office). The Department of Political Affairs, meanwhile, had designated, through Lt. Col. Takase Keiji of General Staff acting as intermediary, that Tokyo College of Commerce (Toshodai, abbreviation of Tokyo shoka daigaku, now Hitotsubashi University) cooperate with the Army's request. A Toshodai Chosabu was to be attached to the Gunsei Sokambu of the Southern Army in Saigon[6] and the Research Institute of the South Manchuria Railway Company (*Mantetsu*) to the 25th Army Gunsei Kambu at Syonan.

President Takase Sotaro of Toshodai, Keiji's elder brother, had been eager for the Institute of Asian Economic Studies, founded in February 1941, to be actively involved in field research on Asian economic affairs, an area in which it had expert knowledge and research experience, and for its staff to participate in the Army's plan. President Takase appointed Professor Akamatsu Kaname, the Institute's director, to head a chosabu team.[7] He in turn recruited colleagues from among the Toshodai's faculty members, most of them Institute associates. They comprised the core of the chosabu, but others from outside the College also joined it.

The Toshodai Chosabu, as the Sokambu Chosabu, was to coordinate and integrate chosabu activities of other Gunsei Kambu administering the occupied territories. Before he was to leave for Malaya, Akamatsu met with staff from other designated institutes to discuss the problem of coordinating research projects but to his disappointment, he found the staff of established research institutes such as the Mantetsu Chosabu and the Institute of East Asian Affairs (Toa Kenkyusho) were unresponsive to his proposal. Akamatsu surmised that they found it presumptuous that their established institutes were to be subordinate to the Toshodai Chosabu, and he felt it would be difficult to carry on coordinated research activities of chosabus with specific problems in their assigned territory.[8]

Before their departure, Toshodai members clarified two things about their status while serving for the Army. They agreed to maintain the academic freedom of scholarly pursuit independent of military aims and to retain their academic status at Toshodai rather than becoming civil administrators (*shiseikan*) or civilian employees (*gunzoku*). The Army acceded to their requests.[9] The departure of the chosabu group was much delayed by increasing security risks on the high seas and a lack of transport,[10] but an advance team headed by Edayoshi Isamu of the Mantetsu team left by air in late November for Syonan, where it arrived on 1 December.

On reporting to Col. Watanabe Wataru, the 25th Army Gunsei Kambu's Director General, Edayoshi said in all candor that the security problems in peninsular Malaya engendered by Communist guerrilla activities made it impossible to carry on in-depth research about rubber estates and tin mines.[11] Accordingly, their research activities were confined to reading seized official documents of the British colonial government to familiarise themselves with Malaya's economic history in order to cope with any problems that might arise. Unable to carry on field work and being confined to Syonan, the Mantetsu members complained of the poor living conditions. The situation had a demoralising effect, and some of them drowned their frustrations in alcohol or quarrelled among themselves. Frequent brawls tarnished the image of the Mantetsu group so much that some Gunsei Kambu officials openly reproached them for their unruly behaviours, saying the chosabu served no good use to the military administration. Edayoshi recalled that the Mantetsu team had acomplished little in field studies before it moved to Sumatra and Burma in April 1943.[12]

The main group of the chosabu, including 40 members of the Toshodai Chosabu, arrived in Saigon on 28 December 1942. The Toshodai Chosabu met with a cool reception from the Sokambu when Lt. Col. Sato Hiroo received the team. Looking at the list of its members, he did not hide his displeasure and disappointment, remarking, "What we need now is natural scientists, not social scientists who serve no good service for our purposes."[13] Indeed, there was only one natural scientist in the team, Harashima Susumu of the Keio University Medical School.

Recalling this cold reception, Iwatake Teruhiko of the Sokambu said some Sokambu officers were skeptical of the Chosabu's usefulness, and wondered how they would be useful. The military wanted studies for exploiting natural resources, not economic studies of which there was no time to implement.[14] They expected the Chosabu to carry out practical and immediately useful studies for *gunsei* objectives, and were particularly disappointed that the Chosabu members were academically inclined. From the beginning, *gunsei* officers regarded the Toshodai Chosabu as useless and some of its members as Marxist economists.[15]

At a meeting held in March 1943 at Akamatsu's request for discussing research projects for 1943, all chosabu heads of the Southern area agreed on the research priorities laid by the Nanpo Seimubu in June of the previous year.

The first priority was to investigate and to win popular support, which had become the most urgent matter. Specifically, the research was to study:

1. the actual state of people's livelihood and the minimum standard of living;
2. the acquisition of daily necessities secured by trade and rationing;
3. in agricultural and industrial production increase;
4. supply and demand of labour resources;
5. policy plans for currency and price controls.

The second priority was the investigation of ways to develop heavy and chemical industries.[16]

Maj. Gen. Takahashi Hitoshi, Director General of the Gunsei Sokambu, spoke to the gathering, reiterating that the investigation should not be academic but practical — geared toward serving *gunsei* objectives. He also stressed cooperation between chosabus so they would not engage in parallel or overlapping studies. Takahashi's request, however, was not heeded by the Mantetsu Chosabu when Akamatsu asked Edayoshi for cooperation.

The Sokambu Chosabu and Its Activities: May 1943–May 1944

In May 1943, the 25th Army was deployed to Sumatra together with the Mantetsu Chosabu. Previouly the 25th Army had engaged in research activities such as reprinting and translating published materials in Syonan. Malaya came under the administration of the Malai Gunsei Kambu directly commanded by the Nanpo Gunsei Sokambu.[17] Malaya became the Toshodai Chosabu's territorial area of research. Setting up its office at Fort Canning, the Toshodai Chosabu began a full scale field research, covering various aspects of Malay society, and prepared 36 reports filed as *Sochoshi* (research reports of the Sokambu Chosabu) (see Appendix 1).

Yamada Isamu, Kawai Mikio and Ohno Seizaburo conducted field works on the industries of Malaya, visiting Malacca, Kuala Lumpur, lpoh, Penang and Alor Star, while Odabashi Sadatoshi directed a study in August about the life of a Minankabau village at Kuala Pilah in Negri Sembilan. In March 1944, Itagaki Yoichi, Yamada Isamu and Yamanaka Tokutaro went to Java, where they were to undertake a field research about agricultural village life. They were, however, unable to get full cooperation from the 16th Army. In early 1944, the Sokambu Chosabu tried to undertake a field study about the household economy of the entire Southern region. The investigation, however, had to be limited to Malaya as a result of uncooperative attitude of the chosabu*s* in Java and Sumatra. The researchers concentrated its studies on Syonan and Penang, and produced the first study of household economy ever undertaken in Malaya.[18] Assisted by Yamada Hideo, Ohono Seizaburo and Utsugi Tadashi, Ishida Ryujiro spent a month in September 1943 studying rice production and distribution at Kluang in Perak, and Yamada Hideo studied the Malayan land system and its relation to the Chinese in October of the same year.

Japan's war situation had been deteriorating since June 1942. The Allied counter-attack in the southwestern Pacific resulted in Japan's disastrous defeat in the naval battle of Midway, its retreat from Guadalcanal, the death, in action, of Adm. Yamamoto Isoroku, Commander-in-Chief, of the Combined Grand Fleet, and the loss of Attu Island in the Aleutian chain. Anti-Japanese resistance was also a growing problem in the occupied areas.

Faced with the adverse tide of the war, the Nanpo Gunsei Sokambu hosted a two-day conference in Syonan of chosabu heads representing the five areas of the Gunsei Kambu on 11–12 October 1943.[19] The meeting, attended by Lt. Gen. Shimizu Noritsune, the *gunsei* Superintendant General, and Maj. Gen. Takahashi, re-evaluated research priorities in order to cope with the changing war situation and the growing security problems. Shimizu emphasised the need to re-examine what the chosabu's role should be and whether its research had met *gunsei* needs. It was of crucial importance, he said, that the chosabu provide results that would be consonant with military needs. Takahashi insisted that the priority be given to the development of mining resources for industrialisation, ethnic studies directed toward food production and labour resources, and research on the Chinese who controlled distribution networks. Although cognisant of the importance of basic studies, Takahashi told the chosabu*s* that their work ought to be combined with practical studies that would help the military deal with current problems.

The Sokambu Chosabu re-examined its activities as demanded by the military. It was originally organised on the premise that Japan would establish firm control over Eastern Asia and then develop the Greater East Asia Co-Prosperity Sphere to sustain protracted hostilities. Accordingly, its mission was to provide the military with long term basic study that could be useful for planning the post-war management of the Southeast Asian economy. With the war entering a critical period, all that changed. The military demanded that Sokambu Chosabu gear its activities to practical research producing immediate results, and unauthorised it to expend resources on long term basic studies.

One week after the October meeting, the Sokambu Chosabu convened in Syonan a two-day conference of science institutes of the Southern Region, and on 14 November established the Science Committee of the Southern Region.[20] Its purpose was to facilitate scientific and technological studies by research and experimental institutes to meet *gunsei* needs, and to coordinate their research activities with similar works being done by the Navy in Taiwan and Japan in order to wage the war. The Committee had five subcommittees: agriculture, mining, chemistry, industry and nationality, to which Toshodai Chosabu personnel were assigned.

The Chosabu of the Malai Gunsei Kambu, 29th Army: January 1944 to August 1945

In January 1944, the 29th Army was organised and deployed, first at Kuala Kangsar and in October at Taiping. The Toshodai Chosabu, located in Kuala Lumpur, was attached to the 29th Army's Malai Gunsei Kambu, which was responsible for administering the five states that came under the Malai Gunsei Kambu's administration after the transfer of the four northern-most states of the former British Malaya to Thailand in 1943 and Johor to the 7th Area Army in Syonan.[21]

Launching chosabu activities under the 29th Army Gunsei Kambu, Akamatsu reaffirmed *gunsei* objectives as laid out in previous October, but he reorganised chosabu personnel, assigning them to 14 sections supervised by 3 departments (see Appendix 2). During this final phase of the Occupation, the chosabu produced 32 *Malai chosa shi* reports (research reports prepared by the Malai Chosabu) (see Appendix 3) and published Fortnightly Report (*Chosabuho*) in 34 issues beginning 1 May 1944 and ending 15 March 1945.

The appointment of Col. Hamada Hiroshi to the post of *gunsei* director general in January 1944 changed the character of the Chosabu from a policy planning body to a policy making body. Hamada had served as a member of the military advisory group to the Wang Ching Wei government prior to his new appointment and had a reputation of being a razor sharp, no nonsense officer. He was said to have once sympathised with the cause of the young officers of the Imperial Way faction (Kodoha),[22] who attempted a *coup d'etat* in February 1936 to rid the army of Control Faction officers (Toseiha) allied with the capitalist big business.

Irritated by exploitative Japanese company representatives and profiteers whose unscrupulous business practices had been driving Chinese out of their businesses and alienating them from the Japanese, Hamada severely castigated them for their behaviours towards indigeous people. He took the unusual step of publishing his scathing statement against them in *Syonan Simbun* (on 31 May 1944), and placed the Chosabu under his direct command. This step was a turning point for the Chosabu, drawing it into the political arena and eventually putting an end to its work as a research body. It terminated its research activities with the publication of the final issue of the fortnightly *Chosabuho* on 15 March 1945.[23] From early summer, Chosabu personnel were more deeply involved in political affairs dealing with Chinese and Malay youths and Islamic issues, all aimed at winning popular support.[24]

Hamada was prepared to listen to Chosabu advice when Itagaki and Suzuki Choei, an Islamic specialist, proposed organising an Islamic council in every state, and he allocated ¥250,000 in August for this purpose.[25] Itagaki and Suzuki invited Islamic leaders to a conference of the All Malay Muslim Supreme Council at Kuala Kangsar on 13–15 December. "The conference was an intrinsic part of the official atempt to solicit unflinching commitment from the religious leaders towards the Japanese war efforts." Itagaki, Suzuki, Watanabe Kan'o of the Chosabu, Burhanuddin Al-Helmy, the Gunsei Kambu advisor on Malay customs and Islamic affairs, the Crown Princes of Johor and Perak and various Gunsei Kambu and Perak state government officials attended the meeting.[26]

Guided by the Chosabu, the conference "effectively aligned the conservative religious elite to the Japanese side". They together with fellow Malay Muslims, pledged to "cooperate with Japan in order to achieve the final aims of the greater Asian war through (a) soliciting donations for war purposes; (b) advising the people to cooperate fully with Dai Nippon; (c) increasing food production; (d) ensuring law and order continued to prevail in Malaya; and (e) praying for the end of the war with victory for Japan".[27]

American forces meanwhile had forced Japanese forces to retreat closer to their homeland — the loss of Saipan (10 July 1944) was followed by the downfall of the Tojo cabinet on 22 August. Japan lost Manila (5 March 1945) and the US forces landed at Iwo Jima (17 March); American troops landed on Okinawa on 1 April, and the British Army recaptured Burma the following month.

In May, Akamatsu and Itagaki met Maj. Gen. Umezu Hirokichi, who had succeeded Hamada, and presented their idea of winning popular support by encouraging the national aspirations of young Malays. Umezu, however, remained uncommitted because, he said, the Japanese government had not yet considered granting independence to Malaya.[28] Akamatsu and Itagaki then took the matter into their own hands. On 4 May, Itagaki visited Col. Kusuda Tanenari, Chief of Staff of the Syonan Defence Army, and asked him to release Ibrahim Yaacob, former leader of the Malay Youth Movement (*Kesatuan Muda Melayu*, KMM), from the Voluntary Army (*Giyugun*) to allow him to lead the Malay people for supporting Japan's war efforts. Kusuda acceded to Itagaki's request. On the following day, Itagaki called on Maj. Mori Fumio, *gunsei* staff officer of the 7th Area Army, and impressed on him the need to employ Ibrahim's talent for organising a youth movement and enhancing Malay national aspirations. Concurring with Itagaki's argument, Mori cabled a telegram to 29th Army headquarters requesting its assistance. Much to Itagaki's surprise, everything went well. The military was so desperate for gaining popular support that it was more than ready to listen to the Chosabu and to follow their suggestions.[29]

On the night of 5 May, Akamatsu and Itagaki met with Ibrahim and urged him to gather his former KMM comrades and discuss a Malay independence movement, which they named the *Kekuatan Ryakat Istimewa Semenanjung* (KRIS, The Strength of Special People on the Peninsula), a Malay version of the Indonesian *Pusat Tenega Ryakat* (Young People's Office).[30] Five days later, Itagaki, Ibrahim and Mustapha bin Hussain visited Umezu. Upon receiving them, Umezu made a statement that flabergasted the visitors. He said:

> The Japanese military has made basic mistakes in the nationality policy towards the Malays. I want to make this point very clearly. Though it may be a little too late to rectify the mistake, I will do my best in encouraging your national aspirations. Because we are still at war, we can not realise your aspirations right now. I am sure that day will not be too far away. Should you have any complaints about *gunsei*, let me hear about them.

Umezu's candid admission drove Ibrahim and Mustapha to dancing wildly with joy, and Ibrahim immediately began recruiting comrades to organise local KRIS offices.[31]

In the meantime, Kirita Naosaku, Uchida Naosaku and Yamagata Tomoo of the Chosabu, using ¥150,000 provided by Hamada, had been engaged since June 1944 in organising a public reading room (Epposho) to deal with Chinese affairs, recruiting Chinese youths and entrepreneurs as advisors and collaborators for the project.[32] The Epposho listened to Chinese complaints, made efforts to rectify the punitive and discriminatory anti-Chinese policy under which they had suffered, and tried to make efficient use of Chinese business experience.[33]

In May 1944, the Epposho established the Syonan Rice Import Association by uniting Teochew and Hokkien Chinese traders, and formed a similar association in Penang — the Rice Import Public Corporation — in June. In cooperation with the Epposho, these two organisations imported rice with junks via Singora and Penang and helped to ease the rice shortage.[34]

Akamatsu and Itagaki took a further step towards integrating the Epposho and KRIS when they formed a central office for guiding indigenous people (*Genjumin Chuo Hodosho*) to coordinate the activities of the two organisations. This office opened in Taiping on 3 July, with Akamatsu as its director, and he assigned Chosabu personnel to local offices of the Epposho and the Hodosho. The Chosabu was dissolved on 3 July.[35]

Japan's surrender on 15 August put an end to the KRIS movement and to the Epposho, in which the Chosabu had played a significant part. The members of the Chosabu were detained until repatriation in early 1946. Itagaki and Akamatsu in the meantime engaged themselves, at the British Military Administration in translating documents the Kempeitai had prepared about Communist activities. Before being interned on Rembang Island in February 1946, Akamatsu and Itagaki presented a complete set of *Sochoshi, Malai Chosashi* and *Chosabuho* to the British Military Administration.

Conclusion

Fukami, who conducted a study of the Southern region's chosabu, raised three questions for evaluating its activities. First, what was the chosabu's significance for the *gunsei* administration? Second, what was its contribution to developing Southeast Asian studies, particularly in Japan? Third, was there any significant study produced in wartime about Southeast Asian society?

Fukami concluded that the Gunsei Kambu had little appreciation, if any at all, of the chosabu, and I would agree with this judgement. Military staff officers looked upon it as a white elephant, and thought the Occupation Administration could be carried out without it. Commenting that chosabu reports had "no effect on *gunsei* policy making", Yamada Hideo attributed the situation to the academic perspective of the reports, which had little relevance to the acute military situation. As a result, staff officers had little appreciation of the chosabu. The deteriorating war situation further devalued chosabu activities.

When the war entered a desperate stage in 1944, the *gunsei* administrators finally allowed the Chosabu to influence on policy making. Ironically, the Chosabu's participation in political affairs and its role in organising groups such as the KRIS and Epposho was a marked departure from its original purpose, which was to provide the Gunsei Kambu with information necessary for policy planning.

Fukami argues that the chosabu contributed little to the development of Southeast Asian studies. After the war, most members of the Toshodai Chosabu team pursued their own academic interests, and in the anti-war and pacifist atmosphere that prevailed in Japan after 1945, many seemed to be hesitant to disclose their wartime role lest they be accused of having participated in that "aggressive war".[36] For more than a decade after 1945, academic circumstances were not conducive for the development of Southeast Asian studies, and only Itagaki, Kirita, H. Yamada, Uchida and Yamagata remained active in the field. In Japan, Southeast Asia only gained recognition as a field of area studies in the 1960s.

As for the research reports, unlike other Gunsei Kambu reports that were mostly destroyed or dispersed after Japan's surrender, a large quantity of Sokambu and Malai Gunsei Kambu chosabu reports have survived because Tokugawa Yoshichika, who served an advisor to the Gunsei Kambu in Malaya from March 1941 to August 1944, kept copies of these materials and donated them to the War History Department of the Institute of National Defence Studies. They are compiled in 65 volumes.[37] It is not known how many reports had been prepared by March 1945, when the Chosabu ceased research activity, and certainly a number of them are missing. The reports in the Tokugawa Collection, together with materials at Hitotsubashi University and interview records of former Chosabu personnel, are substantial sources of information for the study of occupied Malaya. As has been mentioned, the Toshodai staff maintained a scholarly stance in their investigation, and the quality of their reports is high. Many studies are the first of their kind ever produced in Malaya and provide useful information, substantiated by statistics, about the daily life of the occupied people and their society. Reports on the economic conditions and inflation cover such topics as rural and urban life, inflation, minimum standard of living, commodity prices and rice cultivation, and they are of particular value. Since the late 1970s the Tokugawa Collection and other related official papers have been made accessible to scholars. Tapping these documents, Iwatake Teruhiko has published a comprehensive study of the economic policy in occupied Malaya and Java.[38] Ota Koki also used chosabu reports extensively for his numerous articles on *gunsei* studies. Some scholars in Malaya and Singapore have also consulted chosabu papers in connection with their studies of the Japanese Occupation.[39]

Since the Defence Institute's War History Department published *Shiryoshu Nampo no Gunsei* (*Documents Relating to Nampo Gunsei*) in 1985, scholars have found these chosabu reports an indispensable source of reference. Most notable is an increasing interest among Japanese-language teachers who use them for studying Japanese language policy and its implementation in Malaya.[40]

As far as the *gunsei* studies of Malaya are concerned, it is reasonable to conclude that the chosabu reports have made a significant contribution to the understanding of the economic and social situation in occupied Malaya and Singapore.

Notes

1. "Tonan Ajia ni okeru Nippon *Gunsei* no Chosa", *Nanyo Bunka* 15 (1988): 119–49.
2. Hata Ikuhiko, ed., *Nampo Gunsei no Kiko Kambu Gunseikan Ichiran* (Private publication, Dec. 1998), pp. 3–4.
3. *Dai 25gun Gunsei Chosaban Shiryo oyobi Tokeishu*, Feb. to Oct. 1942.
4. Rikugunsho, *Nampo Gunsei Chosa Kenkyu Jisshi Yoryo*, 25 July 1942.
5. Ibid.; Hara Kakuten, *Gendai Ajia Kenkyu Seiritsuronshi: Mantetsu Chosabu, Toa Kenkyusho, IPR no kenkyu* (Tokyo: Keiso Shobo, 1984), pp. 33–4. Interview Kiroku D, *Nippon no Gunsei* 4, Tsuge Hideomi; Tokutei Kenkyu, "Bunka Masatsu", Tokyo Daigaku Kyoyo Gakubu Kokusai Kankei Kenkyushiitsu, 1980, pp. 29–30.
6. Takase Sotaro, p. 568, quoted from Senso no Jidai to *Hitotsubashi*. Showa 12-nen 1gatsu Showa 20nen 8gatsu, Josuikai Gakuenshi Kanko Iinkai, 1989, p. 171. The Army assigned Toa Kenkyusho to the 16th Army in Java, Mantetsu Chosabu to the 15th Army in Burma, Taihaiyo Chosakai to the North Borneo Garrison Army (later the 37th Army), Mitsubishi Chosabu to the 14th Army in the Philippines, Mantetsu Chosabu moved to Sumatra when the 25th Army was deployed there in May 1943.

    The Toshodai Chosabu was said to be envious of Toa Kenkyusho being sent to Java as it wanted to be assigned to the 16th Army, because Itagaki Yoichi had visited Java and Sumatra in a three-month study from Nov. 1940 to Feb. 1941. Rivalling the Navy which had dispatched a research group to the Southern region, the Army hastened to organise an investigation team. Tsuge in Interview Kiroku (Record), p. 26.

7. Akamatsu was at first hesitant to accept the post but his colleague, Sugimoto Eiichi, a Marxist economist, insisted much to his surprise that Akamatsu accept

the post. Kojima Kiyoshi, ed., *Gakumon Henro: Akamatsu Kaname Sensei Tsuito Ronshu* (Tokyo: Sekai Keizai Kenkyu Kyokai, 1975), p. 44.

8. Kojima, *Gakumon Henro*, p. 44. Interview Kiroku D, *Nippon no Gunsei* 6, Itagaki, p. 127.
9. Interview Kiroku D, *Nippon no Gunsei* 6, Itagaki, pp. 119–21.
10. In May the Taiyo Maru carrying several hundreds of civilian employees destined for Syonan was sunk by a submarine attack just off Kyushu.
11. Edayoshi Isamu, *Chosaya Ruten* (Private publication, 1981), pp. 73–4. Edayoshi recalled that while he set up a chosabu, he did not know what sort of research it was supposed to do, its purpose and whether it aimed at general economic studies or complicated ethnic problems.
12. Ibid., pp. 76, 78. Tsuge Hideomi. *Toa Kenkyusho to Watashi* (Tokyo: Keiso Shobo), pp. 144, 151.
13. Interview Kiroku D, *Nippon no Gunsei* 4, Tsuge Hideomi, p. 30.
14. Interview Kiroku D, *Nippon no Gunsei* 5, Iwatake Teruhiko, p. 42. Seki Yoshihiko, who was a chosabu member of the North Borneo Gunseibu, recorded: its staff officer, Lt. Col. Yano Tsuneo, tried in vain to disestablish its chosabu which he thought was unnecessary. *Watashi to Shakai Shugi*, Tokyo, pp. 45–55. Yano became a *gunsei* staff officer of the Nampo Sogun in March 1943.
15. Interview Kiroku D, *Nippon no Gunsei* 6, Itagaki, p. 128. Itagaki Yoichi, ed., *Riron to Keiryo ni Tesshite: Yamada Isamu Sensei Tsuiso Bunshu* (Tokyo: Ronsosha, 1987), p. 35.
16. *Senso no Jidai to Hitotsubashi*, pp. 175–6.
17. In May 1943 the Syonan Gunsei Kambu changed to Malai Gunsei Kambu. Throughout the Occupation period "Malai" was used instead of "Malaya".
18. *Riron to Keiryo*, pp. 33–7. Nippon no Eiryo Malaya/Singapore Senryoki Shiryo Chosa Forum, ed., *Interview Kiroku: Nippon no Eiryo Malaya/Singapore Senryo (1941–1945)* (Tokyo: Ryukei Shosha, 1998), pp. 20–8.
19. Gunsei Sokambu Chosabu, *Chosakikan Shuninsha Kaido Hokokusho*.
20. See official papers relating to this topic in the Tokugawa Collection, vols. 28 and 52.
21. Perlis, Kedah, Kelantan and Trengganu were transferred to Thailand in Sept. 1943 and Johor to the 7th Area Army in Syonan.
22. Interview Kiroku D, *Nippon no Gunsei* 6, Uchida Naosaku, p. 134. *Ueda Jun'ichi: Watashi no Rireki* (Private publication, 1994) p. 247.
23. Chosabuho, no. 34 was its last issue. Only nos. 1–6 are in existence.
24. See my articles, "Japanese Military Administration in Malaya: Its Formation and Evolution in Reference to Sultans, the Islamic Religion, and the Moslem Malays, 1941–1845", *Asian Studies* 7, 1 (1969): 81–110, and "Japanese Policy Towards the Malayan Chinese 1941–1945", *Journal of Southeast Asian Studies* 1, 2 (1970): 61–89.
25. Interview Kiroku D, *Nippon no Gunsei* 6, Itagaki, p. 142. *Itagaki Yoichi: Ajia tono Taiwa* (Private publication, 1968), pp. 159–60.
26. Abu Talib Ahmad, *The Malay Muslims: Islam and the Rising Sun, 1941–1945*, monograph 34, Malaysian Branch of the Royal Asiatic Society, 2003, p. 225.

27. Ibid., p. 226.
28. Itagaki, *Ajia tono Taiwa*, p. 160. The Imperial Conference of 31 May 1943 made the decision that the Japanese government would make Malaya permanent possession. The Political Affairs Section of the Foreign Affairs Ministry drafted a memorandum on 20 Feb. 1945 that said, "It is difficult to grant independence to Malaya by repealing the present military government and replacing it with a new system of government." *Daitoa Senso Kankei Toji* in the Ministry of Foreign Affairs Archives. A translation of the memorandum appears in Cheah Boon Kheng, *Red Star over Malaya*, 2nd edition (Singapore: Singapore University Press, 1987), Appendix A, pp. 302–3. A Foreign Ministry's position paper prepared in June 1945 reconfirmed this conclusion.
29. Itagaki, *Ajia tono Taiwa*, p. 164.
30. Ibid., p. 163. Abu Talib, *The Malay Muslims*, p. 115.
31. Itagaki, *Ajia tono Taiwa*, p. 166. See, *Malayan Nationalism Before UMNO. The Memoirs of Mustaph Hussain* (Kuala Lumpur: Utusan Publications, 2005). Chapter 28.
32. Epposho was named after an organisation with the same name founded in Penang by Sun Yat-sen.
33. Interview Kiroku D, *Nippon no Gunsei* 6, Uchida Naosaku, p. 130. Uchida Naosaku, "Shusen Zengo no Tonan Ajia no Kakyo", Nippon Gaiko Gakkai, ed., *Taiheiyo Senso Shuketsuron* (Tokyo: Tokyo Daigaku Shuppankai, 1958), pp. 486–8.
34. Ibid.
35. Itagaki, *Ajia tono Taiwa*, p. 167.
36. Goto Ken'ichi, *Nippon Senryoki Indonesia Kenkyu* (Tokyo: Ryukei Shosha, 1989), p. 19.
37. Neither the Public Record Office (currently the National Archives) nor the Imperial War Museum in Britain has a record of having received the seized Japanese Military Administration papers. I have tentatively traced the materials to New Dehli, India, where the British Military Administration shipped them to in the post-war period. It is likely that they are in the Archives of the Indian Defence Ministry, which is not accessible to scholars. Itagaki said that before being detained by the British, he and Akamatsu placed a set of 114 chosabu reports in their office to show the British what they had done during the Occupation period.
38. Iwatake Teruhiko, *Nampo Gunseika no Keizai Shisaku: Malai, Sumatra, Java no Kiroku*, 2 vols. (Tokyo: Ryukei Shosha, 2002).
39. Paul H. Kratoska, *The Japanese Occupation of Malaya 1941–1945* (London: Allen & Unwin, 1998), and Abu Talib Ahmad, *The Malay Muslims*.
40. Matsunaga Noriko, *Nippon Gunseika no Malaya ni okeru Nippongo Kyoiku* (Tokyo: Kazama Shobo, 2002).

Appendix 1: *Socho Shi*

1. Mines in Western Malaya, April 1943.
2. Academic Institutions in Malaya (related to *gunsei*), May 1943.
3. Inflation in Malaya, June 1943.
4. Problems of Training and Education in Malaya, June 1943.
5. Living Conditions of Ethnic Groups in Java, July 1943.
6. Problems of Inflation in East Coast Residency, Sumatra, June 1943.
7. Comparison of Climatic Conditions between Thailand and Malaya, July 1943.
8. Currency Problems in Java, July 1943.
9. Problems of Rice Rationing in Malaya, Sept. 1943.
10. A Study on the Delivery Capability of Palm Oil in Sumatra, Sept. 1943.
11. Reference Materials Relating to Religious Schools in Malaya, Sept. 1943.
12. Rice Crop Agriculture in Java, Oct. 1943.
13. A Study of the Real State of the Lowest Living Standard of Ethnic Groups in Syonan Municipality: A Study Focused on Prices, Quantity and Degree of the Need of Daily Necessities According to Various Ethnic Groups, Oct. 1943.
14. Bauxite of Bintang Island, Oct. 1943.
15. Matrilineal Kampong Society and Adat in Negri Sembilan, Oct. 1943.
16. Problems of Currency and Money in Malaya, Oct. 1943.
17. The Real State of Agricultural Life in Malaya (interim report), Oct. 1943.
18. A Medical Study of Labour Power in the Southern Region, Nov. 1943
19. The Delivery Capability of Copra in Malaya and the Policy for its Collection, Dec. 1943.
20. Prospects of Automobile in Malaya, Oct. 1943.
21. A Survey of Rare Elementary Minerals in Malaya, Nov. 1943.
22. Trade Situations in French Indochina and Thailand (missing).
23. Overseas Chinese Remittances to China, Nov. 1943.
24. Withdrawal of Local Money from Circulation, Dec. 1943.
25. The Delivery Capability of Palm Oil and its Bottleneck in Malaya, Dec. 1943.
26. Plans to Strengthen the Sector for Automobile Repair, Dec. 1943.
27. A Population Survey of Syonan Municipality According to Occupations, Dec. 1943.
28. The Present Transportation Situation for Principal Cargo in Malaya, Dec. 1943 (missing).
29. Elementary Education in Post-war Malaya, Dec. 1943.
30. Physical Characteristics of Ethnic Groups in the Southern Region, Jan. 1944.
31. A Study on the Production Situation in Indochina, Part I: Agriculture, Marine and Livestock Products, Jan. 1944 (missing).
32. Production Situation in Indochina, Part II: Mineral products, Jan. 1944 (missing).
33. Production Situation in Indochina, Part III: Industrial products, Jan. 1944 (missing).
34. Technological Capability of the Indigenous Malays, Feb. 1944.
35. Study on Constructing a Railway Network in the Southern Region, Jan. 1944.
36. Counter-measures for Prices in Syonan Municipality, March 1944.

Appendix 2: *Malai Cho Shi*

1. Inflationary Situation in Malaya and its Counter-measures, April 1944.
2. The "Pigtail" Riot of 1912 and the Pahang Insurgency of 1891, May 1944.
3. Problems for Increasing Automobile Transportation Capability in Malaya, May 1944.
4. A Summary of Retail Prices of Daily Necessities in Syonan, May 1944.
5. The Present Situation of Cargo Transportation in Java, June 1944.
6. Progress of Religious Policy under the Military Administration, July 1944.
7. Reference Materials Relating to Sultan's Religious Administration, July 1944.
8. The Land System in Malaya and Overseas Chinese, Oct. 1944.
9. Problems of Utilising and Guiding Religious Customs under the Military Administration, Aug. 1944.
10. Policy for Increasing Food Production in Syonan-to, Oct. 1944.
11. Reorganising Commercial Businesses in Syonan Municipality, Sept. 1944.
12. The Land System in Negri Sembilan and Kampong Farmers (supplement), Nov. 1944.
13. A study on the Labour Situation in Syonan Municipality Focused on Factories Managed by Japanese, Oct. 1944.
14. A Field Study of Agricultural Kampong in the Krian District (a summary report), Sept. 1944.
15. The Administrative Structure of Ethnic Groups in Negri Sembilan and Malacca, Nov. 1944.
16. A Report on the Study of Household Economy (1 November 1943 to 30 April 1944), Oct. 1944.
17. Rice Imports in Malaya Especially in Syonan Municipality, Oct. 1944.
18. A Study of the Labour Distribution along the Railway Running through the Malay Peninsula, Nov. 1944.
19. Problems of the Food Control System in the State of Malacca Especially Abolishing Official Prices, Nov. 1944.
20. The Palm Oil Industry in Malaya, Dec. 1944.
21. The Control System of Perishable Foods in Malaya and the Double Price System, Jan. 1945.
22. A Comprehensive Study of Commodity Prices: Part I, Oct. 1944.
23. Study of Commodity Prices: Part II, missing.
24. Study of Commodity Prices: Part III, Nov. 1944.
25. Study of Commodity Prices: Part IV, 15 Nov. 1944.
26. Study of Commodity Prices: Part V, 1 Dec. 1944.
27. Study of Commodity Prices: Part VI, 15 Dec. 1944.
28. Study of Commodity Prices: Part VII, missing.
29. Part VIII of the same study, 15 Jan. 1945.
30. A Summary of Retail Commodity Prices in Syonan, Nov. 1944.
31. A Summary of Retail Commodity Prices in Syonan, Dec. 1944
32. A Summary of Retail Commodity Prices in Syonan, Jan. 1945.

Appendix 3: *Chosabuho*, nos. 1–6, May–July 1944*

No. 1 (1 May 1944)

1. Chosabu Regulations. Organisation chart.
2. Summaries of Research Reports.
   a. Kannogi Keizo. Problems of clothing in Malaya.
   b. Itagaki Yoichi. On the Sultan's political and religious status in pre-war years — Pahang and Selangor.
   c. Ohno Seizaburo. On Problems of Cooperative Association in Malaya.
3. Field Research Report by Itagaki Yoichi, Yamashita Kakataro Report on Pahang and Selangor
4. Review of Important References Published in *Filippin Chosa Shiryo*, no. 7
5. Bibliography of Books and other References donated and purchased
6. Bibliography of Published Research References

No. 2 (15 May 1944)

1. Reports of Study Meeting by Yamada Hideo, Ohno Seizaburo on Present Condition of an Agricultural Village in Negri Sembilan
2. Report by Yamada Isamu on Field Study in Kuala Lumpur, Penang and on Family Budget
3. Report by Higuchi Goro on Inflation in Malaya and Its Counter-measures
4. Review on Books relating to Malayan Agriculture
5. Statistics of Commodity Prices Prepared by Statistics Section

No. 3 (5 June 1944)

1. Report of Study Meeting by Nogaya Yuji on Policy for Private Schools in Malaya
2. Report of Study Meeting by Izawa Kozo on Industrial Labour Work
3. Study Report by Yamada Hideo on the Land Inheritance in a Matriarchal Tribal Society (Negri Sembilan)
4. Study Report by Izawa Kozo on Change in Absentism among labourers
5. Study Report on Demand of Important Daily Necessities
6. Diary of the Chosabu

No. 4 (20 June 1944)

1. Study Report by Watabe Sumio on Religion and Customs and Problems of Guiding them
2. Field Study Report by Itagaki Yoichi on the Sultan of Perak
3. Survey of Islands under the Administration of Syonan Municipal City and Land Cultivation
4. a. Characteristics of Chinese in Penang reported by Mukai Umeji
   b. Establishing Epposho in Penang reported by Hoshino Shin

    c. The Cultural and Economic Study Office of the Perak State Government by Itagaki Yoichi

    d. Trends of Commodity Prices in Syonan by Nanpuhara Shuichi

No. 5 (5 July 1944)

1. Report by Uchida Naosaku on Manufacturing Enterprises in Penang
2. Report Azuma Sukeo on the Industry Manufacturing Consumer Goods in Syonan Municipal City
3. Report by Nagaya Yuji on Chinese Private Schools in Syonan
4. Report by Suzuki Choei on Inheritance Laws in the Koran
5. Report by Yamada Hideo on the Land System in Malaya
6. Report by Izawa Kozo on Oxcart-driven Cargo in Syonan
7. Chosabu Diary

No. 6 (20 July 1944)

1. Report by Higuchi Goro on the Rationing Organisation of Principal Foods in Syonan
2. Report by Yamada Hidezo, Ohno Seizaburo on a Field Study of Dry Field Farming families in Syonan
3. Report by Kubomura Ryusuke on the Machine and Tool Industry in Syonan
4. Trends of Commodity Prices in Syonan (June)
5. A Comparative Study of Productive Age Population in Various Countries by Odabashi Sadatoshi, Ohmura Junzaburo

---

* The *Chosabuho* was published fortnightly. Only six issues are in existence. Thirty-four reports were printed. The last issue was printed 15 March 1945.

Appendix 4: Organisation Chart of the Chosabu, Malai Military Administration, May 1944

Akamatsu Kaname, Chosabu Director

General Affairs Department
Ishida Ryujiro, Director
Chiba Masao
Mukai Umeji
Odabashi Sadatoshi
Itagaki Yoichi

The following three sections are sub-sections of the General Affairs Department:

1. *Reference Section*
Uchida Naosaku, Head
Aso Fukumaru

2. *Statistics Section*
Yamada Isamu, Head
Kawai Mikio
Tanaka Mitsuo

3. *General Affairs Section*
Kannoki Keizo, Head
Ozaki Kenji
Sudo Kaichi
Hoshi Nobuko
Saeki Satako
Saito Nobuko
Torii Kin
Mohri Sawako

Ethnic Affairs Department
Watanabe Kan'o, Head
Itagaki, Deputy Head

1. Education and Religion: Watanabe, Nagaya Yuji
2. Administration: Itagaki Yoichi, Koga Minoru
3. People's Livelihood and Customs: Mukai, Suzuki Choei, Hoshino Susumu
4. Overseas Chinese: Uchida Naosaku, Matsuura Shigeharu

Economics Department
Akamatsu Kaname, Head
Yamashita, Kakutaro and Kirita Naosaku, Deputy Heads

The following seven sections are sub-sections of Economics Department:

1. *Labour*
Odabashi Sadatoshi
Izawa Kozo
Omura Junzaburo
Ogawa Takao

2. *Agriculture*
Taniyama Seizo
Yamada Hideo
Ohno Seizaburo

3. *Mining*
Azuma Akio
Saji Koji
Kubomura Ryusuke
Utsugi Tadash

4. *Commerce*
Kirita Naosaku
Nagamori Shoji

5. *Transportation*
Imanishi Goro

6. *Currency and Money*
Higuchi Goro
Yamagata Tomoo

7. *Finance*
Yamashita Kakutaro

Third batch of students of Syonan Koa Kunrensho (1942–43)

Kunrensho students exercising marching practice
(August 1942)

Kunrenjo students receiving
graduating certificate
(Malacca Koa Kunrensho)

Japanese officers surrendering their swords
(September 1945)

A student presenting speech at Malai Senior Teacher's College (Jokyu Shihan Gakko) to visiting guests of the Gunsei Kambu, 1943

Malai Senior Teacher's College (Malai Jokyu Shihan Gakko), Simon Road, Syonan

Japanese Surrendered Personnel (JSP) at detention camp

Bones of *sook ching* excavated at Asahan, Malacca

7

The Civilian Women's Internment Camp in Singapore: The World of *POW WOW*

NAKAHARA MICHIKO

The fall of Singapore on 15 February 1942 was the worst military defeat suffered by the British Empire. For Winston Churchill, who ordered British forces to defend Singapore till the last soldier, the surrender of nearly 100,000 British troops to the Imperial Japanese army was a humiliating military and political failure.[1] But worse was to follow. For the next three and a half years, Asian and European prisoners of war and civilian internees suffered unimaginable hardship. Many POWs were sent to Saigon, Burma, Siam, Taiwan, Korea and Japan to perform forced labour under brutal conditions. Women, children and men — who had been living in British Malaya peacefully before the war — were interned as "enemy" civilians in Changi Prison and later in the Sime Road Internment Camp. Changi Prison had been built to house 600 convicts, but as of 8 March 1942, a total of 2,800 European civilians were held there. Among them there were 430 women and children, and the number increased to 700 the following year.

Although many books present histories of warfare, little has been written about the experiences of women and children. Official papers rarely mention women, and few accounts have been written by women. This chapter reconstructs the experiences of civilian women and children interned in British Malaya from 1942 to 1945 on the basis of diaries, reports, memoirs, books, taped interviews and a camp newspaper called *POW WOW* published in the Civilian Women's Internment Camp of Changi Prison from 1 April 1942 until 15 October 1943. *POW WOW* ceased publication when the editor, Freddy Bloom, was arrested by the Kempeitai (Japanese Military Police), who suspected her of involvement in an anti-Japanese attack known as the Double Tenth Incident.

On 30 March 1942, Freddy Bloom wrote in her diary, "Last night, Dr Hopkins and Dr Williams came and asked whether I would edit a camp newspaper."[2] Bloom, who had worked as a journalist before the war, accepted the suggestion, and chose the name *POW WOW* for the publication. The four-to-eight page newspaper appeared without fail every Wednesday in Changi Women's Internment Camp. Bloom and a group of women who helped her could not use the jail printing press and had very little paper, so the publication had to be typed, and a copy was delivered to each cell block. *POW WOW* was passed around and pored over by internees. It was a great source of encouragement for the women, who had been living all over British Malaya and were struggling with the disruption the war had brought to their lives. They were of different nationalities, professions, social backgrounds and religions. *POW WOW* helped shape a sense of community in the camp and provided a semblance of normality, something the women needed to cope with in their extremely poor living conditions. Many of the women internees had spent the 1930s in a British colony controlled by men where they had been addressed respectfully as *mem* or *missie* and assisted by many servants, and internment was the first time they were on their own and able to take charge of their own lives. The women elected their own leaders, organised committees, planned projects, improved their living environment, opened hospitals and schools, taught children, conducted lectures, organised exhibitions and contests and put on various forms of entertainment. By running the internment camp and participating in the decision making process via their negotiations with the Japanese, these women discovered hidden abilities. They learned of their own and other women's talents, and cultivated lasting respect and trust for each other. *POW WOW* provided information on how to survive in camp and on the regulations governing everyday affairs. It also offered items about church activities, entertainment, fashion education, literature, and anything else the editors could think of.

The British Evacuation

The Japanese Imperial army landed in southern Siam (known as Thailand today) and at Kota Bahru in the Malayan state of Kelantan on 8 December 1941, and marching southwards reached Singapore in just over two months. Lt. Gen. Arthur Percival, Commander of the Malaya Command, knew that it would be extremely difficult to defend British Malaya in the event of a Japanese attack. After the war, he openly discussed the complexity and difficulty of defending Malaya, stating that "defence was of very little interest to the great majority of the people of Malaya in those days".[3]

British Malaya had a complex administrative structure. The Straits Settlements — Singapore, Penang and Malacca — was a Crown Colony. Each of the Federated States (Selangor, Perak, Negri Sembilan and Pahang), and the Unfederated States (Johor, Trengganu, Kelantan, Kedah and Perlis) had its own ruler and administrative structure, an arrangement that impeded the British response to crisis situations created by the war. Ethnically the population consisted of Malays, Chinese, Indians, Eurasians, various ethnic minorities and about 20,000 Europeans. The Malays owed loyalty to their rulers, and many neither identified with nor had any sense of belonging to British Malaya. A nascent Malay nationalism amongst Malay intellectuals was just beginning to take shape when the war broke out. Among the Chinese, place of origin and native dialect provided the focus for individual loyalties. Many Chinese residents were more concerned with the war in China than with British Malaya. Support was divided between the Kuomintang and the Communist Party, but their strong overall anti-Japanese leanings did benefit the British. The situation of the Indians was even more complicated, for they were divided by religion, language, profession, caste and political loyalties. Deeply influenced by the political situation in India, a great number of Indians in British Malaya supported the independence movement in their homeland and were therefore anti-British. These complex and divided loyalties made the British cautious in seeking support for the defence of Malaya. Percival wrote, "No liability to military service was imposed upon the Asiatic population. Many of them were of a type unsuitable for training as soldiers, sailors, or airmen...."[4] A considerable number of Japanese also lived in British Malaya, some working in mines or on plantations, others at hotels, restaurants, confectioners, kimono shops and brothels. Japanese dentists, doctors, photographers, barbers, hair stylists and prostitutes were familiar sights in pre-war Singapore.

The Japanese population in Singapore was big enough to have two Japanese-language newspapers of its own. When Percival was asked why he did not give the public more accurate information about the war situation as it arose, Percival explained that the presence of a Japanese press in Singapore made it hard to do so. Press conferences included representatives of the Japanese as well as the English and vernacular press, so that "we either had to request the representative of that paper not to attend — a rather invidious thing to have to do — or else be very careful what we said....

Unfortunately a defended area, such as Malaya was becoming, is not the sort of place where you can easily give away news without prejudicing security."[5] Peter Elphick has noted, however, that the Singapore censors "kept a tight grip on everything published".

> Very few of the ordinary populace of the island were aware of just how badly the military situation on the mainland was going. The news that was released was usually well out of date and full of false optimism. Right up to the end the authorities were reluctant to tell the truth. Had they been more open the number of voluntary evacuees among the European women and children would have been larger and they would have left earlier and almost certainly reached safety.[6]

Warnings the colonial government did issue about the war were not taken seriously, and when European women and children were advised to evacuate, few did so. People could not imagine that the "Asiatic" Japanese military could defeat the British army, or that Singapore could fall to Japan. Moreover, the Asian population of British Malaya regarded the war as very much a battle between the Japanese and the British. The preparations for war were carried out in front of "native Asiatics" who for many decades had been made to believe in the superiority of their British rulers, and the British feared the consequences of appearing weak or vulnerable.

Percival and Shenton Thomas, the Governor of the Straits Settlements and High Commissioner for the Malay States, delayed evacuating British civilians because of the psychological impact an early evacuation might have on the Asian population. However, there were also logistical reasons for the delay, arising in part from confusion between military and civil administration. Percival later admitted that "what was provided was very inadequate throughout Malaya for the needs of the civil population".[7] For example, the number of air raid shelters constructed was insufficient, and while there were concerns over having too many air raid shelters as they were a natural breeding ground for mosquitoes and obstructed traffic, "perhaps with a little more determination and a little more expenditure of money some more adequate shelters could have been provided".[8] A blackout was also difficult to maintain, not only in a city like Singapore but also in the rest of Malaya, because it meant shutting out much needed ventilation or else living in the dark. Buoyed by false optimism, people did not see why they needed to endure such discomfort in the tropical heat. When Singapore experienced its first Japanese air raid, many people remember that the town was lighted up as usual.[9] Lt. Col. C.J. Verdon recalled that even the dockyard of Naval Base in Singapore was ablaze with lights when the first Japanese air attack took place.[10]

As British troops retreated towards Singapore and civilian refugees flowed into the city, European life in Singapore went on much as usual. People shopped and sipped afternoon tea, and in the evenings, they dined and danced under the bright lights of the Raffles Hotel. Dr Cicely Williams, who had escaped from Trengganu by desperate measures and travelled across mountains and jungles to reach Singapore, found the city a very "strange" place. She recalls that petrol was being sold freely and Europeans were keeping to their customs of siesta and afternoon tea, even as Japanese troops were preparing to attack. Sakakibara Masaharu, Staff Officer of the Southern Army in Saigon, wrote in his diary on 11 January that dance halls in Singapore were closed for five days after 7 December, but reopened from 13 December.[11] However, Mrs H.C. Reilly has protested against these criticisms. Responding to accusations that Europeans maintained a leisurely life style even after 8 December 1941, she claims there was a complete blackout in Singapore, and as for allegations that European residents continued with cocktail parties, dancing, golf and tennis: "Never was any statement more unjust!"[12]

A recorded interview with Mrs Colley found in the collection of the Imperial War Museum makes the point, "But we never of course thought, nobody dreamed or did say that Singapore would really — it's — I mean after all it was boasted as an impregnable fortress, we rather believed it."[13] Certainly *The Straits Times*, the premier English-language newspaper in Singapore, contributed to this illusion, publishing stories that underestimated the Japanese war potential and told readers that the British were superior to the Japanese. Percival thought that British prestige would be damaged if "native Asiatics" saw them scurrying to prepare defences against the Japanese, although he himself knew that Singapore was far from "impregnable" if war broke out in the Far East. Percival wrote after the war,

> Nevertheless, an atmosphere of unreality hung over Malaya. In the restaurants, clubs, and places of entertainment, peace-time conditions prevailed. Having just come from England, where austerity had already become the fashion, I must confess to rather an uncomfortable feeling when provided with an almost unlimited amount of food in the hotels and restaurants. In connection with food, committees had twice been appointed to draw up schemes for rationing of food in time of war but had reported that the difficulties were so great that food rationing was impracticable. Eventually a modified scheme was drawn up to cover European foodstuffs, but there was never any proper scheme for Asiatic foodstuffs.[14]

It is not clear whether Shenton Thomas was given full information about the war and grasped the situation correctly. Mrs Molly Reilly, a Cypher clerk at Government House from March 1939 to when Singapore fell, reported that the Governor came into her office on 6 December 1941 and said very solemnly:

> "Well, Mrs Reilly, I have got bad news for you. We are at War!"
> She said, "Well we've been expecting it for a long time now."
> He said, "Oh! But you didn't ask me with whom we were at war."
> She answered, "But of course, you mean Japan", at which he laughed and said, "Ha! I thought I would catch you — No, we are at war with Finland."
>
> As he walked away laughing, I called after him, "Oh! I thought you were going to prepare me to expect a Jap bomb on my head any moment."
>
> At that he returned and said, "What did you say! Japanese bombs in Singapore! You can take it from me there will never be a Japanese bomb dropped in Singapore — there will never be a Japanese set foot in Malaya."
>
> On Monday morning about 4 A.M., 8 December, the Japs bombed Singapore!!!!![15]

The order by the colonial government in Singapore to evacuate European civilians scattered across the entire Malay Peninsula came too late. Some of them were caught behind the battlefront because Japanese troops advanced with incredible speed. Others surrendered, or were captured and killed. Hugh C. Allan of Kuala Muda Estate, Sungai Patani — a member of the Kedah Volunteer Force — was captured at Ipoh. He was ambushed just north of Simpang Pulai, outside Ipoh, on 28 December 1941, along with Oliver Tyndale Powell of Paya Besar Estate, South Kedah, and Eddie Miller of United Patani Estate, Sungai Patani. Powell and Miller, who were both wounded, were interrogated by Japanese officers and then taken away; ten seconds later Allan heard sounds of them being killed. When he turned around, he saw a Japanese soldier wiping his bayonet on the grass. Allan was ordered by the Japanese officers to drive a car to Singapore, where he became a POW.[16] When Japanese troops landed at Patani, all Europeans in Yala district were assembled. There were 27 civilians including 4 European women. They were transported under Japanese guard to Pinyak, where most of the other Europeans in the district had been gathered. They stopped at Kampong Toh and were housed in one of nine bungalows there. The next day a high-ranking Japanese officer visited them, and separated three

Danes, a Pole and a Swede from the party. On the 12th, ten Indian soldiers who had been captured near the border were placed in the bungalow with them. That night the door was opened and a grenade thrown in, followed by two others. Eight members of the group survived, including Mrs van der Straaten, Harry Moor, a Scot, and de Boer, a South African. They hid in the jungle but gave themselves up on 25 February, after a tortuous journey, when they heard that Singapore had fallen. They were taken to Taiping jail where 38 prisoners were held in one room. Mrs van der Straaten, the only woman, was later moved to Kuala Lumpur.[17]

Some civilians, believing that the British would repulse the Japanese, and that victory was a mere few weeks away, hid in the jungle to wait. Two such people were Vincent Baker and his sister Nona. Vincent Baker was General Manager of the Pahang Consolidated Tin Mining Company, which operated the largest tin mine in the world at Sungei Lumbing, with around 8,000 workers. People in Sungei Lumbing called Vincent *tuan besar* (great master). This isolated tin mine was his mini fiefdom and was where he spent more than 30 years of his life. A British officer who visited him said that if the Japanese landed it would be impossible to defend the peninsula. Nevertheless, Vincent told his sister, "Perhaps a few weeks, six months at the longest. Singapore won't fall, and with their long lines of communications the Japs won't be able to last." On 29 December, three weeks after Japanese troops landed at Kota Bahru, Vincent received a telegram from the British Resident in Kuala Lipis ordering him to flood the mine. "For a time Vin was speechless; it was only then that he came face to face with the disintegration of his life's work."[18]

> As the night shift reached the surface, another day was just beginning; the early morning mist was clearing from the sky and to all appearances it was one of a thousand other beautiful tropical mornings. Suddenly the pumps stopped for the first time in over fifty years, the roar of the mill died down and Sungei Lembing lay in an uncanny silence as the sun touched the mountain tops. It was a deathly calm....[19]

Water filled the tunnels and flooded the entire mine. All the bags of tin had already been dumped down the bottom of the mine, and the stocks of fuel oil were dumped in the river. Vincent and Nona entered the jungle, dependent on a Chinese manager at the mine named Cheng Kam.

But the war did not proceed as Vincent Baker envisaged. In February 1943, two Chinese visited them bearing news that Cheng Kam had been threatened by another Chinese over delivering food to Vincent and Nona. To avoid endangering Cheng Kam further, Vincent and Nona went underground, seeking the protection of *orang bukit* (hill people), the guerrilla army of the Malayan Communist Party. They were also penniless, having spent the last of their money to pay Cheng Kam for his services. Vincent died in the jungle before the war ended but Nona survived, living in the jungle with the guerrillas who affectionately termed her Pai Naa, or White Nona.[20]

When the Japanese landed at Kota Bahru on 8 December, George A. de Moubray, the British Adviser to Trengganu, received a telephone call from his counterpart in Kelantan. Mrs de Moubray wrote in her diary that the British Adviser to Kelantan told her husband that war had begun.[21] Japanese troops were attacking on the beach of Kota Bahru. At the beginning, the news from Kelantan was all good, saying things like "The situation is well in hand." There was no information from Singapore. Dr Cicely Williams, who would later become commandant of the Civilian Women's Internment Camp in Changi, was working in Trengganu at the time. On 8 December, she turned on the radio and heard "… have landed at Kota Bahru and confused fighting is going on.…" De Moubray "asked Cicely to stand by the telephone, but no instructions came from anywhere".[22] Dr Williams and Mrs de Moubray, like many others, could not imagine a Japanese victory.[23] On 9 December, they began to receive indications that things were not going satisfactorily, but news reports still insisted that the situation was well in hand. An hour later, telephones in the north went dead. Mrs de Moubray wrote, "At about midday the British Adviser to Kelantan managed to connect with us from Kuala Krai, and he told us that they had had to evacuate Kota Bahru, and the 8th Brigade was falling back on Krai. This meant that our road out north was cut. From that moment the question of all Europeans abandoning the State had to be considered."[24] Mrs de Moubray, Dr Williams and the rest of the European community started their evacuation southwards, moving through the jungle, sailing down rivers and crossing mountains as they headed towards Singapore.

On 13 December, an evacuation order was issued to European residents in Penang. Evacuation had until then never even been a topic of conversation in Penang, and the order seemed completely absurd. Europeans there simply could not believe that British troops had failed to defend Kota Bahru against the Japanese, and had been forced into full retreat. On 14 December, European civilian women and children left for Singapore by boat and train, and British troops and the volunteer army followed two days later. The entire process was sudden and furtive. The wartime Malayan correspondent for the *Times*, Ian Morrison, wrote that, "the evacuation of Penang had a calamitous effect on the Malayan population as a whole", while other commentators said that "a message of defeatism and racial discrimination ... spread among Malayans".[25]

Prior to the evacuation, British civil servants and engineers in the country sent important documents and maps to Singapore, and destroyed much of what remained. But not all maps were saved from the enemy. First rate one-inch to one-mile maps, which had been printed in the Headquarters of the Survey Department in Kuala Lumpur, fell into Japanese hands. C. Noble of the Survey Department wrote, "I have seen captured Japanese Army maps used during the invasion of December 1941 which were, in fact, our own maps overprinted with Japanese characters."[26] The evacuation of the Survey Department was a highly strategic decision. The Department was printing maps right until the week before the invasion of Kuala Lumpur, attempting to meet the sudden increase in demand for maps brought on by the war. It completed 3,500 maps just on time. When the air raid on Kuala Lumpur began, nearly all of the 93 staff at the Survey Department fled, but five remained behind: Noble, Husband, Leckie, Irving and Sworder. As the city was being evacuated, looting began. Private homes, government offices, factories and shops were plundered. Looters carted off cars, machinery, furniture and whatever else they could carry. Noble and his companions packed maps, map materials, zinc plates and glass negatives along with anything else likely to be of use to the enemy into a car and left for Singapore on 7 January. None of them at that time "had any idea that Singapore would fall". In Singapore they encountered the reality of the situation on 11 February. "At 9 A.M., Bridges, who was then in the uniform of a Colonel R.E., called together all the available Europeans of the Department in Mt. Sophia. Having ordered the clerical staff out of the room, he said the news was very grave indeed and that nothing but a miracle could save Singapore. This news came as a very severe shock to all of us. Being the first time we had heard the true state of affairs." "We had not been told of the seriousness of the military situation and such information as was available from newspapers and the radio led us to believe that the Japanese would soon be thrown off the island."[27]

Crates of negatives and other mapping material were loaded on the *SS Ipoh* bound for Australia. Not a single Asian labourer could be found at the docks, so in addition to loading their own cargo, Noble and his colleagues had to assist in getting coal on board. The precious cargo left Singapore just before the island fell to the Japanese. A total of 71 packing cases weighing about eight tons reached Australia. Most of the cases contained fragile glass negatives, and when they were opened it was found that less than one per cent of them had broken.

Evacuees from the northern part of the peninsula flooded into the Kuala Lumpur train station. After the exhausting trip from their homes, they had to wait for hours for trains to Singapore. Josephine Foss, headmistress of Pudu English School, sent her girls "to the station to look after and feed the babies, see to any casualties and — with the help of the Salvation Army — supply meals".[28] Foss herself helped out at the General Hospital, where her job was to talk to the wounded, find out their names and write to their families. The transportation of casualties to Singapore had also started, and boarding school students were being evacuated. Kuala Lumpur was in chaos. Foss was one of the last civilian evacuees to leave the city, departing on 8 January. The British rearguard withdrew on 10 January and the Japanese entered the city on 11 January. In Singapore she started work as a volunteer at a casualty station in the city centre, and found accommodation at the Poh Leung Kuk home on York Hill. The name means "The Preserve of the Virtuous Establishment", and the building provided refuge for women and girls — prostitutes, girls in need of care and orphaned children. The Chinese Protectorate and the local community maintained similar facilities in each major Malayan town.[29] After the surrender of Singapore, the Japanese inspected the Poh Leung Kuk home and appropriated the prostitutes as "comfort girls" for the soldiers. Foss was moved to a boarding house in Katong to join other European women internees. From there she and the other European women were moved to Changi Prison.[30]

Civilian Women's Internment Camp in Changi Prison

Immediately following the British surrender, the Japanese interned more than 400 women in three seaside bungalows in Katong, one of them the property of the Sultan of Trengganu. Gladys G. Tompkins, a nurse, arrived there on 23 February. The house she was to occupy was large, of Chinese design, and had been wrecked and looted. Gladys and the other women had to spend a whole morning cleaning up just to make the house liveable.[31] Sheila Allan arrived with her mother on 28 February. They had not been given reliable information about where to go and had first reported to the Seaview Hotel. There they were told to go to Changi Prison, where they were told to go to Katong. The next morning they had to stand in a long queue for their breakfast.[32] Katherine de Moubray reached Katong on 2 March, and was interned in a "beach house" behind one of the bungalows.[33]

Freddy Bloom arrived on 4 March. She kept a diary in the form of letters to her husband, whom she had only recently married, although she knew the letters would never be posted. Assigned to a house with more than 130 other women, Bloom settled in a garage outside the house. While the houses in Katong were large for private dwellings, even three of them could not accommodate the large number of women and children sent there. She chose her roommates carefully: Katherine de Moubray, Kate Clarke and a woman named Ethel.³⁴

On 8 March, the women were ordered to march from Katong to Changi Prison. Young children, the elderly and the sick were provided with transport, but adults and children older than nine walked the nine miles to Changi Prison, starting at 10 a.m. The women were paraded in front of local "Asiatics", tottering with their heavy trunks in the strong tropical sun. As the exhausted party saw the prison gate they pulled themselves together and began singing "There'll always be an England", and the men already in the prison joined in. Thus began life in Changi Prison.³⁵

Changi Prison had been built by the British Royal Engineers in the mid-1930s to accommodate 600 Asian convicts.³⁶ Coincidentally, one of the internees, Dr Williams, was a cousin of the engineer John Farewell, who had overseen construction of the prison. When the 359 women and 61 children arrived, there were already 2,200 men there, so the total number of internees was 2,620, and the figure increased over the next five months to 2,800.³⁷

The Prison consisted of four blocks, starkly named A, B, C and D. Women were interned in the A block. A typical cell was "eight feet by twelve feet, each containing a cement block [called 'the slab' by internees] and an 'Asiatic' lavatory pan ['squatter']".³⁸ A total of 90 people — 43 women and 47 children — were placed in 18 cells, with three European women occupying a tiny cell originally designed for one convict. The prison building was made of concrete and iron, and had extremely small windows lined with iron bars high up on the walls. The cells were poorly ventilated, creating conditions that were almost unbearable in the hot and humid tropical weather, especially for the aged and the sick, and for children. The cells had no beds, furniture, mattresses, pillows or blankets. Everyone slept on the bare concrete floor. There was no hospital and no special rooms for the sick, apart from a makeshift sanatorium on a veranda. On 25 August 1942, commandants from both the women's and men's sections of Changi Civilian Internment Camp jointly submitted a petition on behalf of some 2,800 female and male internees to the Commander-in-Chief of the "Nipponese Army", asking for amelioration of camp conditions. Using examples from the *Shonan Times*, the petition compared the treatment of internees at Changi with that of internees in other countries. Internees in Manila, for example, were housed in the University of Santo Thomas, where 3,000 people occupied 64 acres, while in Changi Prison, 2,800 people occupied less than eleven acres of concrete buildings and exercise yards. Internees in Hong Kong were housed in villas, and those in Beijing in their own homes.[39]

At Changi, women and men were strictly segregated. Husbands and wives, children and parents were not allowed to see each other, and had to live without any information about their families. At a later date, "relatives" were allowed to see each other for thirty minutes a week, but initially this arrangement excluded wives and husbands as they were not considered relatives, a ruling that baffled the European internees. Josephine Foss wrote, "there was a great iron door on each landing of the prison, and there the poor women would sit and listen and tap to see if by any chance it was their husbands who were tapping back".[40] On the other side, as A.M. Duncan-Wallace wrote in his *Diary of a Civilian Internment in Singapore 1942–1945*, "I used to see poor unhappy men peering through bars in the hope of catching a fleeting glimpse of their wives, day in, day out."[41] To circumvent this policy of complete segregation for spouses, Miss Foss invented the "dustbin parade". Her job was to take the sick to the Japanese prison office everyday, and as she did that she always saw the same Englishman en route. She would ask him to pick a letter, say M, and the following morning all wives who surnames began with M would carry the dust bins into the central yard, and all husbands whose names began with M would be there to empty the bins. No one was allowed to speak, only to touch hands in handing over the dustbin and receiving it back empty.[42] Gladys Tompkins wrote in her diary on 21 September 1942, "Dustbin parade was quite a scream."[43] The internees perfected this scheme to a fine art. Iris G. Parfitt, who published wonderful sketches of her own experience of life in the internment camp in *Jail-Bird Jottings*, wrote about Miss Foss's good work, "No meeting of any kind was allowed between relatives for a long time. Then they were (half an hour a week) for relatives other than husbands and wives! However, Miss J. Foss, Camp Superintendent did good work by carrying notes and messages when ostensibly taking over shoe repairs."[44]

The immediate objective of the Japanese army after landing in northern Malaya was to attack Singapore. They were not prepared to deal with the large number of POWs and civilian internees who fell into their hands, and immediately after the fall of Singapore had to face the serious task of providing accommodation, three daily meals and sanitation facilities for more than 100,000 captives. In the Changi Civilian Internment Camp, internees were given partial control over camp affairs. Each block elected its own commandant and deputy commandant, and chose a member for the central committee that represented all four blocks. Each floor elected a superintendent. Each block also organised committees for health, food, finance, labour, gardening, education, sanitation, entertainment and so on.

Block A elected Dr Elenor Hopkins as its Commandant, and also organised several committees. Miss Foss was in charge of labour. The armband she wore, which bears the Japanese character for labour, is now exhibited in the Imperial War Museum in London. Iris Parfitt was the chairperson of the Entertainment Committee and played a key role in staging all kinds of entertainment in camp. Capitalising on the variety of ages, races, nationalities, professions and social backgrounds of the internees, she put on magnificent entertainments that were remembered as a great source of encouragement, joviality and humour. With the cooperation of her fellow internees, Parfitt succeeded in uncovering the women's hidden abilities and sent out a fortifying message. The entertainment these women provided varied from classical concerts, piano recitals, theatre performances, ballet, comedy, lectures, exhibitions, contests, competitions and even circuses! A woman named Palmar, whose family was in the circus business, taught circus skills to some of the other women, and they presented a show that was so successful it became legendary amongst both female and male internees.[45] A dwarf was impersonated by Ms McKenzie, an orang-utan by Ms Kirkbride, the fat woman was played by Ms Trixie Augur, the half-man half-woman by Judy, the bearded woman by Jefferies. The clowns were Freddy Bloom and Ms Williams, the horse trainer Marion Williams, and the trainers of acrobatic of dogs and seals were Helen and Ms Rank. The circus was hilarious beyond imagination. Spectators were thrown into convulsions of laughter. Performances took place in the central area and were seen by men and women alike.

There had been about 20,000 European civilians resident in Malaya when the war began, the majority of them male Englishmen. Half of them lived in Singapore. Many were civil servants working for the colonial government in fields such as administration, law, education, economy and security. In a sense, the whole of the colonial society moved into the internment camp. Shenton Thomas was there, so were the civil servants, engineers, doctors, university professors, lawyers, artists, accountants, journalists, businessmen, planters, miners, merchants, cooks, waiters, entertainers, policemen and even warders who had worked in Changi Prison before the war.

According to the original Register of Changi Internment Camp, nearly half of the women internees were housewives. Among the rest, the most common professions were nursing, teaching, secretarial or stenographic work, Salvation Army officer, telephone operator and medical doctor.

The original Register of Changi Internment Camp is preserved in the Imperial War Museum in London.[46] It was created when new internees arrived from various places in Malaya after March 1942. The first group of women and children interned at Changi Prison numbered 369 women and 61 children. The book consists of the following parts:

1. Male internees;
2. Female internees;
3. Child internees;
4. Changes, amendments, corrections, increases and decreases in personnel.

There is one page missing from the female internees' section. The following chart (Table 1) on the first group of female and children internees

Table 1: Professions of Female Internees in Changi Civilian Women's Internment Camp

Housewives	180	Masseur	1
Housewives / nurses	13	Ambulance service	1
Housewives / teachers	6	Missionaries	2
Housewives/singing teacher	1	Salvation Army officers	2
Housewives/teacher (retired)	1	Teachers	21
Housewives/telephone operators	2	School mistresses	2
Housewives/dressmaker	1	Riding instructor	1
Housewives/typist	1	Music teacher	1
Housewives/ boarding house	1	Dog trainer	1
Housewives/chemist	1	Boarding house	2
No occupation	25	Hotel manager	1
Doctors (39)	5	Artist	1
Matrons	9	Stenographers	4
Nurses	58	Secretaries	6
Midwife	1	Buyer	1
Health Service	1	Hairdressers	2
X-ray engineer	2	Students	9
Physical Therapist	1	Governor's wife	1
Medical Officer	1		

Source: *Register of Internees in Changi Camp, 1942*, Imperial War Museum.

was made from the original Register.[47] According to the Register, 45 per cent of women were housewives, 34.4 per cent were working women, and 7.3 per cent were working housewives; 6.8 per cent did not indicate a profession.

The ethnicities and nationalities, as indicated by the women included British, Australian, Canadian, New Zealand, Eurasian, Armenian, Greek, Polish, Spanish, Irish, American, Chinese, Burmese, Thai, Javanese, Dutch, Malay, Czech, German, French, Tamil, Iraqi, Turkish, Japanese and Jewish. Iris Parffitt noted, "Japanese internment rules were quite incomprehensible. The only unchangeable rule seemed to be that nothing wiped out the stain of British birth. Women of any other nationality married to British husbands became automatically British. Thus German, Burmese, Javanese, Japanese, Dutch, etc., all were interned as British. But British women married to Germans, Japanese and Chinese or men of any nationality, were also interned as British."[48] Parfitt also mentioned that there were 630 internees at the beginning, among them about 250 Europeans and 380 Eurasians including children. "Less than a dozen European children were interned", she observed.[49] Sheila Allan was a Eurasian internee. Daughter of an Australian father and Thai mother, Sheila herself was classified as Eurasian while her Thai mother was listed as English. One Japanese internee appears in the Register. She was classified as English under the name of Olive Barton, and her husband was W.R. Barton, perhaps a civilian. Her contact name and her address are those of her husband, but a footnote reading "Japanese by birth" reveals her true ethnicity. Beneath her English name, her Japanese name, Yamamoto, was scribbled with a pencil in Japanese. Gladys Tompkins also wrote that there were about 405 women and children internees at the beginning, of whom only 250 were "pure British".[50]

Around Christmas of 1943, more than a hundred women and children of Czech, Dutch, German, French, Tamil, Eurasian, Malay, Javanese, Brazilian, Turkish and Iraqi origins joined the internees. By the end of 1943, the number of internees were 527 women and 116 children. In March 1942, there were 2,600 internees in Changi Internment Camp and in 1945, the number had reached 4,511. In March 1945, about 700, mostly Jewish and Eurasian women and children from Singapore, Penang and Seremban arrived. Needless to say, having women of so many different customs and cultures living closely in an overcrowded prison gave rise to a lot of difficulties. A cartoon, by Parfitt, entitled "Misfortune Makes Strange Bedfellows", illustrated a complicated situation which arose from having so many different nationalities living together in a small space. She drew a Chinese girl adopted by an Irish mother, a child of a Scot and a Thai, a

Malay woman, a Burmese woman, an Iraqi woman wearing a veil, and a black woman dubbed "A little Bit of Scotch Black Label".[51] She particularly lampooned non-white women who were categorised as British through marriage. When Red Cross condensed milk was distributed, Dr Hopkins wrote about the great fuss made by mothers over how the milk was rationed. "Some black and tans have five or seven children with all the extras given — no doubt they are living well and look fat and well here."[52]

In spite of all the hardships they faced, the women in camp sought to establish a sense of normality. Women with professional training, such as doctors, matrons, school mistresses, teachers, nurses, missionaries and wives of colonial civil servants organised committees, established regulations, negotiated with the Japanese and generally ran the camp. Besides basic household chores such as cleaning, cooking, and washing, the committees did many other things. Five doctors and nurses set up a hospital and received patients, although facilities and medicines were extremely poor.[53] School teachers set up a school and a library, and started classes for children. Vegetables were cultivated in the prison garden. The Entertainment Committee was particularly active, organising classes in French, Malay, Japanese and Dutch, dancing, singing, handicraft and painting. They also put on a series of lectures in which women spoke about their areas of specialisation and their experiences. There were contests for short stories, poetry, painting, handicraft and Christmas cards, along with poetry readings, fashion shows, concerts, recitals and plays ranging from Shakespeare to slapstick comedy. For her short story, "Motherless Aileen", Sheila Allan got a special prize — a can of white peaches. According to Allan's diary, her story was picked from amongst the following entries:

> Section (a) Short Stories: there were 26 serious, 8 humorous, 2 detective and 3 ghost stories;
> Section (b) Essays: there were 11 serious and 3 light;
> Section (c) Verse: there were 25 serious and 28 light;
> Section (d) Plays: there were 14 one-act plays.

This means that the women internees, who numbered less than 360, generated an amazing 120 entries.[54] Gladys Tompkins also got a prize — one pound of tea — for handmade Christmas cards.[55]

From 1943, the lecture series were started by lecturers from the men's camp which women were permitted to attend. This provided comfort beyond words for internees starved of intellectual stimulation and pleasure. Women were allowed to listen to the men's orchestral performance and the men's chorus once or twice a month. Unfortunately, these modest pleasures and occasions for human contact were short lived. They were prohibited completely after the Double Tenth incident in October 1943, when the only piano in Changi Prison was also seized. A piano given as a present to Lady Thomas remained in Sime Road Internment Camp, but it was left in an uncovered corridor, exposed to the wind and rain, and was ruined.

It was a struggle just to survive in the overcrowded camp. Basic functions like eating, working, reading, thinking or sleeping became difficult. Apart from the heat, internees faced infestations of mosquitoes, cockroaches and bed bugs, and jarring noises from concrete floors and walls, iron staircases and human voices at all hours of the day and night. Depression and fatigue were common, and some women lost hope, while others became apathetic or fell ill. Nerves were constantly on edge, and the movements of strangers and the incessant noise frayed tempers. One question dominated everyone's thoughts — "when will this end?" Rumours flew around constantly, causing emotions to fluctuate between joy and despair. Most were groundless, but sometimes a rumour turned out to be genuine news received secretly from the men's camp, where a secret radio received news from outside, or brought in from the outside world. Internees' diaries record many of the rumours that circulated, which varied from "the war situation is going in our favour", to "America attacked Japan", "there will be exchange of prisoners", "Red Cross' ration will be delivered today", "meat or butter or sugar or coffee will be distributed tomorrow". Although the women knew that these rumours were mostly baseless, they nevertheless listened eagerly.

The internees were kept busy. They had to collect garbage, clean the building, run the hospital, care for the sick and elderly, operate a school for the children, tend the vegetable garden and carry out repairs. There were many disputes, and trifles could escalate into serious disputes. For example, one young girl kept a dog. To her, the dog was an irreplaceable friend, essential to her survival in this wretched camp, but to others it was a noisy, dirty, smelly creature that should be removed. The issue was put to a vote and the girl won by a narrow margin, but when the food situation became desperate, the dog was taken from her.

Food was a major problem. A petition submitted to the Japanese Supervisor of Changi Prison Internment Camp by the Central Committee of the men's and women's camps on 25 August 1942 drew a stark comparison between the Japanese ration scale for Changi camp and that used by the British for Japanese, European and Asiatic internees.[56] A post-war report by Dr R.A. Pallister stated that the food supplied by the Japanese in Changi was "adequate in quantity, or in food essential to maintain the internees in reasonable health".[57] However, European women and children were unaccustomed to rice as a staple food. Initially some of them could not eat it and threw it away. Instead they consumed canned food or eggs, coconuts, cooking oil, palm sugar and cakes purchased from the camp shop, but supplies of these foods soon ran out. Meals often consisted of little more than meagre quantities of boiled rice, and malnutrition gave rise to deficiency diseases among the internees. People began eating rubber seeds, and by the end of the war the Central Committee was seriously considering breeding snails as a supplementary source of protein.

Table 2: Changi Prison Internment Camp Ration Scale

	Japanese Rations Scale for British Internees	British Rations Scale for Japanese Internees	British Prison Diet for Europeans	British Prison Diet for Other Asiatics
Rice	500	453.5 + 113 for morning congee	340	454
Wheat flour	50		57	
Bread		113	454	113
Dhall				57 per week
Sugar	20	14	28	
Salt	5	28	14	28
Tea	5	14	7	7
Milk	15		57	
Cooking oil	5			
Coconut oil				43
Lard		42.5	28	
Butter			28	
Curry stuff			28	28
Soya sauce				As required
Meat	50	113 four days a week	227	113
Fish		85		85
Vegetable	100	340	283	340
Jam		57		
Cheese		57		
Egg		6 eggs a week	2 eggs per week	
Cigarettes	40 sticks per month			

Note: Figures in grams unless otherwise indicated.

Source: Henry Miller, "Changi Prison Internment Camp", 67/194/5, Imperial War Museum.

Civilian Women's Internment Camp Newspaper: *POW WOW*

In addition to creating their own command structure and running the camp, the women also published *POW WOW*, which provided entertainment and intellectual stimulation for internees and gave them a channel for airing disagreements and discussing issues. It allowed women to recover their dignity or forget for a while their distress and anxiety.

When the war began, Freddy Bloom was a reporter based in Singapore. Born in New York, she had spent three years at Barnard College before transferring to Trinity College in Dublin. Her first marriage was brief and tragic: she was just 26 when her husband died in Penang. In August 1940 the young widow found work with the Malaya Tribune in Singapore, and there she met Philip Bloom, a British doctor serving with the Royal Army Medical Corps. When Japanese air raids started in the early morning of 8 December, the building that housed the *Malaya Tribune* was bombed. Freddy then became an assistant nurse in the General Hospital, helping treat the hundreds of bomb victims, both military and civilian. Wards were overflowing and the corridors were packed. The American Consul advised her to leave, saying it was just a matter of time before Singapore fell. On 6 February, Freddy's 28th birthday, Philip Bloom left work for half an hour and they were married between air raids at the Registry Office.[58] Nine days later Singapore fell and they were interned separately for the next three and a half years.

On 29 March 1942, Dr Hopkins, one of the camp commanders, and Dr Williams approached Freddy and asked her to produce a camp newspaper. Freddy agreed, naming the newspaper *The Changi POW WOW*. Freddy explained the name in an editorial she wrote for the first issue, which appeared on 1 April 1942: "We chose it partly because we liked the idea of a very informal literary get together and partly because we could not resist the feeble pun. To those quibblers who will point out that we are not POWs but internees we say that as long as we are incarcerated in a gaol we are prisoners. And that is all there is to it."[59] She also wrote in her Editorial, "Here are more than four hundred women and children in a rotten situation. They have lost everything that is dear to them and are now herded in a fortress of ugliness. There is no comfort, no beauty, no privacy. Undoubtedly no matter how long it might last it is only an interlude but an interlude of hell. There should be something devoted wholeheartedly and solely to the well-being and happiness of these women."[60] The men's camp also had a newspaper. The first issue was published on 19 February 1942, just two days after male civilians had been interned following the surrender on 15 February, under the title the *Karikal Chronicle*. A number of the male internees were professional journalists, and contributions came thick and fast.[61] The men's side also had many other professionally trained male internees and these included doctors who organised the camp hospital, a chef from Empress of Asia who cooked for the internees and police officers who started an informal camp police force, wearing white armbands as their badge. Administrators and engineers took charge of health, hygiene, education, building and public work.

There were far fewer professionals among the women internees. The names of *POW WOW* staff and their former occupations were:

Committee Notes: Dr E. Hopkins, Camp Representative and
Liaison Officer;

Church Notes: Georgina White, Hospital Matron;

Entertainment News: Betty;

Educational Series: Margaret Williams, Housewife;

Weekly Puzzle Page: Lisa Hunt;

Poems: Edith L. Rattray or Helen Beck, both Housewives

Sketches: Iris Parfitt, School Mistress;

Children's Number: Joan Stanley-Carry, Housewife, Teacher;

My Stars!: The prophet series "My Stars!" is written by the
Old Squaw, who insisted upon remaining incognito;

Collecting, Typing and Compiling: Constance Sleep, Housewife,
Toby Williams;

Article, Fillers: Freddy Bloom, Editor.[62]

Only 5 of the 13 *POW WOW* staff members had professional backgrounds. Without their husbands or "bosses", these women were initially at a loss and felt powerless. Over time, however, the absence of men made the women internees think, plan, decide and act by themselves. While the purpose of *POW WOW* was to provide entertainment and intellectual stimulation for the women and create some sense of cohesion within the camp, it also served a practical function. It was used to organise the camp, establish ground rules, distribute information and discuss various issues as they arose.

Issues of *POW WOW* typically included information of the following sort:

1. *Editorial*
2. *Committee News*

"Information from the Central Committee and Women's Committee, official notice from the Japanese commandant, the answers to the petition letters from the Central Committee. For example, 'CC required to increase more vegetable and milk'. Lieut. Okazaki promised, as the vegetable position was improving, to supply a larger quantity as soon as it was possible to make arrangement with the Japanese Army, also he would try to get further supplies of fresh meat. Milk is very scarce and present tin supplies were available only to children, old people and the sick, but he was also trying to obtain fresh milk." (6/5/42) "CC required communication between wives and husbands. Okazaki answered that it was strictly prohibited. He, however, promised to endeavour to obtain permission for communication." (6/5/42) "Japanese High Command issued the order that black out regulations were to be strictly observed between 8:30 P.M. and 7:30 A.M. The long hours of the black out have apparently created a demand for more entertainment in the camp. A piano sent in by Lieut. Okazaki for our use." (20/5/42) "Notice of three new born babies." (29/7/42) "Lieut. Okazaki handed over the command of the Camp to Mr Asahi Itoshi of Syonan Municipality. Mr Asahi addressed the meeting and stated that the change in command indicated that the civilian authorities were taking over the charge of the Camp in place of Military." (2/9/42) "Complaints on sanitary grounds against the dogs." (14/10/42) "Two new babies." (18/11/42) And so on.

3. *Church News*

Table 3 shows the number of people affiliated with various churches. *Church News* started from issue no. 17 (22/7/42) and continued till the final issue, No. 28 (15/10/43). Worship service became an important function at the women's camp after male ministers were allowed to officiate Sunday service.

4. *Fashion*

The women were hungry for beautiful things, and fashion shows in the camp were always popular. Women produced various ideas for dresses and hats. In one issue, Parfitt published "Fashion Hint", which featured drawings of shorts (29/4/42), while another illustration, called "Taking a walk in Changi", showed hat designs. (13/5/42) Her sketches were always humorous. In June, she drew sketches of handmade chairs in Changi (17/6/42), in July it was shoes. European women in the tropics were accustomed to wearing delicate sandals, but in Changi Prison their shoes were old and broken. (1/7/42)

Table 3

Church of England	180	United Church of Canada	1
Presbyterian & Church of Scotland	27	Christian Science	1
Roman Catholic	67	Theosophist	1
Methodist	7	Swedenborgian	1
Salvation Army	3	Quaker	1
Congregational	2	Russian Orthodox	1
Dutch Protestant	4	Jewish	2
Armenian	6	Buddhist	1
Seven Day Adventist	1	Unspecified	79
Brethren	1		

Occasionally the women were allowed to bathe in the sea, a precious opportunity to leave their concrete cells and enjoy the sunshine, wind, smell of the sea and the cool water. In August 1942, Parfitt sketched beachwear in the style of Maison Changi! (19/8/42)

5. *Education*

Classes for school children started on 24 February 1942. There were 29 teachers for 32 children. (22/4/42) There were also classes for adults covering stenography, French, Malay, Dutch, Japanese, poetry, carolling, contract bridge and other subjects.

6. *Lectures*

Many lectures were organised. After male lecturers were allowed to give lectures in the women's camp, the themes of lectures increased in variety. Some of the topics covered are shown below:

1. Character of the Chinese
2. Radiography
3. Jungle Walk
4. Work of the Red Cross
5. On India
6. Trengganu Today
7. Health Work in Trengganu
8. Girls Reformatory Experience 1910–18
9. War Time Cities
10. Poets in Gaol
11. Pioneer Welfare Work
12. Pioneer Maternity and Child Welfare

13. Work in Singapore
14. Great Flood of Malaya
15. On Tunis
16. International Postal System
17. American Literature
18. Women's Rights in the Legal System
19. Classic Architecture
20. Evolution of Mankind
21. Portuguese Navigation and Discovery
22. How to Choose a House
23. Hinduism
24. Style of Furniture
25. Development of Archaeology
26. Better Understanding of the Bible
27. Birds of Malaya
28. Judaism
29. West Indies
30. From Baghdad to Peshawar
31. Social Change During the Past Hundred Years

7. *Entertainment*

POW WOW contained announcements of recitals, concerts, dances, variety shows, poetry readings and theatrical productions (among them *Rain and Wind, French Without Tears*, and the *Merchant of Venice*). There were also parties for children, Christmas parties, fancy dress parties, magic shows, circuses and fashion shows.

8. *Literature*

POW WOW carried short stories and poems.

9. *Serial Publications*

Articles on a variety of subjects ranging from Astronomy to the "History of Malaya" appeared in instalments.

10. *"Rumour"*

"Rumour" was a humorous, teasing feature that was purely for entertainment. One issue's "Rumour" read as follows: "This week's best rumour: All the fat ladies are being sent to Tokyo to show how well-fed Nipponese Internees are. Send in your pet rumours of the week, please." (26/8/42)

11. *Horoscope and Oneiromancy*

These features were hugely popular among the women, who seized on even the faintest hint of hope for the future and derived a great sense of satisfaction from the explanations of dreams.

12. *Competitions*

POW WOW supported many competitions, reported their results and wrote critiques. There were contests in areas such as dance, designing shoes, making Christmas cards, painting, poetry writing, short story writing, script writing and, in the men's camp, who had the best moustache and tattoo. (Men's camp, 26/8/42)

13. *Reviews*

POW WOW published critiques on the exhibitions, contests, concerts and theatrical performances held in Changi Prison.

14. *Bridge and Mahjong*

These games were very popular in camp, and almost every issue carried an article on bridge.

15. *Birthday Announcements*

Each issue carried birthday congratulations. People celebrating their birthdays in camp invited friends to parties. Cards and small gifts were hand made, and guests received tea and small home made cakes.

16. *Obituaries*

In the civilian camps, 29 people died in 1942, 26 in 1943, 79 in 1944 and 39 in 1945. Life in Changi Prison and Sime Road Camp was difficult, especially for the elderly. There were no medicines and nutrition was poor. Many old people could not cope with the harsh conditions and some lost the will to live.

17. *Advertisements*

POW WOW published advertisements for things that people wanted to buy or sell. For example, there were requests from women wishing to purchase a black skirt, blue or black woollen yarn, a dressing gown, brown or white shirts, short pants, blue woollen yarn for a baby's shoes, a washable dress and a porcelain tea cup with a saucer. Items for sale included shoes, white cloth and Dunlop shoes.

Some issues carried Japanese censorship stamps. On 2 December 1942 and again on 24 February 1943, four lines were deleted, on 1 June 1943, nine lines.[63] The final edition, published on 15 October 1943, made no mention of recent events in Changi Internment Camp: the roll call, investigation and subsequent arrests by the Military Police in connection with the so-called Double Tenth Incident. One week after this issue *POW WOW* appeared, Freddy Bloom was seized by the Military Police. The date was 22 October, and her arrest marked the end of *POW WOW*.

The Double Tenth Incident

At 8.15 in the morning on 10 October 1943 — the tenth day of the tenth month of the year — all internees, women and men, were ordered to parade in the central square of the prison. There was no explanation, and the atmosphere was tense. The whole area was surrounded by the Japanese Military Police with fixed bayonets. All entrances were closed. Every woman was searched and each cell was thoroughly examined, a process that continued until 6 o'clock in the evening. The women stood in the scorching sun without any water or food from morning. Several women fainted. Dr Hopkins repeatedly demanded that the Military Police move the old people and the sick into the shade, and the Japanese eventually agreed to allow them to have coffee.

From the women's camp, Dr Cicely Williams, Freddy Bloom and Mrs D. Nixon were arrested. From that day on, all entertainment was prohibited and camp life became extremely restrictive. Women could no longer listen to records, boil water for tea or bake biscuits. Contact between the women's and men's camps ceased for some months. Joseph Kennedy wrote, "The shadow of the affair of the 'Double Tenth' seemed to hang over Changi for a long period and, in mid-February 1944 Mrs Sleep was noting we have never been free of the Gestapo since last October. Some of them were left in the building and they watch us day and night."[64]

The clampdown in camp was a reaction to sabotage operations against Japanese shipping in Singapore's harbour. In August 1943, a Japanese military vessel anchored in Singapore harbour caught fire, and on 28 September a cargo boat and six oil tankers were blown up. These attacks were carried out by a small group of British and Australian officers, led by Captain Lyon in Australia, who had sailed a fishing boat into the region, but the Japanese

Military Police blamed the British soldiers who had infiltrated Johor. They believed that civilian internees were involved in these subversive activities, in collaboration with local residents. Several considerations led the Military Police to these conclusions. First, the internees included many people who had worked as administrators, engineers, financial experts, policemen and doctors before the war, and had the necessary skills to plan and execute such attacks. Second, a number of internees had close relationships with the local people, and some of them had brought substantial sums of money into the camp when they were interned. Third, because the camp administration was left largely to the internees, there were opportunities for them to conspire against the Japanese. Lastly, the internees were able to get hold of money through the prison black market. At the beginning of the internment, a camp shop had been opened with the permission of the Japanese for the sale of sweets, cigarettes and so on, but this operation was soon dwarfed by the prison's black market mini-economy. In the men's camp, a large number of internees worked outside the camps and brought back things to sell. At one stage, internees were bribing guards and bringing in goods by the truckload.[65] The overall camp situation also seemed conducive to anti-Japanese activity, particularly after the Sikhs replaced Japanese as camp guards in 1942, reducing direct Japanese control over the internment camps.

In the spring of 1943, the tide of war began to turn against the Japanese. The food situation in Malaya and Singapore deteriorated and prices skyrocketed. People in Singapore suffered from the lack of food and goods, and gross inflation. The British army had begun a campaign to penetrate Malaya, and anti-Japanese propaganda was spreading among the local people. Rumours abounded of the British army's imminent return. The Japanese Military Police were convinced that sabotage and anti-Japanese activities were being fomented by the former masters of the colony. It was just a matter of time, the Military Police felt, before the culprits in Changi Civilian Internment Camp were unearthed. The Kempeitai found a radio receiving set in a prison cell, but they were convinced that the internees were hiding a transmitter. Between 10 October 1943 and 12 April 1944, 57 internees were arrested by the Kempeitai, including the three women.[66] In the town, local civilians were also arrested. They were detained in one of three locations: the ex-YMCA building, Central Police Headquarters or a building on Smith Street. Interrogation and torture by the Kempeitai started immediately.

Cells were 3.5 by 5.2 metres, and the Japanese crammed sixteen people into each cell, mixing European and local detainees. The Japanese had strictly forbidden contact between women and men in the internment camp, even between husbands and wives, but now placed them in embarrassingly close proximity. Freddy was put in a men's cell to humiliate her, and when she "looked through the bars across into the cell facing us ... Fifteen men looked back." The cell had a toilet in one corner. "It was European but strangely different. It had no seat and instead of a chain or plug it had an ordinary tap from which the flow of water could be controlled." They had to sit on the floor all the time with their feet crossed and their hands on their laps. They could not lean against the wall. After long time Freddy spoke to the sentry and tried to explain that she wanted to "be excused". He said "If the woman wants to wash, drink or pass water, there is a WC in corner." When she got up and walked to the corner, she reflected, "I could feel each of those men retire within himself in his effort to give me a privacy that was not there."[67] They were not allowed to have towels, soap or handkerchiefs. Bright lights were kept on all night, and they heard the sounds of blows and the shrieks of tortured prisoners day and night. Torture victims were thrown back into their cells, often unconscious and covered in blood, with broken bones and pieces of skin torn off. "One man died after being brought back; he had had no medical attention and his body was not removed for several hours. In these conditions, and in this atmosphere of terror, men and women waited for their summons, at any hour of the day or night, sometimes for months. Driven to breaking point, two of the men tried to commit suicide. One jumped out of a window."[68] Freddy was interrogated but was not tortured, although she was once socked on the jaw by a guard and the blow sent her clear across the room. After the ordeal, she fell ill and suffered repeated heart attacks. When she was released and sent back to Changi Prison, she was near death.

Conclusion

Many details of life in Changi Civilian Women's Internment Camp are revealed in internees' diaries, letters, reports, interviews and *POW WOW*. One thing that remains unclear is the relationship between European and non-European women. Parfitt caricatured non-European women cynically in her cartoons, and was critical of Japanese methods for designating a person's nationality. The diaries of other women, such as Tompkins, contain very few critical comments on non-Europeans. It appears that there was little interaction between the races. European internees at Changi were mostly middle class. As members of a suzerain nation, they had internalised colonialism and held typically colonial attitudes.

There is no doubt, however, that internment changed them. Women, who previously totally depended on their husbands and bosses, elected their own representatives, organised committees and decided everything. While professional women such as doctors, nurses and teachers were accustomed to showing initiative, for ordinary women, internment provided an opportunity to discover their own abilities, achieve many things and assume leadership in various areas. They organised themselves, created their own newspaper, solved problems, settled disputes, injected beauty and laughter into their deprived lives, and made an effort to maintain some semblance of normality. English women tried to maintain the minutiae of their lives before the war, such as elevenses and playing bridge; they baked "cakes" and invited friends over for afternoon tea or a birthday party, and even if the "tea" was just hot water, they might insist on drinking it from a cup with a saucer. Some women continued to use make up, now not to please or attract men since there were none around, but to satisfy themselves. Such things raised their spirits. They might also dress for dinner — changing clothes, combing their hair and applying lipstick — even though dinner was often eaten without tables or chairs, proper tableware or even cutlery. By learning to do things not for somebody else but to please themselves, they gained much-needed encouragement and a boost in self confidence. Reflecting on the experience years later, many internees said that they had discovered their independence, their own strength and a will to survive. Previously, women had not paid much attention to other women. They bored each other with gossip and small talk about their husbands, children and servants. During internment, women began to notice other women, seeing them as independent, and extremely strong and capable. Strong bonds were formed and long after these women had left the Changi Civilian Women's Internment Camp, they said they maintained the same degree of respect for their fellow internees that they had built up during their incarceration.[69]

Notes

1. A.E. Percival, *The War in Malaya* (London: Eyre and Spottiswoode, 1949), pp. 304–5, "On the British side the total number of officers and men who took part in the campaign (excluding the Royal Navy and the Royal Air Force) was a little over 125,000, though the strength in Malaya at any one time was considerably less than this. This number included a large proportion of command, base and lines of communication troops, many of whom belonged to

non-combatant units or were unarmed owing to shortage of personal weapons. At the time of the capitulation the total of British forces in the Singapore fortress area was in the neighbourhood of 85,000, but this again included a large number of administrative troops, some of them non-combatant and all inadequately trained for a fighting role, and also the very poorly trained reinforcements which had recently arrived. We never at any time had more than one squadron of obsolescent light tanks." Peter Elphick, "The Malaya Command Forces", in *Singapore: The Pregnable Fortress* (London: Hodder & Stoughton, 1995), pp. 185–6.

2.   Freddy Bloom, *Dear Philip: A Diary of Captivity, Changi 1942–45* (London: The Bodley Head, 1980), p. 34; Sally Craddock, *Retired Except on Demand: The Life of Dr Cicely Williams* (Oxford: Green College, 1983), p. 103; Mrs K.M. de Moubray, typewritten diary donated to the Imperial War Museum (henceforth IWM), London, entry on Tuesday 31 March 1942; Weekly *POW WOW*, IWM. Dr Hopkins and Dr Williams were medical doctors, and each of them spent time as Commandant of the Civilian Women's Internment Camp.

3.   Percival, *The War in Malaya*, pp. 1–24.

4.   Ibid., p. 75.

5.   Ibid., p. 80.

6.   Elphick, *Singapore: The Pregnable Fortress*, p. 275.

7.   Percival, *The War in Malaya*, p. 76.

8.   Ibid.

9.   Ibid., pp. 83–4.

10. Elphick, *Singapore: The Pregnable Fortress*, p. 273.

11. Sakakibara Masaharu, *Ichi-Chui no Tonan-Ajia Gunnsei Nikki* (Diary of the Southeast Asian Military Administration by a First Lieutenant) (Tokyo: Soshisha, 1998), p. 37.

12. BAM XII/24, Cambridge University Library, p. 5.

13. Interview tape of Mrs Colley, Reel I, IWM.

14. Percival, *The War in Malaya*, p. 83.

15. Reilly, BAM XII/24, Cambridge University Library, p. 1.

16. Harry Miller, *On the Road to Singapore — With the Nips*, IWM 67/194/5, pp. 1–5.

17. Miller, *Massacre at Kampong Toh. How 19 Died In Mine Bungalow*, IWM 67/194/5, pp. 1–4; Joseph Kennedy, *British Civilians and the Japanese War in Malaya and Singapore, 1941–45* (London: Macmillan, 1987), pp. 108–9.

18. Dorothy Thatcher and Robert Cross, *Pai Naa: The Story of Nona Baker* (London: Constable, 1959), p. 25.

19. Ibid.

20. Ibid. An Australian soldier named Arthur Shephard lived through the war with Nona. He was badly wounded and with three other injured men had been left in the jungle. He survived with the help of the Chinese Communist guerrillas. Iain Finlay, *Savage Jungle: An Epic Struggle for Survival* (East Roseville, NSW and New York: Simon and Schuster, 1991); Kennedy, *British Civilians and the Japanese War*, pp. 104–21.

21. de Moubray, Diary, pp. 1–23.

22. Craddock, *Retired Except on Demand*, p. 87.
23. de Moubray, Diary, p. 1.
24. Ibid., p. 2.
25. Kennedy, *British Civilians and the Japanese War*, p. 22.
26. C. Noble, *The Evacuation of Malayan Survey Department Military Maps and Mapping Material from Singapore to Australia*. MSS.Ind.Ocn., s.199.200, Rhodes House Library, Oxford, p. 1.
27. Ibid., pp. 5–6.
28. J.M. Gullick, *Josephine Foss and the Pudu English School, A Pursuit of Excellence* (Kuala Lumpur: Pelanduk Publications, 1988), p. 112.
29. Ibid., pp. 113–4.
30. Ibid., p. 114.
31. Miss G. Tompkins, *Diary Kept by Gladys Tompkins While in Changi Prison*, p. 9, and *Three Wasted Years, Women in Changi Prison* (Hamilton, NZ: Tompkins, 1977).
32. Sheila Allan, *Diary of a Girl in Changi, 1941–45* (Australia: Kangaroo Press, 1994), pp. 35–6.
33. de Moubray, Diary, p. 8.
34. Bloom, *Dear Philip*, p. 15.
35. Gullick, *Josephine Foss*, p. 115; Tompkins, *Diary*, p. 11, 8 Mar. entry.
36. Craddock, *Retired Except on Demand*, p. 100. Dr Williams recalled that the original capacity of Changi prison was 700. Miss Foss wrote that the capacity was 600; Gullick, *A Pursuit of Excellence*, p. 115. The petition letter submitted by the Joint Committee to the Japanese Director of Changi Prison on 25 Aug. 1942 stated that 2,800 internees were imprisoned at the prison which was built to house 600. These figures are probably accurate because the signatories included several ex-warders who had worked in Changi Prison.
37. Miller, "Changi Prison Internment Camp", 25 Aug. 1942, IWM 67/194/5, pp. 1–2; Kennedy, *British Civilians and the Japanese War*, p. 87. Kennedy wrote that the original number of civilian internees at Changi was about 2,600, and that this figure included 349 women and 55 children. About two-thirds of the detainees were white British or Dominion subjects and the rest were American, French, Dutch, Czechs and Norwegians, together with some locally-resident Eurasians and Jews.
38. Iris G. Parfitt, *Jail-Bird Jottings: The Impressions of a Singapore Internee* (Kuala Lumpur: The Economy Printers, 1947), p. 10; Miller, "Model Home and Plan of our Bed-S (censored)itting Room". *B.III.28*, IWM 67/194/2; W. Wynne Mason, "Prisoners of War", in *Official History of New Zealand in the Second World War* (Wellington, New Zealand: War History Branch, Dept. of Internal Affairs, 1954), pp. 177–9.
39. Miller, "Changi Prison Internment Camp".
40. Gullick, *Josephine Foss*, p. 120.
41. A.M. Duncan-Wallace, "Diary of a Civilian Internee in Singapore 1942–1945", Cambridge University Library, p. 2.
42. Gullick, *Josephine Foss*, pp. 119–21.
43. Tompkins, *Diary*, p. 37.
44. Parfitt, *Jail-Bird Jottings*, pp. 11–2.

45. Tompkins, *Three Wasted Years*, pp. 50–1, Mrs Palmar was registered as a 50-year-old housewife.
46. Register of Internees in Changi Camp, 1942, IWM Misc. 1089.
47. A name list of internees was also kept by the Malayan Research Bureau in Sydney, Australia, starting 15 Feb. 1943 and amended until 1944.
48. Parfitt, *Jail-Bird Jottings*, p. 3, "Japanese Internment Rules".
49. Ibid., p. 4, "Internees"; pp. 5–6, "Misfortune Makes Strange Bedfellows".
50. Tompkins, *Three Wasted Years*, p. 35.
51. Parfitt, *Jail-Bird Jottings*, pp. 5–6.
52. Tompkins, *Diary*, p. 47, 27 Dec. 1942 entry.
53. Leslie Bell, *Destined Meeting* (London: Oldhams, 1959), pp. 64–5; Tompkins (in *Three Wasted Years*, p. 33) wrote that there were six female doctors in camp: Dr Eleanor Hopkins, Dr Cicely Williams, Dr Margaret Smallwood, Dr Jeanette Robinson, Dr Patricia Ruth Elliot, and Dr Robbie Worth. Dr Worth's name, however, does not appear in the camp register.
54. Allan, *Diary*, p. 68.
55. Tompkins, *Diary*, p. 47, entry for 27 Dec. 1942.
56. Miller, *Changi Prison Internment Camp*.
57. Kennedy, *British Civilians and the Japanese War*, pp. 89–90.
58. Bloom, *Dear Philip*, p. 34.
59. Bloom, *POW WOW* Editorial, Changi Prison, Singapore, vol. 1, no. 1 (1 Apr. 1942), IWM 66/254/1.
60. Ibid.
61. *Karikal Chronicle*, No. 1, Thursday, 19 Feb. 1942 in Miller, "We Published in Prison", IWM 67/194/2.
62. *POW WOW*, Changi Prison, Singapore, Special Edition 15 Aug. 1942, in documents deposited in the Imperial War Museum by Harry Miller. See IWM 67/194/5. The Imperial War Museum holds a complete set of *POW WOW*.
63. Bloom, *POW WOW*, vol. 1, no. 1 (1 Apr. 1942); no. 39, 30 Dec. 1942 and Vol. II nos. 1 and 28, 15 Oct. 1943, IWM 66/254/1.
64. Kennedy, *British Civilians and the Japanese War*, p. 127.
65. See documents deposited by Harry Miller in the Imperial War Museum, which record the prices of items sold on the Changi black market: (a) Camp Shop Price List, (b) How We Shopped, (c) Black Market, (d) Black Market, Price List of Goods as at Aug. 20, 1942. IWM 67/194/5.
66. Colin Sleeman, ed., *Trial of Sumida Haruzo and Twenty Others* (*The 'Double Tenth' Trial*) (London: William Hodge and Company, 1951), p. xviii; Mason, *Prisoners of War*, pp. 110–2; Tompkins, *Diary*, pp. 50–62, *Three Wasted Years*, p. 72; E.J. Currie, *Double Tenth Investigation*, IWM 87/34/1; W.F.N. Churchill, "To Those Who Laughed", ch. 13, Double Tenth, Misc. 562, Double Tenth Investigation, IWM 85/36/1; Leslie Bell, *Destined Meeting*, op. cit., p. 13; Freddy Bloom, op. cit., 13 October, pp. 113–37, Craddock, op. cit., pp. 110–6.
67. Bloom, *Dear Philip*, pp. 117–9.
68. Kennedy, *British Civilians and the Japanese War*, p. 95.
69. Tapes of interviews with Madame de Jonge, 62/0/7; Mrs Guy, 64/76/6; Mrs Colley, IWM 6229/11.

8

Surrendering Syonan

HENRY FREI

Japan's Unbroken Western Front

The year 1945 started grimly for the inmates of Syonan. Singapore's propaganda daily, *The Syonan Shimbun*, had heralded in the New Year with the ominous statement, "Those who do not fight, shall not eat. Those who do not win, shall not survive!"[1] These stark words reflected the desperation of the Japanese army, which was being forced into retreat by successful Allied attacks, but the portents for Allied prisoners of war were ominous.[2]

In Malaya, Japan's fighting capacity and its military administration remained intact to the very end of the conflict. The Japanese anticipated a British offensive in Malaya, and when the Allies launched their massive counter-offensive in the Pacific in Spring 1944, they made an all-out effort to fortify defences in the strategic and political centre of Japan's Southern war theater. The 7th Area Army was established in Syonan in March 1944 under General Doihara Kenji, who was called in from Tokyo to command Malaya, Sumatra, Java and Borneo.[3] He expected that British and Indian troops would attempt to recapture Syonan in conjunction with Britain's offensive in Burma, perhaps throwing their main strength at the neck of the Malay Peninsula around the Kra Isthmus, or a possible landing at Penang or further down, seeking to isolate the south and retake Singapore.[4] But the British did not come as early as Doihara had expected. U.S. B-29 bombers from Colombo began the first raids on Singapore only in November 1944. By then the battle of Leyte had been won, and U.S. marines were successfully installed in the Philippines.

Japanese Southern Army Headquarters had moved from Syonan to Manila to better monitor the U.S. invasion of the Philippines. After the defeat at Leyte, it retreated to Saigon, but did not return to Syonan. In Saigon, Japan sought to establish Indochina and Thailand as the new defence line. However, the 7th Area Army argued successfully that Syonan should remain the centre of transportation, production and commerce in the South.

The Syonan administration launched a comprehensive stockpiling programme for provisions, especially rice, and weapons, and this effort would see them comfortably through to the end of the war.[5]

In January 1944, the powerful 29th Division was made an independent unit with command over central and upper Malaya. It set up its headquarters at the small town of Taiping in north Malaya. Syonan was given its own defence command under Singapore Defence Commander Lt. Gen. Tasaka Senichi, a force dedicated to the city itself along with neighbouring Johor. General Doihara was now replaced in April as 7th Area Army Commander by the 17th Area Army Commander, Itagaki Seishiro.[6]

British troops reached the Irawaddy river in Burma in spring 1945, and the Japanese General Staff thought their next objective would be to recapture Singapore. They expected a further thrust from the Indian Ocean that would bypass the two small island citadels of Andaman and Nicobar, off the north Sumatran coast, to make a direct landing on the Malayan peninsula somewhere at the latitude of Medan after June 1945, along with a concomitant attack by Australian forces on strategic points in Borneo.[7] The Japanese had made preparations to counter these Allied moves, and a chiefs of staff conference at Saigon in mid-February had decided on the strategic positions the Japanese must hold at all costs in Malaya, Sumatra and Java, and had issued directives for Japan's all-out defence of Singapore.[8]

Lord Louis Mountbatten was indeed yearning for such an offensive. Following the Allied Forces' success at Imphal, they had regained Burma with the fall of Rangoon on 2 May.[9] The next step would be the recapture of Malaya and Singapore, even if it was late in the day of the Pacific War. Okinawa had already fallen, and U.S. forces were planning to invade Japan proper with the help of British troops. Mountbatten believed that there could be no real control of Japan unless Singapore was recaptured and the Straits of Malacca opened, and he argued that Malaya and Singapore should be recaptured before the final assault on mainland Japan, even if this meant a long siege in Singapore.[10] General Douglas MacArthur agreed in principle, as long as the British effort did not interfere with the invasion of Japan, and on 12 May, he approved a British plan to invade Malaya in mid-August.[11]

By the time this decision was taken, however, U.S. forces were already effectively bombing Japan's cities. Mountbatten's request to regain control of former British colonies in the region was now politicised. With Churchill's approval, five Commonwealth divisions assembled in India and trained there in preparation for the second wave of Allied counterattacks, which would include an invasion of Japan in March 1946.[12] Mountbatten needed not only troops earmarked for the Japan offensive, but also ships from the British Pacific Fleet for his Southeast Asian Command. However, to divert ships to the Singapore operation at this stage would weaken the main assault on Japan. Mountbatten's wish to recover Malaya and Singapore was criticised as a belated mopping-up operation in British colonial backwaters.[13]

Casualties in the looming invasion of Japan were expected to reach two million. Every man and ship would be needed. Britain's top Admirals, Somerville and Cunningham, understood very well the urgency of MacArthur's invasion plans, and they both backed full allocation of Britain's forces for the Japan operation. But Mountbatten and Field Marshal Alan Brooke preferred to concentrate on first taking Malaya with Dominion and Indian troops.[14] This internal division could only have benefited Japan's position on the Western front, where its forces remained intact and very powerful.

The Sudden and Unexpected Surrender of Syonan

This situation notwithstanding, it was clear to most people that Japan would lose the war. Saito Eisaburo, the Syonan correspondent of the economic daily *Nihon Keizai Shimbun*, had anticipated this outcome since Japanese setbacks in 1943. When in 1944, he briefly reported back to his main office in Tokyo, the president of the newspaper, Obama Toshie, told him, "We are sure to lose this war. Do not return to Syonan. Unless, of course, if you are determined to die there. Then it's a different matter."[15]

Saito did not want it to be said that he escaped to safety before everyone else. Besides, duty called. He was writing articles for *The Syonan Shimbun* and also broadcasting for the army. He flew back via Hong Kong, barely escaping death when his plane managed to shake off a U.S. fighter. Saito returned to a maelstrom. U.S. B-29 bombing raids on Syonan's military installations had intensified. These planes appeared in large formations at ever shorter intervals. The few neutral Europeans allowed to go about their business freely in Syonan, such as the Swiss and the Danes, climbed on rooftops when the bombers approached. Although their hearts were beating with joy, they had to keep a straight face lest informers or the Japanese arrest them for disloyalty. Hans Schweizer, the unofficial Red Cross delegate from Switzerland, counted ninety bombers in January 1945, and 108 in February.[16]

When Allied bombing increased, the Danes moved up the peninsula and took refuge in the safer Cameron Highlands. The Swiss consul, too, applied for permission to leave the doomed city, but Chief Inspector Sasamoto flatly refused, saying, "Much better you all stay together here." The Japanese had important business with the Swiss, whose consulate was entrusted with looking after British affairs.[17] In March, Singapore's oil installations were bombed and postal links with Japan were broken. For security reasons, in the meantime, all Eurasians were interned along with eight hundred non-European Jews. With each raid, prices soared. Malayan vendors kept saying, "Lagi baik makan sendiri!" (It's better if we eat what we have ourselves!)[18]

The Syonan defence consisted of two independent infantry battalions in the city as a garrison force, one field artillery battalion, two field artillery battalions and two field automatic cannon companies.[19] It was a weak force, yet the Japanese command remained convinced of ultimate victory. They were fighting a hundred-year war, and setbacks were only temporary. They were determined to defend Syonan, even if it meant throwing all their forces into a final pitched battle.[20]

The loss of Burma and the Philippines had a galvanising effect on the Japanese. They now expected British-Indian amphibious forces to invade the Malayan north coast at any time, and Australians to land on the east coast. Collectively, they would move down both sides of Malaya, recreating the huge pincer attack the Japanese had used to attack Singapore four years earlier.[21] To prevent the enemy from reaching Syonan, Japanese forces stationed in northern Malaya had to conduct self-sustaining warfare. It was essential to keep Syonan's Malaya Railway securely connected with Indochina as the main artery and backbone of Japan's Western front.[22]

In late July, the 7th Area Army sponsored a major conference at Batavia, where deadlines were set to prepare Japanese forces to resist the enemy fully, even under the worst conditons.[23] Artillery and close combat trenches were to be completed by 10 September, infantry positions by mid-September, tunnel-type communication trenches by 20 September, and dummy positions — constructed using local labour — by the end of September.[24] Allied working parties were taken by the hundreds across the causeway to Johor and made to build tunnels for weeks on end. They also drove bunkers four metres wide and four metres high into the hills to protect Japanese troops and provide ambush positions.[25]

Syonan municipal authorities were ordered to mobilise every available person for fortification work, using schools and private houses as much as possible.[26] Enemy tanks were to be lured into unfavourable positions for close range anti-tank attacks.[27] Should everything go wrong and Syonan fall, the 7th Army Headquarters would move to Malaya or Sumatra to conduct stubborn holding actions from strategic locations in the interior of Malaya, Sumatra and Java.[28] The Japanese even prepared defences against chemical warfare after receiving erroneous information that poison gas had been used by the enemy on isolated islands in the Pacific.[29]

The defence of Syonan went beyond concern for the individuals. The Southern Army Headquarters in Saigon despatched a 7th Area Army staff officer to Borneo to study Japanese suicide missions that had inflicted heavy casualties on Australian forces at Tarakan in July. The officer's job was to find out why Japanese forces had been less effective during subsequent operations at Brunei, Miri, and Labuan, but the trip ended up costing the man his life, for his plane did not make it back to Singapore.[30]

On land, the plans called for small units to execute close-quarter suicide actions from the enemy's rear.[31] At sea, the Japanese would spring surprise attacks on enemy vessels using "liaison boats" with bombs fixed to their bows. With personnel from the 25th Army in Sumatra as well as some of its own soldiers, the 29th Army used these "explosive ram-boats" effectively to frustrate enemy landings in the Malacca Straits.[32]

Two meetings in Tokyo held on 9 August, however, made all these preparations unnecessary. At eleven in the morning, just when the Prime Minister and the military were discussing the disastrous effects of the atom bomb on Nagasaki and the Soviet invasion of Manchuria, an officer reported the dropping of a second bomb on Nagasaki. An imperial conference was immediately slated for after eleven that night. At the conference, the Emperor decided to surrender.

Beamed abroad a few hours later, Japan's decision was picked up on foreign radio stations in the morning of 10 August.[33] When the 7th Army intercepted the surrender message, the commander of Syonan at first doubted that this was truly the Emperor's wish. General Itagaki was conducting army and navy manoeuvres in Penang island and passed on the radio message to the High Command in Saigon,[34] but he continued air-raid exercises for more than a week, and neither the newspapers nor the radio mentioned the termination of war.[35]

Knowledgeable media men, such as foreign correspondent Saito Eisaburo, were immediately convinced that the Emperor's decision to surrender was genuine. Saito understood that a surrender would endanger thousands of Japanese planters, labourers and businessmen exposed to anti-Japanese elements throughout Malaya, and he began warning these Japanese civilians about the threat they faced. Between 10 and 15 August, he and his colleagues contacted as many of their compatriots as possible, and urged them to go to Singapore using the most direct route available.³⁶ Saito's countrymen still thank him for this invaluable service, particularly in light of Japan's chaotic withdrawal from Manchuria, which claimed tens of thousands of lives and produced war orphans — children abandoned in the hasty retreat — a memory that still haunts Japan today.

On 16 August, the day after the Emperor broadcast his acceptance of the Allied Potsdam ultimatum, the Southern Army Headquarters summoned all commanders to Dalat, near Saigon, to give them instructions on how to comply with the Imperial Rescript (Emperor Hirohito's personal message to the people). The 7th Area Army ordered a halt to military operations, froze all fortification works in the Syonan sector, and demobilised the Malay volunteer force. All army commanders of the 7th Area Army then met in Syonan to clarify the procedures for terminating the war and handing over control to the Allies.³⁷

Meanwhile, the imperial princes flew out in three directions, to what had been the Japanese realm, carrying personal copies of the Imperial Rescript to dispel any doubts about the authenticity of the surrender. On 20 August, Prince Kan'in Haruhito flew into Syonan in a white plane to convey personally the Emperor's decision to surrender.³⁸ The 7th Area Army, through *The Syonan Shimbun*, announced Japan's surrender to the public on the same day. On 24 August, orders went out to relieve each army of operation assignments as of midnight. On 26 August, Lt. Gen. Numata Takazo, Chief of Staff of the Southern Army, flew to Rangoon to meet representatives of the Allied Forces and receive a copy of the instrument of surrender. Numata and Allied representatives discussed the ceremony at which the surrender instrument was to be signed and how to proceed when British and Indian soldiers disembarked at Keppel Harbour on 5 September.³⁹ It was in fact hoped that British and Indian soldiers would arrive earlier, but the delay to 5 September was by order of General MacArthur. Mountbatten had been assigned this date so that his forces would repossess Singapore only after the signing of the formal supreme surrender ceremony in Tokyo on 2 September.

Singapore's Post-War Revival

For a period of time after mid-August, Syonan — now Singapore once again — existed in a deadly twilight. During this seemingly interminable state of limbo, the Japanese disposed of their documents and ammunition, hidden foodstuffs began to circulate, valuable old currency notes reappeared, thieving and looting took place, old debts were settled, bloody punishment meted out and scores of former Japan collaborators called on the Swiss Red Cross and Consulate for protection.[40]

The Japanese now cooperated with the Red Cross delegate, Hans Schweizer, whom they had relentlessly persecuted throughout the Occupation. As Schweizer set about providing relief for internees he was allowed to hold direct negotiations with Maj. Gen. Saito Masatoshi, who was in charge of all POWs, and arranged visits to the one civilian and thirteen military camps to survey the available foodstuffs and medicines. He also persuaded Saito to release twenty tons of undistributed Red Cross parcels.[41]

This courageous man, who before the war was the managing director of Diethelm Trading, had voluntarily served as the Red Cross delegate responsible for liaising with POW camps in Syonan since the British surrender in 1942, but Tokyo suspected him of involvement in Allied espionage. He was interrogated by the Kempeitai, Japan's notorious Military Police, and accused of being a spy, apparently to provide an excuse for the Japanese High Command to prevent Schweizer from carrying out his humanitarian duties as a Red Cross delegate for Malaya.[42]

Similar occurrences happened elsewhere in Southeast Asia. In Java, Sumatra and Borneo, the Japanese went so far as to kill the Swiss Red Cross delegate and his wife for trying to help POWs with small food parcels.[43] On a visit to Syonan in 1943, the head of Japan's own Red Cross Society, Prince Shimadzu Tadatsugu, told Schweizer that even the Red Cross in Japan was forbidden to function during the war. It was the Army's policy not to have Red Cross personnel interfere with the handling of POWs in Southeast Asia.[44]

Schweizer first came under Kempeitai surveillance shortly after the surrender of Singapore in 1942 when he was approached by Colonel Roberts, the acting officer in charge of the Australian Red Cross contingent with the Australian Expeditionary Force, and Sergeant Major Fujibayashi, who was attached to the POW camp. Roberts asked Schweizer if it was possible for Schweizer to extend a loan on behalf of the Red Cross International Commission to the Australian Red Cross Society to buy food for the sick and wounded. Schweizer agreed without hesitation, and immediately tried to set himself up as an official Red Cross delegate to help POWs interned in the camps.[45] In time this resulted in the celebrated weekly run of the "Blue Angel", a 2.5 ton truck loaded with five tonnes of necessities for POW camps. There were interruptions to this service, but it always managed to resume operations. Through this service, Schweizer also managed to contact loyal Indian troops and supply them with medicines.[46]

The Kempeitai watched both Roberts and Schweizer closely. Schweizer had nothing to back him in his negotiations with camp commanders, even when he dared to stretch his point a bit and claim that he was acting under the authority in charge of Australian POWs. On one occasion, he asked for some crutches. The Japanese Medical Army Unit eventually fulfilled the request but warned him that he was asking for far too much, and stopped him from making further visits to the camps.[47] He soon lost contact with Roberts, whom the Japanese had sentenced to death owing to various problems he had with the Kempeitai, although his sentence was later commuted to a long-term prison stay.[48]

One Japanese military official assisted Schweizer, a Sergeant Fujibayashi. With Fujibayashi's help, Schweizer was able to have his telegrams translated into Japanese and sent via the International Red Cross Commission in Yokohama to Red Cross headquarters in Geneva. A second loan for the Australian Red Cross unit was thereby made possible, paid in funds through a Japanese bank in Singapore. Without Fujibayashi's translations, Schweizer would not have gotten a single message out of Syonan. Fujibayashi asked for nothing in return, and it is likely that his honourable efforts saved the lives of a number of POWs and civilian internees. Schweizer once asked Fujibayashi what made him help and take the awful risk of his altruistic actions being misconstrued and treated as treason. Fujibayashi replied grimly, grasping his sword, "I am a good Japanese and will fight for my country until I die. I follow our great Emperor Meiji, who said in one of his poems that one must be magnanimous with a beaten foe."[49]

After the Australian commandos blew up Japanese steamships in Singapore harbour on 10 October 1943, Schweizer was seized by the Japanese Military Police and subjected to interrogation under torture. Fujibayashi intervened and managed to free Schweizer after he had endured a gruelling 12 hours of interrogation. Schweizer was assisted by Fujibayashi for three more years, until Japan's defeat, when the Japanese military finally accepted that he was a genuine Red Cross employee.[50]

Fujibayashi died in prison a few weeks after the British returned to Malaya. For most of this period, Schweizer was not allowed to visit him. Schweizer eventually threatened to approach Lord Mountbatten, and was finally allowed to bring Fujibayashi some cigarettes and a packet of biscuits — the very things Fujibayashi had done his best to help Schweizer get to the British, Dutch, Australian and Indian troops in captivity. But Schweizer's visit came too late. Fujibayashi was already in extremely poor condition after having been treated harshly by British investigators. One of the last things Fujibayashi muttered to Schweizer was, "I am so glad for you, that you were finally able to function as a Red Cross delegate, and thank you...." Two days later, Fujibayashi died. In his memoirs Schweizer says of Fujibayashi, "Yes, he was an instrument of a Higher Power of whom the Japanese people may well be proud, because he made good so much that was wrong...."[51]

When a British armada of battleships, aircraft carriers and cruisers entered Singapore harbour on 5 September, Schweizer was summoned to the Admiral's ship. Lord Mountbatten asked him about events in the city following receipt of the Imperial Rescript and the arrival of the first British troops. Mountbatten particularly wanted to know about the condition of POWs, the confinement of the Japanese Army and civilian administrative officers in camps prepared by the Japanese themselves and the health and state of mind of the population. After rendering an account, Schweizer was handed telegrams from various international commissions, the headquarters of the British and Australian Red Cross, along with the remarkable messages from the Colonial Office in London expressing satisfaction and deep gratitude for his endurance.[52]

A British military administration now took over the running of the country. Not everyone in Singapore was enchanted to see the British back. Lee Kip Lin, a student, went down to the Tanjong Pagar docks on 5 September to watch the 5th Indian Division land. Silence greeted the disembarking troops. The Indian soldiers wondered, "Are we liberators or are we conquerors?!" One of them broke the silence by asking the crowd, "Well, are you glad?" Six pairs of hands clapped and one person shouted "Hurrah". Most Chinese simply wondered what the Indian soldier was saying, and what the clapping was about.[53] Later in the evening, in downtown Singapore, there were cheers in the streets and considerable enthusiasm over the white faces pouring in. But something bothered Lee Kip Lin. "It annoyed me to see some of the British officers," he remembers, because in the eyes of some he saw the same arrogance as before the war.[54] On Surrender Day, 12 September, huge crowds showed up to watch the capitulation ceremony on the steps of City Hall. The atmosphere was carnival-like, and Lord Mountbatten rode grandly through the crowd in an open car to thunderous applause.

General Itagaki led six generals of the Southern Army up the steps of City Hall, where they signed the British surrender instrument at 1.41 p.m.

The nine-minute ceremony concluded 1,304 days of Japanese Occupation that had begun on 15 February 1942 at 6.20 p.m. when General Percival surrendered to the Japanese. General Itagaki stepped out from the surrender chambers into the scorching sun to face a huge crowd booing him terribly. They were endlessly shouting abusively in Japanese, "Bakero! (fool)", echoing words that Japanese soldiers had often used in speaking to people in Singapore.[55] Itagaki was hanged on 23 December 1948 in Tokyo three years later as A-class war criminal.

After the surrender, working parties made up of Japanese soldiers went into the city. Their immediate task was to clear bomb wreckage and rebuild the wharves at Tanjong Pagar. They did a lot of cleaning and also collected night soil. Lan Khong Kon remembers that many Chinese spat in their faces. Others scolded them.

Reports differ as to how the British treated them. Lan reports that the British were kind to the Japanese, and on the whole did not allow people to ill-treat them.[56] This was not always confirmed on the Japanese side. Many female Japanese were sent to work at army hospitals, and one nurse, Minetomo Fumi, reported irrational behaviour by British personnel against the Japanese. Minetomo was serving at Yamato Hospital where she treated many Japanese labourers for heatstroke. Knowing some English, she was asked to be an interpreter at Alexandra Hospital when the British took over. It proved to be a tough job. The hospital had been the scene of a massacre at the fall of Singapore in February 1942. Minetomo was cleaning the hospital with thirty Japanese soldiers when a British colonel arrived to handle the takeover. A British matron and some Indian combat soldiers were with him. The matron had worked in the hospital before the war and had escaped to Australia. She hated the Japanese, and asked Minetomo many harsh questions. Eventually she became hysterical and began brandishing a Japanese sword, threatening to kill them all.

At Yamato Hospital, Minetomo interpreted for the incoming British lieutenant who was to take charge of the hospital. He also hated the Japanese, not because of personal experiences, but on account of Japan having been an Axis country. The lieutenant had lost many friends in the battle of Dunkirk. Minetomo tried to placate him, "This is a hospital. The war is over. Let us help each other to survive." The lieutenant calmed down and became reasonable.[57]

One person Minetomo met at Yamato Hospital was Captain Ueda Kunitaro. He had just returned from a war crimes trial at Kluang, where he had been held on erroneous charges. He had been wrongfully arrested and sent north on a cargo train. The judge had apologised for the mistake, but left Ueda to make his own way back to Singapore. He had been lucky to hitch a ride on an ambulance, and had disguised himself as a doctor to survive the long and hazardous journey through the communist infested jungle. This was the reason he was taken to Yamato Hospital before rejoining his work unit at Changi.[58]

His comrades were happy to see him back alive. Because he had survived the trial, they felt that he should lead their working party to Tengah Airfield, which the Japanese called Jigoku Tenga or "Tengah Hell". The place was notorious for hardship.[59] When Ueda arrived at "Tengah Hell" with twelve hundred men, tommy guns were trained on them and they were made to stand for hours in the pouring rain. A British officer eventually emerged. He approached Ueda and barked at him, "Bow! Bow!" Ueda understood this to mean, "Show that you surrender! I want to see you surrender!" The officer asked the Japanese prisoners their names and then made them wait another three to four hours in the rain.

Finally, the Japanese were given small grass cutters and ordered to cut the grass. Soldiers had to cut 100 square metres, non-commissioned officers doubled that size and officers 300 square metres. They were kept doing this until 8 p.m., going without food the entire time. Then they were made to march at double time back to their camp at Bukit Timah, seven kilometres away. Many collapsed by the road side. A jeep later came and picked them up.

This treatment continued for a week. In that short time, the soldiers were attacked by malaria, dengue fever and beri-beri, and the number of Ueda's fit soldiers dropped to five hundred. After all the grass had been cut, the soldiers were allocated sundry jobs. They cleaned toilets, did carpentry and paint jobs, and had to go to the aerodrome each day. Only five or six were allowed to remain at camp in the sick bay or help in the kitchen. And while the men worked at Tengah aerodrome, the British went into the Japanese camp and stole many things, including Ueda's shoes.[60]

The Japanese had ordered Australian working parties to build a shrine during the Occupation, and the British adjutant now ordered the Japanese to build a church for the Royal Airforce soldiers. Around this time, the Japanese prisoners were also given half a day of rest per week. Things were getting better. Buoyed by the improvement in their working conditions, the prisoners collected bricks enthusiastically and completed the church by Christmas. Archbishop Beardley of the Church of England came to Tengah aerodrome specially to open the church. However, as Ueda remembers sadly, "Only one bloody Japanese soldier and myself were allowed to attend the opening ceremony."

Twenty to thirty priests later came to see the church. The British adjutant asked Ueda and his men to arrange presents for the visiting priests. The Japanese captives decided to carve small wooden boxes. The adjutant ordered that words be carved onto the boxes. "What words should we use?" asked Ueda. The adjutant replied, "God is love". So these words were carved in Japanese characters — *Kami wa ai ni nari*. The soldiers carved for three nights without sleeping. One of the boxes is still kept by Mr Cliff Cooper in Australia.

After the opening of the church, the British treated the Japanese prisoners better. The prisoners no longer had to run from their camp to the airfield but were transported by lorry, and the sick were no longer forced to work. Despite the initial harsh treatment, the working parties in Singapore may have fared better than the bulk of the Japanese Army who were interned on Rembang Island, where 20 per cent of the 59,900 internees contracted malaria, dysentery or beri-beri. In 1946, General Numata reported 56 deaths "in recent months".[61]

The Allies were not guilty of anything resembling the extreme and systematic ill-treatment of POWs in Japanese-run camps during the war. But the treatment accorded many Japanese POWs could have been more in keeping with international law and Red Cross principles than was the case. Schweizer later learnt that many Japanese troops were retained as labour well into 1947, often under quite unsatisfactory conditions, resulting in a number of deaths. As the man entrusted with observing that Red Cross principles were applied by British authorities, Schweizer has painful memories of the British return. "I [have] felt bad ever since for having been too confiding in my own white race for whom I had fought and risked my life innumerable times during three and a half years."[62]

Schweizer remembers many British officers as being high-handed, shameful and highly objectionable. They behaved like an army of liberation occupying enemy territory, when in fact they had not had to fire a single shot to recover their colony, a place that had for three and a half years suffered from the very arrogance and unscrupulous behaviour that the returning British now displayed.[63]

Such scathing memories of a neutral bystander notwithstanding, many Japanese POWs saw a certain logic in the reversal of roles after the Japanese surrender. They understood the wrath of the British and of the local people. When Private Tsujimoto Sanosuke trooped across the causeway to Johor, en route to the island of Rembang, onlookers threw stones at him. "It was understandable," he says today, "I would have done the same. Many of them had lost their parents, children or husbands during the Japanese Occupation."[64] Even though Tsujimoto was a Japanese soldier, he privately felt good when he heard that Japan had lost the war. Japan had gotten too arrogant, he thought. They had done bad things against the local people. His age in Japanese history had been a thoroughly militaristic one. He felt that the Japanese deserved the punishment they endured on the uninhabited island of Rembang. Languishing on the barren rocks of this island, about a third of the size of Singapore, the Japanese lived on leaves, a little water in the morning and tapioca. They had no other vegetables and no tobacco. About ten in Tsujimoto's unit died because of the absence of health care. Around 1,000 POWs from Rembang were charged with war crimes; 760 were sentenced to death and around 600 died of ill health or from mental breakdowns, including suicide.

Three men in Tsujimoto's unit of 250 had killed themselves immediately upon hearing the news that Japan had surrendered without a battle. That no foreign infantry had challenged Japan's Malayan front was an unbearable humiliation. Forty men in Tsujimoto's unit developed severe neuroses and died because of that.[65] Even after the Japanese were freed, some committed suicide. When Tsujimoto was repatriated in May 1946, on a ship packed with 1,800 men bound for Nagoya, two men threw themselves overboard as they approached their homeland.[66]

Conclusion

Sailing out in the opposite direction of Japan-bound ships was Russell Braddon, heading for a more fortunate land. He pondered the big dent the war in Malaya had made in each of their lives. With the sudden surrender of Syonan, the careful fabric of the personal life of the Japanese, built up over almost four years of occupation, disintegrated in a single moment. All the singular ties created under the special and insane circumstances of war evaporated. Braddon realised that this feeling of disintegration bothered him greatly because he felt that the war was not truly over. This was not a real surrender, Braddon thought. "For us and the undefeated Japanese all over Southeast Asia, the war has not ended. It has only stopped momentarily." Braddon could not forget the words of an indoctrinated Japanese soldier, "War finish hundred years." Braddon believed this. The Syonan surrender was simply an interlude. The opening of the war had played itself out. Five years had passed, but there were another 95 to go.[67]

With the benefit of hindsight, we know that Braddon's conclusion was interesting but wrong. Perhaps he would tell his story differently today. Singapore, which became Syonan and then Singapore again, proved to be a tremendous catalyst in modern regional history, even in world history. It played a vital part in a drastically changed world order. The military personnel who participated in the war did not die or suffer in vain. Ultimately, Japan's militaristic apparatus, based on fifty years of indoctrinating the masses, was destroyed. The Japanese departed from the region, and later returned as traders and tourists, without guns. The end of the war was also the beginning of Great Britain's final farewell from the region, which held the seeds for the birth of new nation states in Southeast Asia.

In a drastic way, the war was also Australia's initiation to the realities of Asia. But rather than confront Asia, as Braddon thought would be the case, Australia began to seek Asia. It dismantled White Australia, and its intellectuals and politicians — along with Japanese intellectuals — began pioneering an Asia Pacific regionalism. Today, Japan holds a stable and peaceful position in the region, and Australia continues to aspire to a mature role as an Australasiatic Pacific Rim country.

Despite the many positive changes brought about by the surrender of Syonan, a small uncertainty of mine remains. I wonder if the Allied veterans of the war have managed over the past fifty years to forgive their former captors. Let me illustrate with a personal anecdote. On 15 February 1992, at the Fifty Year Commemoration of the Fall of Singapore, I attended an impressive ceremony at the Allied graves by Kranji war memorial at seven in the morning, just after sunrise. Watching the various representatives lay their wreaths was a most touching and emotional commemoration. Nevertheless, at the end I had a slight feeling that something was missing.

The day before I had been asked to guide a group of Japanese to Kranji war memorial. I knew that many Japanese had wanted to participate in the commemoration the following day, but it was made known to them that they would not be welcome. The group I finally brought to Kranji to lay flowers at the memorial, almost furtively, on the day before the ceremony, had just three participants. The BBC accompanied us and captured the scene for their video programme "Unfortunate Incidents".

The next day I approached an Australian veteran soldier after the ceremony, and suggested that it would have been good if a Japanese could have gone up the stairs and laid a wreath for all those who died, for I knew that there were so many Japanese who felt deeply about the war and its sacrifices. The soldier turned to me and said incredulously, "No, absolutely not. That would have been the last thing to do. We don't forget, and we certainly don't forgive."

Later that same day, Changi Prison was opened as a rare exception to visiting ex-Allied personnel and their families. I hitched a ride in on a bus full of British ex-servicemen. The animated elderly man sitting next to me was a former naval officer. He had been a Royal engineer on a British warship, and was most outspoken as we wandered through the prison examining the famous cells of Changi prison. On the way out, he was interviewed by Singapore television. He told the reporter, "Well, we may forget for the simple fact that we grow old, and our memory may fail us for purely biological reasons; but, no, of course not, we do not forgive."

At noon, the Singaporean Chinese held their own memorial service at their civilian war monument by the sea, as they did each year on 15 February. The monument stands in memory of civilians the Japanese massacred following the British surrender. After the Nanjing killings, the Singapore massacre ranks as the worst single atrocity of the Pacific War. In Singapore a media campaign was used to lure unsuspecting Chinese males into a trap. Press advertisements and radio messages summoned Chinese males to various check points for "inspections". When the men turned up, many of them were hauled off on lorries to beaches where they were slaughtered. The number of victims varies between 6,000 (which is the Japanese figure) to 50,000 (the Chinese figure).

In spite of these atrocities, at the commemoration ceremony I witnessed, the Chinese, the Japanese ambassador and Japanese residents participated side by side — the first time Japanese had been invited to a war memorial ceremony in 50 years. Dressed in black, the Japanese were solemn, and grateful for the extended hand of reconciliation. They sought to atone for the past and looked towards the future with new trust. After the commemoration service, the little group in black was exposed to relentless questioning from the press. The Japanese representatives apologised — if one ever can apologise adequately for such an event — and the Chinese demonstrated their forgiveness. Many Chinese had been victims of the Japanese, as the Allied POWs had been, and while the Chinese could not forget, they were willing to forgive. It made me think. It still does.

Notes

1. Hans Schweizer-Iten, *One Hundred Years of the Swiss Club and the Swiss Community of Singapore 1871–1971* (Singapore: Swiss Club, 1980), p. 214.
2. Russell Braddon, *The Naked Island* (London: Pan Books, 1955), pp. 280–3.

3. Interview with former Colonel Imaoka Yutaka, former staff officer of the 7th Area Army at his home in Yokohama, 6 May 1995; with additional recollections he provided for Japanese monograph no. 162, "Southwest Area Operations Record (7th Area Army) April 1944–Aug. 1945", prepared by the Information and Historical Record Division of the First Demobilisation Bureau, Feb. 1951 (henceforth JM 162), p. 3.
4. Ibid., pp. 9–10.
5. Ibid., pp. 18b–21.
6. Ibid., pp. 34, 39.
7. Ibid., pp. 39–40.
8. Ibid., pp. 42–4.
9. D.G.E. Hall, *A History of South-East Asia* (London: Macmillan, 1981), p. 869.
10. David Day, *Reluctant Nation: Australia and the Allied Defeat of Japan 1942–5* (Oxford: Oxford University Press, 1992), pp. 283, 298, 300.
11. Cables, joint staff mission to chiefs of staff, 6 and 30 April and 12 May 1945, and chiefs of staff to Mountbatten, 16 May 1945, PREM 3/149/11, 3/149/10 and 3/160/8, Public Record Office, London, in ibid., p. 283.
12. Extract from Cable UK Delegation to Foreign Office, 23 June 1945, CRS M100, Australian Archives, in ibid., p. 297.
13. Ibid., pp. 283, 349.
14. Ibid.
15. Interview with Saito Eisaburo, Tokyo, 15 Oct. 1994.
16. Schweizer, *One Hundred Years of the Swiss Club*, pp. 214–5.
17. Ibid., p. 216.
18. Ibid., pp. 214–5.
19. JM 162, p. 55.
20. "Malay Operations Record: 29th Army, Jan. 1944–Aug. 1945", Japanese monograph no. 167, based on the recollections and notes of Maj. Gen. Fujimura Masuzo and Maj. Gen. Kawahara Naokazu, former chiefs of staff of the 29th Army, concerning Malaya operations after the establishment of the 29th Army in Jan. 1944, and compiled by the Historical Record Division of the First Demobilisation Bureau, May 1951 (henceforth JM 167), p. 51.
21. Ibid., pp. 43–4.
22. JM 162, pp. 59–60.
23. Ibid., p. 186.
24. Ibid., pp. 167–8.
25. Braddon, *The Naked Island*, p. 280.
26. JM 162, p. 170.
27. Ibid., p. 174.
28. Ibid., p. 74.
29. Ibid., pp. 55–6.
30. Ibid., pp. 73–4.
31. Ibid., p. 167.
32. Ibid., p. 57.
33. John Toland, *The Rising Sun: The Decline and Fall of the Japanese Empire* (New York: Bantam Books, 1971), pp. 908–20.

34. JM 167, p. 52; JM 162, p. 87.
35. Schweizer, *One Hundred Years of the Swiss Club*, p. 217.
36. Interview with Saito Eisaburo, Tokyo, 15 Oct. 1994.
37. Monograph no. 162, p. 87.
38. Schweizer, *One Hundred Years of the Swiss Club*, p. 217.
39. Imaoka, "Southwest Area Operations Record (7th Area Army)", pp. 87–8; John Hayter, *Priest in Prison: Four Years of Life in Japanese-Occupied Singapore* (Singapore: Graham Brash, 1991), pp. 241–2.
40. Schweizer, *One Hundred Years of the Swiss Club*, pp. 217–8.
41. Ibid., pp. 218–9, 222.
42. Ibid., p. 411.
43. Schweizer, *Dark Days in Singapore: Experiences of a Delegate of the International Committee of the Red Cross During the Japanese Occupation of Singapore and Malaya 1942–1945*, Part 3 (Singapore, 1992), p. 30.
44. Schweizer, *One Hundred Years of the Swiss Club*, p. 411.
45. Ibid., p. 412.
46. Ibid., p. 413. Schweizer, *Dark Days in Singapore*, pp. 30–1.
47. Schweizer, *One Hundred Years of the Swiss Club*, p. 412.
48. Ibid., pp. 412–3.
49. Ibid., p. 413.
50. Ibid., pp. 413–4.
51. Ibid., p. 415.
52. Ibid., p. 220.
53. Lee Geok Boi, *Syonan: Singapore under the Japanese 1942–1945* (Singapore: Landmark Books, 1992), p. 121.
54. Ibid.
55. Ibid.
56. Ibid.
57. Interview with Minetomo Fumi, Tokyo, 5 Sept. 1993.
58. Interview with Ueda Kunitaro, Tokyo, 17 Oct. 1993.
59. Ibid.
60. Ibid.
61. WO 203/4587, British War Office, London, in Meirion and Susie Harries, *Soldiers of the Sun: The Rise and Fall of the Imperial Japanese Army* (New York: Random House, 1992), p. 460. For the repatriation movements, see Koseisho engokyoku (Ministry of Health and Welfare), *Hikiage to engo sanjunen no ayumi* (Repatriation and Support over the Past Thirty Years) (Tokyo: Koseisho, 1978).
62. Schweizer, *One Hundred Years of the Swiss Club*, p. 225.
63. Ibid., p. 224.
64. Interview with Tsujimoto Sanosuke, Reel 2, Oral History Department, National Archives of Singapore.
65. Ibid.
66. Ibid.
67. Braddon, *The Naked Island*, pp. 282–3.

9

Massacre of Chinese in Singapore and Its Coverage in Postwar Japan

HAYASHI HIROFUMI

Introduction

Shortly after the British forces surrendered in Singapore on 15 February 1942, the Japanese military began an operation, called *Kakyo Shukusei* or *Dai Kensho* in Japanese and known in the Chinese community of Singapore as the *Sook Ching* (Purge through Purification), in which many local Chinese were massacred.[1] Although the killings have been investigated extensively by scholars in Malaysia and Singapore, the sources available to them are limited, and Japanese documents have not been fully utilised in such research. One purpose of this chapter is to consider what Japanese sources can contribute to an understanding of what took place.

The first point to be considered is why the massacre took place, and the second is how the massacre has been presented in postwar Japan. Although even ex-Kempeitai officers involved have admitted the killings were inhumane and unlawful, little attention has been paid to the episode. While there has been valuable research carried out on the Japanese military administration of Malaya and Singapore, no reliable study has appeared in Japan. Moreover, while the Singapore Massacre is well known to scholars in Japan, similar killings carried out in the Malay Peninsula only came to the attention of the Japanese public in the late 1980s after I discovered documents relating to the Japanese military units involved.

Why did the Japanese Military Massacre the Chinese in Singapore?

Aspects of the Massacre

On the night of 17 February 1942, Maj. Gen. Kawamura Saburo, an infantry brigade commander, was placed in charge of Japan's Singapore Garrison. The next morning, he appeared at the Army Headquarters and was ordered by the 25th Army commander, Lt. Gen. Yamashita Tomoyuki, to carry out mopping-up operations. He received further detailed instructions from the chief of staff, Lt. Gen. Suzuki Sosaku, and a staff officer, Lt. Col. Tsuji Masanobu. Kawamura then held consultations with the Kempeitai commander, Lt. Col. Oishi Masayuki. The plan for a Purge through Purification of the Chinese population was drawn up in the course of these meetings. Under this scheme, Chinese males between the ages of 18 and 50 were ordered to report to mass screening centres for inspection. Those regarded as anti-Japanese were detained, loaded onto lorries, and taken away to the coast or to other isolated places where they were machine-gunned and bayoneted to death.[2] In my survey of official documents of the Japanese military at the time, I found two sources that give a figure for the number massacred. One is Kawamura's diary that shows the figure of 5,000.[3] The other is an issue of the *Intelligence Record of 25th Army* (No. 62, dated 28 May 1942) prepared by the staff section of the 25th Army.[4] This secret record states that the number was missing as a result of bombing and the purge was 11,110. This second record is important because it was drawn up as a secret document shortly after the purge took place. However, as this description is ambiguous and offers no basis for the figure, its credibility is open to question. This issue remains unsettled.

The mass-screening was carried out mainly by Kempeitai personnel between 21 and 23 February in urban areas, and by the Imperial Guards Division at the end of February in suburban districts. Most accounts of the killings include a map that shows the island divided into four sections, and explain that three divisions, the Imperial Guards, the 5th Division, and the 18th Division carried out the mass screening in suburban districts.[5] However, on 21 February, the 25th Army ordered both the 5th and the 18th Divisions to move up into the Malay Peninsula and carry out mopping-up operations there.[6] The order assigned the Imperial Guards Division to mass-screening of non-urban areas of Singapore, and made the 5th and the 18th Divisions responsible for the rest of the Malay Peninsula. According to war diaries and other documents relating to these two divisions, neither played a role in the mass screening in Singapore. The British war crimes trial prosecuted the commander of the Imperial Guards Division, Lt. Gen. Nishimura Takuma, on charges related to the Singapore Massacre, but not the commanders of the 5th or the 18th Divisions. This version of events is correct, and the conventional map is wrong.

With regard to the background of the massacre, it is important to stress that the Purge through Purification was planned before Japanese troops landed in Singapore. The military government section of the 25th Army had already drawn up a plan entitled, "Policy Principles toward Overseas Chinese" on or around 28 December 1941.[7] This guidance stated that anyone who would not obey or cooperate should no longer be allowed to live. It is clear that the headquarters of the 25th Army had decided on a harsh policy toward the Chinese population of Singapore and Malaya from the beginning of the war. According to Onishi Satoru,[8] a Kempeitai officer who was in charge of Jalan Besar screening centre, Kempeitai commander Oishi Masayuki was instructed by the chief of staff, Suzuki Sosaku, at Keluang, Johor, to prepare for a purge operation following the capture of Singapore. Although the exact date of this instruction is not known, the Army headquarters was stationed in Keluang from 28 January to 4 February 1942.

Rebuttal of the Defense

Let us, for the moment, consider the justification or defense for the actions of the Japanese army presented by some writers and researchers in Japan.

One of the major points is that the Chinese volunteer forces, such as the Dalforce, fought fiercely and caused many casualties among the Japanese. This is supposed to have inflamed Japanese anger and led to reprisals against local Chinese.[9] Most of the British volunteers, such as the Straits Settlements Volunteer Forces (SSVF), Federated Malay States Volunteer Forces (FMSVF), were not in fact thrown into battle but stayed back in Singapore. As for the Dalforce, about 600 personnel of four companies from among the 1,250-strong nine companies were sent to the battle front. Around 30 per cent of the Dalforce personnel either died in action or were later killed during the Purge through Purification.[10] It is generally said in Singapore that the Dalforce personnel fought fiercely.[11] Although I do not question their bravery, their role seems much exaggerated. The volunteers of the Dalforce were equipped only with outdated weapons. Japanese military histories make no reference to Chinese volunteers during the battle of Singapore, and report that the opposition put up by British forces was weaker than expected. The greatest threat to the Japanese was artillery bombardment.[12]

During the second half of the 1940s and during the war crimes trials of 1947, no Japanese claimed that losses suffered by Japanese forces at the hand of Chinese volunteers contributed to the massacre. As noted above, the 25th Army had planned the mass screening even before the battle of Singapore. This sequence of events clearly rebuts the argument.

A second point raised is that the Chinese in Malaya were passing intelligence to the British and that Chinese guerrillas were engaged in subversive activities against Japanese forces during the Malayan campaign, for example by flashing signals to British airplanes. The Kempeitai of the 25th Army was on the alert for such activities during the Malayan campaign, but made only two arrests. Kempeitai officer Onishi Satoru said in his memoirs that they had been unable to find any evidence of the use of flash signals and that it was technologically impossible. Thus, this line of argument is refuted by a military officer who was directly involved in the events.[13]

A third explanation offered for the massacre is that anti-Japanese Chinese were preparing for an armed insurrection, and that the law and order situation was deteriorating in Singapore. It claims that a purge was necessary to restore public order, and this point was raised at the war crimes trial in Singapore.[14] One piece of evidence cited by the defense during the trial was an entry in Kawamura's personal diary for 19 February that ostensibly said looting still continued in the city. The same evidence was presented to the Tokyo War Crimes Tribunal. However, the diary actually says that order in the city was improving.[15] The extract used during the trials was prepared by a task force of the Japanese army set up to take counter-measures against war crimes prosecutions by the Allied forces. It is clear that the evidence was manipulated.

Otani Keijiro, a Kempeitai lieutenant colonel in charge of public security in Singapore from the beginning of March 1942, also rejected this line of defense, rebutting Japanese excuses and severely criticising the Japanese atrocities in Singapore.[16] Onishi likewise stated that he had not expected hostile Chinese to begin an anti-Japanese campaign, at least not in the short term, because public security in Singapore was getting better.[17]

The fourth argument is that staff officer Tsuji Masanobu was the mastermind behind the massacre, and that he personally planned and carried it out. Although Tsuji was a key figure in these events, I believe that researchers have overestimated his role. At the time of the war crimes trials, Tsuji had not been arrested. As soon as the war ended, he escaped from Thailand to China, where he came under the protection of the Kuomintang government because he cooperated with them in fighting the communists. He later secretly returned to Japan in May 1948 where he was protected by the US military, namely G2 of GHQ.[18] In this situation, the defense counsel attempted to pin all responsibility on Tsuji alone. This point will be discussed in further detail later.

Reasons for the Massacre

Let us now examine the reasons why such atrocities were carried out by the Japanese in Singapore. I limit the discussion to internal factors of Japanese military and society.

In the first place, it should be noted that the Japanese occupation of Singapore began ten years after the start of Japan's war of aggression against China. After the Manchurian Incident in 1931, Japan invaded and occupied Manchuria, setting up the puppet state of "Manchukuo" (State of the Manchus) in 1932. The Japanese army faced a strong anti-Japanese campaign and public order, as a result, remained unstable and to which it responded by conducting frequent punitive operations against anti-Japanese guerrillas and their supporters. Under normal circumstances, those arrested in these operations should have been apprehended and brought to trial for punishment. However, Japan forced Manchukuo to enact a law in September 1932 that granted authority to army officers, both Japanese and Manchurian, and police officers to execute anti-Japanese activists on the spot without trial. This method of execution was usually called *Genju Shobun* (Harsh Disposal) or *Genchi Shobun* (Disposal on the Spot) by the Japanese military.[19] Once this law was in place, the Japanese military and military police killed suspects on the spot during punitive operations without trial or investigation. Those killed included not only guerrillas but also civilians, including children, women, and aged people unable to bear arms. Such inhuman methods were made legal in Manchuria. Further, such methods prevailed among the Japanese military, and *Genju Shobun* was regularly used throughout China during the war.[20]

Yamashita Tomoyuki, 25th Army commander directing the invasion of Malaya, played an important role in the evolution of the *Genju Shobun* method. As chief of staff of the North China Area Army in 1938–39, he formulated an operational plan for mopping-up in northern China that made use of *Genju Shobun* in Manchuria by way of the Provost Marshal, China who had been stationed in Manchuria as a Supreme Adviser to the Military Government Section of Manchukuo.[21] At the time, the Chinese communists had a number of strongholds in northern China. After Yamashita was transferred, the plan undertook an intensive cleanup operation called the *Sanguang* (Kill All, Loot All, and Burn All; the Chinese character for *Sanguang* is used as a Japanese word that literally means three lights) Operations in 1940; which involved unbridled killing, looting, and burning during which numerous people were massacred and deported. Yamashita was the link that connected Japanese atrocities in Manchuria and North China with those in Singapore.

During the final phase of the war, Yamashita was appointed commander of the 14th Area Army in the Philippines, where he surrendered to US forces at the end of the war. While he had trouble with anti-Japanese guerillas in the Philippines, he commented to the deputy chief of staff that he had dealt harshly with the local population in Singapore, so they became docile.[22]

The army order that began the "Purge through Purification" in Singapore and Malaya was issued to the Singapore Garrison Commander, Kawamura by Army Commander Yamashita. When Kawamura presented Yamashita a report of the operations on 23 February, Yamashita expressed his appreciation for Kawamura's efforts and instructed him to continue the purge if needed.[23] Yamashita was not a puppet of Tsuji but an active instigator of the Singapore Massacre.

A third important point is that the headquarters of the 25th Army included other hardliners aside from Tsuji and Yamashita. A notable example was the deputy chief of the military government of Singapore and Malaya, Colonel Watanabe Wataru.[24] He was the mastermind behind the forcible donation of $50 million and the "Implementation Guidance for Manipulating Overseas Chinese", which set out the fatal consequences of non-compliance. His earlier career included time spent as chief of a secret military agency in both Beijing and Harbin. His speech delivered at the War College in 1941 and other statements in 1942 advocated the use of strong pressure against those who "bent their knees" to the British and thereby betrayed East Asia. The lesson he derived from his experience in China was that Japan should deal harshly with the Chinese population from the outset. As a result, the Chinese population of Singapore was regarded as anti-Japanese even before the Japanese military landed.

In a sense, Japanese aggression in Southeast Asia was an extension of the Sino-Japanese War.

Fourth, among Japanese military officers and men there was a culture of prejudice and discrimination toward the Chinese and other Asian people. These attitudes had deepened following the Sino-Japanese War of 1894–95 and were deeply embedded within the Japanese population as a whole by the 1930s.

A final consideration is the notion of "preventive killing". In Japan, preventive arrest was legalised in 1941 through a revision of *Chian Iji Ho* [Maintenance of Public Order Law], which allowed communists and others holding dangerous thoughts to be arrested and held in custody even if no crime had been committed. A number of detainees were tortured to death by the police, in particular the *Tokko* special political police. The Singapore Massacre bears a close parallel to this method of preventive arrest and summary execution.

It is clear that the Singapore Massacre was not the conduct of a few evil people, but rather a product of a long period of Japanese aggression against China and other Asian countries.

Narratives of the Singapore Massacre in Postwar Japan

Negative Campaign against War Crimes Trials in the 1950s

Although the Singapore Massacre has not generated much interest among the Japanese people in the postwar period, there has been some discussion of what took place. In this section, I will discuss the evolving narratives of the Singapore Massacre in postwar Japan.

Singapore Garrison Commander Kawamura Saburo published his reminiscences in 1952, at a time when Japan was recovering its independence.[25] This book contains his diaries, personal letters, and other materials. In one letter to his family, he expressed his condolences to the victims of Singapore and prayed for the repose of their souls. The foreword to the book was written by Tsuji, who managed to escape punishment after the war, and Tsuji showed no regrets and offered no apology to the victims. Although I do not know who asked Tsuji to contribute the foreword, I believe his text accurately reflects the atmosphere in Japan at the time as described below.

During the 1950s, the Japanese government, members of parliament, and private organisations waged a nationwide campaign for the release of war criminals held in custody at Sugamo Prison in Tokyo.[26] Both conservatives and progressives took part in the campaign, arguing that minor war criminals were victims of the war, not true criminals. A Japanese government committee was in charge of recommending the parole and release of war criminals to the Allied Nations. The committee's recommendations are still closed to the public in Japan, but can be read in the national archives of the U.K. and U.S.A.

As an example of this committee's recommendations in 1952, the British government was asked to consider parole for Onishi Satoru, who took part in the Singapore Massacre as a Kempeitai officer and was sentenced to life imprisonment by a British war crimes trial.[27] The recommendation says that the figure of 5,000 victims of the Singapore Massacre was untrue and that his war crimes trial was not an act of reprisal. Although this recommendation was not approved by the British government, it reflects the Japanese government's failure to admit that mass murder had occurred in Singapore.[28] Among the Japanese people, the war crimes trials were, and still are, regarded as mock trials of little value.

Japanese Response to Accusations by Singaporeans in the 1960s

Beginning in 1962, numerous human remains dating from the Occupation were found in various locations around Singapore. Prolonged discussions between the Singapore and Japanese governments relating to these deaths led to a settlement in 1967, a matter that was reported in the Japanese newspapers, but only as minor news. For example, the *Nihon Keizai Shimbun* stated that a Japanese official involved in the negotiations as saying that no executions by shooting happened in Malaysia.[29] The *Asahi Shimbun* reported that it was hardly conceivable that the Japanese military committed atrocities in Indonesia and Thailand.[30] Another *Asahi* report criticised the Chinese Chamber of Commerce in Singapore, saying it should not stoke hatred by propagating stories of barbarity by the Japanese military during the war.[31]

In 2003, the Japanese Ministry of Foreign Affairs released documents relating to the negotiations between Singapore and Japan during this period.[32] The Japanese government had made use of a report prepared in 1946 by an army committee chaired by Sugita Ichiji, a staff officer with the 25th Army. To counter the war crimes prosecutions, the report admitted that about 5,000 people had been executed, but excused the killings on several counts.[33]

This figure, according to a written opinion by an official at the Ministry of Justice who was in charge of detained war criminals, was an exaggeration; the correct figure might be about 800. The *Asahi Shimbun* reported this number with apparent approval.[34] Additional figures come from the Ministry of Foreign Affairs, which accepted that the Japanese military had committed mass murder in Singapore, but some Japanese foreign ministry documents state that the number of victims was 3,000, while others use 5,000. One ex-foreign ministry official sent a letter to the Foreign Minister saying that Japan should repent and apologise in all sincerity, but this attitude was exceptional among officials.

On the negotiations with Singapore, the Japanese government rejected demands for reparations but agreed to make a "gesture of atonement" by providing funds in other ways. What the Japanese government feared most was economic damage as a result of a boycott or sabotage by the local Chinese should Singapore's demands be rejected. The agreement with Singapore was signed on the same day as a similar agreement with Malaysia. Singapore was to receive 25 million Singapore dollars as a free gift and another 25 million Singapore dollars in credit, while Malaysia was to receive 25 million Malaysia dollars as a free gift.[35]

To the last, the Japanese government refused to admit legal responsibility for the massacre or to carry out a survey. The mass media in Japan did not examine what had happened in Singapore and Malaya during the war. It is no exaggeration to say that the Japanese media at that time showed no inclination whatsoever to confront Japan's war crimes or war responsibility.

Publications in the 1970s

There were, however, some honest responses in the years that followed. In 1967 Professor Ienaga Saburo, famous for his history textbook lawsuit against the Japanese government, published a book entitled *The Pacific War* which dealt with the Singapore Massacre.[36] In 1970, the monthly journal *Chugoku* [China] published a feature called, "Blood Debt: Chinese Massacre in Singapore", the first extended treatment in Japan of the Singapore Massacre.[37] The piece was mostly written by Professor Tanaka Hiroshi.

The 1970s also saw publication of reminiscences by some of those directly involved in the Massacre, and by people who witnessed or heard about it, including *Nihon Kempei Seishi* [The Official History of the Japanese Kempeitai] by the Zenkoku Kenyukai Rengokai [Joint Association of National Kempei Veterans],[38] *Kempei* by Otani Keijiro, and *Hiroku Shonan Kakyo Shukusei Jiken* [Untold Story of the Syonan Chinese Massacre Incident] by Onishi Satoru. Onishi Satoru was a Kempeitai section commander who had taken part in the Massacre. In his book he admitted that the "purification" was a serious crime against humanity, but he claimed that number of victims was actually around 1,000.[39] Otani's book severely criticises the Japanese military, stating that the "purification" was an act of tyranny and claiming that the action should be criticised from a human perspective.[40]

Although veterans' associations usually justify or deny that inhuman acts had taken place, the Joint Association of National Kempei Veterans has admitted that the massacre was an inhuman act.[41] A few writers who were stationed or visited Singapore during the war have also published memoirs in which they record what they had heard about the Singapore Massacre.[42] On the whole, nobody denied that the Japanese purge in Singapore was an atrocity against humanity and historians began to pay attention to the episode. However, it failed to catch the attention of the Japanese people.

Development of Research in the 1980s and 1990s

The situation changed in 1982, when the Ministry of Education ordered the deletion of passages relating to Japanese atrocities in Asia from school textbooks, and instructed textbook writers to replace the term "aggression" with less emotive terms, such as "advance".[43] This decision was severely criticised both at home and abroad, and the issue generated interest in Japan regarding the behaviour of the Japanese military in other Asian countries during the war. A growing number of historians began to conduct research into Japanese atrocities, including the Nanjing Massacre.[44]

In 1984, while the textbook controversy continued, a bulky book called *Malayan Chinese Resistance to Japan 1937–1945: Selected Source Materials* was published in Singapore. Sections of this volume were translated into Japanese in 1986 under the title *Nihongun Senryoka no Singapore* [Singapore under Japanese Occupation], allowing Japanese to read in their own language the testimony of Singaporeans concerning wartime events.[45] The main translator was Professor Tanaka Hiroshi, mentioned earlier as the author of a magazine feature about the Singapore Massacre.

Another significant publication was a 1987 booklet by Takashima Nobuyoshi, then a high school teacher and now a professor at Ryukyu University, entitled *Tabi Shiyo Tonan-Ajia e* [Let's travel to Southeast Asia].[46] Based on information Takashima collected during repeated visits to Malaysia and Singapore beginning in the early 1980s, the booklet discussed atrocities and provided details of the "Memorial to the Civilian Victims of the Japanese Occupation" and of an exhibition of victims' mementos at the Sun Yat Sen Villa. The volume served as a guidebook for Japanese wishing to understand wartime events or visit sites of Japanese atrocities. In 1983 he began organising study tours to historical sites related to Japanese Occupation and to places where massacres occurred in Malaysia and Singapore.

In 1987, I located official military documents in the Library of the National Institute for Defense Studies, Defense Agency that included operational orders and official diaries related to the massacres of Chinese in Negri Sembilan and Malacca in 1942. Newspapers throughout Japan reported these findings, the first time public attention had been focused on the killings in Malaya.[47] The document showed that troops from Hiroshima had been involved in atrocities in Negri Sembilan and this information came as a major shock to the people of Hiroshima, who had thought themselves as victims of the atomic bomb and had never imagined that their fathers or husbands had been involved in the massacres in Malaya.[48]

In 1988, several citizens' groups jointly invited Chinese survivors from Malaysia to visit Japan, and held rallies where Japanese citizens listened to their testimony. A book that included these statements was published in 1989.[49] Also in 1988, the Negri Sembilan Chinese Assembly Hall published a book in Chinese called the *Collected Materials of Suffering of Chinese in Negeri Sembilan during the Japanese Occupation*, and the following year Professor Takashima and I published a Japanese translation of this volume.[50] Another source of information was the history textbook used in Singapore by students in lower secondary school, *Social and Economic History of Modern Singapore 2*, which was translated into Japanese in 1988. The material it contained concerning the occupation attracted the attention of Japanese readers, particularly teachers and researchers.[51]

As might be expected, there was a backlash to these initiatives. It was claimed that Japanese troops killed only guerrillas and their supporters, and that the number was much smaller than reported. Responding to these allegations, I published a book in 1992 entitled *Kakyo Gyakusatu: Nihongun Shihaika no Marei Hanto* [Chinese Massacres: The Malay Peninsula under Japanese Occupation][52] that substantiated in detail the activities of the Japanese military in Negri Sembilan during March 1942, when several thousand Chinese were massacred. Since then there has been no rebuttal by those who would not concede the massacres in Malaya apart from personal attacks and corrections of trifling details that have no effect on the central argument.[53]

In 1996, the Singapore Heritage Society's book, *SYONAN: Singapore under the Japanese, 1942–1945* was translated into Japanese.[54] This book introduced to Japanese readers the living conditions and suffering of Singaporeans under the Japanese occupation in a comprehensive way.

Further information appeared in a book I published entitled, *Sabakareta Senso Hanzai: Igirisu no Tainichi Senpan Saiban* [Tried War Crimes; British War Crimes Trials of Japanese]. This volume contains an account of the Syonan Massacre based on British, Chinese and Japanese documents.[55]

The Rightist Backlash and the School Textbook Issue after the Year 2000

In the 1990s, some Japanese high school history textbooks began to provide information on the massacres in Singapore and Malaya, although they devoted only one or two lines to the events. More recently, chauvinistic campaigns and sentiments have become rampant in Japan. A number of ultra right books now claim that the Nanjing Massacre is a fabrication, that the Japanese military took good care of comfort women, and so on. Under pressure from the Ministry of Education, the Liberal Democratic Party, and other right-wingers, statements in school textbooks about Japanese atrocities have become less common, and the Minister of Education said in 2004 that it was desirable for descriptions of Japanese atrocities to be dropped.[56] Moreover, teachers who give lessons about Japanese aggression and army atrocities are often subjected to criticism by local assembly members or municipal education boards.

Descriptions of the Singapore massacre in high school history textbooks are particularly rare. According to research in the 1990s, just 8 out of a total of 26 textbooks referred to the event.[57] The most widely used textbook states simply that "atrocities took place in Singapore and elsewhere".[58] Other textbooks say that the Japanese army massacred tens of thousands of overseas Chinese in Singapore and Malaya, but even these descriptions are limited to one or two lines, and give no details. Anyone who dared set a question about the atrocities for a university entrance examination could expect attacks not only from right-wingers but also from MPs belonging to the ruling Liberal Democratic Party.

The situation is similar with regard to junior high schools history textbooks. In the eight textbooks approved by the Ministry of Education in April 2005 for use from 2006, descriptions of Korean forced labour have all but disappeared, as has the term "comfort women". Overall, references to Japanese aggression and atrocities have been drastically reduced under pressure from the Ministry of Education, the Liberal Democratic Party, and the right-leaning mass media. If the current ultra-nationalistic trend strengthens, it seems likely that even the few descriptions of the Singapore massacre that do exist will be eliminated in the near future.

Conclusion

Work by Singaporean and other researchers has produced information about the Singapore massacre, but it seems to me that there is room for further research. In particular, what seems to be lacking is collation of documents in the various languages: English, Chinese, and Japanese. While Singapore citizens have accounts of the Massacre and the suffering caused by the Japanese occupation, students in Japan are unable to imagine what happened in Singapore and Malaya during the Japanese Occupation. Few Japanese students have any opportunity to learn about the Occupation, and the many Japanese who visit Singapore each year generally have no awareness of the killings or of the wartime suffering of Singaporeans. It is difficult to redress the balance, but if Japan is to achieve full reconciliation with the people of Singapore and other Southeast Asian countries and gain their trust, steps in the right direction must be taken.

Notes

1. The Japanese term "Shukusei" was used by the Japanese Army at the time. In Chinese community of Singapore it is usually called "Sook Ching".

2. Regarding details of the decision-making in the 25th Army, see Hayashi Hirofumi, *Sabakareta Senso Hanzai* [Tried War Crimes: British War Crimes Trials of Japanese] (Tokyo: Iwanami Shoten, 1998) and "Singaporu Kakyo Shukusei" [Massacre of Chinese in Singapore], *Nature-People-Society: Science and the Humanities*, Kanto-Gakuin University, no. 40, Jan. 2006.

3. Kawamura's diary is preserved in the Public Record Office in Kew Gardens in London.

4. This document is preserved in the Library of the National Institute for Defense Studies [LNIDS], Defense Agency, Tokyo.

5. For example, National Archives of Singapore, *The Japanese Occupation, 1942–1945* (Singapore: Times, 1996), p. 68.

6. The operational order of the 25th Army and the order of the 5th Division dated 21 February 1942 in LNIDS.

7. "Kakyo Kosaku Jisshi Yoryo [Policy Principles toward Overseas Chinese]" in LNIDS.

8. Onishi Satoru, *Hiroku Shonan Kakyo Shukusei Jiken* [Untold Story of the Syonan Chinese Massacre Incident] (Tokyo: Kongo Shuppan, 1977), pp. 69 and 78.

9. This claim is prevalent among researchers in Japan. It is believed even by those who are not right-wingers. I have not clarified who put forward this reason for first time.

10. The Dalforce file in "British Military Administration, Chinese Affairs, 1945–1946" (National Archives of Singapore).

11. There are numerous books with such assertion, in particular, books in Chinese.

12. Rikujo Jieitai Kanbu Gakko [Ground Staff College, Ground Self-Defense Force], *Marei Sakusen* [The Malay Campaign] (Tokyo: Hara Shobo, 1996), pp. 240–1.

13. Onishi, *Hiroku Shonan Kakyo Shukusei Jiken*, pp. 87–8.

14. Furyo Kankei Chosa Chuo Iinkai [Central Board of Inquiry on POWs], "Singaporu niokeru Kakyo Shodan Jokyo Chosho" [Record of Investigation on the Execution of Overseas Chinese in Singapore], 23 Oct. 1945. Reprinted in Nagai Hitoshi (ed.), *Senso Hanzai Chosa Shiryo* [Documents on War Crimes Investigation] (Tokyo: Higashi Shuppan, 1995).

15. See Hayashi Hirofumi, *Sabakareta Senso Hanzai*, p. 224.

16. Otani Keijiro, *Kempei* [The Military Police] (Tokyo: Shin-Jinbutsu Oraisha, 1973), p. 189.

17. Onishi, *Hiroku Shonan Kakyo Shukusei Jiken*, p. 86.

18. The intelligence files on Tsuji are preserved in Boxes 457 and 458, Personal Files of the Investigative Records Repository, Record Group 319 (The Army Staff), US National Archives and Records Administration.

19. Asada Kyoji and Kobayashi Hideo (eds.), *Nihon Teikokushugi no Manshu Shihai* [Administration of Manchuria by the Japanese Imperialism] (Tokyo: Jicho-Sha, 1986), p. 180.

20. See Onishi, *Hiroku Shonan Kakyo Shukusei Jiken*, pp. 88–92.

21. Boeicho Boei Kenkyusho Senshi-bu [Military History Department, National Institute of Defense Studies, Defense Agency], *Hokushi no Chian-sen*, Part 1 [Security Operation in North China] (Tokyo: Asagumo Shinbunsha, 1968), pp. 114–30.

22. Kojima Hoburu, *Shisetu Yamashita Tomoyuki* [Historical Narrative Yamashita Tomoyuki] (Tokyo: Bungei Shunjusha, 1969), p. 325.

23. Kawamura's diary. See also Hayashi, *Sabakareta Senso Hanzai*, p. 220.

24. See Akashi Yoji, "Watanabe Gunsei" [Military Administration by Watanabe], in *Nihon Senryoka no Eiryo Mare Shingaporu* [Malaya and Singapore under the Japanese Occupation, 1941–45], ed. Akashi Yoji (Tokyo: Iwanami Shoten, 2001).

25. Kawamura Saburo, *Jusan Kaidan wo Noboru* [Walking up Thirteen Steps of the Stairs] (Tokyo: Ato Shobo, 1952).

26. See Hayashi Hirofumi, *BC-kyu Senpan Saiban* [Class B & C War Crimes Trials] (Tokyo: Iwanami Shoten, 2005), Ch. 6.

27. FO371/105435(National Archives, UK).

28. Later, he was released in 1957.

29. *Nihon Keizai Shimbun*, 3 Nov. 1966.

30. *Asahi Shimbun*, 20 Sept. 1967.

31. *Asahi Shimbun*, 18 Sept. 1963.

32. These documents are open to the public at the Diplomatic Record Office of the Ministry of Foreign Affairs.

33. See endnote 14.

34. *Asahi Shimbun*, 29 Sept. 1963.

35. Hara Fujio, "Mareishia, Shingaporu no Baisho Mondai" [Reparation Problem with Singapore and Malaysia], *Senso Sekinin Kenkyu* [The Report on Japan's War Responsibility], no. 10, Dec. 1995.
36. Ienaga Saburo, *Taiheiyo Senso* [The Pacific War] (Tokyo: Iwanami Shoten, 1967).
37. "Kessai: Singaporu no Chugokujin Gyakusatsu Jiken" [Blood Debt: Chinese Massacre in Singapore], in *Chugoku* [China], vol. 76 (Mar. 1970).
38. Tokyo: Private Press, 1976.
39. Onishi, *Hiroku Shonan Kakyo Shukusei Jiken*, pp. 93–7.
40. Otani Keijiro, *Kempei*, p. 189.
41. Zenkoku Kenyukai Rengokai, *Nihon Kempei Seishi*, p. 979.
42. For example, Terasaki Hiroshi, *Senso no Yokogao* [Profile of the War] (Tokyo: Taihei Shuppan, 1974), Nakajima Kenzo, *Kaiso no Bungaku* [Literature of Recollection], vol. 5 (Tokyo: Heibonsha, 1977), Omata Yukio, *Zoku Shinryaku* [Sequel: Aggression] (Tokyo: Tokuma Shoten, 1982), and so on.
43. See Rekishigaku Kenkyukai [The Historical Science Society of Japan], *Rekishika wa naze Shinryaku ni kodawaruka* [Why Historian adhere to Aggression] (Tokyo: Aoki Shoten, 1982).
44. Composed of historians and journalists, Nankin Jiken Chosa Kenkyu Kai [The Society for the Study of the Nanjin Massacre] was established in 1984. It remains active, although the scope of research has been extended to Japanese atrocities in China and the rest of Southeast Asia.
45. Tokyo: Aoki Shoten, 1986.
46. Tokyo: Iwanami Shoten, 1987.
47. This article was delivered by the Kyodo News Service and came forth on newspapers on 8 Dec. 1987.
48. As mentioned before, the 5th Division conducted the Purge through Purification throughout Malay Peninsula except Johor. The headquarters of the Division in peacetime was situated in Hiroshima and soldiers were conscripted in Hiroshima and neighboring prefectures.
49. Senso Giseisha wo Kokoro ni Kizamukai [The Society of Keeping War Victims in our Heart], *Nihongun no Mareisia Jumin Gyakusatu* [The Massacres of Malaysian Local Population by the Japanese Military] (Osaka: Toho Shuppan, 1989).
50. Originally published in 1988. The Japanese translation was as follows: Takashima Nobuyoshi & Hayashi Hirofumi (eds.), *Maraya no Nihongun* [The Japanese Army in Malaya] (Tokyo: Aoki Shoten, 1989).
51. Ishiwata Nobuo and Masuo Keizo (eds.), *Gaikoku no Kyokasho no nakano Nihon to Nihonjin* [Japan and the Japanese in a Foreign Textbook] (Tokyo: Ikkosha, 1988).
52. Tokyo: Suzusawa Shoten, 1992. As for arguments of right-wingers, see Chapter 8 of this book.
53. See, for example, two articles by Hata Ikuhiko in the journal *Seiron*, Aug. and Oct. 1992 and Professor Takashima's and my responses in the same journal on two occasions in Sept. and Nov. 1992.
54. Tokyo: Gaifusha, 1996.

55. Tokyo: Iwanami Shoten, 1998.
56. See Hayashi Hirofumi, "Nihon no Haigaiteki Nashonarizumu wa naze taito shitaka" [Why the Japanese Chauvinistic Nationalism has gained power] in VAWW-NET Japan (ed.), *Kesareta Sabaki: NHK Bangumi Kaihen to Seiji Kainyu Jiken* [Deleted Judgment: Interpolation of the NHK's TV Program and the Politician's Intervention] (Tokyo: Gaifusha, 2005).
57. Zenkoku Rekishi Kyoiku Kenkyu Kyogikai [The National Council for Education of History] (ed.), *Nihonshi Yogo-shu* [Lexicon of the Japanese History Textbook] (Tokyo: Yamakawa Shoten, 2000), p. 291.
58. *Shosetsu Nihonshi* [The Details of Japanese History] (Tokyo: Yamakawa Shoten, 2001), p. 332.

10

An Annotated Bibliographical Study of the Japanese Occupation of Malaya/Singapore, 1941–45

AKASHI YOJI

For three years and eight months during the Asia-Pacific War, Japan occupied virtually the entire expanse of Southeast Asia. The Occupation had an impact on postwar political, social and psychological developments of the peoples in the region.

The Japanese military administration of Malaya/Singapore thoroughly controlled every aspect of the society because the Imperial Conference of 31 May 1943 decided to incorporate the former British colony as a permanent possession of the empire. Preparing for the colonisation, the Malay Military Administration (*Malai Gunseikkambu*) implemented a thorough going programme of Japanising the occupied people and the society with an indoctrination in Japanese spirit (*Nippon seishin*) and emperor worship.

Despite its impact on Malaya/Singapore, the Occupation received, comparatively speaking, little attention from Japanese and Malayan/Singaporean academic circles for many years. In contrast, academics in the United States, Britain and the Netherlands began examining its effects in the early 1950s.

Willard H. Elsbree's work,[1] published in 1953, was the first attempt to interpret the political significance of the Occupation for postwar nations in South East Asia, and it was followed, during the 1950s and the 1960s, by additional academic works by western scholars, among them, F.C. Jones (1954),[2] M.A. Aziz (1955),[3] Harry J. Benda (1958),[4] Josef Silverstein (1966),[5] Dorothy Guyot (1966),[6] and George S. Kanahele (1967).[7]

In Japan, studies of the Occupation and its administration remained "frozen" for 11 years because of a strong current of postwar anti-war pacifism in the country, and decline in the pre-war and wartime fever for *Nanyo* (the South Seas). Japanese anti-military sentiment was so strong that any writings relating to World War II and the region, apart from debunking Japan's Occupation practices, were unpopular. Furthermore, both academics and non-academics were afraid of speaking about their activities in the Occupation administrations, or of writing about their experiences. Studies of the Occupation thus remained, for more than a decade, "taboo" in such an environment in the Japanese academic circles in the postwar period.

However, a breakthrough appeared in 1959 when two Japanese, who had served in the Naval Civil Administration in Jakarta, Kishi Koichi and Nishijima Shigetada, published a study of the Japanese Military Administration of Indonesia[8] under a grant from the Rockefeller Foundation. As Nishijima said in 1956, it had been "folly" to engage in studies probing into Japanese wartime activities in Indonesia. This pioneering and highly significant work received scant attention in the Japanese scholarly circles, where the topic had remained taboo. In 1961 and 1963, Itagaki Yoichi of Hitotsubashi University, a former research associate with the *Malai Gunseikkambu's* Research Department, published an article in English about Japanese policy for Malaya and a second one about Islam in Malaya and Sumatra. Five years later, Ota Tsunezo, who had served in the Military Administration of Burma, published a documented monograph on the Occupation there.[9]

By the late 1960s, the strong anti-military sentiment of the immediate post-war years had abated as the Japanese regained their national confidence through reconstruction of the war-torn economy and in successfully hosting the 1964 Tokyo Olympic Games. The Japanese were gradually emerging from the trauma and dejection of the defeat in World War II.

With the publication of *Daitoa senso zenshi* (General History of the Greater East Asia War)[10] in 1965, written by a former colonel of the Imperial General Staff, and of *Marei shinko sakusen* (Malayan Campaign)[11] in 1966, the first volume of an official war history series project undertaken by the Defence Agency's History Department, studies of the war became less of a taboo subject. Access, though still restricted then, to Japanese Imperial Army and Navy documents returned from the United States, and to the Tokugawa *gunsei* (military government) collection both in the War History Department Archives, enabled academics and non-academics to examine archival sources and opened the door for researchers to study the Occupation *gunsei*.

In 1966, Akashi Yoji became the first academic to obtain official access to the Department's Archives to carry out *gunsei* studies. He also

conducted interviews with former Japanese military and civilian officials of
the *Malai Gunseikambu*. He presented his research result, "Japanese Military
Administration in Malaya — Its formation and evolution in reference
to the sultans, the Islamic religion, and Moslem Malays, 1941–1945" at
the 1968 Kuala Lumpur International Association of Historians of Asia
(IAHA) Conference.[12] But *gunsei* studies are far from being recognised in
the Japanese academic circles as a proper genre in historiography in contrast
to the western academic world where the topic falls within an established
field of studies.

The following chart, which is a record of memoirs, autobiographies,
documents, biographies, monographs, and articles published in Japanese from
1946 to 2005, illustrates the point discussed above. In the period between
1946 and 1974, war related publications were relatively few, reflecting limited
public interest in war literature. In contrast, there was a sharp rise in the
period of 1975–99, particularly in the categories of documents, monographs,
biographies and articles. Translated literature concerning the battle for
Malaya and Singapore and biographical studies of Japanese generals written
by British and Australians also appeared in this period.

**Published Literature Relating to the Japanese Gunsei Period in
Malaya and Singapore**

Years	Diary, Memoir	Document, Monograph Biography, Article	Translation	Total
1946–49	1	0	0	1
1950–54	7	1	0	8
1955–59	5	0	1	6
1960–64	3	3	0	6
1965–69	5	6	0	11
1970–74	5	6	2	13
1975–79	15	31	0	46
1980–84	8	27	2	37
1985–89	7	47	3	57
1990–94	3	43	4	50
1995–99	4	28	3	35
2000–5	1	8	0	9
Total	64	200	15	279

In the 1975–99 period, former *gunsei* officials, soldiers, academics, and non-academics, freed from the trauma of the defeat in war, were less hesitant about making their wartime experiences public in a positive term, and journalists were also writing about what Japanese did positively and negatively in occupied Malaya/Singapore. After 30 years it was no longer folly to study about the *gunsei* period of Malaya/Singapore, and by using newly discovered primary sources, scholars and journalists have cast light on various unexplored aspects of the Occupation years. By the year 2000, however, an interest in the Occupation years seems to have reached a saturation point as indicated above by a decrease in the number of publications after that date.

In 1978, a three-year Culture Conflict project was organised with support from the Japanese Ministry of Education, and one of its objectives was to carry out oral recorded interviews with former military men and civilians who participated in the *gunsei* in Southeast Asia. As a member of the project's Malaysian team, Akashi interviewed some 40 persons. The selected recorded interviews were published in 1980 and 1981.[13]

Tapping the Defence Agency's archival materials and based upon his own experience, Iwatake Teruhiko, a former *Malai Gunseikkambu* official, published in 1981 a comprehensive study of the economic policies in occupied Malaya and Indonesia.[14]

In 1983, Sodei Rinjiro of Hosei University convened a symposium for a comparative study of the U.S. Occupation of Japan and the Japanese Occupation of Southeast Asian countries (Indonesia, Malaysia, and the Philippines). Some 40 Japanese and foreign scholars participated in the conference.[15] Also the Japan Association of Southeast Asian History organised, in 1990, a panel on the Japanese Occupation of Southeast Asia. Southeast Asian occupation *gunsei* studies by 1990 had been established in Japan as a genre in historiography.

Beginning in 1988, the study of the Occupation of Southeast Asia was further enhanced by "forums" established with support from Toyota Foundation grant, beginning with Indonesia, the Philippines, Malaya/Singapore, Burma, and East Timor. The Forum, concerned with Occupied Malaya/Singapore, started in 1994 with a team of Southeast Asianists and military historians. During its 4-year lifespan, the Forum searched systematically for documents in archives and libraries in Australia, Britain, India, Malaysia, and Singapore and the United States as well as in Japan. It also collected diaries and memoirs in private possession, and interviewed some 50 persons involved in the Malaya/Singapore Occupation *gunsei* as part of an oral history project. These collected primary sources are invaluable for researchers of *gunsei*.

The Forum has published a monograph,[16] an interview record,[17] selected papers on education,[18] Watanabe's memoirs and diary,[19] *Nippon-go* textbooks,[20] and reprints of North Borneo *gunsei* yearbooks of 1942 and 1943, all in Japanese.[21] A bibliographical references on *gunsei* and Japanese Malayan (Malaysia) relations in English, Chinese, Japanese, and Malay languages, published and unpublished in pre-war, intra-war, and postwar years, is now being prepared for publication in late 2007. It is hoped that additional unpublished private diaries and memoirs collected by the Forum will be published in the future.

Since 1970, a number of Malaysian and foreign scholars have published research on the history of occupied Malaya/Singapore. G.P. Ramachandra,[22] Halinah Bamadhaj,[23] Cheah Boon Kheng,[24] Paul H. Kratoska,[25] and Abu Talib Ahmad[26] have written theses or published monographs and articles delving into the impact of the Occupation on Malayan and Singapore postwar politics, economy, society, religion, and ethnic relations. Also the National Archives of Singapore (in 1981) and Universiti Sains Malaysia (in 1983) respectively undertook an oral history project to gather first-hand accounts of the Occupation. However, no definitive work of the Japanese Occupation history has yet been written.

Why were studies of the Occupation of Malaya and Singapore delayed? First, for the Japanese, the postwar anti-military environment was not conducive for the study of the Occupation or, for that matter, of the Asia-Pacific War generally. The people who took part in the Occupation were afraid of writing about it lest they might be attacked for having collaborated with the military, and few universities offered classes in Southeast Asian studies in the 1950s. As a result, few Southeast Asianists were trained. In the early 1960s interest in Southeast Asia was revived with the establishment of the government-affiliated Institute of Asian Economic Affairs in Tokyo in 1960, followed in 1963 by the Center of Southeast Asian Studies at Kyoto University and the Japan Association of Southeast Asian History in 1965. These developments led to the emergence of a generation of students of Southeast Asian affairs. Equipped with language training, they, unfettered from personal links to wartime activities, have examined the Occupation *gunsei*.

Second, locating and then gaining access to archival sources was problematic for many years. An enormous quantity of *gunsei* papers was destroyed after the surrender by military orders, and many of the surviving documents that were seized by the British Military Administration have been missing since. My search in 1996 for them led me to the Archives of the Indian Defence Ministry but access to whatever they may have, was denied.

Third, Japanese repatriates were not allowed to take any written records including diaries and memos when they embarked for home. Some privileged high-ranking officials who returned to Japan before the war's end carried back official papers and diaries but much of this material was incinerated in air raids towards the end of the conflict. Marquis Tokugawa Yoshichika, an advisor to the *Malai Gunseikkambu* from March 1942 to June 1944, Watanabe Wataru (see p. 256) and Sakakibara Masaharu (see p. 257), were a few officials who were able to bring back official documents, and the Tokugawa collection forms the principal part of the Defence Agency's holding on *gunsei* materials at its War History Department Archives.

Lastly, although the War History Department has relaxed regulations in opening its collection to the public, access to personal diaries and memoirs is still restricted or denied for reasons of privacy. Another problem is a lapse of time more than 60 years since the end of the war. By the time a systematic oral history recording project was started in 1978, many senior military and civilian officers as well as soldiers had passed away and memories of mid-ranking officials, who were by then in their early 70s, were growing hazy. Since then their death toll has been high, and hardly any person who had participated in the Occupation period *gunsei* is alive today.

In the following pages I will introduce selected *gunsei* sources, commenting briefly on each of them.

I. Official Documents

1. *The Tokugawa Collection (Tokugawa shiryo)*

This large and important collection, donated by Tokugawa Yoshichika, is housed in the Defence Agency's War History Archives in Tokyo. The collection comprises 126 volumes containing 374 items largely sorted by subjects. Tokugawa turned the collection over to the War History Archives in 1957, which made it available to the public in the 1970s. Apart from the 12 items relating to Burma, Java, North Borneo, Sumatra and Thailand, the rest of the holdings is related to Malaya/Singapore administered by the *Tomi Gunseikkambu*[27] and later by the *Malai Gunseikkambu*. Most of them were once classified documents.

More important papers included in the collection are: *Senji geppo* (Wartime monthly reports) March 1942 to March 1944; *Gunsei junpo*

(Ten-day reports, Nos. 1–25), 10 April 1942 to 20 December 1942; *Tomi koho* and *Malai koho* (*Tomi* public notices and *Malai* public notices), Nos. 1–21, 1 November 1942 to 15 April 1943, 15 May 1943 to 29 January 1944; speeches and minutes of conferences of governors, department heads, *gunsei* executive directors, police, education, and sultans and Muslim leaders; papers relating to administrative and economic policies prepared by the Army Ministry; various statistics; and numerous field research reports on agriculture, living conditions, education, economic affairs, finance, inflation, industry, and religion.

Tomi koho,[28] *Malai koho*,[29] and *Gunsei geppo*[30] have been edited by Kurasawa Aiko and published, while selected papers on education[31] and field research reports[32] edited by Akashi in 22 volumes were published in 2007. The Gunsei Research Department's field work reports prepared by academics of Tokyo *Shoka Daigaku* (now Hitotsubashi University) are of a high standard, and include many studies not conducted during the British colonial period. They are very useful for the study of the daily life of the occupied people.

2. *The Watanabe Collection (Watanabe Wataru gunsei shiryo)*

The Watanabe papers are in the possession of Col. Watanabe Wataru who, as the first director general of the *Malai Gunseikkambu*, was the architect of the *Malai gunsei* from November 1941 to March 1943. Documents edited by Akashi in 2 volumes (volumes 3 and 4 of the 5 volume Watanabe Collection) include 44 items, 10 of which are also found in the Tokugawa collection. A unique feature of the Watanabe papers is that they include a number of policy papers drafted in the formative months of the *gunsei* period by Watanabe himself with the assistance of his trusted adviser, Takase Toru. About one-half of the drafts were prepared in the period between December 1941 and July 1942. These early papers reveal Watanabe's *gunsei* philosophy and the rationale underlying his policies in the areas of financial, Chinese and sultanate affairs. His position on the disposition of enemy property, particularly the controversial rubber question, is of interest as it created a schism within his office. Another paper that attracts attention is Tokugawa's advice given in November 1941 to Watanabe on dealing with the sultan. Tokugawa was of the opinion that the Malay sultans should be persuaded to surrender their power to the Japanese emperor as the Tokugawa *shogun* did to the Meiji emperor in the Restoration of 1868.

Volume 5 of the Watanabe Collection contains the *Gunsei* Yearbook covering the period from March 1942 to March 1943 for Malaya and Sumatra.[33] It is a general survey of *gunsei* policy and its implementation, and consists of 8 sections: general remarks, *gunsei* outlines, domestic affairs, transportation, finance and monetary affairs, trade, industry, and local government. It was published by Ryukei Shosha in 1998.

3. *The Sakakibara Collection*[34]

This collection, discovered in 1997, was in the possession of Lt. Sakakibara Masaharu, who was a staff officer in the Office of *Gunsei Sokambu* of the Southern Army from November 1941 to May 1943. Viscount Sakakibara, as a privileged member of the peerage, had access to classified *gunsei* papers and was able to retain them in his possession when he completed his tour of duty. The papers were edited in 9 volumes by Akashi and published by Ryukei Shosha in 2005. Included in the collection are some 150 items divided into 6 sections: classified papers that were opened to the public in the 1970s, classified papers that are treated as official documents, minutes of conferences, policies drafted that are treated as official documents, minutes of conferences, policies drafted by *Gunsei Sokambu*, reports prepared by non-government organisations and individuals, and Sakakibara's personal diary. The majority of the papers are concerned with the economic affairs of occupied countries in the Southern regions. The Sakakibara papers are an indispensable source of information for the study of overall *gunsei* policy in the region and are particularly valuable as a source of statistics otherwise not readily available.

II. Official Publications

1. The Defence Agency's War History Department founded in 1956 undertook the task of compiling an Asia Pacific War history series. The first volume of this multi-volume study of the war was *Marei Shinko Sakusen* (Malayan campaign), published in 1966. Other books relating to Malaya/ Singapore are: *Hito/Marei Homen Kaigun Shinko Sakusen* (Naval operations in the Philippines and Malaya), published in 1969; *Nampo Shinko Rikugun Koku Sakusen* (Army-Air Force operations in the Southern area), published in 1990; *Nansei Homen Rikugun Sakusen — Marei Ran'in no Boei* (Army operations in the South western theatre — Defence of Malaya and the Dutch East Indies), published in 1976; and *Nampo no Gunsei* (Military

Administration of the Southern area), published in 1985. These volumes, based on official army and navy documents, memoirs, diaries, and interviews, represent the official version of the war history as seen from the Japanese side, or more specifically interpreted by former staff officers of the Imperial Armed Forces. Written by amateur historians, it is descriptive rather than analytical in approach. The series was published in 103 volumes by Asagumo Shinbunsha, Tokyo.

III. Diaries and Memoirs (unpublished and published)

The Archives of the War History Department hold numerous personal diaries and memoirs of the former officers of the Imperial Armed Forces. Access to many of these materials is restricted because of the wishes of the donors. The following sources are relevant to Malaya/Singapore.

1. *Inada Masazumi (Inada Diary, unpublished)*

Lt. Gen. Inada served in Syonan as the deputy chief of staff of the Southern Army for nine months (February to October 1943). His unpublished diary tells us how he conceived the idea of organising the *Giyugun* (voluntary army) that was formed in October 1943 under the command of Ibrahim Yaacob, prewar leader of the *Kesatuan Malayu Muda* (KMM or Young Malay Union). He was critical of the lax morals of the officers and soldiers who enjoyed their leisure time as if there were no war going on.

2. *Ishii Akiho (Nampo Gunsei Diary, unpublished)*

Col. Ishii was a staff officer in charge of *gunsei* and intelligence for the Southern Army from November 1941 to December 1942. Based on his experience in administering occupied China, Ishii drafted a set of *gunsei* principles giving priority to the acquisition of strategic raw materials vital for national defence and self-sufficiency of the Occupation forces. These principles were incorporated in *Nampo Senryochi Gyosei Jisshi Yoryo*, 20 November 1941. To realise these goals, the local people had to endure economic hardships. He said that this was the lesson he learned from the Sino-Japanese war in which he encountered constant bickering over the question whether military requirements or those of the *gunsei* should be given priority. According to Ishii, on 31 December 1941 Gen. Yamashita Tomoyuki, commander of the 25th Army, expressed his desire to separate

Sumatra from Java and incorporate it into the Japanese territorial possessions together with Malaya. Though the Southern Army and the central Army authorities were skeptical of making these countries Japanese possessions, they agreed in late June 1942 with the 25th Army's request to administer Malaya and Sumatra together.

3. *Imaoka Yutaka (Nampo no Kaiso, Memoirs, unpublished)*

Col. Imaoka was a *gunsei* staff officer of the Southern Army and later of the 7th Area Army in Syonan between August 1943 and August 1945. When he arrived there, he, like Inada, found a relaxed mood in the army headquarters, where there was no sense of urgency, as if there were no fighting going on around them. Even low ranking officers, he wrote, drove captured automobiles and high-ranking officers whiled away the afternoons, playing golf. Confronting the *gunsei* administration, he said, were two serious problems: fortifying the defence of Malaya/Singapore against an impending Allied invasion and securing food supplies, especially rice.

4. *Fujimura Masuzo (Fujimura Kaisoroku, Memoirs, unpublished)*

Col. Fujimura succeeded Watanabe Wataru in March 1943 and later became the *Gunseikan* (Superintendent) of the *Malai Gunseikkambu* and chief of staff of the 29th Army. He characterised the *Malai gunsei* as a *Kakyo* (Overseas Chinese) *gunsei*, differentiating it from other *gunsei* areas. According to Fujimura, the *Kakyo* question was always a foremost problem in the *Malai gunsei* because it was the *Kakyo* who organised an anti-Japanese army, the *Kayko* who cooperated with the *gunsei*, and the *Kakyo* who opposed cooperation with the *gunsei*. During his tenure in office, the most serious problems he faced were securing rice supply, recruiting labourers for the construction of the Burma-Thai railway and the Kra Isthmus railway, and controlling inflation.

5. *Kushida Masao (Kushida Nikki and Kaisoroku, Diary and Memoir, unpublished)*

Col. Kushida served as a staff officer in the Imperial General Headquarters and as a staff officer in charge of operations of the 7th Area Army and the Southern Army (April 1943–August 1945). His diary of 1942 records his frequent contacts with the *Malai gunsei* administrators with whom he formulated a hard line *gunsei* policy. In his memoirs written in 1948, he characterised the Asia-Pacific War in positive term, saying that it inspired indigenous people to liberate themselves from western domination and to gain independence.

6. *Kunitake Teruhiko (Marei Sakusen no Kiroku, Record of Malay Operations, unpublished)*

Maj. Kunitake was a junior operations staff officer of the 25th Army who infiltrated British Malaya in early 1941 for intelligence gathering. After having observed the British defence posture in the Peninsula Malaya and Singapore, he reported that Singapore could be successfully attacked from the north. Tsuji Masanobu and Kunitake designed the operational plans based on this approach and carried them out exactly as planned.

7. *Mori Fumio (Gunsei Shubo, Memo, unpublished)*

Maj. Mori was a *gunsei* staff officer with the 7th Area Army. The memo includes extensive *gunsei* statistical data on economic matters in Malaya/Singapore, Java, and Sumatra, including industry, transportation, defence, education, and inter-regional trade during the years 1944–45. It is an extremely useful source of information. Kurasawa Akiko is editing it for publication.

8. *Sukegawa Seiji (Sukegawa Nikki 1943, Diary, unpublished)*

Maj. Gen. Sukegawa was the governor of Kedah/Perlis from March 1942 to October 1943. His diary records in detail, personal activities such as visiting the *kampongs* frequently to meet people, helping them to grow cash crops, and introducing an experimental planting of *Horai* rice, a strain developed in Taiwan for double cropping. Because information about Kedah is scarce, the diary is useful but the entry for 1942 is missing.

9. *Sakakibara Masaharu (Ichi chui no Tonan Ajia Gunsei Nikki, Diary, published). Tokyo: Soshisha.*

As was discussed earlier, Sakakibara served in the General Headquarters of the Southern Amy as a *gunsei* staff officer. The diary, as a primary source, is valuable and rare in that he criticises, without mincing words, *gunsei* policies and its implementation expressing his opinions with *honne* (frank opinion). Throughout the diary, he recorded critically of the unbecoming behaviour of victory-intoxicated Japanese soldiers and officers who visited bars and comfort stations frequently. The diary is more than a personal record of what he thought. It is valuable for his opinions of the *gunsei* as a student of political science and what *gunsei* ought to be. The diary is rich in information and is written logically and analytically. It was published in 1998 with Kurasawa's comments and will be translated into *Bahasa Melayu* with the assistance of Sakakibara's granddaughter.

10. *Taniguchi Takeji (Gekido no Seiki — Ichi Senpan Kempei no Kaiso, Memoirs, published). Tokyo: Taipinkai.*

Taniguchi, Kempeitai captain of the 29th Army in Taiping, was the commander of a fighting unit engaged in the mopping-up operations against the MPAJA (Malayan People Anti-Japanese Army) and Force 136 in Grik and the Bidor/Tapah areas. The book was published in 1997. He recalls his negotiations with MPAJA officers, right after the Japanese surrender, who said that they would not attack surrendered Japanese as they were no longer the enemy.

11. *Seki Michisuke (Sei mo Shi mo. Memoirs, published). Tokyo: Bungeisha.*

Seki served in the 2nd Field Army Kempeitai and in the 29th Army Kempeitai. He talks about his wartime experience of engaging in the battle of Malaya/Singapore, of carrying out what he personally believed to be the unjustifiable *sook ching* in Singapore, of fighting the MPAJA in Johor, Negri Sembilan, and Perak, of serving Suhbas Chandra Bose as an escort police, and of negotiating for a postwar armistice with the MPAJA's ranking member whom he thought was Chin Peng, secretary of the Perak district of the Malayan Communist Party. His memoirs were published in 2002. Seki had visited the Peace Village of ex-MPAJA soldiers in southern Thailand, where he had talks with Chin Peng's deputy. They reminisced about their fighting days in Perak. He also met Chin Peng in Bangkok in 2005.

12. *Onishi Satoru (Hiroku Syonan Kakyo Shukusei Kiroku, Memoir, published). Tokyo: Kongo Shuppansha, 1977.*

Onishi is one of the best-known Kempeitai officers associated with the *sook ching* of Singapore Chinese in February–March 1942 as well as with a special police unit fighting MPAJA guerillas and Force 136. According to Onishi, an order for liquidating the anti-Japanese Chinese was issued around 25 January 1942 to the Kempeitai commander. Though the Kempeitai had strong reservations about carrying out the *sook ching* order, which was ordered by a higher command, it had to be obeyed without question. Onishi believed that Tsuji Masanobu masterminded the *sook ching* and together with Asaeda Shigeharu, he agitated for carrying out a thorough killing field. Onishi has insisted that the Chinese victims from the *sook ching* numbered no more than 2,000.

13. *Ishibe Toshiro (Seishun Kempei Kashikan Ishibe Memo, Memoirs, published)*

Like Seki, Ishibe served in the 2nd Field Army Kempeitai and Onishi's counter espionage unit. The accuracy of his recorded activities in his memoirs is questionable, particularly in respect to dates and individual names. This is due to his failing memory. Tan Chong Tee, a former intelligence agent of Force 136 and the author of *Force 136* (1995), has accused Ishibe of fabricating stories, telling lies about his activities in the 1943–44 anti-Force 136 operations, and of glossing over brutal tortures committed by the Kempeitai on arrested Force 136 members including himself. Historians must be careful when evaluating Ishibe's account. It was published privately in 1990.

14. *Taipinkai, ed. Marai yo Harukanari (Reminiscences of the 29th Army Kempeitai, published). Tokyo: Taipinkai.*

Eighty-three former Kempeitai members contributed their account of life in prison as war criminals or suspected war criminals in the postwar years. They eulogised their deceased comrades as well as executed comrades and recalled their part in the war. The book was published in 1989.

15. *Nanpokai, ed. Nanpo no Omoide (Reminiscences of members of the South Seas Development Bank, unpublished)*

Fifty-seven staff members of the Bank of Japan were dispatched to the occupied Southern areas to open the *Nanpo Kaihatsu Kinko* (South Development Bank) during the war. Their recollections of their experiences in Malaya, North Borneo, and Sumatra form part of the articles. The book was privately distributed in 1969.

16. *Marei wo Katarukai, ed. Marei no Kaiso, (Reminiscences, unpublished)*

Thirty-one former members of the *Malai Gunseikkambu* contributed essays on finance, agriculture, commerce, economy, education, transportation, petroleum, security, MPAJA activities, distribution, and mass media. Data on the economic statistics for 1944 and 1945 are most useful because these statistical figures are not readily available elsewhere. It was privately distributed in 1976.

17. *Sekidokai, ed. Sekidohyo (Reminiscences, published).* *Tokyo: Sekidokai.*

The book is a compilation of recollections of the people who served in the *Malai Gunseikkambu* and the Sumatra *Gunseikkambu*. Sixty-two persons contributed essays, telling tidbits of episodes on the less stuffy side of the *gunsei*. The book was published in 1975 to commemorate the 30th anniversary of the war's end. It is informative about the *gunsei* seen through the eyes of civilians. Some 70 articles were contributed, of which two-thirds dealt with the *gunsei* in Sumatra under the 25th Army.

18. *Odachi Shigeo Denki Kankokai, ed.* Tsuioku no Odachi Shigeo *(Memories of Odachi Shigeo)*

Odachi's former subordinates who served with him during the Syonan period have reminisced about him as the mayor. *Tsuioku*'s companion book, *Odachi Shigeo* describes him criticising carpet baggers, Watanabe's hard line *gunsei* policy towards the Chinese, and his ban on English usage. The two volumes were pressed in 1956 for private distribution.

19. *Nakano Koyukai, ed. Rikugun Nakano Gakko (Reminiscences, published)*

The book is an authentic account of the history of Army intelligence operations by Nakano School's graduates. Chapters 3–6 and 12 discuss their activities in Malaya and Borneo. There is an interesting chapter on counter intelligence operations in Penang for India. The Army in cooperation with the Navy, set up a school for training INA soldiers. A number of Indian agents infiltrated into India by submarines and aeroplanes as well as over land through Burma. Most of them were arrested shortly after they reached India without accomplishing their mission. It was pressed in 1978 for private distribution.

20. Nakajima Kenzo. (Ukatensei no Maki: Kaiso no Bungaku (Reminiscences, published). Tokyo: Heibonsha.

Nakajima helped recruit such well known *bunkajin* (intellectuals) members as Ibuse Masuji,[35] Jimbo Kotaro,[36] and others for the propaganda unit of the 25th Army. He himself served in it until December 1942. Nakajima was active as a teacher at *Syonan Nippon Gakuen* for teaching *Nippon-go* and *Nippon seishin*. In June he drafted a "Declaration for *Nippon-go* Emphasis Week" and the propaganda unit urged citizens to learn, use, and speak *Nippon-go*. After returning to Japan, Nakajima actively engaged in lecturing about *Nanyo* at *Nippon-go* teacher training school established by the government for dispatching them to the occupied Southern area. It was published in 1977.

Ibuse published a number of articles and books about his experiences in Syonan. His works are less propagandistic and depict the life and the people of Syonan through the eyes of a novelist.

Jimbo, as the principal of *Syonan Nippon Gakuen*, is a rabid nationalist propagating Nippon seishin, culture and emperor worship. In his book, *Syonan Nippon Gakuen*, published in 1943, he extolled the superiority of Japanese culture which students ought to emulate.

21. Tamura Hideyuki. Gunseika no Perashu no Keisatsu (Reminiscences, privately distributed)

Tamura was a police officer stationed in Perak and Syonan from May 1942 to the war's end. During that period, he served as the police chief of Perak state, director of the police training school, and director of the anti-air raid section of the *Malai Gunseikkambu*. In collaboration with his former colleagues, Tamura has reconstructed the record of the police campaigns against the MPAJA. The information provided in the book is an authentic account of police actions against the MPAJA's best trained 5th Battalion. Tamura recounts the Communists' fierce activities of harassing and attacking local police stations and of the Japanese countermeasures against them. According to him, the fierce fighting resulted in the deaths of six Japanese police officers with 29 local policemen died in action and more than 200 collaborators killed or missing.

He also recorded the Communist attacks on local police stations attempting to seize arms, and the inhumane treatment of captured Japanese police officers in the hands of vengeful MPAJA soldiers during the Communist reign of terror following the surrender. It was printed in 1980.

22. *Shingaporu Shiseikai, ed. Syonan Tokubetsushi Shi (Reminiscences, published). Tokyo: Shingaporu Shiseikai.*

This is a record of collected memories of the people who had served in the Syonan Special Municipal Office. The book is intended not only to record "our memories for posterity but also to tell the truth of what we did in Syonan to the people concerned, because there have been many misunderstandings about the administration of Syonan". It is divided into two parts. The first part recounts the city's administrative policy and a general survey of the history of the administration. The second part discusses individual topics — personnel, finance, accounting, administrations of economy, welfare and hygiene, education, police, civil engineering, enemy property, and life in the detention camps. Sixty-three persons contributed articles. In this synopsis, they wanted to convey a message that under a given wartime condition, they tried to protect as best as they could the lives of 800,000 citizens in the city. It was published in 1986.

23. *Kanazawa Kin. Omoidasu Kotonado (Reminiscences, privately pressed)*

Kanazawa was a former official of *Kokusai Gakuyukai* (International Friendship Association), which looked after *Nanpo Tokubetsu Ryugakusei* (scholarship students from the Southern Area). Twelve Malays from Malaya and Singapore were sent to Japan in 1943–44. After studying *Nippon-go* and culture for 10 months at the *Gakuyukai*, they went to different parts of Japan for further study at colleges, the police academy, and the military academy. Three Malay students passed away in Japan; Nk Yusof in the atomic bombing of Hiroshima, Syed Omar at a hospital in Kyoto after having survived the effects of the atomic bomb for three weeks, and Syed Mansoor at a hospital in Fukuoka of tuberculosis in December 1946. Five Malay students including Ungku Abdul Aziz[37] were also sent to Japan in 1943 under the Tokugawa scholarship programme. It was privately pressed in 1973.

24. *Shinozaki Mamoru. Shingaporu Senryo Kiroku (Memoirs, published). Tokyo: Hara shobo.*

Shinozaki, a former member of the Japanese Consulate General in pre-war Singapore and an official of the Syonan Special Municipality, has written of his experiences working in the Education section and later the Welfare section. He recounts his being imprisoned in Changi Prison for espionage activities to help Maj. Kunitake; witnessing the *sook ching* and the $50 million extortion; inducing Lim Boon Keng to organise the Overseas Chinese Association and issuing *Ankyosho* (ID card), helping evacuate Chinese and Eurasians from Syonan to Endàu and Bàhàu, and testifying and defending Japanese war criminals in postwar military trials.

The Japanese version is somewhat inconsistent with his English version, *My Wartime Experiences in Singapore*, which was published by the Institute of Southeast Asian Studies, Singapore in 1973. The Japanese edition was published in 1976.

25. Matsumoto Naoji. Daihon'ei Haken no Kishatachi (Reminiscences, published). Toyama: Katsura Shobo.

Looking back on the days when he was a war correspondent in the Malayan campaign, Matsumoto, a former leftist, is contrite for having served as a propaganda mouth-piece for the military. He describes cruelties and crimes committed by the Japanese soldiers as well as the sufferings of the people which he witnessed, while covering war news.

Matsumoto recounts episodes about his association with comrades like Ibuse Masuji and Satomi Kinzo.[38] It was published in 1993.

26. Tsuji Masanobu. Shingaporu (Memoirs, published). Tokyo: Tozainanbokusha.

Col. Tsuji Masanobu, "the killer they called a god" or a "god of operations", was a staff officer in charge of operations of the 25th Army and was said to be the man who planned and executed the Malayan operations. Though his colleagues acknowledge Tsuji's brilliant planning for the conquest of Singapore, some of them have charged that Tsuji credited the victory to himself alone and disregarded contributions rendered by his staff and field commanders.

Tsuji was believed to be the instigator of the *sook ching*, but he managed to elude British war crimes investigators and returned secretly to Japan in 1948. He remained in hiding until 1950 when the Allied Powers dropped war crime charges against him. He became a member of National Diet but disappeared in 1961 in Laos and is believed to have been killed, allegedly by Laotian communists. His memoir was published in 1952.

27. Tokugawa Yoshichika Nikki (Diary, unpublished)

Tokugawa's diary was discovered in 1983 in the U.S. National Archives where it had been kept since 1945. U.S. prosecutors seized it to investigate his wartime activities for possible indictment against him as a war criminal.

The diary is a valuable source about his activities as a *gunsei* advisor of the *Malai Gunseikkambu* and his role in considerably influencing Watanabe's hard line policies towards the Chinese, the sultan, and the Japanisation of the indigenous people through *Nippon-go* education. The diary reveals, for instance, his frequent meetings with Watanabe's brain trust, Takase Toru, who masterminded the $50 million extortion; and his part in persuading the sultans to surrender their powers to the Japanese emperor and in naming a new sultan of Trengganu.[39]

28. *Watanabe Wataru. Nichi-Bei-Ei senso Sanka Nisshi (Diary published). Tokyo: Ryukei Shosha. 1998.*

His dairy, recorded in eight notebooks, comprises the first two volumes of his 5-volume work cited in the Document section (p. 256). It is an indispensable primary source about the Malay *gunsei* in the first year. The diary begins with entry on 1 December 1941 and ends on 28 October 1944, when Watanabe was appointed a brigade commander in Inner Mongolia. The diary is helpful for an understanding of his administrative philosophy and rationale derived from his long military career as a political officer for administering occupied China.

Watanabe elaborates his administrative rationale in dealing with the occupied people, particularly the Chinese, the sultan and the *penghulus*, with a hard line policy. The diary reveals his constant bickering with bureaucrats whom Watanabe criticised for their bureaucratic inefficiency and sectionalism. On the other hand, they found him obnoxious for his unbureaucratic style of drafting and executing policies with only a small group of hand-picked cohorts.

Watanabe's diary did not hide his personal liking and disliking of his superiors and colleagues. Except for Gen. Yamashita, whom he held in high esteem, Watanabe found others feather-headed and lacking in administrative philosophy. With Yamashita's support of his *gunsei*, Watanabe exercised so much power that he regretted Yamashita's departure from Singapore.

29. *Yamashita Tomoyuki. Sento Nikki (Battle Diary, unpublished)*

Gen. Yamashita, the "Tiger of Malaya" and the "Conqueror of Singapore", kept a battle record during his command of the 25th Army. He recorded often his impatience and irritation when front line commanders were making little progress in battle. He blamed it on their poor leadership. He personally directed his staff officers to deploy troops in order to attack the enemy's rear.

It is of interest to note that Yamashita found Tsuji to be egocentric, crafty, and unworthy of trust. Though Yamashita did not like Tsuji's outrageous behaviour, he appeared confident of utilising this talented staff officer.

Regarding the "Yes" or "No" demand to Gen. Percival, Yamashita was regretful that it was reported erroneously by the media that he intimidated the defeated British commander at the surrender negotiations. The truth of the matter is that Yamashita became so impatient with the feet dragging negotiations while the military situation was becoming so critical that it was imperative to force an unconditional surrender on the British immediately. Growing impatient of a civilian interpreter's clumsy translations, Yamashita shouted at the translator, not at Percival, to convey his demand. He was burdened, until the last moment of his life, with the erroneous report of the negotiations by the mass media.

30. *Ochi Harumi. Marei Senki (Memoirs, published). Tokyo: Tosho shuppan.*

Ochi, as a platoon commander of the 11th Battalion, the 5th Division, took part in every major battle of the Malayan campaign from the beginning to the end, after landing at Singora on 8 December. His battalion fought all the way, capturing every inch of the enemy territory at Jittra, Kampar, Slim, Gemas, and Bukit Timah.

Describing the battle scenes graphically, his account brought home the reality of the fierce fighting at the front line. It was published in 1973.

He also published a companion book, *Kyoran no Singapore* (Tokyo: Hara Shobo, 1967), in which he depicted the frenzied life of Syonan in the closing months of the war.

31. *Iwakuro Hideo. Singapore sokogeki (Battle Record). Tokyo: Kojinsha, 2000.*

Col. Iwakuro was a regiment commander of the Imperial Guards Division. His troops were engaged in the battles at Muar, Bakri, Parit Sulong,

Batu Pahat, Rengit, and Singapore. The regiment received a citation from Yamashita for wiping out the enemy at Bakri. Iwakuro was relieved of his command after having sustained a wound in the battle at Rengit. After recovering from the wound, he succeeded Fujiwara Iwaichi as chief of the *Iwakuro kikan* in charge of the Indian National Army.

32. *Arai Mitsuo. Singaporu Senki (My War Record, published). Tokyo: Tosho shuppansha, 1984.*

Warrant Officer Arai fought in China, Malaya, and Burma while working at the headquarters of the 114th Regiment command, 18th Division. The Division's main force, commanded by Lt. Gen. Mutaguchi Renya, joined Yamashita's Army on 30 January 1941 for the assault of Singapore. His account supplements and corrects erroneous information about the regiment's role in the assault. Arai did not record the killing of staff and patients at Alexandra Hospital that was committed by soldiers of the Division.

33. *Tsuchikane Tominosuke. Singaporu e no Michi (My War Record, 2 volumes, published). Tokyo: Sogeisha.*

Tsuchikane, sergeant first class, served in the 4th Regiment, Imperial Guards Division and took part in the Malayan campaign from December 1941 to February 1942. He stationed in Sumatra from March 1942 until the war's end. His account of the battles he fought, seen through the eyes of a front line soldier, provides us with a rare view about how his comrades fought their way to Singapore. It was published in 1977.

34. *Kawamura Saburo. Jusan Kaidan wo Noboru — Senpan Shokeisha no Kiroku (Diary of a War Criminal, published). Tokyo: Ato Shobo.*

Maj. Gen. Kawamura, as a commander of the Syonan garrison army, was charged for the war crimes of the *sook ching* in Singapore. The diary begins on 14 September 1946, the day he was arrested and ends on 25 June 1947, the day of his execution. He recorded every day of his war crime trials and of his reflections on the trials after being sentenced to death by hanging. The book contains letters he sent to his wife and children during the trials and while awaiting his execution. In these letters Kawamura explains to his wife and children how he was wrongfully indicted for the *sook ching* of which he had some reservation, but he had to obey the order without question. He wrote these letters as his last will to the family members. He assured them of his innocence and advised his children on the conduct of their lives.

The day he faced the gallows, Kawamura submitted letters addressed to the supreme commander of the British Army and chairman of the Singapore Overseas Chinese Association. In the letter to the British commander, he protested against the injustice of the war crimes trials which he saw as an act of revenge and an appeasement to the Chinese community. In his letter to the Singapore Overseas Chinese Association, he said he would be glad to die if his execution would alleviate Chinese hatred towards the Japanese. He hoped for the coming of a day of mutual trust and understanding.

It is ironical that the book, published in 1952, was prefaced by Tsuji Masanobu who masterminded the massacres for which Kawamura was held responsible and executed.

35. *Fujiwara Iwaichi. F Kitan (Memoirs, published).* *Tokyo: Hara Shobo.*

In October 1941, Maj. Fujiwara was sent to Bangkok as an intelligence agent to deal with Indian and Malayan affairs. As chief of the *F Kikan*, he helped organise the Indian National Army, with volunteers of Indian POWs, commanded by Mohan Singh. The book is the account of an idealistic young officer who, seeing himself as a "Japanese Lawrence of Arabia", carried on the wartime propaganda slogan, "Asia for Asians". Fujiwara's significant role in organising the INA and furthering the cause of Indian nationalism is an important chapter in its history.

Fujiwara's own account, though subjective and uncritical, is a valuable addition to the discussion on this important topic. It was published in 1966.

36. *Takumi Hiroshi. Kota Baru Tekizen Joriku. Warera kaku Tatakaeri* *Shigaporu Koryakusen (Reminiscences, published). Tokyo: Press Tokyo.*

Maj. Gen. Takumi, brigade commander, 18th Division, recorded his battles beginning with the landing at Kota Bharu on 8 December 1941 and onto Singapore. It was published in 1968.

IV. Secondary Publications

1. *Akashi Yoji*

Akashi published three articles about the *Kempeitai's* mop-up operations (*Gunji Shigaku* vol. 28, no. 3, 1992), education (*Kokuritsu Kyoiku Kenkyusho Kiyo*, no. 121, 1992), and *Koa Kunrenjo and Nanpo Tokubetsu Ryugakusei* (*Indonesia, sono Bunka Shakai to Nippon*, 1979). Waseda Daigaku Shuppankai.

2. *Iwatake Teruhiko. Nanpo Gunseika no Keizai Shisaku (Marai/ Sumatora/Jaba no Kiroku), 2 volumes Economic Policies for the Occupied Southern Region (Malaya, Sumatra, and Java) (published) (Tokyo: Ryukei Shosha).*

Iwatake was a former official in charge of material logistics and industry at the *Nanpo Sogun Gunseikkambu* serving from February 1942 to August 1944.

Combining his own experience with archival materials such as the Tokugawa Collection, the Kishi Papers, and the Nishijima Collection as well as interviews with more than 30 former colleagues, Iwatake has produced a comprehensive work on economic policies drafted and implemented at the *gunsei*'s highest level.

In volume 1, after defining what the *gunsei* is, Iwatake discusses the process of planning *gunsei* policy and organisation (Chapter 1); shipping materials vital for national defence to Japan, inter-regional trade and exchange of goods and trans-regional exchange of materials with China, Manchuria, and the Axis Powers (Chapter 2); rubber estate administrative policy in Malaya/Sumatra and Java, and "Grow-more-food" policy in Malaya and Java (Chapter 3); industrialisation policy for self-sufficiency (Chapter 4); currency, finance, monetary policies, and inflation countermeasures (Chapter 5); and the end of the *gunsei* and its remedial measures (Chapter 6).

Volume 2 consists of a list of statistics, tables, bibliography, and principal *gunsei* papers and ordinances. It was privately pressed in 1983 and published in 1995.

Iwatake's 1989 companion work, *Nanpo Gunsei Ronshu* (Tokyo: Gannando, 1989), a collection of five articles, supplements *Nanpo Gunsei no Keizai Shisaku*. Of particular interest is an article comparing the two types of the administration in Malaya under the hard line Watanabe/Yamashita *gunsei* and in Java under soft line Imamura/Nakayama *gunsei*.

3. *Egawa Yoshiro. Nanpo Tokubetsu Ryugakusei Shohei Jigyo no Kenkyu (A Study of the Special Scholarship Programme for Students of the Southern Regions) Tokyo: Ryukei Shosha, 1997.*

The former prime minister of Brunei, Pengiran Yusuf, a former *Nanpo Tokubetsu Ryugakusei*, visited Hiroshima University in 1982 where he, as one of the victims, spoke about the atomic bombing. The visit motivated Egawa to carry out a study on the students who came to Japan in 1943–44 for education and training under a Southeast Asian student scholarship programme. In his book, he wrote about the founding of the programme, the selection procedures, and *Nippon-go* and cultural learning taught at the International Friendship Association. Egawa also examined their education and lives at universities and in postwar Japan, and the historical significance of the programme.

His study of the 12 students from Malaya and Singapore and the many pictures of their youthful days are interesting.

Egawa's book should be read together with Kadono Hiroko's book, *Tonan Ajia no Otototach.* (Expanded edition published in 2002. Tokyo: Akatsuki Inshokan.) Kadono was the students' "big sister" and *Nippon-go* teacher. She has reminisced about the wartime days of sharing joys and hardships with them and her warm association with them lasting to this day. Her portrayal of the Malay and Singapore students is very warm, and the reprinted letters from Tunku Abdullah[40] and Raja Nong Chik[41] are heart warming.

Another book related to the Southeast Asian scholarship students from Malaya is Nakayama Shiro's book, *Ten no Hitsuji* (Tokyo: Sankosha 1982.). He wrote about Syed Omar who died at Kyoto University hospital on 3 September 1945 from the effects of the atomic bombing in Hiroshima.

4. *Ota Koki*

He has published 22 articles relating to the Japanese *gunsei* in Southeast Asia. There are three studies concerning Malaya, "Marei, Sumatora no Nippon Gunsei Soshiki (The Gunsei Organisation in Malaya and Sumatra)", in *Seiji Keizaishi*, no. 259, 1987; "Rikugun Nanpo Gunseika no Doko Taisaku (The Army's Gunsei Policy Toward the Sultan)", in *Gunji shigaku* vol. 16, no. 1, 1980; and "Nanpo ni okeru Nippon Gunsei kankei Bunken Mokuroku: Mareishia (Bibliography of Nippon Gunsei in the Southern Regions)", in *Gunji Shigaku* vol. 28, no. 3, 1992.

**5. Onda Shigetake. Ningen no Kiroku. Marei-sen. 2 volumes.
Tokyo: Gendaishi Shuppansha.**

To prepare materials for his book, Onda, an editorial writer of the *Chugoku Shimbun* in Hiroshima, the home of the 5th Division, interviewed former veterans of the 9th and the 21st Brigades, commanded by Kawamura Saburo and Sugiura Eikichi, of the 5th Division. He also examined the brigades' battle reports and the veterans' diaries. He narrates, blow by blow, the battles in graphic vividness. Onda criticises Yamashita's commandship when the general, sitting at the command post away from the battle front and getting impatient of the slow progress of the battle at Gemas, made an unwarranted criticism in saying that a front line commander lacked a fighting spirit. Yamashita was just another "elite bureaucratic general", Onda says, who had little understanding of soldiers fighting a fierce battle at the front lines. The book is not only a record of the Malayan campaign but is also a human story, not found in official battle reports, of front line soldiers who had experienced glory and sorrow of the war. It was published in 1977.

**6. Nagai Shin'ichi. Gendai Mareishia Seiji Kenkyu (A Study of
Contemporary Malaysian Politics). Tokyo: Ajia Keizai Kenkushyo, 1998.**

Chapters 2 and 3 respectively deal with the Malay nationalist movement and the Malay Communist Party before and during the Occupation period. Of particular interest is Ibrahim Yaacob's contact with Kaite Yoshi, a *Domei* Wireless Service reporter in Singapore, who introduced Ibrahim to Tsurumi Ken, Consulate General in Singapore. Tsurumi later handed S$25,000 to Ibrahim to enable him to buy up the *Warta Malaya*, turning the newspaper into an anti-British propaganda mouth-piece. This episode is known as *"Kame Kosaku"*. See Malay side of the *Kosaku* discussed by Mustapha Hussain, *Malay Nationalism before UMNO* (Kuala Lumpur: Utusan Publication 2005).

Based on an interview with Ibrahim, Nagai discussed, on some length, the collaboration of the *Barisan Muda* organised by Onan Siraj and Mustapha Hussain of the Malay Youth Movement (Kesatuan Melayu Muda) with the *F Kikan* in the early stages of the Malayan campaign. The *F Kikan*, however, was not successful in mobilising Malay support, largely because most of Malay leaders had been arrested by the British police and the *F Kikan* then turned its main attention to Indian affairs.

*7. Habu Yoshiaki, alias Haji Abu Hurairah Habu Abdullah. Nipponjin yo
Arigato (Thank You to the Japanese). Tokyo: Nippon Kyoiku Shinbunsha.*

Habu's account is based on a series of interviews with Raja Dato Nong
Chik who studied in wartime Japan as a scholarship student from Malaya.
Nong Chik attributed his spiritual awakening in nationalism and Malaysian
independence to the Japanese who defeated the British. Nong Chik has
expressed regret that many young Japanese today have the slightest interest
in the Great East Asia War, in which their grandfathers had shed their
blood for helping Asian people to gain their national independence, and
which changed the political map of postwar Southeast Asia. He urged that
Japanese students should be taught about it. It was published in 1989.

*8. Takashima Nobuyuki and Hayashi Hirofumi, ed. Maraya no
Nippongun: Nuguri Sunbiran shu ni okeru Kajin Gyakusatsu (The Japanese
Army in Malaya: Massacre of Chinese in Negri Sembilan).
Tokyo: Aoki shoten, 1989.*

This work, originally written in Chinese, relates how in March 1942,
Japanese soldiers killed Chinese villagers in Negri Sembilan. Takashima
Nobuyuki, professor at Ryukyu University in Okinawa, had this book
translated and published in 1989. In the same year, *Nippongun no Mareishia
Jumin Gyakusatsu* was published as the 3rd volume of *Senso Giseisha wo Kokoro
ni Kizamukai* in its *Ajia no Koe* series. This work relates how in March 1942,
Japanese soldiers massacred 2,400 people in 27 places in Negri Sembilan.

   These studies castigate the Japanese troops for their brutal behaviors
during wartime, showing gruesome pictures of the scenes.

*9. Nakajima Michi, Nichu Senso Imada Owarazu: Marei Gyakusatsu no
Nazo (The Sino-Japanese War Has not Yet Ended: Riddle of the Massacre in
Malaya). Tokyo: Bungei shunshu.*

Nakajima, the daughter-in-law of Lt. Gen. Matsui Takuro, commander
of the 5th Division, published the book in the defence of the honour of
the 5th Division's soldiers who spearheaded mop-up operation against the
MPAJA's anti-Japanese activities in Negri Sembilan.

   She refuted the account of the indiscriminating *sook ching* allegedly
carried out by soldiers of the 5th Division in March 1942 at Titi, Parit
Tinggi, Jelundong, Sungei Lui and Senaling, exposed by Takashima and
Hayashi. For four and half years she worked on the book travelling to

Malaysia and retracing activities of the 5th Division, especially those of the 11th Regiment. She interviewed numerous veterans of the 7th Company of the Regiment and a survivor of the "mop-up" operation. Considering that the Japanese soldiers tended to inflate the number of the enemies killed in their battle reports, she disputed the figure killed in these villages, as cited in *Maraya no Nippongun* (p. 224). Furthermore, she said those killed were "hostile elements" and the killing was a necessary measure to maintain the security of the occupied area. It was published in 1991.

10. Hayashi Hirofumi. Kakyo Gyakusatsu. Nippongun Shihaika no Marei Hanto (The Massacre of Chinese: The Malay Peninsula under Japanese Control). Tokyo: Suzusawa Shoten.

Hayashi was working on the book about the same time when Nakajima was also doing her research but the conclusions they reached were diametrically opposite. His detailed and painstaking study showed little shadow of doubt about the killing fields in March 1942 in Negri Sembilan. The strength of the book is that his analysis is substantiated by testimonies of numerous Chinese survivors and soldiers of the Japanese army.

Hayashi takes Nakajima to task on such issues as the number of the victims she claimed was inflated and the mop-up operation carried out in Negri Sembilan based on Lai Teck's squeal, informing the *Kempeitai* that the villagers were all anti-Japanese guerillas. How can Nakajima justify, Hayashi asks, the killings of innocent children and women? Nakajima's book, according to Hayashi, is nothing but an apologia, based solely upon interviews with the former soldiers of the 7th Company who were keen to defend the honour of the 5th Division. It was published in 1992.

Hayashi also published *Sabakareta Senso hanzai. Igirisu no tai-Nichi senpan* (Tried War Crimes. British War Crimes Trials of the Japanese). Tokyo: Iwanami Shoten, 1998 and *BC Kuràsu Senpan Saiban* (Trials of BC Class War Crimes). Tokyo: Iwanami Shoten. Iwanami Shinsho 952, 2005.

11. Nippon no Eiryo Maraya/Shingaporu Senryoki Shiryo Chosa Forum. ed. Interview Kiroku: Eiryo Maraya/Shigapore Senryo (1941–45) (Recorded Interviews: Occupied British Malaya and Singapore). Tokyo: Ryukei Shosha.

The forum, supported by the Toyota Foundation's research fund from 1974 to 1977, conducted a series of interviews with former Japanese military and civilian officials as well as Malays and Chinese. The book is a selected record of interviews with 34 people. The interviewees were an assortment of officials engaged in research, agriculture, propaganda, police and the *Kempeitai* fighting against the MCP/MPAJA, Syonan city administration, the INA, education, and *Koa kunrenjo*; the two Japanese civilians who joined and stayed with the MPAJA in the jungle until 1989; the Malay students in Japan; and Malays and Chinese living in Kota Tinggi and North Borneo during the war. It was published in 1999.

12. *Akashi Yoji. ed. Nippon Senryoka no Eiryo Maraya/Singaporu (Japanese Occupied British Malaya and Singapore).*
Tokyo: Iwanami Shoten.

The book consists of eight articles contributed by members of the above forum. The topics are: the rationale of the Watanabe *gunsei* and its policy implementation (Akashi Yoji). MCP leaders during the anti-Japanese resistance period (Hara Fujio), the Singapore *sook ching* (Masutani Satoru), railway operations (Ota Koki), economic policy focused on procurement and Japanese-owned rubber estates (Yoshimura Mako), petroleum in Sumatra and Borneo (Yamazaki Isao), woman detainees in Changi Prison (Nakahara Michiko), and the Japanese surrender in Syonan (Henry Frei). It was published in 2001. An English edition will be published by the National University of Singapore Press in 2008. The articles by Masutani and Yamazabi are replaced by Hayashi Hirofumi's article on the *sook ching* in the English edition.

13. *Oki Shuji. Yamashita Tomoyuki (Biography). Published in 1968.*
Tokyo: Akita shoten.

Kojima Noboru. Shisetsu Yamashita Tomoyuki (Biography). Published in 1969.
Tokyo: Bungei Shunshusha.

Yasuoka Masatake. Ningen Yamashita Tomoyuki (Biography). Published in 2000.
Tokyo: Kojinsha.

Fukuda Kazuya. Yamashita Tomoyuki (Biography). Published in 2004.
Tokyo: Bungei Shunshusha.

Yamashita is the best known general of the Imperial Japanese Army since the Russo-Japanese War of 1904–1905 and the most written about military figure in the history of the Japanese Army. Since his execution in January 1946 in Manila, scores of books and articles have been written about him. One common theme in Yamashita's biographies is that he was a tragic general nurtured by the modern Japanese military system. He is depicted as a lonely and sensitive man of reason and prudence, contrary to the popular image of the "Tiger of Malaya", the sobriquet resulting from his imposing appearance with the sharp glaring eyes, portrayed at the surrender negotiations with Lt. Gen. Arthur Percival, though he did not like the sobriquet.

Fukuda characterises Yamashita as the "last hero who conquered Singapore, putting an end to the European domination of Asia", and as a "man whose honour was disgraced by war crime charges and as a man condemned to death by hanging, stripped of all military honours and uniform". Yamashita, although he played a significant role in the Imperial Army, symbolises the demise of the Japanese Imperial Army in which he was nurtured.

14. *Takayama Shinobu. Hattori Takushiro to Tsuji Masanobu. (Biography). Published in 1975.*

Tatamiya Eitaro. Sanbo Tsuji Masanobu Kiden. (Biography). Published in 1976. Tokyo: Fuyo shobo.

Sugimori Hisahide. Sanbo Tsuji Masanobu. (Biography). Published in 1982. Tokyo: Kawaide shobo shinsha.

Ikude Hisashi. Akuma teki Sakusen Sanbo Tsuji Masanobu. (Biography). Published in 1993. Tokyo: Kojinsha.

Tsuji is one of the staff officers most written about, particularly for his notoriety. In the Nomonhan Incident in 1939, the Malayan campaign, and the battles of the Philippines in 1942, and Guadalcanal in 1942–43, Tsuji earned a notorious reputation. In these biographical studies, Tsuji is portrayed as an eccentric and egocentric man known for his overconfidence and strong convictions. In the battle field he often acted like a front line field commander rather than a staff officer and his arbitrary behaviour caused a clash with fellow and superior officers creating confusion in the command system.

Of Tsuji's defiant behaviour against senior officers, Yamashita confided in his diary that: "This man is an egocentric and conceited person who has too much confidence in his own ability. In short, he is a crafty small fry

harmful for the good of the state." Col. Iketani Hanjiro, Tsuji's immediate
senior officer in the 25th Army, also criticised Tsuji's self-conceit for claiming
the successful Malayan campaign as his own achievement and his dishonest
for blaming others for faults in the campaign.

15. *Nakajima Masato. Bosatsu no Kiseki. Shingaporu Kakyo Gyakusatsu
Jiken (Premeditated Murder. Massacre of Chinese in Singapore). Published
in 1985. Tokyo: Kodansha.*

*Sakuramoto Tomio. Daihon'ei Hapyo Singaporu wa Kanraku seri
(Statement Announced by Imperial Army Headquarters. Singapore Has
Been Conquered). Published in 1986.
Tokyo: Awoki Shoten.*

*Kobayashi Masahiro. Shingaporu no Nippongun (The Japanese Army in
Singapore). Published in 1986.
Tokyo: Heiwa Bunka.*

These three books deal with the fall of Singapore and the *sook ching*. Nakajima,
a critic, has published the book based on interviews mostly with Chinese in
Singapore and on articles in the local newspapers, while Kobayashi, a former
teacher of the Japanese School in Singapore, has written the book based on
published accounts he found in Singapore. Their works have brought out into
relief the real image of Singapore during the *sook ching* period. There are a
number of factual errors and misunderstandings in both books, particularly
in Nakajima's book in which we find obvious fabrications. Having heard
from a Chinese who claimed he saw the document, *Kakyo sook ching* (plan
for *sook ching*), at the 25th Army headquarters in Singapore, Nakajima,
too eager to disclose what he believed to be new evidence, fabricated that
such a document did exist. The fact of the matter is that there was no
such document, and that the Chinese informer was never in Singapore, but
instead he was in Ipoh during the Occupation period.

Sakuramoto, a poet, who has been probing the war responsibility of the
intelligentsia (*bunkajin*), has maintained that it is meaningful to re-examine
wartime speeches and activities of well known intellectuals (writers, poets,
painters, film makers, academics and journalists), who joined in a chorus of
government propaganda for supporting the war. Intoxicated by the news of
the British surrender in Singapore, they celebrated the victory with speeches
and writings, willingly serving as cat's-paw propagandists for the military.
The re-examination of their wartime speeches and activities is necessary as

a lesson for not repeating the same mistake, and for the intelligentsia to account for their wartime responsibility.

The three authors have reminded the reader of Japan's responsibility for wartime atrocities and of a perception gap in historical truth between the Japanese and the Occupied people of Southeast Asia. Hence, there is need for teaching objective war history to younger Japanese in schools.

16. *Katano Shoji. 1484-nichi Marai/Shingaporu Nippon Gunsei no Kenkyu (1484 Days: A Study of the Japanese Gunsei in Malaya and Singapore). Tokyo: Nippon Mareiisha Kyokai.*

Katano, a former junior agricultural officer of the Perak state government, first wrote a draft in 1957 and revised it based on archival materials in Japanese, Chinese, and Malay languages. It is supplemented by interviews with his former Malaysian friends in London, Brisbane and Sydney.

The book, consisting of 12 chapters, is a descriptive general history of the Occupation period, surveying its policies for the administrative system, research activities, enemy property, education, religion, culture, inflation, industry, local government and agriculture. The last two chapters cover such topics as the surrender, life in detention camps, war crimes, the military administration in north Borneo, and reports on living conditions of various ethnic groups and rice cultivation in Java, and on Sumatra and Banka/Billiton islands.

This volume is useful for its numerous statistics, tables, and charts not readily available in other sources, but it is marred by careless editorial work that overlooked many minor typographical and factual errors. It was published in 2001.

Conclusion

As mentioned earlier, the study of Japan's Occupation of Southeast Asia by Japanese historians began comparatively late, while in the western academic circles, scholars undertook the studies much earlier, probing into the impact of the Occupation on postwar political, economic and social changes in the occupied countries.

For many years, Harry Benda's transformation thesis had remained influential until the early 1980s. Younger scholars, like Alfred McCoy,[42] challenged the Benda thesis and raised the question of whether the Occupation really disrupted and transformed irrevocably many aspects of the occupied society. Instead, McCoy has introduced a new thesis arguing that some aspects of the political and social system remained unchanged and maintained continuity in the postwar society.

Japanese historians and political scientists had taken the Benda thesis for granted. The study of the Japanese Occupation were first undertaken in 1959 by Kishi and Nishijima, whose work on occupied Indonesia followed the line of the transformation thesis. The Kishi/Nishijima study generated an interest in the topic among younger Japanese historians represented by Goto Ken'ichi and Kurasawa Aiko.

On the other hand, the studies of the Japanese Occupation of Malaya/Singapore had been left untouched until the late 1960s. This is partly because Japanese scholars who took part in the Occupation had remained hesitant to engage in the study lest they be accused of being wartime collaborators with the military. In addition, the outbreak of the 1962 "blood debt" incident in Singapore and Malaysia added a psychological pressure on them to think twice about engaging in the study of the wartime Occupation. Consequently, they had hesitated to encourage their graduate students to engage in the study. The polemics of the academic argument on transformation or continuity still have not reached a consensus among the Japanese circles of specialists. In an article, "Japanese occupation of Malaya: Interruption or Transformation", Akashi has argued that the Japanese Occupation brought about a considerable change in the political, social, and psychological outlooks of the Malaysian people.[43]

With access to the Defence Agency's Archives, Akashi and Iwatake pioneered, in the late 1960s and the 1970s, the studies of the Japanese military administration of Malaya/Singapore. Since then, the study have been advanced by a systematic oral history project conducted by Akashi and our Forum in the 1980s and the 1990s. During these years, many new materials such as official papers, private diaries and memoirs were discovered, providing *gunsei* studies with more information and enabling us to gain a new insight.

In the meantime, scholars in Malaysia and Singapore like Cheah Boon Kheng, Paul Kratoska, Lim Pui Huen, and Abu Talib Ahmad, aided by numerous archival and published materials in English, Chinese, and Malay as well as oral history records, have produced monographs and articles. These in-depth scholarly studies in Japan and abroad on the question of "disruption or continuity" will provide additional fuel to keep the polemics alive. This bibliographical study of the Japanese Occupation of Malaya/Singapore reveals that, in contrast to the popular notion, the topic has been relatively well researched.

Problems, however, still remain. First, the wall of language barrier is still high, particularly for Malaysian and Singaporean researchers whose language ability prevents them from reading the Japanese materials now available in many volumes. Moreover, these official papers are written in a literary style, requiring foreign scholars to equip with a considerable knowledge of Japanese, and private diaries and memoirs are often written in each author's characteristic handwriting. As a result, it taxes the reader's energy to decipher the meaning. On the other hand, English and *Bahasa* Melayu are less of a problem for the Japanese researchers studying Malaysian affairs because they have a working knowledge of the languages or they have a language proficiency acquired at universities.

Second, translation of the Japanese language documents published or unpublished into English or *Bahasa* Melayu and vice versa is necessary for a comprehensive study of this important period. However the translation of voluminous Japanese documents is an enormous project that will require a huge amount of fund and energy. Nonetheless, some of the more important selected papers, dairies, and memoirs should be translated. If this is not possible in the foreseeable future, Japanese scholars should be encouraged to publish their works in English.

Third, the Japanese Occupation years in Peninsular Malaya and Singapore have been studied rather intensively. In contrast, there have been fewer studies done so far about North Borneo (Sarawak and Sabah). Ooi Keat Gin and Bob Reece are a few scholars undertaking the research focusing on Sarawak. Japanese literary sources about the North Borneo military administration are also very scarce. During our Forum project, we have been able to discover only two volumes of the yearbook of the North Borneo Military Administration for 1942 and 1943. Hara Fujio edited and published them in 1997. According to a former ranking official of the North Borneo Military Administration with whom I corresponded, the whereabouts of all 57 research papers are unknown and they are still missing to this date. It is known that its research department had produced 35 reports between April 1942 and January 1943 before the arrival of research associates of *Taiheiyo Kyokai* (Pacific Affairs Society) that was attached to the Administration. The latter had produced, as of January 1944, 22 reports by the end of December 1943. There has been practically no serious research on Sabah except for several memoirs published in Japanese.

It is much desired that scholars in Japan and Malaya/Singapore should encourage for exchanging of information and sharing it for the scholarly advancement of the *gunsei* study.

Notes

This article was originally published in Japanese.

1. Willard H. Elsbree, *Japan's Role in Southeast Asian Nationalist Movements, 1940 to 1945* (Cambridge, Mass.: Harvard University Press, 1953).
2. Francis Clifford Jones, *Japan's New Order in East Asia: Its Rise and Fall, 1937–44* (London: Oxford University Press, 1954).
3. Muhammed Abdul Aziz, *Japan's Colonialism and Indonesia* (The Hague: M. Njihoff, 1955).
4. Harry J. Benda, *The Crescent and the Rising Sun: Indonesian Islam under the Japanese Occupation, 1942–1945* (The Hague: W. van Hoeve, 1958).
5. Josef Silverstein (ed.), *Southeast Asia in World War II: Four Essays* (New Haven: Southeast Asian Studies, Yale University, Detroit, 1966).
6. Dorothy H. Guyot, "The Political Impact of the Japanese Occupation of Burma", Ph.D. Diss., Yale University, 1968.
7. George S. Kanahele, "Japanese Occupation of Indonesia: Prelude to Independence", Ph.D. Diss., Cornell University, 1969.
8. Waseda Daigaku Okuma Kinen Shakai Kagaku Kenkyusho. *Indonesia ni okeru Nippon gunsei no kenkyu* (Tokyo: Kinokuniya Shoten, 1959).
9. Kennedy G. Tregonning (ed.), "Japanese Policy for Malaya under the Occupation", *Papers on Malayan History* (Singapore: Journal of South-East Asian History, 1962); "Japanese Islamic Policy: Sumatra and Malaya", *Intisari* II, no. 3, n.d. Ota Tsunezo, *Biruma ni Okeru Nippon Gunseishi no Kenkyu* (Tokyo: Yoshikawa Kobundo, 1967).
10. The author, Hattori Takushiro, was a staff officer in charge of operations at the Imperial Army Headquarters during the war.
11. The author, former Colonel Fuwa Hiroshi, was a staff officer in charge of operations of the field armies including the 7th Area Army.
12. The paper was subsequently published in *Asian Studies* 7 (April 1969), The University of the Philippines.
13. *Interview Kiroku* D. *Nippon no Gunsei* and D. *Nippon no Gunsei/6.* Tokutei Kenkyu "Bunka masatsu". Tokyo Daigaku Kyoyo Gakubu Kokusai Kankeiron Kenkyushitsu.
14. Nanpo Gunseika no Keizai Shisaku — Marai/Sumatra/Jaba no Kiroku, 2 vols. (Tokyo: Ryukei Shosa).
15. Sekaishi no naka no Nippon Senryo (Tokyo: Nippon Hyoronsha, 1985).
16. Akashi Yoji (ed.), *Nippon Senryoka no Eiryo Maraya/Shingaporu* (Tokyo: Iwanami Shoten, 2001).
17. *Nippon no Eiryo Maraya/Shigaporu Senryo (1941–1945)* (Tokyo: Ryukei Shosha, 1998).
18. Akashi Yoji (ed.), *Gunseika ni okeru Maraya/Shingaporu kyoiku jijoshi, shiryo (1941–1945),* 2 vols. (Tokyo: Ryukei shosha, 1999).
19. Akashi Yoji (ed.), *Watanabe Wataru Shosho Gunsei Kankeishi, Shiryo,* 5 vols. (Tokyo: Ryukei Shosha, 1998).
20. Akashi Yoji and Miyawaki Hiroyuki (eds.), *Nippongo Kyokasho. Nippon no Eiryo Maraya/Shigaporu Senryoki, 1941–1945,* 6 vols. (Tokyo: Ryukei Shosha, 2002).

The edited Nippongo textbooks complement Matsunaga Noriko's study, *Nippon Gunseika ni okeru Nippongo Kyoiku.* (Tokyo: Kazama Shosho, 2002). Relating to the *gunsei* topic, Akashi Yoji and Ishii Hitoshi (eds.), *Daitoa Kensetsu Shingikai Kenkei Shiryo* (The Council for the Construction of Greater East Asia), 4 volumes compiled by Daitoa Kensetsu Sinjikai (published by Ryukei Shosha in 1996) is an important reference. The Council was established in January 1942 and chaired by Prime Minister Tojo Hideki. Its members were prominent political, business, and academic leaders. The Council was organised with eight panels: Basic principles for the construction of Greater East Asia; Education; Population and nationality; Basic economic policy; Industry (Mining, Technology, Electric power); Agriculture, Forestry, Marine, and Dairy; Monetary, Finance, and Trade; and Transportation.

Based on the policy papers prepared by the panels, the Council drafted policy recommendations for the government to implement them.

21. Hara Fujio (ed.), *Kita Boruneo Gunsei Gaiyo*, 2 vols. (Tokyo: Ryukei Shosha, 1997).
22. G.P. Ramachandra. "The Indian Independence Movement in Malaya, 1942–1945", M.A. Thesis, Department of History, University of Malaya, 1971.
23. Halinah Bamadhaj, "The Impact of the Japanese Occupation of Malaya on Malay Society and Politics (1941–1945)", M.A. Thesis, Department of History, University of Auckland, 1975.
24. Cheah Boon Kheng, *Red Star over Malaya: Resistance and Social Conflict During and After the Japanese Occupation of Malaya, 1941–1946* (Singapore: Singapore University Press, 1983).
25. Paul H. Kratoska. *The Japanese Occupation of Malaya: A Social and Economic History* (London: C. Hurst, 1998).
26. Abu Talib Ahmad, *Malay Muslims, Islam and the Rising Sun: 1941–1945* (Kuala Lumpur: Malaysian Branch of the Royal Asiatic Society, 2003).
27. *Tomi* is the code name for the 25th Army.
28. Tomi Gunseikkambu, *Tomi Koho* (Tokyo: Ryukei shosha, 1990).
29. Malai Gunseikkambu, *Malai Koho* (Tokyo: Ryukei shosha, 1990).
30. Malai Gunseikkambu, *Gunsei Geppo*, 5 vols. (Tokyo: Ryukei shosha, 2000). *Gunsei geppo* was originally titled *Senji geppo.*
31. Akashi (ed.), *Gunseika ni okeru Maraya/Singapor.* Kyoiku Jijoshi, Shiryo (Tokyo: Ryukei Shosha, 2000).
32. Akashi Yoji (ed.), *Nanpogun Gunsei Sokambu Chosabu/Malai Gunsei Kambu Chosabu. Hokokusho 1943–1945*, 22 vols. (Tokyo: Ryukei Shosha, 2006).
33. The Yearbook had been edited by April 1943, but its printing was delayed until October 1943 owing to the deployment of the 25th Army to Sumatra.
34. Akashi Yoji (ed.), *Sakakibarake Shozo Nanpogun Gunsei Sokambu Kankei Monjo*, 9 vols. (Tokyo: Ryukei shosha, 2004).
35. Ibuse Masuji, under a pseudonym, briefly edited the Japanese language edition of the *Syonan Shimbun*. A principal work is *Choyo no koto.* Tokyo: Kodansha, 1996.
36. Jimbo Kotaro was a poet. He published *Syonan Nippon Gakuen* in which he reminiscences about teaching pupils Japanese discipline, emperor worship, and *Nippon seishin.* Tokyo: Ai-no Jigyosha, 1943.

37. Ungku Aziz is a royal member of the family of Sultan Ibrahim of Johor and former vice chancellor of the University of Malaya.
38. Satomi Kinzo was a former leftist and draft dodger. Drafted as a punitive measure into military service after having surrendered himself to the police, he was killed in action while covering battle in the Philippines.
39. According to his autobiography, *Saigo no Tonosama* (Tokyo: Kodansha, 1973), Tokugawa volunteered his service in order to protect the property and welfare of the sultans. He had been a close friend of Sultan Ibrahim of Johor since the early 1920s, and invited him to visit Japan in 1934. During this visit the emperor received the Sultan in an audience in Tokyo. Otabe Yuji, author of *Tokugawa Yoshichika no 15-nen Senso* (Tokyo: Aoki shoten, 1988), was critical of Tokugawa by pointing out contradictions of what he had said in his autobiography. The new sultan succeeded his deceased father in September 1942.
40. Tunku Abdullah is the eldest son of Malaysia's first *Agong* or king.
41. Raja Nong Chik was a senator in the Malaysian Parliament. For his services in promoting Japan and Malaysian relations, the government of Japan honoured by bestowing upon him the First Order of the Rising Sun.
42. Alfred McCoy (ed.), *Southeast Asia under Japanese Occupation* (New Haven: Yale University Southeast Asia Studies, 1980).
43. McCoy (ed.), *Southeast Asia under Japanese Occupation*.

Index